CANADA AND COLONIALISM

1898 Canadian stamp showing the British Empire with Canada at its centre. It boasts, "We Hold a Vaster Empire Than Has Been." | *Copyright Canada Post Corporation, Library and Archives Canada, RG3, 1989-565 CPA*

JIM REYNOLDS

CANADA AND COLONIALISM

An Unfinished History

PURICH
BOOKS

UBC Press is a Benetech Global Certified Accessible™ publisher. The epub version of this book meets stringent accessibility standards, ensuring it is available to people with diverse needs.

Purich Books, an imprint of UBC Press
The University of British Columbia
www.purichbooks.ca

Printed in Canada on FSC-certified ancient-forest-free paper (100% post-consumer recycled) that is processed chlorine- and acid-free, with vegetable-based inks.

Library and Archives Canada Cataloguing in Publication

Title: Canada and colonialism : an unfinished history / Jim Reynolds.

Names: Reynolds, James I., author.

Description: Includes bibliographical references and index.

Identifiers: Canadiana (print) 20230586619 | Canadiana (ebook) 20230587488 | ISBN 9780774880947 (softcover) | ISBN 9780774880954 (PDF) | ISBN 9780774880961 (EPUB)

Subjects: LCSH: Canada—Politics and government—1763–1867. | LCSH: Canada—Politics and government—1867– | LCSH: Canada—History—1763–1867. | LCSH: Canada—History—1867– | LCSH: Canada—Colonization. | LCSH: Indigenous peoples—Canada—Government relations—History. | LCSH: Canada—Relations—Great Britain—History. | LCSH: Great Britain—Relations—Canada—History.

Classification: LCC FC165 .R49 2024 | DDC 971—dc23

Canada Council   Conseil des arts
for the Arts   du Canada

Canadä

BRITISH COLUMBIA
ARTS COUNCIL

BRITISH
COLUMBIA

UBC Press gratefully acknowledges the financial support for our publishing program of the Government of Canada, the Canada Council for the Arts, and the British Columbia Arts Council.

UBC Press is situated on the traditional, ancestral, and unceded territory of the xʷməθkʷəy̓əm (Musqueam) people. This land has always been a place of learning for the xʷməθkʷəy̓əm, who have passed on their culture, history, and traditions for millennia, from one generation to the next.

Contents

Note on Terminology

Anyone writing on history, legal issues, and Indigenous peoples enters a minefield when it comes to terminology and the need to balance historical accuracy with shifting social norms about what is considered acceptable language. Many authors and publishers struggle with this issue, and there is no consensus on the best approach to dealing with outdated terminology.[1] This book sets out to explore how Canada's legal and political relationship with Indigenous peoples remains rooted in its colonial past. In this book, "Indigenous" generally refers to the original peoples of a territory. However, "Indigenous" is not a term that was widely used either by the colonized or the colonizers during much of the time period explored in this book. The colonized used words in their own language to describe themselves or their language rather than a general term for all Indigenous peoples. Sometimes, the colonizers used these words and sometimes they used their own terms that may or may not have been similar and that may have referred to more than one Indigenous group or confused them.

In what is now the Americas, a particular problem was the use of "Indian" to refer to the original inhabitants of these lands, resulting from the error of European explorers who thought they had landed in South Asia. "Indian" is now widely regarded as an offensive term when used to refer to the original peoples of North America. In Canada, the term has generally been replaced by "Indigenous peoples," a term which encompasses First Nations, Inuit, and Métis peoples. "Aboriginal" is the term used in Canada's constitution and that remains enshrined in Canadian law; I use it in this book when referring to current Canadian legal contexts. Like "Indigenous," "Aboriginal" encompasses First Nations, Inuit, and Métis peoples. However, it should be noted that only First Nations were subjected to systematic colonization through the various versions of the *Indian Act* discussed in Chapter 6.

In this book, I generally use the terms "Indigenous," "Aboriginal, "First Nations," "Métis," and "Inuit." In the context of Canada rather than the Indian subcontinent, I use "Indian" only in quoted materials or to reflect historical or legal usage (such as in the terms *Indian Act*, Indian agent, and Department of Indian Affairs); other dated terms used to categorize people from different races also appear in quotations from historical sources. As this book examines, scientific racism divided human beings into different races while cultural evolutionists argued that different races were at different stages of civilization (with the "white race" being the most advanced). The belief in white racial and cultural supremacy was widespread and used to justify the colonialism explored in this book. Some of the original historical material included is offensive and no doubt many readers will find some sections challenging to read, particularly if they are not used to reading historical materials. While my intention is not to cause harm or discomfort, because racism was fundamental to colonialism, and racist language was wielded as a tool to justify it, this book includes examples of racism from many different sources to preserve historical accuracy and provide a sense of the times. My hope is that the overall aims of this book, which include revealing how this racism at the heart of colonialism still has an impact on the lives of Indigenous people, will help readers move through the uncomfortable emotions the use of this historical language may evoke. Ideally, my hope is that this book will contribute to efforts to dismantle the systemic racism that persists in Canada to this day.

CANADA AND COLONIALISM

Introduction

Anyone in Canada reading a newspaper, watching television, listening to the radio, or using the internet will see daily references to "colonialism," usually in the context of Indigenous matters. This book explores Canada's historical connections with colonialism and how they continue to have an impact. It seeks to provide a general account of what I consider to be the essential history of Canadian colonialism. Endnotes provide references for those wishing to pursue particular topics in more depth.

Colonialism is a process that results in the control of one people's territory by another. In the Canadian context, this means primarily French and British settlers taking control from Indigenous peoples. It also refers to Canada's and Canadians' support for the British Empire, which dominated many of the world's peoples for hundreds of years. The main argument presented in this book is that colonialism is deep-seated in Canada. The control of Indigenous peoples in Canada formed part of a broader, worldwide process in which Canada and Canadians participated. This process was rooted in a shared economic goal, belief in racial and cultural superiority, and a readiness to use force if other preferred measures, such as treaty making, did not succeed.

Earlier generations of Canadians (who identified as British as much as Canadian) were well aware of this imperial background. For example, the Truth and Reconciliation Commission (TRC), which investigated the residential school system for Indigenous children in Canada, observed that "the men and women who established the schools celebrated [the] link between their work and the growth of European empires."[1] The architects of Canadian Indian policy and the western treaties that transformed the nation were ardent imperialists as were most of their contemporaries. My sense, however, is that this background is not as well understood by contemporary Canadians as it should be, despite many contemporary efforts to "decolonize." This book seeks to describe the broader process of colonialism, including control of the territories of Indigenous peoples in Canada by the British colonists and their Canadian descendants.

Most of the material in the following pages is historical, relating to events and people of long ago. Few people in Canada today advocate the racism, cultural supremacy, and willingness to use force that were central to the imperial project. Since 1971, when Prime Minister Pierre Elliott Trudeau announced multiculturalism as an official government policy – the first of its kind in the world – it has replaced identification with the British World.[2] So why write a book about the painful past? There is, of course, the usual reason of wanting to know more about how we got to where we are today. More fundamentally, the past continues to have an impact on our present. As Eric Hobsbawm, the eminent British historian, wrote, "We swim in the past as fish do in water, and cannot escape from it."[3] The sun gradually set on the British Empire beginning with the Second World War and, with it, Canada's role in supporting it. However, a legacy of that history was a system of control over Indigenous peoples in Canada that remains. An understanding of that history is necessary to better understand the current situation of Indigenous peoples in Canada. Their impoverished economic circumstances and the failure of Canadian governments to fully recognize their rights are better understood in the broader context of Canada's history as part of the British Empire and its treatment of Indigenous peoples. As the TRC noted, the experience of Indigenous peoples in Canada had much in common with the experiences of Indigenous peoples in other colonized lands.[4] The current public focus on residential schools and on such doctrines as discovery/*terra nullius* (which were used to justify colonialism), although necessary, does not tell the whole story.

A greater understanding of the history of the relationship between Canada and the British Empire enables us to see the progress made in recent decades in transitioning from supporting racial and cultural superiority to becoming a multicultural and more egalitarian country. This progress encourages us to continue the effort to make the necessary fundamental changes required to bring about reconciliation and decolonize Canada in a way acceptable to Indigenous peoples. Knowledge of the history of colonization is also required for the process to be successful. In the words of the TRC, "No process of reconciliation or decolonization can take place without first recognizing and addressing the legacy of colonialism."[5]

Canadian prime ministers have made statements stressing Canada's role as a colony rather than an imperial power. In 1960, Prime Minister John Diefenbaker addressed the UN General Assembly, telling members, "There are few that can speak with the authority of Canada on the subject of colonialism for Canada was once a colony of both France and the United Kingdom. We were the first country which evolved over 100 years ago by constitutional processes from colonial status to independence without severing the family connection."[6] Fifty years later, Prime Minister Stephen Harper said, "We ... have no history of colonialism." In 2016, his successor, Prime Minister Justin Trudeau, told students at New York University that Canada has "a capacity to engage in the world in difficult places without some of the baggage that so many other Western countries have, either colonial pasts or perceptions of American imperialism, as a critique that's often out there."[7]

In the twentieth century, Canadian officials lectured Indigenous groups in other countries who were demanding independence from colonial governments. They told them to copy Canada and go slowly and not be overly demanding or critical of the colonial powers, whose rights should be respected.[8] At the end of the First World War, George Foster, minister of trade and one of Canada's delegates to the Treaty of Versailles, wrote that "'self-determination' is translated into the dreams and hope, or the mischievous propaganda, of sections of humanity, large and small. The result would be, carried to the limit, a world of small, ill-regulated, weak and antagonistic communities."[9] External Affairs minister Lester Pearson told the House of Commons in January 1957: "The old colonialism is disappearing inevitably and, if the process is orderly, desirably; but that is all the more reason why those countries which still have direct responsibilities for non-self-governing territories should not be made to feel at the United Nations or elsewhere that they are oppressors to be deprived arbitrarily of their rights or indeed their reputations."[10] According to Asa McKercher, a historian at the Royal Military College, in the 1950s and 1960s, "officials in Ottawa felt that the process from colony to nation should proceed at a slow *Canadian* pace."[11] In August 1962, Prime Minister Diefenbaker stated he desired "early independence for all dependent people" but went on to declare that "the orderly achievement of freedom and independence for all people in all lands will not be brought about through hasty and impractical measures, adopted in response to emotional and immoderate demands."[12]

These statements create a false impression that Canada was a colony of the British Empire like any other. As this book shows, Canada is a leading example of settler colonialism, by which settlers from overseas take over the lands of Indigenous peoples and rule them as subject peoples. Canada possessed internal self-government from the mid-nineteenth century; chose to remain a dominion rather than request independence until almost a century later; did not have to struggle to gain independence for itself; and supported the subjugation of Indigenous peoples in the Empire, including in Canada itself. Canadians actively participated in colonial conquest and rule, and worked in and promoted the Empire. There was no anti-imperialist movement of any size. Prominent Canadians, and Canadians generally, were enthusiastic imperialists, supporting and participating in imperial campaigns in India, Africa, and elsewhere, as well as in the Canadian West. Even today, the imperial link is reflected by the British monarch automatically becoming Canada's monarch and head of state, as illustrated by the succession of Charles III in 2022 without Canadians having any choice, even though polling has indicated that a majority of them do not want Canada to continue as a monarchy.[13]

It is correct that Canada was not an external imperial power. It did not have its own colonies, unlike Australia, New Zealand, and South Africa, all of which acquired former German colonies following the First World War. The reason was not that Canada rejected having colonies in principle. In fact, especially from the 1880s to 1919, there was serious Canadian interest in proposals to give it control of the British colonies in the West Indies.[14] Prime Minister Robert Borden, a strong supporter of the Empire and the proposal, said in 1916, "The responsibilities of governing subject races would probably exercise a broadening influence upon our people as the Dominion thus constituted would closely resemble in its problems and its duties the Empire as a whole."[15] Joseph Pope, the under-secretary of External Affairs, prepared a confidential report on the annexation of the West Indies to Canada. It listed advantages, including compensation for sacrifices made defending the Empire. However, there were objections to be considered: "First and foremost there is the negro question." Limits would have to be placed on the franchise to "exclude a very considerable proportion of the black population."[16] Borden was so concerned that West Indians might insist upon representation in Parliament that he dropped the proposal.[17] It may also be noted that some writers employing the concept of informal empire have argued that Canada's economic and military activities in other countries, especially in parts of Latin America and the Caribbean, make it an imperial power.[18]

Canada had its place in the *Colonial Office List*, an annual publication containing a wealth of historical and statistical information about each colony. In 1901, for example, it could be found between British Honduras and the Cape of Good Hope. But Canada was not just another part of the Empire. It was central to it. Newfoundland was the first colony established outside the British Isles. Canada led the way for other settler colonies in gaining internal self-government and uniting its different colonies. Geographically, it was at the core of an Empire stretching from the Atlantic to the Pacific. It provided an essential link between the United Kingdom (UK) and the Asian colonies from 1886 following the construction of the Canadian Pacific Railway across the country. The railway formed part of an "All-Red Route" entirely within the Empire that stretched from London to cities in Canada, Hong Kong, Australia, and New Zealand.[19] The Royal Navy policed the Atlantic from Halifax on Canada's East Coast and the Pacific from Esquimalt on the west coast. Canada was the successful eldest child of Mother England, the epitome of what a settler colony might become.[20]

Canada never removed itself from the Empire or made a declaration of independence. Although few would dispute Canada's current independence, even the date of that independence remains uncertain. The preamble to the *British North America Act 1867* (renamed the *Constitution Act, 1867*) refers to promoting "the interests of the British Empire," and section 132 describes Canada as "part of the British Empire"; these provisions have never been repealed. UK legislation continues to set out the Canadian constitution. For example, the *Constitution Act 1982*, which contains the Canadian Charter of Rights and Freedoms and is often referenced as marking the date of Canada's independence, is a schedule (appendix) to a statute passed by the UK Parliament. In a sense, the Empire left Canada when the United Kingdom's attention turned toward Europe in 1960 (not a permanent union, as it transpired), leaving Canada in a state of arrested constitutional development that has not been fully resolved with the constitutional changes made in 1982, including the so-called patriation of the constitution.

The United Kingdom's responsibility for its imperialist history has aroused considerable controversy, but any discussion of Canada's responsibility has been largely avoided.[21] As noted above, the impression is sometimes created that Canada has no history of colonialism or even that non-Indigenous Canadians were part of the colonized rather than the colonizers. Honesty alone requires greater acknowledgment of Canada's past as a participant in the British Empire and of the role played by Canadians as part of that empire and the British World. That support, and the racist and white supremacist views of Canadian imperialists, should be acknowledged.

My interest in the British Empire and Canadian colonialism is both personal and professional. I was born in England shortly after decolonization had begun with the independence of India, Pakistan, and Burma in 1947. My wife (raised in Singapore) and I subsequently immigrated to Canada, where our sons were born. I spent over forty years as a lawyer in Vancouver, acting primarily for Indigenous groups. My practice often caused me to wonder how the Canadian government had gained such control over most aspects of Indigenous peoples' lives and lands. I was shocked to discover that they were still living under discriminatory laws – the *Indian Act*, the first version of which had been passed over a century earlier, during the height of the British Empire. These laws meant that they required the approval of the Canadian government to deal with their reserve lands, those small parts of their traditional land still in their possession. Indigenous groups were not even party to leases of those lands, which were signed in the Crown's name as the landlord. At that time, governments denied that Indigenous peoples had any Aboriginal rights or title. When those rights were finally defined by the courts beginning in the 1970s, they included onerous restrictions and requirements.

The colonial status of Indigenous peoples in Canada was brought home to me early in my career through my involvement in a case for the Musqueam of Vancouver. In the 1950s, an exclusive golf and country club had obtained a seventy-five-year-lease (still in existence) from the federal government for one-third of the Musqueam's small reserve on terrible terms not even disclosed to the band. The facts of the case raised fundamental questions about the nature of Canadian colonialism. An English-born former residential school principal employed by the Department of Indian Affairs had negotiated the lease with the experienced businessmen of the golf club. How did he and they have so much power, and band members so little, over lands that the Musqueam had occupied for thousands of years? At the time of the lease, the band members did not even have the right to vote.[22]

As this brief biographical background demonstrates, I have lived in the shadow of the British Empire, and I am by no means alone in this regard. Most Canadians will have grown up in parts of the former Empire. More importantly, as I show in this book, we all still live with the shadow that it casts over the relationship between Indigenous and non-Indigenous people.

The main points I make in *Canada and Colonialism* can be summarized as follows:

1 Canada was a central part of the British Empire and the British World. This fact is critical to its history and current circumstances and, in particular, to the legal position of Indigenous peoples.

2 The British Empire was divided into "the British," who were the rulers/colonizers, and the "Indigenous peoples," who were the ruled/colonized. Fundamental features of British rule included belief in racial and cultural superiority, accompanied by a willingness to use overwhelming force to achieve and maintain that rule, but with a preference to use more peaceful means, especially treaties.

3 Canadians were part of the colonizing British and were enthusiastic supporters of imperial expansion. They considered themselves as much the proprietors of the British Empire as those living in the United Kingdom – it was *their* Empire as well.

4 Because Canada was a member of the British World, self-government came easily and early to the country in the mid-nineteenth century.

5 In contrast, the Indigenous peoples of other colonies, such as India, were ruled despotically until the mid-twentieth century.

6 Canadian self-government included rule over Indigenous peoples. Canadians established a system of internal colonialism, primarily administered by Indian agents under successive versions of the *Indian Act* that formed part of the broader system of imperial rule.

7 Independence was available at Canada's option from the second half of the nineteenth century.

8 In contrast, Britain resisted self-government and independence for Indigenous peoples throughout the Empire. It was not until almost the second half of the twentieth century that Indigenous peoples in British India ceased to be ruled by the British ("decolonization" as usually understood).

9 Self-government for Indigenous peoples in Canada has still not been fully recognized. They will not become independent or decolonized in the usual sense since the descendants and successors of the French and British settlers and other immigrants are, and will remain, overwhelmingly the majority.

10 It is for Indigenous peoples to say what they consider to be decolonization.

The book concentrates on the period since 1830 with only brief references to earlier years for context. For the reasons set out in Chapter 1, the 1830s were critical in establishing Britain as a ruling or imperial power over, rather than a trading partner and ally of, Indigenous peoples in both British North America (later Canada) and India, the major part of the non-white or Dependent Empire. This period also marked the enormous expansion of the Empire (including in Canada), which reached its height over the next century before receding in the following decades with self-government and independence for Indigenous peoples, except in former settler colonies such as Canada, where they were now a minority.

I also concentrate on formal colonialism or imperialism – defined as the rule of Indigenous peoples by a foreign power – rather than other more informal expressions of colonialism, such as effective control by economic power or cultural influence. The term "colonialism" is sometimes used to refer only to imperialism through the settlement of populations from the mother country (the original meaning), but it is now generally used for all types of rule of Indigenous peoples by a foreign power, and "colonies" includes territories acquired by methods other than settlement.[23]

The general scheme of this book is as follows. Chapters 1 to 4 set the scene and deal more generally with the British Empire. Chapter 1 provides a historical outline of Canadian history within the context of the British Empire and events in other colonies, especially India. This outline gives a timeline to orient the reader and link developments occurring at different times in different areas. The chapter also provides definitions of some key terms. Chapter 2 seeks to provide the essential elements of the British Empire, describing its expansion and extent, and the distinction between the British, who were the rulers/colonizers, and the Indigenous peoples, who were the ruled/colonized. It examines how this distinction was justified mainly by belief in racial and cultural superiority. Chapter 2 also describes the principal methods used to establish that rule: settlement, treaties, and force. Chapter 3 discusses a fundamental difference between colonies settled by the British in which they became a majority, such as Canada, and those where there were relatively few settlers who remained a minority, such as India. Canada obtained self-government easily and early during the mid-nineteenth century, but India was ruled despotically from London. Chapter 4 then examines the rulers and their rule in non-settler colonies.

Chapter 5 turns more specifically to the role of Canada and Canadians in the Empire as part of the British World and as supporters of colonial rule. One element of self-government for Canada included rule over the Indigenous peoples of the country and their lands. Chapter 6 covers the system of internal colonialism created through the various versions of the *Indian Act* and the Indian agents who administered that legislation. Until the advent of apartheid in South Africa, no other British colony appears to have established such a comprehensive system of control over Indigenous peoples.

The remaining chapters deal in more detail with self-government and independence. As discussed in Chapter 7, independence was available at Canada's option from the second half of the nineteenth century. Non-white colonies, led by India, had to fight for their independence, which did not occur until the middle of the twentieth century. Developments in the relationship between governments and Indigenous peoples in Canada since 1970 and steps toward Indigenous self-government and "reconciliation" are also covered. Finally, the Conclusion discusses the legacy of the British Empire and what "decolonization" might mean in the Canadian context.

1

Historical Overview

The Royal Commission on Aboriginal Peoples (RCAP) was created in 1991 to find ways to rebuild the relationship between Indigenous peoples and the Canadian government following years of civil unrest and disagreement over the constitution. In its review of the history of the relationship between Indigenous peoples and the imperial and colonial governments (referred to as "the Crown"), the Royal Commission divided the history of Canada into four main stages, which overlapped and occurred at different times in different regions.[1] The stages are:

1 Separate Worlds
2 Contact and Co-operation
3 Displacement and Assimilation
4 Negotiation and Renewal (now known as Reconciliation).

The separate worlds stage refers to the time before contact, which differed considerably depending on geographical location. During the contact and co-operation stage, the Crown regarded Indigenous peoples as independent nations and warriors/allies. During the displacement and assimilation stage, it treated them as subjects to be ruled and as wards of the state. Finally, during the reconciliation stage, the Crown recognizes Indigenous peoples have special enforceable legal rights but does so without overturning the essentially colonial nature of the relationship.

The Early Stages

The first stage was the era of separate worlds, which lasted until approximately 1500. Indigenous and non-Indigenous societies developed in isolation from each other. Differences in physical and social environments inevitably meant differences in culture and forms of social organization. "On both sides of the Atlantic, however, groups with long traditions of government emerged, organizing themselves into different social and political forms according to their traditions and the needs imposed by their environments," explained the final RCAP report.[2] This first stage ended with the arrival of early explorers. Jacques Cartier sailed up the St. Lawrence in 1534, erected a cross and claimed the land for the French, leading to the later establishment of New France. Such dates of arrival ("discovery") and symbolic acts of taking possession were used in competing claims of sovereignty by European nations. Claims were also sometimes advanced on the basis that the lands were unoccupied or occupied by non-Christians and so could be treated as *terra nullius* (land belonging to nobody).

After Cartier, more French, British and other European explorers, traders, and settlers crossed the Atlantic and met the Indigenous Nations who controlled the territories now comprising Canada. In 1583, the first British attempt to establish a colony occurred when Sir Humphrey Gilbert sailed from England and claimed possession of Newfoundland for the British Queen.

These voyages led to the contact and co-operation period, which lasted until the late eighteenth and early nineteenth centuries in eastern Canada. "Although there were exceptions, there were many instances of mutual tolerance and respect during this long period."[3] The social, cultural, and political differences between the two societies were mostly respected. "Each was regarded as distinct and autonomous, left to govern its own internal affairs but co-operating in areas of mutual interest and, occasionally and increasingly, linked in various trading relationships and other forms of nation-to-nation alliances."[4]

The term "nation" was generally used by Europeans to refer to Indigenous groups, reflecting this acknowledgment of autonomy. There was a high degree of co-operation in the form of trading and military alliances. One important alliance, initially concluded in 1613 between the Iroquois and the Dutch, was later assumed by the British. It is referred to as the Covenant Chain and recorded in the Two-Row Wampum Belt.[5] The Belt symbolized the separate and equal nature of the relationship aimed at peaceful co-existence and co-operation. Treaties of Peace and Friendship were signed in the colonies on the East Coast, such as the 1760 treaty with the Mi'kmaq. These treaties did not generally purport to transfer any land. Indigenous people assisted the newcomers, helping them survive in the unfamiliar environment, and this stage also saw intermarriage and mutual cultural adaption. Despite the generally positive relationship, there were also many incidents of Indigenous resistance and of conflict between Indigenous people and newcomers, a growth of the non-Indigenous population, and a steep decline in the Indigenous population due to newly introduced diseases for which Indigenous people had no natural immunity.

During this stage of contact and co-operation, the British were in a struggle for supremacy with the French to extend their influence in and increase their control over North America, particularly the trade in furs. This rivalry continued until the British conquest of New France and the Treaty of Paris in 1763, which effectively ended the presence of France as a colonial power in North America. First Nations often held the balance of power in this conflict, and they could use their bargaining power to their advantage. Sometimes they actively supported one side against the other. Sometimes they remained neutral. The price for their support or neutrality was often "presents" or trading preferences.[6] In an effort to retain the goodwill of their Indigenous allies, the British Crown issued the Royal Proclamation of 1763. This prohibited settlers from claiming land from Indigenous peoples unless and until it was first surrendered to the Crown. This proclamation set out the practice of acquiring land by treaties with Indigenous peoples. However, over time, the proclamation was forgotten and governments ceased negotiating land treaties, leaving parts of the Canadian West and North unceded and so subject to continuing Aboriginal property interests.[7]

The position of First Nations worsened with the ending of hostilities between Britain and France. As noted by historian Olive Dickason, "Instead of holding the balance of power between two imperial rivals as they had when France was present, Indians now found themselves jockeying for position between an imperial power, Great Britain, and her restive Thirteen Colonies, who would soon gain their independence as the United States of America."[8]

The revolt of British settlers in the thirteen southern colonies between 1775 and 1783 led to the departure of those colonies from the British Empire and the formation of the United States of America. Despite the apparent catastrophe for the Empire, the loss of the thirteen American colonies was balanced by adding new colonies in North America and expanding the Empire in Asia, Australasia, and southern Africa.

Fighting resumed between the British and their former subjects during the War of 1812. The end of this war in 1815 led to a fundamental change in the relationship between the British and Indigenous Nations. The latter's role as warriors and allies became irrelevant to Britain's interests. Although British fears of possible US invasion were to continue for several decades, there was no longer any significant threat to British supremacy in their remaining North American colonies ("British North America"). As noted by historian John Leslie:

> Following the War of 1812, the strategic importance of Indian warriors to British regular forces declined and by the early 1820s the warrior image had been replaced by that of an expensive social nuisance. Since Indian people no longer fulfilled their traditional military role in colonial society, Imperial authorities, particularly those at the Treasury and Colonial Office, began to question whether the Indian department should continue to exist. Concurrently, other interested persons and parties called not for the abolition of the department, but rather for a change in approach which would encourage the department to cease exploiting Indian people and begin assisting them to achieve a degree of social and economic advancement comparable to the non-Native population.[9]

The new situation led to a series of major investigations of "Indian affairs" in the Canadas, commencing with the Darling Report in 1828.[10]

The Other Colonies

Meanwhile, in the Caribbean, British colonies had their early history in piracy, trade, the slave trade, and conflicts with other European nations. Settlements were established in the seventeenth century, some as the result of military success, as with Jamaica in 1655. Slaves from western Africa provided a source of labour for crops, especially sugar, for the European market. The slave trade came to an end in the British Empire in 1807, although slavery itself was not generally abolished in the British Empire until 1833 (it continued in some areas, such as northern Nigeria, for almost another century).[11]

In areas where the climate was considered suitable for Europeans, expansion of the Empire took the form of settlement, as in Canada. This settlement led to the dispossession of Indigenous peoples from their lands, which were then converted by settlers into new societies resembling those found in the British Isles ("settler colonialism"). The settlers continued to identify themselves and be recognized as "British." Captain Cook explored New

Zealand in 1769 and eastern Australia in 1770. Settlement followed a few years later. Cape Province in southern Africa was also considered suitable for settlement after it was formally ceded by the Dutch in 1814. However, British interests in Africa were limited and connected primarily to the slave trade in western Africa.

The East India Company (EIC or "the Company") was founded in 1599. Like the Hudson's Bay Company (HBC), which controlled the land in Canada that drained into Hudson's Bay ("Rupert's Land") under a charter granted in 1670 by King Charles II, the EIC was formed for trading purposes and enjoyed a monopoly in its territory.[12] Also like the HBC, it entered into a variety of arrangements with local groups to further its interests and impede competitors. However, unlike the HBC, which remained predominantly a commercial company (though it had some governmental responsibilities, especially in Red River Colony and on Vancouver Island[13]), the EIC increasingly shed its commercial role between 1765 and 1833 to become a tax collector and government. Through the Company, which had its own army and courts, Britain ruled territory in India that expanded from isolated forts to extensive lands as the result of military conquest and alliances and agreements with existing Indian rulers.

The Company's success in the Battle of Plassey in 1757, over Siraj-ad-Daula, the Nawab, or ruler, of Bengal, and his French allies, was critical to this transformation of the British from traders to the new rulers. The Treaty of Paris in 1763, which had ceded French territories in North America to Britain (there was a lively debate on whether Britain should give up Canada to obtain Guadeloupe),[14] also recognized British claims to paramountcy in key Indian states, including Bengal. Two years later after his defeat at the hands of the British at the Battle of Buxar, Shah Alam II, the Mughal emperor, conferred legitimacy on the EIC by granting it the *diwani,* the right to collect taxes in his name. He still controlled much of the Indian subcontinent despite competition for power from the EIC and the Maratha Empire. The *diwani* was another critical step in changing the role of the EIC from trading company to ruler. The UK Parliament passed legislation that reflected this change. In 1784, a Board of Control was created for the Company, answerable to Parliament, and later legislation extended government control. By that time, the aged and blind Mughal emperor had fallen under the control of the Marathas. The capture by the EIC of the Mughal capital of Delhi in 1803 removed the emperor from control and as a potential threat to the British. He and his successors then became puppet rulers under the "protection" of the EIC. Ten years later, the

Canada and Colonialism

Company lost its trading monopoly, and, in 1833, its charter was amended so that it substantially ceased to trade and became an arm of the British government to rule British India. As in British North America, the nature of the British-Indigenous relationship had fundamentally changed, and the contact and co-operation stage was over.

Displacement and Assimilation

In the colony of Upper Canada, the Darling Report of 1828 promoted what became known as the civilization and assimilation program. It recommended this program be based on establishing reserves where Indigenous people could be educated, converted to Christianity, and transformed into sedentary farmers, thus ending their nomadic habits.[15] The plan was approved by the Colonial Secretary, the responsible minister in the UK government, in 1830. This approval reflected a significant policy change. This change was described a few years later by a commission of inquiry, the Bagot Commission, which reported in 1845: "The policy of the Government towards this race was directed rather to securing their services in times of war, than to reclaiming them from barbarism and encouraging them in the adoption of the habits and arts of civilization ... Since 1830, a more enlightened policy has been pursued ... and much has been done ... to promote their civilization."[16] Indigenous people were no longer regarded as members of independent nations and allies but as subjects to be ruled. Under the guise of "civilization," Indigenous people were no longer to be treated as warriors but as child-like wards of the state, unable to manage their affairs. The goals of the policy were civilization and assimilation, and until it was successful, Indigenous people were to be kept on reserves, isolated from the settler population, and denied the self-government that the settlers were to enjoy as a result of the recommendations in the Durham Report of 1839, which is explored in Chapter 3.[17]

In effect, a system of "internal colonialism" was implemented with the settlers as the colonizers and the Indigenous peoples as the colonized. The new policy was later reflected in legislation such as the *Gradual Civilization Act,* passed in 1857.[18] Its passage introduced the displacement and assimilation stage, the third stage identified by the Royal Commission on Aboriginal Peoples, which is the crucial period for the purposes of this account of the British Empire's impact on Canada.

Under the new Indian policy, the dominant settler society was no longer willing to respect the distinctiveness of Indigenous peoples. Instead, it made repeated attempts to assimilate Indigenous peoples into mainstream society. It also weakened their traditional political structures and control over their lands and resources, which the government increasingly assumed. Most of the details of this new policy were implemented through the *Indian Act*, the first iteration of which was written by senior officials in the Department of Indian Affairs, passed by politicians in 1876, and administered by Indian agents.

During the displacement and assimilation stage, critical aspects of the new relationship between Indigenous peoples and the Canadian government were formalized. Most of the significant developments made during the current reconciliation stage to try to repair the relationship between Indigenous peoples and the government have been attempts to alleviate the consequences of this earlier stage. Unfortunately, they have been only partially successful.

Self-Government and Independence for the Settler Colonies

As Indigenous peoples lost their independence and power in the early decades of the nineteenth century, the ever more numerous British settlers gained greater power and became increasingly independent from the UK government. As settlement spread westward, Indigenous peoples soon became a minority. By the 1840s, it was apparent that Britain had no stomach to use force if its remaining North American colonies decided to follow their southern neighbours. Settler revolts in both Upper and Lower Canada (now Ontario and Quebec) in 1837 led to a report by an English lord (the "Durham Report") that recommended internal self-government on the English model, with a government responsible to an elected legislature ("responsible government"). The recommendation limited the powers of the Crown, which were exercised by the governor general acting as the monarch's representative. Full internal self-government was readily conceded over the following decades, but jurisdiction over defence and foreign affairs was kept within the power of the imperial government in London. Until the early twentieth century, there was no push by the colonists to take on the expense of these portfolios and greater independence.

As part of self-government for the settlers, the British imperial government formally abandoned any responsibility for Indigenous peoples. Instead, it transferred control over Indian affairs to the government of Upper Canada in 1860. Other Canadian colonies also took over the systems of administration that had been set up to rule over Indigenous peoples. This internal colonialism was intensified by ever-increasing regulation under the *Indian Act*, which remains in place today in a modified form.

In 1867, with the encouragement and blessing of the imperial government, four of the colonies in British North America formed Canada ("Confederation"). The other colonies joined later, between 1870 and 1949. Through a prolonged process of devolution, the imperial government transferred its remaining powers to Canada, which became increasingly independent. Control over foreign affairs was confirmed in 1931 by the *Statute of Westminster*, and this is generally considered the date of Canadian independence. However, the ability to change the constitution without British involvement didn't happen until 1982, with the signing of the *Constitution Act* of that year passed by the UK Parliament. To this day, the UK monarch remains the Canadian head of state, and there has been no formal declaration of independence.

Broadly speaking, British colonies in Australia and New Zealand followed the Canadian pattern. Migration increased over the nineteenth century. Settler colonies were established that displaced and disrupted the Indigenous peoples, who were soon outnumbered. The settlers dramatically changed the environment where they settled. Powers of internal self-government were granted by the imperial government to the British colonists, modelled on responsible government in the Canadian colonies. The Australian colonies were slower to follow the Canadian model of confederation, but this took place in 1901. New Zealand, like Newfoundland, opted not to join the federal union. It remains independent, unlike Newfoundland, which joined Canada in 1949. These colonies became known as "dominions," using the title conferred on Canada in 1867 at Confederation. Together with Canada and South Africa, these dominions were increasingly recognized as partners with the UK in running and benefitting from the Empire. From 1887 their representatives met periodically with UK representatives at colonial conferences to discuss their relationship. The 1926 conference was especially significant as it recognized that, in theory at least, the dominions were autonomous, equal with the UK and free to overrule UK legislation and make their own foreign policy. This freedom was formally recorded in the *Statute of Westminster* in 1931.

British India

In contrast to these settler colonies were colonies where Indigenous peoples continued to form the majority of the population and where, with some exceptions, British and other European residents were sojourners and not settlers. Most looked forward to returning "home," perhaps after several decades in the colony. These non-settler colonies were called "dependencies," and collectively "the Dependent Empire."[19]

British India was the biggest part of the Dependent Empire with the longest history. Its predominantly Hindu and Muslim population made up about 75 percent of the Empire's total population. India was not seen as a possible site of British settlement except possibly in cooler northern mountain regions such as Kashmir. According to Bampfylde Fuller, a retired member of the Indian Civil Service, "Speaking generally, Europeans can live in India only as birds of passage ... Children may be born in India without detriment; if sent to Europe before sexual maturity approaches they show no sign of degeneration. But if they remain in India until and after this critical period in their lives, they appear to lose their energy of mind and body ... India enfeebles white races that cling to her breasts."[20] Europeans were a tiny percentage of the population.

Until the 1857 "mutiny" or rebellion in northern India, the East India Company continued to rule as, in theory, an agent of the Mughal emperor but, in practice, on behalf of the British government. The rebellion led to the deposition of the emperor. Its causes were complex, but in the view of a contemporary Indian magistrate, they all resulted from the exclusion of Indians from the legislative process. This exclusion meant the rulers were ignorant of the feelings of the Indians, leading to bad will.[21] The EIC was replaced by the British government, which ruled British India through a government in India headed by the governor general/viceroy and an administration carried on by the Indian Civil Service. The viceroy was responsible only to the India Office in London, led by a Secretary of State for India answerable to Parliament. By 1886, British India had grown to include what is now India, Pakistan, Bangladesh, and Burma.[22]

British rule was despotic. Until the early twentieth century, the viceroy had virtually unlimited power and was able to rule autocratically without any significant Indian representation in the executive and legislative councils that advised him. There was, however, a system of "indirect rule" in some areas using Indigenous rulers under British control, as distinct from "direct rule" where there was no such intermediary. The exclusion of Indians from government led to the formation of a self-rule movement in the later decades of the nineteenth century. At first, it sought dominion status for India, following the Canadian model. This would make it equal to the settler colonies. In the face of government refusal and suppression, Indians increasingly demanded complete independence through a largely peaceful campaign of protest and civil disobedience. Limited self-government was not granted until 1936 and then only at the provincial level. Independence came in 1947.

Africa

The British colonies in Africa were diverse and had elements of both settler and non-settler colonies. The British Empire did not grow substantially in Africa until the later decades of the nineteenth century and had a brief life there compared with North America and India, ending with independence in the 1960s. However, the changes brought by the British and other European empires were profound and fundamentally changed the continent.[23] Following the UK's abolition of the slave trade in 1807, the British navy sought to prevent the trade in the Atlantic, and more territory was acquired on the West African coast for this purpose. Merchants set up trading posts in coastal areas, but at first they rarely ventured inland. Later, they obtained control of the interior, mainly to exploit the raw materials.

During the "scramble for Africa," commencing in the 1880s, European politicians and diplomats carved up the continent between their nations. Their ignorance of local conditions was acknowledged by the British prime minister Lord Salisbury: "We have been giving away mountains and rivers and lakes to each other, only hindered by the small impediment that we never knew exactly where they were."[24] Traditional peoples were brought together in new, sometimes antagonistic, groupings and within boundaries that remain today, sometimes separating Indigenous Nations. Canadian soldiers, engineers, and surveyors played a major role in the expansion of the Empire, especially in West Africa.

Most African colonies were not considered suitable for European settlement, as the tropical climate and diseases made it difficult for Europeans to live there permanently. Like India and other areas of Asia, the African colonies formed part of the Dependent Empire.[25] West Africa was accepted as "a black man's country," to be exploited for its resources and ruled, but not settled, by Europeans. As in India, but unlike North America, relatively little land was taken from African possession. Raw materials and labour were the objectives. The inhabitants were also taxed to provide revenue to pay for the government.

In place of the self-government enjoyed by white settlers in the dominions, Indigenous peoples were ruled despotically, although limited powers were often delegated to local sub-rulers through a system of indirect rule. Harry Johnston, a prominent British explorer of Africa and colonial administrator who was a key player in the scramble, saw these areas as "plantation colonies." Echoing the racist beliefs of his time, he stated that these were "to be governed as India is governed, despotically but wisely, and with the first aim of securing good government and a reasonable degree of civilization to a large population of races inferior to the European."[26]

In contrast, some areas of southern, central, and eastern Africa, especially in the highlands of Kenya, were identified as being very suitable for European settlement. These areas were considered, like Canada, to be "a white man's country," where children could be freely reared "to form a native European race."[27] Thousands of Britons (including some Canadians) settled here, and the existing population was displaced. The settlers looked to Canada as a model for constitutional development and lobbied vigorously for self-government. They wanted to be free of Colonial Office interference so they could better secure their control over land, taxation, labour conditions for Black workers, and the franchise. They were successful in gaining self-government for themselves in South Africa and what became Southern Rhodesia (now Zimbabwe), although not in Kenya, Northern Rhodesia (now Zambia), and Nyasaland (now Malawi).

What distinguished the European settlements in southern and eastern Africa from their counterparts in North America, Australia, and New Zealand was that the settlers remained outnumbered by the Indigenous peoples on whom they depended for labour. In the other settler-controlled societies, Indigenous peoples could be marginalized and ignored, but this was not possible in Africa. Some non-British white settlers in Africa posed a serious challenge to the imperial government. Conflict in southern Africa with the Afrikaners or Boers (descendants of Dutch, German, and French settlers) over land, gold, and diamonds led to the Boer Wars of 1880–81 and 1899–1902, in which Canadian contingents participated. The British were victorious. However, the Afrikaners, who outnumbered the British residents, controlled the Union of South Africa, established in 1909, which united the Afrikaans and British colonies in a manner similar to the Canadian Confederation. The Union of South Africa acquired self-government powers. Dominion status was also granted, and South Africa was included in the *Statute of Westminster*.

African independence movements were encouraged by the success in India. Independence for most African colonies followed that in India by a decade or so, commencing with the Gold Coast (Ghana) in 1957. However, independence for the settler colonies was more complex. Various measures were used to maintain the supremacy of the settlers, but independence and majority rule eventually came, including in Southern Rhodesia in 1980 (after a settler rebellion and civil war) and in South Africa in 1994 (after decades of peaceful protests, sabotage, and attacks on police and military targets combined with international support, including boycotts that made South Africa a pariah on the global stage).

◄◄ • ►►

By 1970, the British Empire had shrunk to a tiny remnant of its former self. Indigenous peoples of former colonies had received self-government and independence, except in the settler colonies, including Canada. Here the shadow of the Empire lingered. To this day, Indigenous peoples in Canada have no express constitutionally recognized right of self-government, and independence is not an option. However, under pressure from Indigenous groups, Aboriginal and treaty rights have been recognized, including the right to land. There has also been negotiation of modern treaties and a greater willingness to address some of the harm caused by colonialism. These changes form part of a process sometimes termed "reconciliation" and sometimes "decolonization." These processes would have been inconceivable to the imperialists who helped establish the Empire.

The Essentials of the Empire

Canada's two-cent stamp for Christmas 1898 was a map of the world with the British Empire boldly coloured red from Australia in the west to Africa and India in the east (see page ii). Canada was at the centre, having pride of place, its size exaggerated by the Mercator projection.[1] By comparison, the British Islands were given no prominence. The boast "We Hold a Vaster Empire Than Has Been" written across the bottom of the stamp was derived from Sir Lewis Morris's "A Song of Empire," which had proclaimed (again, with some exaggeration), "Nigh half the race of man is subject to our Queen! Nigh half the wide, wide earth is ours in fee!"[2] The song was written to celebrate Queen Victoria's Golden Jubilee, held in 1887. The design of the stamp was by Canada's postmaster-general, Sir William Mulock, and followed a discussion at a conference in London on a uniform postal rate for the Empire. The image on the stamp was similar to a map prepared by prominent Canadian imperialist George Parkin to be used in Canadian schools to show Canada's central place in the Empire. The wording reflected the fact that most Canadians were British and so shared ownership of the Empire with fellow Britons in the UK, Australia, New Zealand, and parts of Africa and Asia.

Imperialists loved to describe the large number of countries over which the Union Jack flew to signify British rule. At its greatest territorial breadth in the 1930s, the Empire comprised about a quarter of the globe. It was, indeed, the largest empire that the world had seen or would see (if we exclude informal empires of economic or cultural influence rather than rule). So what were the essential elements that characterized this global empire?

The Expansion of the Empire

In his book *Our British Empire*, the famous Canadian writer and imperialist Stephen Leacock traces the expansion of the British Empire back to John Cabot's voyage of 1497 to the coast of what was to become British North America and later Canada. Leacock considers Newfoundland the oldest colony, following Sir Humphrey Gilbert's taking possession in 1583, although he notes the competing claim of Bermuda.[3] Newfoundland's claim recently received a boost from historian Lizzie Collingham in her account of how the Empire was shaped by a search for food. She traces the history of the fishing industry in that colony and how it helped fund, crew, and sustain later voyages. In her words, "The British Empire was born on Newfoundland's stony beaches."[4]

The date of the Empire's end is also a matter of debate. The return of Hong Kong to China in 1997 is often used as the marker, giving the Empire a life of five hundred years if we ignore the scattered remnants of rocks and islands that still make up the fourteen British Overseas Territories. Historians often divide the British Empire chronologically into the First and Second Empires, with the loss of the American colonies in 1776 marking the end of the First Empire.

The British colonies in what became Canada formed part of this First Empire. They were overshadowed by their rebellious neighbours and fellow British subjects to the south, who first demonstrated that the Empire had more to fear from colonizing settlers than colonized Indigenous peoples. The loyal colonies, and the new colonies that subsequently joined them to form Canada, remained part of what became known as the Second Empire. This new Empire was centred on India – the Jewel in the Crown.

Sometimes historians identify a Third British Empire, which began with the change in status of Canada and the other settler colonies to become dominions and, in theory, autonomous equal partners with the United Kingdom.[5] A Fourth Empire has also been identified, commencing with Britain's new focus after the Second World War on economic development in Africa and Southeast Asia.[6]

The political and ideological height of the Empire was during the reign of Queen Victoria from 1837 to 1901.[7] The start of many significant developments can be dated to the 1830s and 1840s: slavery was abolished throughout much of the Empire; the commercial activities of the East India Company were terminated in India; migration from the UK to the colonies became more popular and better organized; the Privy Council in London became the supreme court for the Empire; the Colonial Service was born to administer over the colonies; the Durham Report, which led to internal self-government for Canada and other settler colonies, was written; the "civilization" program for Indigenous peoples in Canada was approved; an early predecessor of the *Indian Act* was passed; the first residential school was opened in Canada; the report of the Select Committee report on Aboriginal Tribes, with its stress on a humanitarian approach, was published in the UK and applied to all of its colonies; and the domination of new regions of the world was extended with greater vigour.

In 1860, the territorial extent of the Empire was 9.5 million square miles.[8] It reached its political zenith at the end of Victoria's reign. The South African War of 1899 to 1902, called the Boer War at the time, led to a frenzy of imperial fervour throughout the United Kingdom and the settler colonies, including Canada. After the First World War, there was further expansion when the British Empire added German colonies in Africa and the Pacific. But the era of empire-building or High Imperialism was effectively over. And yet, its shadow remains.

The Global Mosaic

The British Empire developed without an overarching plan or vision and lacked consistency. Leacock noted it had no corporate existence, no uniform system of money, no Empire bank, consolidated public debt, or command of public lands or natural resources; no uniform control of navigation, commerce, immigration, or land settlement.[9]

Leacock and another Canadian author, George Woodcock, give some idea of the extent and variety of the Empire in 1930 in their books. Echoing the famous boast of imperialists, Leacock writes, "The sun never sets on the British Empire. It tries to, but it can't."[10] Woodcock describes the reach of the Empire:

> In [1930,] His Majesty's gunboats sailed unchallenged up the rivers of China and His Majesty's representatives ruled *de jure* or *de facto* over the lands of the Pharaoh and the Great Moghul, over Jerusalem and Babylon and Baghdad, over the Rockies and the Himalayas and the Mountains of the Moon, over tropical jungles in four continents and frozen wastes in the Arctic and the Antarctic, over Rajput princes claiming the ancestry of the sun and Cypriot heirs of the glory that was Greece and palaeolithic hunters wandering the deserts of Africa and Australia.[11]

The Empire then comprised almost one-quarter of the land area of the world – around 13 million square miles.[12] About 7.5 million square miles made up the self-governing dominions of Canada, South Africa, Australia, and New Zealand. British India, ruled from the India Office in London, accounted for another almost 2 million square miles. The balance was made up of African and other colonies and protectorates administered by the Colonial or Foreign Offices. About 500 million people lived in the Empire, or about a quarter of the global population. Only 70 million were of European ancestry.

The Empire has been described as "a global mosaic of almost ungraspable complexity and staggering contrasts."[13] The variety was immense: every part of the world, every manner of primary products and raw materials needed for manufacture, and almost every race of people, language, laws, religion, and culture.[14] It included a surprising number of government structures, including self-governing nations like Canada, despotic governors with legislatures comprised of officials and nominated or elected members, powers supposedly granted by local rulers, mandates from the League of Nations, and shared power (or "condominiums") with other nations.[15] Although proposals for Canada to annex West Indian colonies were never implemented, Australia had its own colonial possessions in New Guinea.[16] Jan Morris, the historian and writer, observed that there were "paramountcies, suzerainties, protectorates, leases, concessions, partitions, areas of interest, no-man's-lands and related hinterlands."[17] According to one estimate, the Empire covered "one continent, a hundred peninsulas, five hundred promontories, a thousand lakes, two thousand rivers, ten thousand islands."[18] This vast area was shown coloured red on maps displayed in schools from Calgary to Kalgoorlie.

Summarizing this diversity, one colonial official wrote in 1938, "The most obvious characteristic of this Colonial Empire is, without doubt, its variety. No geographical continuity binds together these diverse territories, no similarity of climate or situation. The units vary in size, from vast continental countries like Nigeria to small oceanic islands; they vary in history, in civilisation, in constitutional developments and in form of government."[19]

The absence of consistency in form of government partially reflected the lack of firm central control from London. From the early nineteenth century, power had been exercised by the governments of the settler colonies, such as Canada, which became internally self-governing. In the rest of the Empire (the Dependent Empire), powers were delegated to the governors appointed by the British government. They ruled despotically through a dizzying variety of governance models, although often using local agents under a system known as "indirect rule." The Parliament in London had ultimate authority but limited interest in colonial affairs, so it intervened only rarely and mainly on matters that concerned the Empire as a whole. The India Office and the Colonial Office were the main central authorities, although they shared their imperial powers with the Foreign Office and several other departments.

Leacock and others called for more unity and even an imperial parliament with representatives from the white colonies as well as the United Kingdom – an imperial federation – but they failed. R.B. Bennett, who later became Canadian prime minister, was an enthusiastic supporter. As an MP, he declared to Parliament in 1913, "I preach a new parliament, an Imperial parliament, where Canadians, Australians, South Africans, and New Zealanders shall sit side by side with the English, Welsh and Scotch and Irish, and legislate for this great Imperial Empire."[20] There were many other Canadian politicians who were vocal in their support, but as Charles Dilke, an English politician, pointed out, they regarded it as safe "to talk enthusiastically about Imperial Federation in the abstract, provided it is understood that no serious practical action is to be taken towards that end."[21] Their opponents, led by Liberal leaders Wilfrid Laurier and Mackenzie King, preferred a looser form of imperialism – a voluntary association rather than a federation. Laurier delivered the death blows at imperial conferences of representatives from the UK and the settler colonies. In private correspondence, he described the proposal for an imperial parliament possessing taxation powers as "absurd and unworkable."[22] He warned the Canadian Parliament in 1892 that representation in London meant assuming responsibility for the almost perpetual imperial wars, although he conceded the idea had "grandeur."[23] By 1930, the opponents had been successful. Their opposition to a stronger, more centralized Empire may have been partly responsible for the end of the Empire that was to occur within a few decades.

Despite this overall lack of consistency and central control, many common elements such as legal systems, civil services, culture, banking, and commercial practices originated in British practice. These common elements resulted in a world system with extensive links that meant the component parts worked well together and were made stronger. Also, the UK Parliament could pass laws that overrode colonial laws. The Judicial Committee of the Privy Council in London, composed mainly of English judges, acted as the final court of appeal whether the dispute involved the common law of most of Canada, the civil law of Quebec, the Roman-Dutch law of South Africa and Ceylon, Islamic law, Indian religious laws, or one of the Indigenous laws of Africa.[24] One of its more interesting decisions involved Quebec religious law. The court ordered a burial in a Catholic cemetery in Montreal which the church had refused because of the deceased's political views.[25] (In the end, the French Canadian bishop prevailed over the British judges by simply deconsecrating the burial

Canada and Colonialism

site.) The court's decisions on Canada's constitution had greater impact, especially those concerning the division of powers between the federal and provincial governments, by denying the federal government's power to pass much social legislation in the 1930s.[26]

Above the variety of constitutional structures, there was (at least in theory) one path leading to self-government within the Empire (or, as it became known, the Commonwealth). This path began with being a Crown colony with despotic rule by a governor, then adding representative institutions, then responsible government, and eventually achieving the final stage of full autonomy within the Empire (dominion status). Canada had pioneered that path, which was always a proud boast of Canadians. This was "the meaning and purpose" of the Empire according to its enthusiastic boosters, such as historian Reginald Coupland.[27] The despotism of the day would lead to some vague future freedom based on the Canadian model. But, of course, imperialists thought the process would take decades and perhaps centuries for some parts of the Empire. For them, it was always a promise of jam tomorrow not today.

Those parts of the Empire were to be found in the non-white colonies or, as they were called at the time, the dependent colonies or territories. They were to be ruled despotically until they were ready for dominion status. This division into self-governing, majority white, settler dominions, such as Canada, and majority non-white, dependent colonies was fundamental and widely acknowledged. Few British people, however, thought it necessary to take much notice of the Indigenous peoples within the settler colonies. Even fewer would have taken seriously any claim by the Indigenous peoples to self-government. After any initial resistance had been overcome, their fate was to be ruled by the settlers, followed by their eventual extinction or assimilation. In 1904, Lord Minto, the governor general, said the "very difficult question" of "Canada's management of her Indians ... [had been] practically worked out."[28] In the words of one commentator in 1907, "the native problem has settled itself by exhaustion."[29]

Economic Motives

The dominant motivation for the Empire is usually recognized as being economic.[30] Certainly, the leaders of independence movements had little doubt of this. Kwame Nkrumah, political theorist and the first prime minister of Ghana, wrote in 1942 that "the aim of all colonial governments in Africa and elsewhere has been the struggle for raw materials; and not only this, but the colonies have become the dumping ground, and the colonial peoples the false recipients of manufactured goods ... This is colonialism in a nutshell."[31] In *Burmese Days,* George Orwell, the famous novelist and a former police officer in Burma, summed up the situation with his usual insight and clarity: "'My dear doctor,' said Flory, 'how can you make out that we are in this country for any purpose except to steal? It's so simple. The official holds the Burman down while the businessman goes through his pockets.'"[32] Orwell later explained that "the high standard of life we enjoy in England depends upon our keeping a tight hold on the Empire, particularly the tropical portions of it such as India and Africa. Under the capitalist system, in order that England might live in comparative comfort, a hundred million Indians must live on the verge of starvation."[33]

More thoughtful imperialists, such as the colonial administrator Lord Lugard, conceded, "It would be absurd to deny that the initial motive for the penetration of Africa by Western civilisation was (with the exception of the religious missions) the satisfaction of its material necessities, and not pure altruism."[34] Margery Perham, Lugard's biographer and another expert on colonial administration, agreed that the British Empire "through most of its duration, like all other empires, had been created and conducted mainly in the interests of the ruling power."[35] Coupland admitted that Europe demanded the economic development. However, ever the Empire booster, Coupland believed it was the duty of trusteeship to see that such development did no more injury to Africa than it had done to Europe (an odd twist on the "do no harm" principle).[36] Economic motives varied from those of individuals who spent their working lives in distant colonies to those of powerful corporations such as the East India Company, the Hudson's Bay Company, and the British South Africa Company, which accumulated great wealth for their shareholders.

With a few notable exceptions, there was widespread agreement that European nations had a right to the resources of the Dependent Empire.[37] Bernard Shaw, the Irish playwright and a Fabian socialist, wrote that the notion that a nation has a right to do what it pleases with its own territory without reference to the interests of the rest of the world "is no more tenable from the International Socialist point of view ... than the notion that a landlord has a right to do what he likes with his estate without reference to the interests of his neighbours."[38] Harry Johnstone, a colonial administrator, was colourful in his support of the views of the majority: "Whatever a few poets – dreamy enthusiasts sure of bed and board, theorists who write in a spirit of perversity – may pretend, the world at large is arriving at a pitch of intolerance of the lotos eater. It wants him to can or cask his lotos berries and ship them overseas in exchange for manufactured goods."[39] Sydney Olivier, who was both a Fabian and a colonial administrator, wrote, "Freedom of access to and exploitation of natural resources is now generally recognized as a common right of mankind."[40]

Within the settler colonies, this sense of entitlement led to the settlers demanding access to the resources of those colonies with limited regard for the claims of the Indigenous peoples.[41] Future Canadian prime minister Wilfrid Laurier argued that "it was not contrary to moral law to take possession, and even forcible possession, of territories which were roamed over rather than possessed by savage tribes."[42] Leacock thought that "without accepting the brutal code of the right of the strongest, one may in all reasonableness recognize the right of civilized nations to the acquisition of territory which is only 'squatted upon' by wandering savages."[43]

Racism

As the comments from Laurier and Leacock reveal, if economics provided the motivation for the Empire, with its division into the British as the rulers and the Indigenous peoples as the ruled, beliefs in racial and cultural supremacy provided the justification. However painful it may be for some readers to see these racist beliefs repeated here, it is impossible to avoid dealing with racism in any discussion of the Empire. As Indian politician Shashi Tharoor comments, it "was central to the imperial project: it was widespread, flagrant and profoundly insulting, and it worsened as British power grew."[44]

Racist beliefs were widespread and varied but, for convenience, can be divided into "scientific racism" and "cultural racism." They overlapped and a person might believe in both. "Scientific" racists thought that there were different races possessing differing levels of intellectual and moral abilities. The French nobleman and writer Arthur Gobineau was a prominent exponent of the theory who had great influence both in Europe and North America. His book, *Essai sur l'inégalité des races humaines*, published in 1853, set out his theory that the white race was superior and that racial mixing led to the decline of civilization.[45] As we shall see, such beliefs were held by prominent Canadians, such as John A. Macdonald, the first prime minister of Canada, and British imperialists such as John Buchan, who became a popular governor general of Canada.[46]

Belief in white superiority was reflected in the theory of cultural evolution that saw different races on different levels of the ladder ranging from "savagery" to "civilization," with European societies on the top rung. This theory was often seen as an application of the theory of biological evolution developed by Charles Darwin and Alfred Wallace in the mid-nineteenth century. It formed part of the new discipline of anthropology, created in the latter half of the century, especially by Edward Tylor in England. He advanced the theory that "the savage state in some measure represents an early condition of mankind, out of which the higher culture has gradually been developed or evolved."[47]

The colonial administrator C.L. Temple summarized the theory: "The native is a human being like ourselves, but in a different stage of development ... The whirligig of time has brought us from five hundred to a thousand years ahead of them in the process of evolution, that is all."[48] Another colonial administrator, Harry Johnstone, was so convinced of its validity that in his book *The Backward Peoples,* he produced a detailed table listing nations and peoples based on a mathematical appraisal according to their level of cultural maturity. He started with Great Britain, the white colonies, the United States, Western European nations, and Japan at 100 percent. He then descended to the Indigenous peoples of Dutch New Guinea and French Central Africa at 75 percent. Black South Africa and most of the rest of Africa had a grade of 90 percent. A score of 95 percent or below meant that self-government was not presently an option. He claimed, "The Backward peoples have mostly stopped in some rut, some siding of human culture, whereas the White Man during the last thousand years has gone speeding ahead till he has attained the powers and outlook of a demi-god."[49]

Historian Eric Hobsbawm has observed that racism pervaded imperialist thought to an extent that is hard to appreciate today.[50] But with some exceptions, such as southern and eastern Africa and the *Indian Act* in Canada, discrimination was not the official policy. Following the 1857 Indian Rebellion, an uprising against the rule of the British East India Company, Queen Victoria's Proclamation of 1858 declared her will that "Our subjects of whatever Race or Creed be freely and impartially admitted to Offices in Our Service, the Duties of which they may be qualified, by their education, ability and integrity, duly to discharge."[51] When Lord Stanley, as governor general, opened the park named after him in Vancouver in 1888, he dedicated it to "the use and enjoyment of peoples of all colours, creeds, and customs, for all time."[52] In 1921, Winston Churchill, who was then the Colonial Secretary, addressed the Dominion premiers: "I think there is only one ideal that the British Empire can set before itself, and that is that there should be no barrier of race, colour or creed which should prevent any man by merit from reaching any station if he is fitted for it."[53] This was mere rhetoric.

Churchill himself was a racist in private and sometimes in public. This is clear from *Churchill's Empire* by Richard Toye. He had an "unashamed belief in white superiority, a conviction which, for him, did not lessen the need to act humanely towards supposedly inferior races that might, in their own way, be worthy of admiration."[54] He made statements such as "I hate people with slit-eyes and pig-tails," and referred to Africans as degraded, "brutish children."[55] The dispossession of Indigenous peoples in North America and Australia did not concern him: "I do not admit ... that a great wrong has been done to the Red Indians of America ... I do not admit that a wrong has been done to these people by the fact that a stronger race, a higher-grade race, or, at any rate, a more worldly wise race to put it that way, has come in and taken their place."[56]

Nearly every speech and book by British residents, politicians, colonial officials, soldiers, and historians on imperial matters reflected racism to a greater or lesser extent, as shown in the following examples. Writing of her experiences as a griffin, or newly arrived Englishwoman to India, in 1836, Julia Maitland said it was painful to witness the rudeness and contempt with which the English treated the local people.[57] Winwood Reade, a Victorian adventurer and historian who had an impact on Churchill's thinking,[58] thought that the possible extermination of Africans to facilitate white settlement must be accepted with composure.[59] Garnet Wolseley, a famous imperial soldier with a close connection to Canada, "found the town negro an objectionable animal." Wolseley felt he would have been more useful if slavery had not been abolished, since he was clearly intended to be the white man's servant.[60]

Lord Milner, a leading colonial official, assured an audience of white South Africans in 1903 that "political equality of white and black is impossible. The white man must rule because he is elevated by many, many steps above the black man."[61] In his 1905 guide for those intending to go to the West African coast, Alan Field of the Colonial Political Service described Africans "in the lump [as] lazy, feckless, sensual, and beyond all fancying, superstitious," although there were any number of exceptions.[62] For politicians we can quote former British Conservative prime minister Arthur Balfour, who spoke for most of his fellow countrymen when he said, during the debate on the Union of South Africa in 1910: "All men are, from some points of view, equal; but to suppose that the races of Africa are in any sense equal to men of European descent, so far as government, or society, or the higher interests of civilization are concerned is really, I think, an absurdity."[63] To give another example, in his classic work on colonial administration in 1922, Lord Lugard saw the typical African as "full of personal vanity, with little sense of veracity."[64]

As members of the British World, most Canadians shared this belief in their racial superiority in their attitude toward Indigenous peoples throughout the Empire, including in Canada itself. Historian Phillip Buckner points out that most of the emigrants from Britain who poured into Canada in the nineteenth century were relatively liberal and took pride in the abolition of slavery. "But they were not cultural relativists. Most were committed to ... a belief in the innate superiority of the British character. They had limited sympathy for the native peoples and as scientific racism grew stronger in late nineteenth-century Britain it also became more pronounced in British colonies overseas."[65]

George Simpson, the governor of the Hudson's Bay Company, made a typical comment in 1825 when he described the Indigenous people of the Columbia River Valley as "indolent and lazy to the extreme."[66] Likewise, Victoria's *British Colonist* newspaper declared in 1861, "Their habits of indolence, roaming propensities, and natural repugnance for manual labour, together with a thievish disposition which appears to be inherently characteristic of the Indian race, totally disqualifies them from ever becoming either useful or desirable citizens."[67]

Racist views were shared by the politicians of all parties who made the laws, including the various versions of the *Indian Act* that we shall consider in Chapter 6.[68] The Conservative prime minister John Macdonald, who was also the minister responsible for Indian Affairs, believed in biological racism, telling Parliament in 1885 that "the Aryan races will not wholesomely amalgamate with the Africans or the Asiatics," and warning against "mongrel races."[69] The debate on plans to extend the vote to some Indigenous peoples in 1886 brought forth a burst of racist comments, referring to "Indians" going from "a scalping party to the polls" and having insufficient intelligence to use the vote.[70] Debates on the exclusion of immigrants from China and India were likewise full of racist comments.[71] Liberal leader Mackenzie King developed policies to maintain Canada as "a white man's country."[72] James Woodsworth, a progressive politician and one of the founders of what became the New Democratic Party, expressed his appreciation in 1909 that there was no "negro problem" in Canada.[73]

Sam Steele, famous for his role as a Mountie in controlling the Klondike Gold Rush, and who fought in the South African War or Boer War, which ended in 1902, recorded his negative views about Africans. They were "by nature untruthful and few are capable of gratitude for any kind act. Admonition by the cat-o'-nine-tails is the only thing understood."[74] Writing in 1940, Stephen Leacock said no one should doubt the superiority of the "white races." Like Macdonald, he was a biological racist: "The Eastern and Western races cannot unite. Biologists tell us where they intermarry their progeny is an ill-joined product, two brains rattling in one skull." Like most of his countrymen, he opposed non-white immigration, fearing "a yellow Canada." Imperial

Stephen Leacock, leading writer, gentle humourist, and racist imperialist, as an old man. | *Yousuf Karsh, Library and Archives Canada, PA-160312*

federation, which he advocated, could not include Indians. "Still less could it include the black subjects of the Queen, now multiplying in Africa."[75] He saw world history as "the question of the Aryan civilization of the West and the uncivilized, or at best semi-civilized people of the Orient." The British Empire, including Canada, was the front line of the white race in this battle.[76]

Racism was rampant in Canada until at least 1945, as evidenced by school textbooks.[77] In his book *The Red Man's on the Warpath*, historian Scott Sheffield compares the images of Indigenous peoples in Canada held by the public and by Indian Affairs officials before, during, and immediately after the Second World War. He finds generally negative views, although the public's image tended to be more romantic.[78] As late as 1951, Lester Pearson, then Secretary of State for External Affairs, made a speech to the Canadian Club in which he compared the Cold War to the situation "which confronted our fore-fathers in early colonial days when they ploughed the land with a rifle slung on the shoulder. If they stuck to the plough and left the rifle at home, they would have been easy victims for any savages lurking in the woods."[79]

Racist views did not preclude sympathy for the plight of Indigenous peoples, although this sympathy was not universal. George Grant, a prominent imperialist, lamented, "Poor creatures! not much use have they ever made of the land; but yet, in admitting the settler, they sign their own death warrants!" He went on to maintain, "It is too late to argue the question; the red man ... is being civilised off the ground ... His wild, wandering life is inconsistent with modern requirements."[80] Prime Minister Macdonald told Parliament in 1880, "We must remember that they are the original owners of the soil, of which they have been dispossessed by the covetousness or ambition of our ancestors ... the Indians have been great sufferers by the discovery of America, and the transfer to it of a large white population. We are bound to protect them."[81] Even a hardened soldier like Garnet Wolseley, who fought Indigenous peoples around the Empire, including during the Red River Resistance of 1869–70, could express regret: "I have never encountered any Indian tribes without experiencing a feeling of remorse not only for having robbed them of their hunting grounds, but still more for killing them off with the fatal poison of whiskey."[82]

But some were not moved. In an early history of Canada written in 1850, John McMullen described Indigenous peoples before the arrival of Europeans. He concluded, "A poor and thinly scattered community of improvident savages has been succeeded by an orderly, industrious, and enterprising people ... Canada must ere long attain to a high position in the scale of nations, and thus leave little room for regret that ... the rule of the fierce Indian has forever passed *away*."[83]

What led to such racist views? Some, perhaps most, were biological racists who believed that the inferiority of other races arose from their genes. As such, they could never expect to be equal. Others were cultural evolutionists who thought that environmental reasons led to differing levels of evolution and, over time, other races might become equal. We shall consider this approach shortly. There were other explanations. One was fear in areas where Europeans were a small, privileged, but vulnerable minority. They needed displays of subservience and conformity from "the subject peoples" to demonstrate their superiority and so assuage their insecurity.[84] Another explanation was identified by George Trevelyan, a Victorian writer on the British in India: "No one can estimate very highly the moral and intellectual qualities of people among whom he resides for the sole purpose of turning them to pecuniary account."[85] In other words, supposed racial inferiority justified conquest and exploitation.

Canada and Colonialism

Trevelyan also noted that some Europeans who were ranked low in their own class-ridden society could achieve some feeling of self-worth by ill-treating Indians: "A native of rank ... will be flouted and kicked about by any planter's assistant or sub-deputy railway-contractor whose path he may chance to cross."[86] The relevance of class was also noted by Arthur Berriedale Keith, a professor of Sanskrit as well as law at the University of Edinburgh. He was highly critical of the restrictions placed by Canada and the other settler colonies on immigration by non-Europeans. He suggested that "a certain lack of culture and good breeding on the part of the average inhabitant of a Dominion renders him incapable of appreciating the fact that .. it is ludicrous to classify, as mentally he often does, every kind of man of colour as a coolie."[87]

Since the official policy in most of the Empire was against formal legal discrimination, racism often relied on unofficial policies and attitudes that effectively discriminated in practice. In reference to people from India, Leacock gloated, "We would never dream of letting in Indians, touchables or untouchables. We forbid their immigration, not by law but by a lawyer's trick."[88] This was a reference to the regulation requiring immigrants to arrive directly from their country of origin, which effectively excluded Indians since no vessels made direct journeys between India and Canada. The colonial services that administered the Empire had racial criteria for recruitment but were reluctant to publicize discriminatory restrictions and went to great lengths to obscure them.

In practice, "pure European descent" was generally required for positions of authority. Therefore, one Canadian applicant to the Colonial Service caused anxiety in 1927 as he was not of such descent. The head of recruitment, Ralph Furse, wrote that it would be unwise to appoint anyone "who from a knowledge of their antecedents, or from their personal appearance, might be suspected of having a mixture of non-European (I mean of course, coloured) blood." The following year, a "West Indian Negro" residing in Canada applied via the recruitment board there for a position with the Nigerian Government Railway. Furse told a contact in Canada that this was a "very difficult question, and one about which we have to be extremely circumspect."[89] One common form of discrimination on both racial and class grounds was the vague criterion of "character." It was widely used to deny appointment or promotion to those not of an upper-middle-class, exclusively European background.

There were, of course, degrees of racism ranging from the segregation and brutality of southern Africa to benevolent paternalism. Ronald Hyam, a historian, suggests that we should distinguish between "racism" and racial prejudice – the former being what many people today would refer to as "structural racism" and the latter "individual racism." Racism, Hyam argues, should be restricted to the abnormal systematization of racial prejudice into institution-alized discrimination or exploitation. Examples would include South Africa before multiracial elections, the "White Australian" immigration policy (also effectively the Canadian policy until the 1960s), and, presumably, Canada's *Indian Act*. Throughout most of the Empire, there was "no legal separation but an insidious hierarchical social convention."[90] Paternalism was widespread. Indigenous peoples were seen as childlike and requiring the firm guidance of those who knew what was best for them, as summed up in the civilizing mission or "the White Man's Burden" considered below. George Orwell describes a paternal official in *Burmese Days:* "He had no prejudices against Orientals; indeed, he was deeply fond of them. Provided they were given no freedom he thought them the most charming people alive. It always pained him to see them wantonly insulted."[91]

It should also be recognized that, as acknowledged by Tharoor, some Euro-peans could rise above the prejudices of their age to treat Indigenous peoples with compassion, curiosity, and respect.[92] Among them, for example, were Allan Octavian Hume, who was a member of the Indian Civil Service, an expert on Indian birds, and one of the founders of the Indian National Congress, which was to lead India to independence; and Annie Besant, who became the president of the Congress. Based on his review of debates in the Canadian House of Commons from 1880 to 1920, one writer concludes that "it was scarcely possible to stand in the House to make a speech denigrating a 'race,' without someone rising in principled objection to remarks that they considered un-British, unchristian, illiberal, or just plain prejudiced."[93] However, such op-position appears to have been in the minority and often motivated by good manners rather than a belief in equality.

Cultural Superiority and the Civilizing Mission

Related to racism was a feeling of cultural superiority. One writer has pointed out that some British administrators in India "may have been racially aloof and even dismissive, but they were not racist in the sense that they considered racial differences to be permanent and innate. They believed they belonged not to a superior race but to a more advanced civilization."[94] (Of course, to those who were considered inferior, it was probably irrelevant if their treatment was based on a belief in racial or cultural supremacy or both.) This sense of cultural superiority was expressed by Thomas Macaulay, politician and historian, who wrote a famous memorandum in 1835 on education in India, arguing for the creation of "a class of persons, Indians in blood and colour but English in taste,

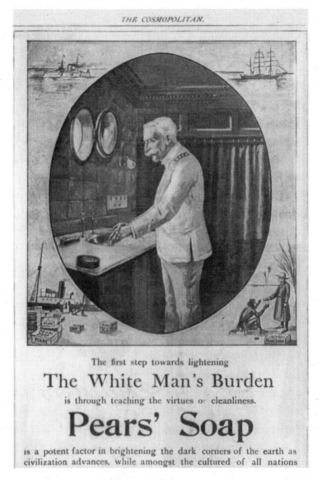

This Pears' Soap advertisement promoted cleanliness – achieved through the use of Pears' soap – as a means of easing "the White Man's Burden" of advancing civilization. | McClure's Magazine, *October 1899, via Wikimedia Commons*

in opinions, in morals, and in intellect." This was required due to the inferiority of Oriental culture: "A single shelf of a good European library was worth the whole native literature of India and Arabia."[95] Canadians shared this sense of cultural superiority. Politician Frank Oliver, who served as head of the Department of Indian Affairs, said in 1917, "We claim that this Empire of ours is the most perfect fruit of the civilization of which we are a part. Our claim is that it stands today at the head of white civilization. It can only retain that position by being maintained by a white civilization."[96]

To the Victorians, their superior technology was tangible proof that the British were at a higher stage of cultural evolution than the "backward" Indigenous peoples. This disparity was vividly shown at world fairs by dividing the world into pavilions for European nations, which displayed and celebrated the technological progress being made by them, and "native villages" showing Indigenous peoples in their traditional villages.[97] For example, the 1895 African Exhibition at the Crystal Palace in London included eighty Somalis wearing animal skins and living in a kraal, where they slept and ate.[98] Introducing the benefits of new technologies to primitive lands was a very practical application of the civilizing mission. In this case, imperialism would result in a charitable, Christian sharing of the benefits of Britain's superior civilization.

The rationale for Empire preferred by most imperialists is that it was an altruistic endeavour, perhaps even a religious obligation, to bring civilization and Christianity to the less fortunate of the world. It imposed a duty of self-sacrifice to serve humanity. The civilizing mission was usually characterized as a trust and even a sacred trust. The origins of this view were worthy and sincere and went back, like much else in the development of the Second Empire, to England in the 1830s and 1840s.[99] This was the zenith of humanitarianism, most often associated with the movement for the abolition of slavery throughout the Empire (including the colonies of British North America), which was largely successful in 1833.[100] This movement was very paternalistic and downplayed the role that slave revolts played in achieving emancipation. During the debate on the abolition legislation, the movement's Parliamentary leader, Fowell Buxton, a wealthy brewer, told the slaves, "out of duty, gratitude and self-interest," to "trust implicitly to that great nation and paternal Government who are labouring for your release."[101]

Concern also extended to the condition of Indigenous peoples in the colonies. Buxton noted in 1834, "My attention has been drawn of late to the wickedness of our proceedings as a nation, towards the ignorant and barbarous natives of countries on which we seize." To do justice, it had to be admitted that "as our settlements must be attended with some evils to them, it is our duty to give them compensation for those evils, by imparting the truths of Christianity and the arts of civilised life."[102] Another religious writer, William Howitt, claimed that "the numbers of negroes in slavery are but as a drop in the bucket compared to the numbers of aborigines who are perishing beneath our iron and unchristian policy" in the colonies.[103] The Aborigines Protection Society was founded in 1836 in response to such concern. Humanitarian principles extended into the Colonial Office under Lord Glenelg, Secretary of State for War and the Colonies; James Stephen, the head of the Colonial Service; and Stephen's successor, Herman Merivale.[104]

The high-water mark of humanitarianism concerning Indigenous peoples was the report of the Parliamentary committee on Aboriginal tribes under the chairmanship of Buxton, which sat for eighteen months and reported in 1837.[105] This committee was paternalistic in the extreme and reflected a belief in the superiority of British civilization. It considered settlement in the colonies to be "a benevolent and laudable object."[106] Nevertheless, it was very critical of colonial expansion in practice, which had been "a source of many calamities to uncivilized nations. Too often, their territory has been usurped; their property seized; their numbers diminished; their character debased; the spread of civilization impeded. European vices and diseases have been introduced amongst them."[107] These assertions were backed up by reports from different colonies. In Newfoundland, for example, it was accounted "a meritorious act" to kill an Indigenous person, and this was a factor in the extinguishment of the Beothuk people.[108] The committee said a more friendly and just policy "would materially contribute to and promote the civil and commercial interests of Great Britain."[109] It made nine key proposals, including withdrawing all Indigenous issues from colonial legislatures and leaving them with the governor and the central government in London, and prohibiting treaties between local governments and tribes. These proposals recognized the conflicts of interest between settlers and the protection of Indigenous peoples. We will see that they were not followed, with predictable results.

The humanitarian movement largely ceased to have a significant effect by the late 1850s. Historian Ronald Hyam links this decline to the spread of settlers: "Everywhere the settlers were gaining ground, and this was fatal to the humanitarian project. As concessions to white-dominated self-government multiplied, the metropolitan government was left with very little practical influence."[110] Despite the declining influence of the humanitarians, they were not without some impact, both genuine and rhetorical. Margery Perham, the colonial expert, said in 1961 that "the standard they left has never been wholly lost. It became part of Britain's public life, maintained by individuals of all parties or none, and especially by the churches, and the tradition has acted as a strong palliative, if not a cure, for the evils to which empire was prone."[111] But the impact of the movement should not be exaggerated. Eric Williams, the historian who led Trinidad and Tobago to independence, said in his seminal study of slavery published in 1944, "The humanitarians were the spearhead of the onslaught which destroyed the West Indian system and freed the Negro.

But their importance has been seriously misunderstood and exaggerated by men who have sacrificed scholarship to sentimentality."[112]

Trusteeship provided the veil of duty and service while justifying imperial rule.[113] Speaking of India, Prime Minister Lloyd George said in 1922, "We accepted the trust. We must execute it. No honourable man gets rid of a trust the first time the beneficiaries lose their temper with him and think they can manage the thing themselves better. We have no right to part with our responsibilities."[114] A similar statement was made over thirty years later by Oliver Lyttelton, the Secretary of State for the Colonies, about Central Africa: "We consider that we have a duty laid upon our shoulders as trustees, and if these duties mean anything, they mean that on occasions one must go forward even when some of the beneficiaries of the trust are not in accordance with one's views."[115] One writer noted in 1940 that, since the mandate system of the League of Nations was introduced in 1919 with the reference in Article 22 of its Covenant to the well-being of Indigenous people forming "a sacred trust of civilization," "the governing principle behind all colonial administration is that of trusteeship."[116]

Historian Kenton Storey has described rhetorical humanitarianism as "the strategic, and often cynical, use of humanitarian language to promote the interests of colonists while, at the same time, asserting the need to protect Indigenous peoples."[117] It required a high level of verbal and moral dexterity. But it failed to persuade Indigenous leaders and other critics of the Empire. Nnamdi Azikiwe, the first president of Nigeria, referred to what he called "aggressive altruism."[118] Jawaharlal Nehru, the first prime minister of India, said nothing astonished him so much "as the way the British people manage to combine their material interests with their moral fervour."[119] And Kwame Nkrumah, the first prime minister of Ghana, denounced humanitarianism as "deception, hypocrisy, oppression and exploitation" and an attempt "to cover the eyes of colonial peoples with the veil of imperialist chicanery."[120]

An American critic of British rule in India wrote, "Hypocrisy was added to brutality, while the robbery went on."[121] Orwell referred to "the lie that we're here to uplift our poor black brothers instead of to rob them."[122] Referring back to the origins of the Empire in the piracy of Henry Morgan and Walter Raleigh, some critics accused the humanitarians of "hoisting the Cross in place of the Jolly Roger, but without changing the sailing orders."[123] The actual experience of the colonized subjects of the Dependent Empire was very different from the humanitarian vision of the civilizing mission.

Some colonial residents and administrators were honest enough to admit the hypocrisy. George Trevelyan wrote in 1895, "There is not a single non-official person in India with whom I have conversed on public questions who

Canada and Colonialism

would not consider the sentiment that we hold India for the benefit of the inhabitants of India a loathsome un-English piece of cant."[124] Likewise, William Johnson Hicks, Home Secretary, said in 1928, "We did not conquer India for the benefit of the Indians. I know it is said in missionary meetings that we conquered India to raise the level of Indians. That is cant. We conquered India as an outlet for the goods of Great Britain. We conquered India by the sword and by the sword we shall hold it."[125]

Most of the leading imperialists promoted the civilizing mission or trusteeship. Thomas Macaulay famously expressed it at the conclusion of his speech in 1833 on the new charter for the East India Company:

> It may be that ... by good government we may educate our subjects into a capacity for better government, that, having become instructed in European knowledge, they may, in some future age, demand European institutions. Whether such a day will ever come I know not. But never will I attempt to avert or to retard it. Whenever it comes, it will be the proudest day in English history.[126]

"Protection" and "civilization" were the duties of colonial government, as described by Herman Merivale in his lectures on imperial policy. He gave these lectures in the 1840s as an Oxford professor before he joined the Colonial Office and then the India Office as a senior official.[127] Likewise, Queen Victoria thought the mission of Britain was "to protect the poor natives and to advance civilization."[128]

Joseph Chamberlain, a leading imperialist politician, gave a speech on the true conception of the Empire in 1897, declaring that "the sense of possession has given place to a different sentiment – the sense of obligation. We feel now that our rule over these territories can only be justified if we can show that it adds to the happiness and prosperity of the people ... In carrying out this work of civilisation we are fulfilling what I believe to be our national mission."[129] Speaking in the 1930s, Winston Churchill, another leading imperialist politician, referred to "our mission of bearing peace, civilisation and good government to the utmost ends of the earth."[130] He was proud the Indian people had been "lifted to a civilisation and to a level of peace, order, sanitation and progress far above anything they could possibly have achieved themselves or could maintain."[131]

The idea of the civilizing mission was widespread in Canada both in relation to the Empire generally and within Canada. Canadian imperialists were often infused with religious emotion that they channelled into calls for Canada to join in the British destiny of bringing the light of civilization and Christianity to the dark places in the world.[132] In 1867, during a lecture at Stratford, Ontario, the Rev. James George exclaimed that Britain "has been called to India for mighty purposes. God will not let her retire till she has accomplished *her destiny* there. She has to attend as a physician to a people who are sinking into the decrepitude of a worn-out civilization, with all the inherent vices of the worst forms of Paganism."[133] George Parkin, one of the leading Canadian imperialists, agreed. In his view, Britain "has assumed vast responsibilities in the government of the weak and alien races – responsibilities which she cannot now throw off, even if she wish to, without a loss of national honour. With increasing force the public conscience insists that her rule should be for the good of the ruled."[134] One Canadian politician explained, "We believe there are other races under the flag more backward than ours, struggling towards the light, who need [the British system of government], to come into the full stature of manhood as we have done."[135] Some Canadians took up the challenge and became missionaries overseas.[136]

Canadian settlers and governments adopted and applied the concept of the civilizing mission or wardship to justify their rule over Indigenous peoples in Canada. In 1868, Gilbert Sproat, an early settler in British Columbia, referred to "a wise and paternal action of the Crown" on behalf of the Indigenous peoples.[137] Joseph Trutch, a colonial official who was active in reducing the size of reserves in the province, wrote in 1870 that "the Indians have, in fact, been held to be the special wards of the Crown," and "in the exercise of this guardianship" the government had set aside the reserves.[138] Giving his report on the *Indian Act* of 1876, David Laird, minister of the Interior and superintendent-general of Indian Affairs, said, "Our Indian legislation generally rests on the principle, that the aborigines are to be kept in a condition of tutelage and treated as wards or children of the State."[139]

A speech by an Indian reserve commissioner to an Indigenous audience on Vancouver Island in 1876 expressed the prevailing self-satisfied view of the improvement of Indigenous peoples:

Many years ago you were in darkness killing each other and making slaves was your trade. The Land was of no value to you. The trees were of no value to you. The coal was of no value to you. The white man came he improved the land [and] you can follow his example – He cuts the trees and pays you to help him. He takes the coal out of the ground and he pays you to help him – You are improving fast. The Government protects you, you are rich – You live in peace and have everything you want.[140]

Canada and Colonialism

This sense of mission accomplished was expressed more romantically in "Pontiac," an 1893 poem by William Kirby:

> *We grow and prosper, and unenvied rise,*
> *And in the social race win many a prize,*
> *Our wigwams change to houses, wood and stone;*
> *Our forests turn to fields, our gardens glow*
> *With fruits and flowers – our barns are full of corn;*
> *The cattle in our pastures well repay*
> *The mighty game we hunted with the bow*
> *In our wild days of freedom long ago;*
> *Now casting off the skins and mantles rude*
> *Of our old life, we don the seemly garb*
> *Of Christian men and women, worship God,*
> *And make the laws that govern us, and stand*
> *Not wards, but freemen, of this glorious land.*[141]

The belief in wardship continued into the twentieth century. In 1916, Arthur Meighen, Solicitor General (and also later prime minister) of Canada, said in connection with the "surrender" (the release of a First Nation's legal interest in a reserve) of St. Peter's Reserve near Winnipeg: "The Government of Canada represents the Indians; the Indians are our wards, and we are making the settlement as their guardians."[142] Another Solicitor General, Hugh Guthrie, explained in 1920 the general inability of Indigenous people on reserves to vote on the grounds that they were wards of the state: "Indians who are living on a reserve and who are receiving the bounty of the Government are the wards of the Government and they have nearly always been disqualified under our Dominion Franchise Acts."[143]

Not everyone agreed that the civilizing mission had been a success. According to the British politician Ramsay MacDonald in 1907, "The history of the Indians in North America ... is too often a sorry comment on the white man's civilisation, and it presents to the Imperialist writer a multitude of awkward episodes which do not fit in with his panegyrics on how we have borne our responsibility for our native brethren."[144] The political scientist Harold Laski complained, "The idea of 'trusteeship' ... which has become so fashionable in our own day, is too flattering to the results obtained. It is hardly compatible with the historic incidence of the facts. It is a word whose sound is too noble for the squalid results too often attained."[145]

The reality was that, in most cases, insufficient steps were taken to "civilize" or educate Indigenous peoples beyond a basic level required for them to be better workers. Moreover, the few who were better educated were often regarded with hostility by colonial authorities and excluded from positions of power and economic advancement.

Jomo Kenyatta, who led Kenya to independence, wrote that Africans "are in the intolerable position when the European invasion destroys the very basis of their old tribal way of life, and yet offers them no place on the new society except as serfs doomed to labour for bare existence."[146] As stated by a character in *Les Blancs*, a 1994 play by Lorraine Hansberry, "the struggle here has not been to push the African into the Twentieth Century – but at all costs to keep him *away* from it! ... The problem, therefore, has been how *not* to educate him at all and – at the same time – teach him just enough to turn a dial and know which mining lever to raise."[147] Such development as took place was generally intended primarily for the benefit of the colonizers.

Opposition to "civilized" or "educated natives" was especially strong in Africa. The Colonial Secretary instructed officials in 1873: "I would have nothing to do with the 'educated natives' as a body. I would treat with the hereditary chiefs only, and endeavour as far as possible to rule through them."[148] The visceral hatred of western-educated "natives" is very apparent in the novels set in Africa written by John Buchan, a future governor general of Canada, and those set in India written by Sara Jeannette Duncan, a Canadian novelist. It reflected a general view that such "civilized" people would threaten the future of the Empire. As early as 1876, Lord Salisbury, the Secretary of State for India, described educated Indians as "an opposition in quiet times, rebels in time of trouble."[149] Indeed, this assessment was not inaccurate; educated Indians were a threat and would become leaders of the independence movement. Regardless, this hostility and the reluctance to give them any authority made a mockery of "the civilizing mission."

Residential schools in Canada, discussed in Chapter 6, also illustrated the hollowness of the "civilizing mission," which was their supposed justification. The conclusion of the Truth and Reconciliation Commission (TRC) in its report of 2015 was that "it is clear that even by the standards of the period in which they operated, residential schools failed to provide students with an adequate education and the promised vocational training."[150] Teachers were poorly qualified and trained, and there were no clear educational goals. As a result, students left the schools lacking the skills to succeed in their home communities or the broader labour market. In addition to their studies, they were expected to work within and outside the schools to make up for inadequate funding. Canada provided another example of this hollowness in the case of agriculture on Indian reserves in Saskatchewan. As shown by historian Sarah Carter in her study *Lost Harvests,* "although the government publicly proclaimed that its aim was to assist Indians to adopt agriculture, little was done to put this course into effect. In fact government policies acted to retard agriculture on the reserves."[151] They prevented the use of technology and promoted surrenders of the land. Such surrenders were often made to receive necessary supplies and to pay for housing and infrastructure on reserves, as well as for money.[152]

How Was Rule Over Indigenous Peoples Achieved?

William Blackstone, an influential English jurist, summarized the main ways the Empire acquired new lands in his *Commentaries* published in 1765: "Plantations, or colonies in distant countries, are either such where the lands are claimed by right of occupancy only, by finding them desert and uncultivated, and peopling them from the mother-country; or where, when already cultivated, they have been either gained by conquest, or ceded to us by treaties."[153] The first method of occupancy or "peopling them from the mother-country" was through settlement, even where nobody could seriously maintain that the lands were "desert and uncultivated." The second was cession (the transfer of rights or land by a nation) through treaties, and the third was conquest. These methods were not mutually exclusive. For example, much of eastern Canada was ceded by France in 1763 under the Treaty of Paris following the conquest of New France. A belt-and-suspenders approach was often taken. Also, the use of these methods was often gradual. A trading relationship might be followed by treaties, then settlement, the use of force, and conquest. Indigenous peoples may not have fully realized what was happening before it became too late to effectively resist.

Settlement

A distinguishing feature of the British Empire was the role played by migration to those parts considered suitable for settlement by Europeans, primarily for climatic reasons. Niall Ferguson, a historian, points out that no other country came close to exporting so many of its inhabitants: "The indispensable foundation of the Empire was mass migration."[154] The most significant and lasting legacy of the Empire was the settlement of people primarily from the United Kingdom to Canada and the other settler colonies.[155] However, it is essential to note at the outset that this was only one aspect of the overall process of colonization. The other side of the coin was, of course, the disruption, dispossession, and domination of the Indigenous peoples. Another historian, Ashley Jackson, states, "The burgeoning settler states were premised on the decline, subjugation and dispossession of their indigenous inhabitants. Not to compute that as a fundamental aspect of an imperial culture is to lose sight of the wood for the trees."[156] Settlement worked as a form of demographic dispossession as Indigenous peoples were overwhelmed by the waves of settlers that rolled over their lands.

We should also acknowledge that the Empire led to the mass movement of people of non-British ancestry and, in particular, those from Africa and India. Some of it was involuntary even after the abolition of the slave trade, which led to millions being transported.[157] The historian Ronald Hyam estimates that the Empire spread Indian communities into fifty-three countries.[158] These included Canada, although the Canadian government took steps to prevent immigration, as will be shown in Chapter 5. Internal migration of Indigenous peoples within colonies occurred as groups moved to take advantage of new opportunities or were dispossessed. In Canada, the Anishinaabe, the Iroquois, the Cree, and some other groups moved west with the fur trade.[159]

British migration and settlement were not a smooth, even process. They have been insightfully examined by James Belich, a professor of imperial and Commonwealth history, in *Replenishing the Earth*. He describes four types or stages: "incremental colonization, explosive colonization, recolonization, and decolonization."[160] At first, migration and settlement were slow and not a primary purpose of the Empire. Then, in 1823, Robert Wilmot-Horton, undersecretary for war and the colonies, wrote a report, *Outline of a Plan of Emigration to Upper Canada*, urging the assisted migration of paupers to be settled principally in Upper Canada. Later, migration became explosive as it was no longer thought of as the removal of undesirable elements (the "shovelling out of paupers"). Instead, it was seen as a desirable redistribution of the British population to new and, it was hoped, better Britains within a British World.[161] In a strong defence of colonization, the London *Times* argued in 1862, "Every emigrant becomes a far more productive customer when set down on a new soil than when he was struggling for existence at home." It continued, "There is no wiser policy for a country like ours than to take possession of the waste places of the earth, and give our crowded populations the power of settling in them under our own laws, modified, if need be, to suit their particular exigencies."[162] Lorenzo Veracini, an Australian author on settler colonialism, writes that "the turning point in the story of the global settler revolution was when schemes for the assisted emigration of paupers became schemes for the assisted emigration of a section of the whole of society."[163]

These CPR posters promoted immigration and the sale of ready-made farms to British boys and farmers. | *CRHA/Exporail, Canadian Pacific Railway Company Fonds*

Explosive migration did not last, as the economic cycle turned and bust followed boom. Exports to the United Kingdom came to the rescue of failing local economies. This stage led to strengthened and tightened relations that Belich describes as a "recolonization." The final stage of decolonization "consisted in the demise of recolonization in the mid-twentieth century and the emergence of real as against nominal Dominion independence."[164] Of course, this model does not apply exactly to all those areas settled by the British, but it appears to have general application to Canada.

Treaties

The British preferred to base their claim to land on acquisition by ostensible agreement – a cession of land and sovereignty from someone with a plausible claim to sign the treaty. This preference applied even when lands had already been occupied by British settlement, causing the dispossession of Indigenous peoples. Land and powers to govern were granted by local rulers throughout North America, Asia, and Africa. Sometimes Britain first decided who those rulers were, using a combination of intrigue and military force. In many cases, the lack of alternatives to a treaty was apparent, and, in some cases, coercion was explicit. John Mackenzie, a missionary, recorded the view of "an intelligent native" in Africa, who said with contempt that some of his people thought the English mode of warfare was "by 'papers' and agents and courts."[165] Major A.B. Thruston, who "negotiated" treaties in Africa during the last decades of the nineteenth century, described the "amiable farce" that might be involved:

> The chief does not understand a word of it, but he looks pleased as he receives another present of beads; a mark is made on a printed treaty by the chief, and another by the interpreter; the vagrant, who professes to be the representative of a great Empire, signs his name. The chief takes the paper, but with some hesitation, as he regards the whole performance as a new and therefore dangerous piece of witchcraft. The boat sails away, and the new ally and protégé of England or France immediately throws the treaty into the fire.[166]

Thruston noted that he had a supply of blank treaties on which the local ruler could place his X. A similar practice was followed in colonial British Columbia, where marks were placed on blank pages and the text added later.[167]

One of the most prominent and celebrated imperialists was Frederick Lugard, who had a prestigious career as a soldier, explorer, colonial administrator, and theorist of imperialism.[168] Early in his career he recorded in his diary how he acquired part of Uganda for his employer, the Imperial East Africa Company, from the Kabaka, or king, of Buganda by coercing him into signing a treaty: "Much discussion and even uproar arose at times but I scowled and looked as fierce as I could and insisted on reading it right through."[169] In return for the Company's "protection," a Resident appointed by it was to have complete control over the affairs of the country. The Kabaka tried to avoid signing, but Lugard demanded that he make his mark: "He did it with a bad grace, just dashing the pen at the paper and making a blot, but I made him go at it again and make a cross, and on the 2nd copy he made a proper cross." As was often the case, there was a Maxim machine gun nearby that Lugard checked before the meeting. He was frank about the enforced nature of this "agreement" – "The treaty was certainly obtained against his will" – and added that all or most so-called treaties signed in Africa would not bear close investigation.[170]

Canada and Colonialism

Treaties were often signed reluctantly and under the threat of force. This photo from the Cook Island Annexation Ceremony of 1900 shows the anxiety of Queen Makea, the Indigenous leader, and the overwhelming power of the colonial forces. | *Alexander Turnbull Library, Wellington, New Zealand, PAColl-4235 via Wikimedia Commons*

Later, in his best-selling book *The Dual Mandate,* published after his retirement as a colonial governor, Lugard was frankly dismissive of treaties:

> Treaties were produced by the cartload in all the approved forms of legal verbiage – impossible of translation by ill-educated interpreters. It mattered not that tribal chiefs had no power to dispose of communal rights, or that those few powerful potentates who might perhaps claim such authority looked on the white man's ambassador with contempt, and could hardly be expected to hand over their sovereignty and lands or other assets had they understood what was asked of them.[171]

He explained how they were obtained by small gifts, a show of force, and vague promises that were not recorded and later ignored. They were based on "make-believe" and "naked deception."

The lack of authority of "chiefs" to make treaties under the Indigenous laws was a serious defect that was simply ignored. In the words of another experienced colonial administrator, "All those acts of native chiefs which, by means of treaties made with strangers, alienated the tribal lands are, in my opinion, according to native laws and custom, *ultra vires*" (beyond their authority).[172] The legal effect of treaties under international law was also uncertain.[173] Further, they were not enforceable in courts by the Indigenous group unless expressly incorporated into the local law.[174] A Nova Scotia court held in 1929 that an Indian group was composed of "uncivilized people or savages" lacking legal capacity to enter into a valid treaty.[175] It was most unlikely that the chiefs had a clear understanding of what they were granting, since they were unfamiliar with the English language and legal technicalities, which would have been very different from their own legal traditions. This lack of understanding meant they were unable to incorporate their own intentions into the documents.

In Canada, a priority of the new government after Confederation in 1867 was the signing of treaties with Indigenous groups to allow settlement to proceed westward peacefully.[176] The importance of treaties increased with (a) the acquisition of Rupert's Land and the North-Western Territory from the Hudson's Bay Company in 1870; (b) the *Dominion Lands Act* of 1872, which provided for land grants to encourage settlement; and (c) the National Policy implemented by Prime Minister John A. Macdonald in 1879 to promote western settlement and development. Starting in the first half of the nineteenth century with treaties in southwestern Ontario and parts of Vancouver Island, followed by the eleven numbered treaties in western Canada from 1871 to 1930, governments entered into land treaties with Indigenous groups. These treaties differed significantly from the earlier peace and friendship treaties that had been signed in eastern Canada, because they were obviously intended, at least according to the written English-language versions, to be surrenders of vast areas of land (except for small parcels retained as reserves) in return for nominal payments and other benefits, such as agricultural supplies meant to turn hunters into farmers as part of the civilization and assimilation policy.

The connection between the British Empire generally and the rule of Indigenous peoples in Canada during the critical years of the nineteenth century was encapsulated in the life of Alexander Morris. Born in Perth, Ontario, he was the chief negotiator of the numbered treaties, lieutenant governor of Manitoba and the North-West Territories from 1872 to 1876 (until 1877 for Manitoba), and an ardent imperialist.[177] He declared his attachment to the Empire in an essay published in 1855: "The inhabitants of Canada are bound to Britain by the ties of common interest, common origin and filial attachment."[178] Three years later, he gave a lecture entitled "Nova Britannia" in which he enthusiastically supported the idea of a Greater Britain that, of course, included Canada:

Canada and Colonialism

The caption for this 1871 illustration describes an "Indian Chief haranguing" his people at the treaty signing at Stone Fort, Manitoba, 1871. | *Peter Winkworth Collection of Canadiana, Library and Archives Canada, R9266-3764c*

Alexander Morris, treaty negotiator and avid imperialist who saw treaties as a means of opening up the "advantages of civilized life." | *Topley Studio, Library and Archives Canada, PA-026334*

"The impress of the British mind is stamped upon and reproduced, in what are in the lapse of time destined eventually to be great kindred nations, bound together by the ties of origin and by parental and filial affection."[179] It was "plain to the most superficial observer that there is an overriding purpose in all this. Surely these English-speaking nations have a mission to discharge to the human race."[180]

An important part of that mission consisted of the treaties that were negotiated to acquire land for settlement in the prairie provinces after the acquisition of land by Canada from the Hudson's Bay Company. His book *The Treaties of Canada with the Indians,* published in 1880, describes those treaties, which he noted "comprehend the whole future of the Indians and of their relations to the Dominion."[181] In the preface, he summarized the goal of civilization that was the foundation of Indian policy and explained:

> I have prepared this collection of the treaties ... in the hope that I may thereby contribute to the completion of a work, in which I had considerable part, that, of, by treaties, securing the good will of the Indian tribes, and by the helpful hand of the Dominion, opening up to them, a future of promise, based upon the foundations of instruction and the many other advantages of civilized life.

These treaties were subject to the objections noted above that applied to many treaties signed in the British Empire.[182] With some exceptions, the Indigenous peoples did not fully understand the legal significance, since they lacked equivalent concepts to a surrender of rights in their own language and thought they were only agreeing to shared use of the lands.[183] In addition, they did not generally understand English and were illiterate. Further, the federal government usually appointed the translators who explained the treaty contents to the Indigenous signers, and there was no independent legal advice. This lack of informed consent led to a gross inequality of bargaining power. Another cause of inequality was the desperate plight of the Indigenous peoples of the prairies following the spread of diseases and the disappearance of the buffalo, which caused widespread starvation. There was also the lawlessness arising from groups of frontiersmen and whiskey traders who posed a danger to Indigenous peoples, which resulted in a massacre at Cypress Hills in southern Saskatchewan in 1873.[184] The federal government exploited these circumstances to obtain treaties.[185] According to D.M. Cameron, an opposition member of Parliament, there was "a mad and reckless and inhuman policy of submission shaped by a policy of starvation."[186] Treaties were written in advance of the negotiations, and the Indigenous "signatories" held the pen while the government officials

Canada and Colonialism

Members of the North-West Mounted Police, dressed in uniforms based on those of the British Army, and members of First Nations at a treaty signing in Regina, Saskatchewan, in 1885. | *O.B. Buell, Library and Archives Canada, PA-118751*

made their marks for them. British or Canadian soldiers or paramilitary police were prominent at treaty signings, sending an obvious message about the power relationship.

Oral promises were not always put in writing: "They promised everything. They wrote bloody little," according to Indigenous leader Harold Cardinal.[187] The gross unfairness of the terms has also been criticized.[188] In return for the surrender of rights to vast areas, Indigenous Nations received benefits such as small annual payments, agricultural implements, and schools. The provisions dealing with reserves and hunting and fishing cannot be regarded as benefits since they were simply exceptions to the surrender. In 1968, the Manitoba Indian Brotherhood accused the government officials of having "committed a legal fraud in a very sophisticated manner upon unsophisticated, unsuspecting, illiterate, uninformed natives."[189] This charge, however, overlooks the extent to which the Indigenous groups sought, with some success, to influence the outcome of the negotiations, and their recognition that their old way of life could not survive in the face of ever-increasing non-Indigenous settlement.[190]

Despite the best efforts of Indigenous negotiators to obtain better terms, they were faced with the hard fact that "it was clear that white settlement would

Mistahimaskwa (Big Bear) in chains during his imprisonment following the North-West Resistance of 1885. He opposed treaties and became the victim of frontier justice. | *O.B. Buell, Library and Archives Canada, C-001873*

come whether the Indians consented or not ... By the treaties, the Indians were essentially giving consent to what was inevitable. It is this fact which gives the sense of unreality to the treaty-making procedure more, really, than the culturally weaker position of the Indians in negotiating legal documents."[191] When the first of the numbered treaties was being made, Adams George Archibald, first lieutenant governor of Manitoba and the North-West Territories, explained that "whether they wished it or not, immigrants would come in and fill up the country ... If they thought it better to have no treaty at all, they might do without one, but they must make up their minds; if there was to be a treaty, it must be on a basis like that offered."[192] In short, it was a take-it-or-leave-it situation. Some chiefs, such as Cree Chief Mistahimaskwa (Big Bear), resisted signing as long as they could and sought better terms but, in the end, recognized there was no other alternative to starvation. Mistahimaskwa subsequently played a passive role in the North-West Resistance of 1885, was found guilty of treason despite his lack of involvement in the fighting, was imprisoned, and died within a couple of years.[193] It is difficult to think that his opposition to settlement and treaties played no role in the

Canada and Colonialism

thinking of the jury made up of settlers who found him guilty after only fifteen minutes of deliberation.

None of the objections to treaties mattered: the colonizers had a piece of paper to justify their rule and the seizure of land and resources and so expand the Empire.

Force

The third method of land acquisition was conquest or force. In 1914, Winston Churchill, who was then First Lord of the Admiralty, told his cabinet colleagues that Britain's vast and splendid possessions were "mainly acquired by violence, largely maintained by force."[194] Violence was used to conquer, fight "small wars" against Indigenous groups, put down revolts and political opposition, and maintain law and order.[195] Sometimes it was carried out by settlers and not sanctioned by the state. Conflict often occurred when the true meaning of an "agreement" was understood, and Indigenous peoples sought to resist the resulting European invasion. This happened, for example, in the 1890s, after associates of the arch-imperialist Cecil Rhodes extracted a flimsy agreement from King Lobengula of the Ndebele in highly dubious circumstances. The agreement was then used to get a charter for Rhodes's company to control what was to become Zimbabwe.[196] Sometimes force was deemed necessary to prevent or put down a mutiny or civil unrest, such as the civil disobedience and protests that persistently accompanied imperial rule in one area or another. Like racism and cultural supremacy, force or the threat of force was pervasive. Not without reason, Ernest Jones, the Chartist leader, wrote of the British Empire that "On its colonies the sun never sets, but the blood never dries."[197]

The Harvard historian Caroline Elkins has studied the Empire's legacy of violence and estimates that there were over 250 separate armed conflicts in the British Empire during the nineteenth century, with at least one in any given year.[198] She sees violence as "endemic to the structure and systems of British rule ... Without it, Britain could not have maintained its sovereign claims to its colonies."[199] Her recent book *Legacy of Violence* examines in detail what she describes as "legalized lawlessness": exceptional state-directed violence when ordinary laws proved insufficient for maintaining order and control, especially during the end-of-empire period of the twentieth century.[200] Another recent book by Erik Linstrum also examines such violence. He maintains that "a willingness to resort to exemplary, extrajudicial, and spectacular violence that did not clearly distinguish between combatants and civilians" was normal rather than exceptional during counterinsurgency campaigns.[201] Elizabeth Kolsky, a historian of British India, concluded that "law normalized the violence [including by private individuals] that sustained British dominance ... Violence was not an exceptional but an ordinary part of British rule in the subcontinent."[202] When faced with determined opposition, the colonial authorities used a full range of repressive measures: curfews, flogging, starvation, terror, torture, detention, deportation, collective punishment, destruction and confiscation of property, censorship, banning of political activities and groups, martial law, states of emergency, suspension of liberties, forced labour, and executions.

Imperialists believed in the use of force. Probably the most famous imperial soldier was Wolseley, who served throughout the Empire, including in Canada, India, China, and Africa. Gilbert and Sullivan used him as "the Very Model of a Modern Major-General" in the *Pirates of Penzance*. One writer estimates that in Wolseley's first twenty-five years of Army life, he tried to get himself killed in a war every three years.[203] His memoirs record his beliefs on imperial and other matters as well as his achievements. He observed of the Indian Army: "There must be no delay, no hesitation to nip in the bud all incipient mutiny. The hand of iron in a soft silk glove can alone keep such an army in order at any time ... We won India by the sword and ... that sword must be always kept sharp and ready for use at any moment."[204]

Joseph Chamberlain, the leading imperialist and promoter of imperial federalism, explained in 1897 that although he regretted the loss of life, especially the "more precious" lives of the colonizers, "You cannot have omelettes without breaking eggs; you cannot destroy the practices of barbarism, of slavery, of superstition ... without the use of force."[205] A British commissioner in East Africa declared in that year, "These people must learn submission by the bullet – it is the only school."[206] At about the same time, Colonel C.E. Callwell wrote his classic book *Small Wars*, which were wars to extend and preserve the Empire (and *big* wars for the defenders of Indigenous lands). He set out the military and psychological objectives of war against Indigenous peoples: "The object is not only to prove to the opposing force unmistakably which is the stronger, but also to inflict punishment on those who have taken up arms."[207] The "enemy must be made to feel a moral inferiority throughout."[208] "Fanatics and savages ... must be thoroughly brought to book and cowed or they will rise again."[209] He described this deterrence as having a "moral effect." Psychological warfare remained an essential part of the imperial system, especially after 1945.[210]

Most of the time, force was kept in the background, hinted at by the presence of military officials and exercises. But it was still a powerful deterrent and a vital part of the picture. Staged demonstrations of superior force were sometimes used to prove the futility of resistance, such as using explosives to blow

Canada and Colonialism

up a wagon or a machine gun to mow down crops.[211] Following the expansion of the Empire during the Victorian era, the role of the army in waging "small wars" against Indigenous resistance declined. It was held more in reserve to be used to restore or maintain order that had broken down through rebellion, riots, or protests that the civil authorities could not control. Sometimes martial law or states of emergency were proclaimed and enforced by the army in conjunction with the police services. The role was more policing than military but still relied on the use of force.[212]

Canadian imperialists shared the belief in militarism.[213] They supported imperialist campaigns throughout the Empire and urged greater military preparedness for Canada. Some based their arguments on Darwinian principles of natural selection and the survival of the strong against the weak. War was seen as a necessity to implement the civilizing mission and introduce Christianity. Compared with other parts of the British Empire, like India and Africa, and in the American West, state-sanctioned violence was not used as much in Canada to gain and keep control over Indigenous peoples. Nevertheless, force was always in the background as a deterrent, to be used on the rare occasions that it became necessary.[214] In 1863, a British naval gunboat fired on an Indigenous village on Penelakut Island near Vancouver Island after some settlers had been attacked.[215] In the British Columbia interior, six Tsilhqot'in leaders were executed in 1864 and 1865 following a confrontation with road construction workers over colonial expansion into their territory.

The North-West Mounted Police (the NWMP), founded in 1873, was a paramilitary force whose role quickly evolved to include keeping Indigenous peoples on their reserves and preventing Indigenous rebellion. Prime Minister Macdonald told Parliament in 1885:

> There must be a continual, hourly pressure upon the Indians to hold them upon their reserves ... The duty of the [North-West Mounted] police is, therefore, a continuous one, and an increasing one, and the increase in the number of white settlers adds to the difficulty ... Recent events have shown that the force is overworked; that they are obliged to watch every reserve, in order to keep the Indians on the reserves.[216]

As with other officials, such as Indian agents and residential school teachers, the powers of the police were extensive, and there was little possibility of redress for abuse. A leading NWMP officer, Sam Steele, noted in his memoirs that the minister of justice maintained they "could arrest an Indian at any time or place. They were wards and we were officers of the Crown, therefore, there

NWMP officers at Dawson City, Yukon, 1900. The Mounties were a paramilitary force responsible for maintaining order on the frontier, including keeping Indians on their reserves following the 1885 North-West Resistance. | *H.J. Goetzman, Library and Archives Canada, PA-202188*

was no chance of a miscarriage of justice."[217] Claims that the Empire was bringing law and order to Indigenous peoples should be seen in the context of such thinking.

The North-West Resistance of 1885 was fought mainly by Métis and a few First Nations allies against Canadian forces.[218] Its suppression resulted in the deaths of hundreds of people and the final subjugation of First Nations in western Canada.[219] Non-Indigenous settlement could then proceed apace. The executions and prison sentences imposed were intended to punish, coerce, and reform not only those directly impacted but also the entire Indigenous peoples of the territories newly acquired by the Canadian government.[220] After the execution of the Métis leader Louis Riel and eight other Indigenous men following the resistance of 1885, Macdonald wrote, "The execution of Riel and of the Indians will, I hope, have a good effect on the Métis and convince the Indians that the white man governs."[221] He had earlier compared Riel with the leader of the insurgents in the Sudan, which was then an imperial preoccupation, saying he was "a sort of half-breed Mahdi."[222] We can see from his words the strong

Canada and Colonialism

A Maxim gun was included in Christmas celebrations in Yukon, 1899. The gun had an honoured place in the dining room, where it could be kept warm. | *Glenbow Library and Archives Collection, Libraries and Cultural Resources Digital Collections, University of Calgary, CU185193.*

and clear connection between imperialism, racism, the use of force, and Canadian Indian policy.

Some weapons used by imperial forces could not but strike terror in the minds of Indigenous peoples. Their shields and weaponry were no match for machinery such as the Maxim gun, which could fire five hundred rounds a minute. Hilaire Belloc, the poet and satirist, wrote:

> *Whatever happens we have got*
> *The Maxim gun and they have not.*[223]

There was limited sympathy from some imperialists for the victims of these fearsome weapons. In an article on the Union of South Africa, formed after the Boer War, Stephen Leacock mocked those who fondly thought that Africans should have the vote, and continued, with apparent approval, "The South Africans think that they understand the native. And the first tenet of their gospel is that he must be kept in his place ... If the native revolts they mean to shoot him into marmalade with machine guns. Such is their simple creed."[224] Another commentator, writing in the *Canadian Magazine* in 1899, thought that although there could be brief sympathy with Indigenous people for not understanding how those "who are racking them fore and aft with grape and canister are the best friends they have," civilization had done them more good than harm, "even if whole tribes had to be blotted out in the process."[225]

William Stairs was a Canadian soldier and graduate of the Royal Military College in Kingston, Ontario, who served in the British Army. He also worked for King Leopold of the Belgians, then in competition with Cecil Rhodes to gain control of the Congo.[226] His gentle appearance belied his barbarity. A doctor who accompanied Stairs on his expedition to the Congo, where some of the worst excesses of imperialism occurred, described him as a "tall, fair, and delicate-looking young man."[227] In his diary, Stairs gives an account of his use of the Maxim gun: "I cleaned the Maxim gun up thoroughly and fired some 20 or 30 rounds at some howling natives on the opposite bank."[228] He callously describes the terror that ended a peaceful scene in an African village, with women cooking and children playing. "All was as it was every day until our discharge of bullets, when the usual uproar and screaming of women took place."[229] Repeated instances of burning down houses, destroying crops, taking animals, and cutting off human heads and hands are recounted. His exploits were honoured in both England and his native Halifax, Nova Scotia, which he nostalgically remembered in his diary.

The use of force by the empire against white settlers had been abandoned after the rebellions in Upper and Lower Canada in 1837, with the significant exception of the wars with the Boers or Afrikaners in South Africa, in which Canada and other settler colonies played major roles. We will see several statements from the 1840s onwards that indicate membership in the Empire was voluntary for the white settlers when we look at Canada's path toward independence in Chapter 7. For now, we can note the comment by Bernard Shaw in 1900: "It will hardly be disputed by any sane person that we cannot permanently hold Australasia, Canada or South Africa by military force against the will of the white inhabitants,"[230] and the comment by a Colonial Office official in 1942 that "it seems unthinkable that any British government would bring military force to bear upon a community of our own blood."[231]

Given the depth of racism, violence, and authoritarianism associated with the Empire, some of its more severe critics in the 1930s and 1940s compared it to the fascism that was then so prominent and threatening. The term "colonial fascism" was coined by George Padmore to describe the connection. The West Indian critic said the colonies were the breeding ground for the fascist mentality

Canada and Colonialism

William Stairs, mercenary and imperial hero. | *Reprinted from Joseph Moloney,* With Captain Stairs to Katanga *(London: Sampson Low, Marston, 1893)*

being let loose in Europe. He compared the lack of liberty of Kenyan Africans to that of the Jews of Germany.[232] The philosopher Bertrand Russell expressed a similar idea: "In British imperialism, as practised in Asia and Africa, all the impulses that seem repulsive in German nationalism have found vent. The Empire has been a cesspool for British moral refuse."[233] John Strachey, later a Labour cabinet minister, described fascism as "Imperialism raised to a pitch of frenzy hitherto unknown."[234] The connection was stressed by Indigenous leaders. Kenyatta said in 1937 that it was time to cry "Down with Fascist rule in the Colonies."[235] Writing from his prison cell in 1944, Jawaharlal Nehru, a leader of the Indian independence movement, referred to Nazi ideology and said, "We in India have known racialism in all its forms ever since the commencement of British rule. The whole ideology of this rule was that of the Herrenvolk and the Master Race ... the idea of a master race is inherent in imperialism."[236]

Fascists also saw the connection. Adolf Hitler declared in the Reichstag, "I have never left room for any doubt of my belief that the existence of [the British Empire] is an inestimable factor of value for the whole of human and cultural and economic life ... For this work I have a sincere admiration."[237] His own ambitions were, of course, to create a continental empire to the east to create a living space or *Lebensraum*.[238] But he saw the analogy with the colonization of North America and said Germans should look on their eastern neighbours as "Redskins."[239] William Joyce ("Lord Haw-Haw"), the American-born fascist leader executed for treason in 1946, devoted a chapter in his book *Twilight over England* to maintaining that, given the violence used in the British Empire, Britain was in no position to criticize Germany.[240] A German newspaper used a similar argument in response to Canadian criticism by referring to Canada's treatment of Indigenous peoples.[241]

Given what we now know about the state-directed horrors that took place under the Nazi regime, fascism is too harsh a judgment to be applied to the British Empire generally.[242] Fascism, at least as practised by the Nazis, saw racial domination and genocide as ends in themselves, and humanitarianism as an unacceptable weakness. With isolated exceptions, this was not true of the British Empire. However, as Hannah Arendt points out in her classic work *The Origins of Totalitarianism,* which devotes Part 2 to imperialism, it is justifiable to consider imperialism as "a preparatory stage for the coming catastrophes." She observes that, in the case of the British Empire, "lying under anybody's nose were many of the elements which gathered together could create a totalitarian government on the basis of racism."[243] Although not mentioned by her, one specific element that might have been used was the race-based *Indian Act* in Canada and, indeed, the equivalent laws in the United States were one source of the Nazi race laws.[244] She concludes that, fortunately, moderation prevailed and British imperialism never became fascist.

Some British imperialists saw merit in the type of authoritarian rule developed by the fascists. Rudyard Kipling, the great propagandist of imperialism, believed in "a strong man governing alone" and, in the words of a sympathetic biographer, could "never see a democratic institution without wanting to heave half a brick at it."[245] In 1929, John Buchan, later a much praised governor general of Canada, described fascism as a bold experiment that was fruitful in constructive statesmanship.[246]

As it was, the British were ingenious in developing their own unique governance systems to suit their needs, creating self-governing white settler colonies that were loyal to empire while despotically overseeing non-white colonies.

Canada and Colonialism

3

Self-Rule and Despotism

On July 1, 1911, the *Illustrated London News,* a leading journal that celebrated imperialism, published a detailed account of the coronation of George V as King and Emperor of India, with many majestic photos of the occasion. One of the most striking shows rows of Indian troops and Canadian North-West Mounted Police side by side. The photo is in black and white, but it is not difficult to imagine the Mounties in their uniform of scarlet tunic, blue trousers, and brown western hats, and the Indian troops with brightly coloured turbans and uniforms, all of them mounted on horseback and riding in carefully spaced lines. The photo conveys all the pomp and pageantry of the Empire that was so important to its appeal and survival. The *News* saw a powerful symbolic message and added a caption that read:

> A pleasantly symbolical unrehearsed effect was seen in Queen Victoria Street during passage of the Royal Progress. In order to facilitate the advance of the State Carriage, the Indians and the North-West Mounted Police were ordered to ride in parallel columns. The people recognized with delight that it contained a happy imperial augury. The greatest Dependency and the greatest Dominion, East and West, were seen marching shoulder to shoulder, thus anticipating a meeting which Kipling postponed till the Day of Judgement.[1]

The distinction between dependencies such as India and dominions such as Canada was fundamental to the Empire. Indeed, there were two overlapping

INDIA AND CANADA SHOULDER TO SHOULDER IN THE ROYAL PROGRESS:
AND ROYAL ARTILLERY IN THE PROCESSION.

OUR GREATEST DOMINION AND OUR GREATEST DEPENDENCY SIDE BY SIDE: NORTH-WEST MOUNTED POLICE (CANADA)
AND INDIAN TROOPS IN DOUBLE FORMATION NOT TO DELAY THE KING'S CARRIAGE.

Members of the Canadian NWMP and Indian Army ride side by side at the 1911 coronation of George V as King and Emperor of India. | Illustrated London News, *July 1, 1911*

empires: one enjoying self-government for the colonizing settlers, including rule over Indigenous peoples, and the other ruled despotically by foreign rulers. Alfred Milner, an intellectual and political leader of imperialism, made the distinction between "new nations sprung from [Britain's] loins," such as Canada and Australia, and "the Dependent Empire," with over 400 million non-British people to whom Britain had striven to extend the blessings of civilized government.[2] This chapter explores these different parts of the Empire. "The greatest Dependency and the greatest Dominion" may have met on that day, but they did not do so on equal terms.

Dominions and Dependencies

There was a critical distinction between settler colonies (called dominions from 1907) and other colonies. Settler colonies had self-government and were partners in the British rule of the Dependent Empire, with the power to rule the Indigenous peoples within their own territories. But colonies forming part of the Dependent Empire were subject to outside despotic rule (as were the Indigenous peoples within the settler colonies). In 1937, a critic of the Empire,

Leonard Barnes, summarized the situation: "What we have to notice is that the free states of the Empire are the states inhabited by the white minority of 70 millions, while the unfree states are those inhabited by the coloured majority of 430 millions. This rigid colour bar is ... a vital and essential part of the present imperial structure."[3] There was general agreement in the British World, including Canada, that the dependent colonies were not the equals of the self-governing dominions. Lord Curzon, former viceroy of India, complained in 1909 that "the patriotic inhabitants of our colonies, taking their cue from England, have seemed to regard India as occupying a lower plane of Imperial importance to themselves."[4] For example, one Canadian parliamentarian noted in 1914 that "India is not part of the empire as we are ... it is not on the same basis in the empire as we are."[5] Another observed, "India ... stands in a different relation to the empire from Canada, South Africa, New Zealand, or any of the other overseas dominions ... The Empire of India is in a different class from the Dominion of Canada."[6]

Self-government meant that settler colonies could impose tariffs to protect their economies from competition from other parts of the Empire, including the UK. In contrast, the dependent territories were ruled in the interests of the British. They were seen primarily as sources of raw materials for British industry and markets for manufactured products. Another crucial difference was the imposition of taxation to pay the cost of the Empire, especially for the military. India was described in 1882 by Lord Salisbury, a former Secretary of State for India, as "an English barrack in the Oriental Seas from which we may draw any number of troops without paying for them."[7] The burden was placed unfairly on the shoulders of the Dependent Empire, while the settler colonies refused it despite the benefits conferred on them. In 1893, a Canadian member of Parliament noted that "the mother country ... gives us protection of its army and navy and diplomatic service free of charge."[8] A Labour politician, the future prime minister Ramsay MacDonald, soundly criticized this unfairness in his 1910 book on India:

> Nine-tenths of the charge of the Army in India is an Imperial charge. Canada, South Africa, and Australia should bear it as much as India. It is a piece of the most bitter cynicism to find the Imperial doors of our colonies shut in the faces of these poor people [Canada and other settler colonies refused to allow Indian immigration, although Indians, like Canadians, were British Subjects – separate citizenship did not exist] who bear such an inordinate share of the cost of Imperial maintenance, and at whose expense these Dominions are protected from the fear of war.[9]

As Indian politician Shashi Tharoor points out in his critique of British India, in 1922, about two-thirds of the total revenues of the Government of India (derived from taxation on Indians) was used for overseas activities.[10]

Although the distinction between the settler colonies, or dominions, and the Dependent Empire may have been largely forgotten by Canadians, it was insisted upon by contemporary writers. In his enormously popular book published in 1883, *The Expansion of England*, which had a big impact in developing the idea of a Greater Britain or a British World, considered in Chapter 5, the historian John Robert Seeley stressed this distinction and the greater importance of settler colonies. The enormous population of India did not form part of Greater Britain in the same sense as those 10 million Englishmen who lived outside the British Islands: "The latter are of our own blood, and are therefore united with us by the strongest tie. The former are of alien race and religion, and are bound to us only by the tie of conquest ... When we inquire then into the Greater Britain of the future we ought to think much more of our Colonial than of our Indian Empire."[11] Joseph Chamberlain, the Secretary of State for the Colonies and a leading imperialist, made the distinction, in a lecture given in 1897, between self-governing colonies such as Canada, united to the United Kingdom by a sentiment of kinship, and those where the non-white population was the majority and to whom there was a sense of obligation.[12]

Writing in 1891 on "Canada and the Canadian Question," the prominent historian and political commentator Goldwin Smith said that the term "Empire" should not be applied to Canada and other self-governing British colonies but only to India, the Crown colonies, and military stations.[13] A few years later, in his book on nationalism in the settler colonies, Richard Jebb said, "The modern starting-point of constructive imperialism must be the admission that it is impossible to imagine any parallelism whatever between the connection of England with India and the other dependencies on the one hand, and with the colonial States on the other hand."[14] The distinction was neatly made by Canadian author Sara Jeannette Duncan, in one of her novels, between "the parts we can plough" and "all that we hold by the sword."[15]

Commentators argued that the distinction between settler colonies and the other colonies meant they should be regarded differently. John Hobson, an influential critic of imperialism as practised in the Dependent Empire, was at pains to praise settler colonialism. There was "a radical distinction between true colonialism [settler colonialism] and imperialism." Unlike imperialism, settler colonialism was not a drain on British resources but a strength. "Migration to, and colonization of, sparsely peopled lands by inhabitants of thickly peopled lands [was] a natural and wholly beneficial movement."[16] In 1905,

Jebb thought that there was some urgency to deal with the emergence of nationalism in the settler colonies to avoid their drifting apart altogether. "On the other hand, there is no irrepressible demand for any change in the connection of England with the subject dependencies."[17] Thirty-five years later, Stephen Leacock was firmly of the view that the future of the Empire rested with Canada and other settler colonies: "Now no one can believe that the future of the British Empire rests on its possession and development of its tropical dependencies. The course of civilization moves northward. Everything turns on the development of the Temperate Zones."[18]

Self-Government for the Dominions

As we will see shortly, the East India Company official and philosopher John Stuart Mill advocated despotism for the Dependent Empire. In contrast, he supported the "fullest measure of internal self-government" for "colonies of European race," including the disposal of public lands.[19] This was the general view. There was some mild dissent in 1872 when Benjamin Disraeli, leader of the Conservative opposition, gave a famous speech at Crystal Palace in which he was critical of the Liberal government for having granted self-government without conditions.[20] He made clear his support in principle: "I cannot conceive how our distant colonies can have their affairs administered except by self-government." However, self-government "ought to have been conceded as part of a great policy of Imperial consolidation." Conditions should have included an imperial tariff, security that land in the colonies would be available for the use of emigrants, and defence arrangements.[21]

A fundamental problem of federations is how to resolve conflicts between the central federal government, which has jurisdiction over matters common to the nation as a whole (such as foreign affairs and defence), and regional governments, which have jurisdiction over more local matters. At times, in Canada, it seems that who has the power to govern is of greater weight than good government. A similar problem faced the British Empire, which can be seen as an informal, loose federation of the United Kingdom and the settler colonies. There were issues of imperial concern, such as foreign affairs and defence, and other issues of internal concern to each colony. How to reconcile central control of topics common to the Empire as a whole and autonomous colonial control of topics internal to each settler colony? Where to draw the dividing line? How to allocate responsibility for the costs? This conflict had led to a settler rebellion and the loss of the Thirteen Colonies that formed the United States. How was a similar fate to be avoided for the other settler colonies?

The solution was found in the idea of responsible government. Under representative government, a governor made decisions that he reported to London. He was supported by advice from an executive council that he appointed and a legislature representing settlers that could criticize but not control him. Under responsible government, he would be required to act according to the wishes of an executive that would consist mainly of elected representatives. They were responsible to the legislature, which could replace them. This arrangement was, in essence, the importation of the cabinet system of government recently implemented in the UK. The colonial governments were to have autonomy over the colony's internal affairs, and the UK government would have primary responsibility for matters common to the Empire as a whole. This solution helped to keep the Empire together for about a century.

It is crucial to recognize that internal self-government for settler colonies sacrificed the imperial responsibility for Indigenous peoples on the altar of "colonial freedom." Indigenous peoples were not represented in the legislatures (except the Māori in New Zealand and "coloured" people in Cape Colony) and were, in any event, outnumbered (except in Africa). This imperial abdication was the sinister side of self-government. Settler populations that campaigned so vigorously for freedom from control denied this freedom to Indigenous peoples, as we shall see in Chapter 6 with respect to Canada. Settler self-government led to apartheid in South Africa, including the abolition of the franchise for "coloured" people.[22] It was welcomed by Stephen Leacock since, without it, the country "could have been overwhelmed in a night by the vast shadows of the black race."[23] Self-government was also welcomed by some imperial politicians because it enabled them to wash their hands of accountability for openly racist policies.[24]

Responsible government has been celebrated as a prominent Canadian achievement. So far as the settler colonies were concerned, it had its birth in the colonies of British North America.[25] Rebellions in Upper and Lower Canada in 1837 were the triggers. Stephen Leacock described them as "a damp squib in the military sense, but ominous with meaning."[26] But hundreds of people died, and they preoccupied the senior official in the Colonial Office, James Stephen. He complained to his wife, "Oh Canada, what wrongs have I done thee that thou thus pursuest me in my house & my office, my walks & my dreams?," no doubt having nightmares over the possibility of another North American secession.[27]

This concern led to an inquiry and report by Lord Durham, which has been widely praised.[28] It has been described as "one of the most vigorous and perceptive expositions of the principles and practices of free government in

Canada and Colonialism

Lord Durham, the romantic figure whose report led to the establishment of the system of responsible government in Canada. | *Library and Archives Canada, 1970-127-1*

the history of the English-speaking peoples,"[29] "one of the classics of British constitutional history,"[30] "a signal development in Imperial governance,"[31] having "a good claim to be the book that saved the Empire,"[32] "the most famous single document in the history of the Commonwealth,"[33] and "a handbook of white colonial development under the Union Jack."[34] Part of the lasting influence of the report is due to the romantic and charismatic personality of its lead author (although some claimed others wrote it) and his early death before it could be implemented. Reflecting his extravagant lifestyle, Durham was accompanied on his trip to British North America by an army of servants, including a musical band, as well as cases of silver and trophies.[35]

So far as self-government was concerned, the Durham Report undoubtedly had merit for saying what had to be done in language that stands out, in such usually dry constitutional documents, for its readability. Durham was critical of the existing form of representative government. Since the elected politicians were not in control of the executive or in office, they had little incentive to show moderation. He recommended that "the government of the Colony should henceforth be carried on in conformity with the views of the majority of the Assembly." Accordingly, "the Crown must ... consent to carry [on the government] by means of those in whom [the] representative body has confidence" and introduce "a system of responsible government as would give the people a real control over its own destinies."[36] The governor would cease to be a despot. Instead, he would act in accordance with the advice of ministers, like the constitutional monarch he represented.

The report received praise, although not universal, from colonial politicians. Most prominent was Joseph Howe in Nova Scotia, who wrote a series of letters to the British prime minister calling for its implementation. In one, he noted that it had circulated for some months in the colonies. "Every intelligent Colonist" agreed that the absence of rulers responsible to those whom they are called to govern was the cause of many, if not all, colonial evils and disputes. "The remedy pointed out, while it possesses the merits of being extremely simple and eminently British, the making them so responsible – is the only cure for those evils short of arrant quackery – the only secure foundation upon which the power of the Crown can be established on this continent, so as to defy internal machinations and foreign assault."[37] (We may note, in passing, that Howe was later to oppose the union of the colonies, another recommendation in the report.)

Nova Scotia was the first of the colonies to officially receive responsible government in 1848, and the others soon followed, although British Columbia had to wait until it joined Canada in 1872.[38] Newfoundland (not then part of Canada) lost it in 1934 when financial problems led to government by appointed British and Newfoundland civil servants.[39]

Despite the Durham Report's fame, it is a matter of dispute how much the report influenced the subsequent development of self-government. Historian Ged Martin argues that its supposed importance is a myth; it had little influence, and the ultimate form of self-government bore only a general relationship to the ideas of Durham. He suggests Durham's romantic life and early death explain the report's fame: "A dramatic life ends in tragic but grand catharsis, the hero becomes a demigod ... Durham secured his place in the imperial pantheon not so much by his Report as by his death."[40]

The report was very brief on the critical division of powers between the imperial and the colonial governments. After first acknowledging that his proposal would "place the internal government of the colony in the hands of the colonists themselves," he continued:

I know not in what respect it can be desirable that we should interfere with their internal legislation in matters which do not affect their relations with the

Canada and Colonialism

mother country. The matters which so concern us are very few. The constitution of the form of government – the regulation of foreign relations, and of the trade with the mother country, the other British Colonies, and foreign nations – and the disposal of the public lands, are the only points on which the mother country requires a control.[41]

It will be seen that Indigenous relations are not listed as matters to be excluded from colonial control. Indeed, the report is silent on Indigenous issues.[42] Durham described the French and English as "two nations warring in the bosom of a single state."[43] But he paid no attention to the Indigenous Nations and their interests. They, and each of the excluded subjects, subsequently fell under colonial control.

The silence in the Durham Report is surprising, as a fundamental aspect of government in the settler colonies was whether the imperial government in London or the colonial government should have control over Indigenous peoples. Only a couple of years earlier, the 1837 Select Committee on Aboriginal Tribes had recommended that power should remain with the imperial government in London and the governor who reported to London:

The protection of the Aborigines should be considered as a duty peculiarly belonging and appropriate to the executive government, as administered either in this country or by the governors of the respective colonies. This is not a trust which could conveniently be confided to the local legislatures. In proportion as those bodies are qualified for the right discharge of their proper functions, they will be unfit for the performance of this office.[44]

In his 1840s lectures on the colonies, Herman Merivale, the Oxford professor who later became the senior official in the Colonial Office, said that he thought "even the most jealous friends of colonial freedom must acquiesce" in this recommendation.[45] Merivale saw as one of the most useful functions of a distant central authority – counterbalancing to a certain extent its disadvantages – its ability to arbitrate dispassionately between groups having so many mutual subjects of irritation.[46] During a parliamentary debate in 1858 on the government of British Columbia, the Duke of Newcastle, later Colonial Secretary, said that the protection of Indigenous peoples was "one of the paramount duties" of the imperial government.[47]

In practice, the will and power of the central government to protect Indigenous groups were minimal. As some recent writers have pointed out, "The realpolitik of running an empire meant that settlers were granted liberties at the expense of Indigenous peoples."[48] In 1861, Mill explained the practical politics regarding the situation in India. English residents thought it "monstrous that any rights of the natives should stand in the way of their smallest pretensions."[49] They, and not "the natives," had the ear of the public at home, with predictable results:

> And when the resident English bring the batteries of English political action to bear upon any of the bulwarks erected to protect the natives against their encroachments, the executive, with their real but faint velleities of something better, generally find it safer to their parliamentary interest, and at any rate less troublesome, to give up the disputed position than to defend it.[50]

The phrase "real but faint velleities" sums up the repeated failures of the imperial government to take effective action to protect its "wards," even when it retained formal responsibility. In the North American colonies, practical authority over Indigenous affairs was in the hands of the settlers, with the policy differing from one colony to another but always favouring the settlers.

Formal authority over Indigenous peoples was soon transferred despite the recommendation of the Select Committee. In the case of the Province of Canada (now Ontario and Quebec), this took place in 1860. Part of the motivation was that the imperial government did not want to bear the cost of enforcing colonial policies directed against Indigenous peoples and their lands, especially in light of the protracted wars in New Zealand with the Māori.[51] Despite his earlier endorsement (as a professor) of the Select Committee's recommendation for central control, Merivale was a key player as a senior colonial administrator in the transfer of responsibility. After receiving the report of a commission in 1858 that inquired into Indian affairs in the Province of Canada, he concluded that it would be advantageous to "get rid of the responsibility of the Home Government," and prepared the dispatch that gave effective control to the provincial government.[52] This happened despite protests from Indigenous leaders that "they [did] not wish to be given over from the Imperial Government to the care of the Provincial one." They even went so far as to offer to pay the British Government the costs of running the Indian Department themselves: "If their Great Mother the Queen objects [to] paying the expenses of Maintaining the Department they will consent to do so provided they are not transferred from the Great Mother's care to the Provincial authorities."[53]

Control of land was also, of course, central to the settler colonial project. As expressed by one writer, "territoriality is settler colonialism's specific, irreducible element."[54] As we have seen, Lord Durham recommended against allowing the colonial governments to control land.[55] But in practice, they had already obtained such control. A Colonial Land and Emigration Commission was set up in 1840 to provide central coordination of land disposals and emigration throughout the Empire.[56] Some of the proceeds of land sales were to be used to fund emigration. Its work in the North American colonies was limited, as recognized in the instructions to the Commission from the Secretary of State, who noted that land in Prince Edward Island had been almost wholly taken up. In Upper Canada and New Brunswick, "the sale of waste land was vested in local authorities" with whom "the Crown had no right of interference." A similar offer had been made to Nova Scotia and Newfoundland, while in Lower Canada the question "must be regarded in abeyance."[57] Imperial control was soon formally transferred. In 1852, Sir John Pakington, Secretary of State for War and the Colonies, wrote in a dispatch to Governor Grey in New Zealand, following a dispute over land in that colony: "I wish to state my full concurrence ... as to the great difficulty of framing regulations in this country for the management of land in the Colonies. I have, therefore, been very anxious to establish, as far as possible, the principle of local control."[58]

The control of land by settlers was to have devastating consequences for Indigenous peoples. However, it is unlikely that the ultimate outcome would have significantly differed even if the Imperial government had retained control, given its failure to use its powers to protect them. Settler control of land was soon exercised as the newly united colonies expanded west in 1870 to include the vast territories of Rupert's Land and the North-Western Territory (collectively renamed the North-West Territories). This was a major expression of colonization over an area roughly the size of Western Europe.[59] Canada now extended to the border with the colony of British Columbia on the west coast, which was added in 1871. Overnight and without any consultation let alone consent, the policy of non-interference of the Hudson's Bay Company with regard to the internal affairs of Indigenous peoples in the territories was replaced by the very active rule of the new Canadian government that sought to destroy the "tribal system" with its self-government.

Confederation in 1867 was a crucial step toward greater collective powers of self-government for the North American colonies.[60] It is important to note that the bringing together of most British colonies in North America did not mean independence or any desire to separate from the Empire. Quite the opposite. The officials in the Colonial Office actively guided the process leading to the union of the North American colonies and have been described as the "silent framers."[61] Stephen Leacock represented the steps to union colourfully, with Great Britain as a mother hen herding the colonies into a coop with a peck here and a push there: "in they came, and they couldn't get out."[62] As explained by the Colonial Secretary, Lord Carnarvon, to delegates from Nova Scotia and New Brunswick, Confederation would confer greater strength on the mother country.[63] When he introduced the legislation that implemented the union into the UK Parliament, he said, "We are laying the foundations of a great state, perhaps one which at a future day may overshadow this country."[64] But this was no cause for jealousy since it would grow large in the great shadow of its mother. However, the debate on the legislation illustrated the general lack of interest of the UK Parliament in colonial affairs. In the words of historian Donald Creighton, "When the debate on the British North America Act was on, the English Parliament could scarcely conceal its excruciating boredom; and when the ordeal was over, it turned with great relief to a really national problem – the English dog tax."[65] We may note, in passing, that as the imperial government was assisting the British North American colonies in deepening their self-government, it was reinstating direct rule in Jamaica, thereby circumscribing the island's autonomy.[66]

Strengthening the imperial connection was also a major motivation of the Canadian politicians involved.[67] The first of the Quebec Resolutions passed in 1864 by the colonial leaders, which led to Confederation, set out the objective of "a federal union under the Crown of Great Britain," and the third spoke of "the perpetuation of our connection with the Mother Country." John A. Macdonald, as Attorney General, referred to the argument, "not a strong one ... that [Confederation] is an advance towards independence ... I have no apprehension of that kind. I believe it will have a contrary effect." He continued, "Instead of looking upon us as a merely dependent colony, England will have in us a friendly nation – a subordinate but still a powerful people – to stand by her in North America in peace or in war." He concluded by saying that Confederation offered the opportunity "of founding a great nation under the fostering care of Great Britain, and our Sovereign Lady, Queen Victoria."[68] Another Father of Confederation, George Brown, the president of the executive committee, said legislators could look forward to the day when "one united government under the British flag shall extend from shore to shore."[69] Likewise, Charles Tupper of Nova Scotia declared, "If there is any sentiment that was ever strong in the breast of our people, it is a disinclination to be separated in any way whatever from the British Empire."[70] Ordinary Canadians recognized Confederation as an imperial as well as a national event. At a celebration in Brantford, Ontario, "Rule Britannia" was sung by a chorus of over one thousand voices on July 1, 1867.[71]

Canadian Confederation inspired similar federations of settler colonies in Australia and South Africa, and even a possible imperial federation of the UK and settler colonies.[72] In 1873, Gilbert Sproat, the Agent-General in London for British Columbia, made a daring argument for the UK to join Canada in a union using the Canadian Confederation as a model – a kind of reverse take-over.[73] This did not come about but, in 1887, the prominent imperialist Joseph Chamberlain did say, to cries of "hear, hear," "It may well be that the Confederation of Canada may be the lamp to light our pathway to the Confederation of the British Empire."[74]

We should recognize that the internal self-government of the settler population remained subject to some constraints. The imperial parliament in London was supreme and could override any colonial laws. Colonial legislation was invalid if contrary to imperial legislation.[75] The UK appointed the governor general, and the Privy Council was the final court of appeal. The strict constitutional position on the approval of legislation was summarized in 1922 by Arthur Berriedale Keith, the leading constitutional scholar of the Empire: "The assent of the Governor is essential to the validity of any measure of the legislature; he may withhold it, or reserve a bill for the signification of the royal pleasure, when, unless especially assented to by the Crown by Order in Council, it falls to the ground, while, even if the Governor assents, the Crown may disallow the act."[76]

In practice, these powers were rarely exercised, and then only when imperial interests were obviously impacted. Soon they ceased to be used at all.[77] In the case of Canada, disallowance was last exercised in 1873, and the bill in question (which regulated parliamentary powers) was later re-enacted after consultations. In 1891, Goldwin Smith wrote, "Of dominion over the Colony barely a rag remains to the mother country, and even that remnant is grudged and is being constantly nibbled away."[78] Likewise, Keith explained that "the history of the development of the Imperial relations is a record of the gradual disuse of control of Dominion legislation by the Imperial Government, while the means of such control remained unrepealed and potentially available."[79] (In fact, even today the powers of reservation and disallowance of federal legislation by the UK government can be found in Sections 55 and 56 of the *Constitution Act, 1867.*) More important than formal constraints on legislative ability was the continuing dependence on the UK for defence, foreign affairs, export markets, and finance. As late as 1938, the Canadian minister of defence said that Canada was still effectively a British dependency, since it was reliant on the British to defend it.[80]

Imperial Representatives

The number of imperial representatives diminished as the North American colonies received self-government, united to become a single country, and took control of defence. Jobs for imperial officials in Canada became limited to the senior military officer commanding the Canadian militia until 1908, and the governor general, who represented not just the monarchy but also the British government, until the 1920s.

The duty of the imperial officer commanding the Canadian militia was primarily to coordinate defence plans and uphold and improve the militia's competence. He also had ceremonial duties.[81] Many had disputes with Canadian politicians, who sometimes thought Canada was being drawn into conflicts in other parts of the Empire not of direct interest to them. As a result, a few officers were recalled prematurely. The first Canadian-born commanding officer of the Canadian militia, William Otter, was appointed in 1908.

The most famous imperial military officer to serve in Canada was Garnet Wolseley, who arrived in 1861 as a twenty-eight-year-old lieutenant-colonel, and was posted to a militia training school outside Montreal. He stayed for almost ten years, including a leave to investigate the American Civil War. Having been in command of the British forces and Canadian militia sent to put down the Red River Resistance in 1869, the first of two Métis-led uprisings against the Canadian government's territorial expansion, Wolseley had developed an admiration for the skills of the voyageurs. He later called upon them to take his soldiers down the Nile during the futile campaign to rescue General Gordon in 1885.[82] His memoirs enthusiastically recall his time in Canada.[83] He described Montreal as "an elysium of bliss for young officers, the only trouble being to keep single."[84] One specific result of that time was a soldier's pocket book, first published in 1869 and written in Montreal.[85] Summarizing his philosophy, he declared, "Soldiers, like missionaries, must be fanatics."[86] His memoirs bemoan the return to England in 1870, for financial reasons, of the last British regular forces to serve in Canada.[87]

The job of the governor general was largely ceremonial, as continues to be the case. Before self-government, the governor of a Canadian colony had considerable powers. After internal self-government was granted, he was expected to act on the advice of ministers and generally had little discretion. This impotence was in marked contrast to the despotic powers enjoyed by governors in the Dependent Empire. An exception occurred in 1926, when Canada's governor general, Lord Byng, refused Prime Minister Mackenzie King's request for a dissolution of Parliament, resulting in a constitutional

Canada and Colonialism

"The man who wont stop"

Lord Wolseley, Gilbert and Sullivan's "Very Model of a Modern Major-General" and imperial hero, who had close links to Canada. | Vanity Fair, *1874*

crisis.[88] Agreement was subsequently reached at imperial conferences that governors general should be appointed on the advice of the Canadian prime minister and should no longer represent the UK government. The first Canadian citizen was not chosen until 1952, and the first Indigenous person not until 2021.[89] Given the largely ceremonial nature of the appointment, merit counted for little. What was important was that the appointee represented imperial values and the upper class of British society. He had to have the right birth, breeding, and background, including a top "public" (that is, private) school and an Oxbridge education and membership in an exclusive London club.[90] A peerage was part of the package, so the "commoner" John Buchan was made a lord before his arrival.

The Canadian governors general included some prominent imperialists. For example, both Connaught and Minto were involved in the 1885 Sudan campaign.[91] Several went on to hold the plum job of governor general/viceroy of

India. According to one writer, "The trajectory from ... the governor-generalship of Canada to the viceroyalty of India soon became a familiar one for noblemen in rather straitened circumstances."[92] Dufferin held both positions in the late 1800s, as did Lansdowne. Minto became viceroy of India after being governor general of Canada, as did Willingdon, who had been governor of Bombay and Madras before becoming governor general of Canada.

The official account of Earl Grey, governor general of Canada between 1904 and 1911, as it appears on the website of the current governor general, speaks of him in glowing terms:

> Earl Grey was a very active Governor General. He was in constant contact with the Prime Minister, offering ideas for social reform. He sought greater political inclusion for all, and worked to reach as many ordinary Canadians as possible. In fact, he was so dedicated and involved that then-prime minister Sir Wilfrid Laurier said Lord Grey gave "his whole heart, his whole soul, and his whole life to Canada."[93]

The account mentions that he donated the Grey Cup to the Canadian Football League and made other worthy contributions. However, there is only a brief mention of his role as a prominent imperialist: "He travelled extensively throughout the British Empire, and was Administrator of Rhodesia from 1896–97. He also gained commercial experience as the Director of the British South Africa Company from 1898 to 1904." In fact, after initially opposing the Company, he subsequently became a devoted supporter of Cecil Rhodes, its founder.[94] He actively implemented the aggressive and violent imperialist policies formulated by Rhodes. As administrator in Rhodesia, he was responsible for punitive measures against African resistance, explaining, "Until we catch them and thoroughly convince them that this country is to be the country of the white, and not the black, man we must go on hammering and hunting them."[95] He participated in this violence himself. According to his private secretary, "He rides through the veldt seeking whom he may shoot and has to be restrained from committing most inexcusable murders."[96] Despite what it says on the governor general's website, the "greater political inclusion for all" was not to include Indigenous peoples in Africa or Canada.

In recent years, much praise has been bestowed on John Buchan, Lord Tweedsmuir. He was the first governor general to be appointed after the Canadian prime minister determined who should fulfill that role.[97] Buchan was the author of about one hundred books covering adventure stories, other novels, history, law, and current affairs. His most famous book was the spy thriller *The*

Lord Grey, governor general of Canada and prominent imperialist. According to his secretary, he had "to be restrained from committing most inexcusable murders" in Rhodesia. | Vanity Fair, *1898*

Thirty-Nine Steps, which was made into a film by Alfred Hitchcock. Buchan was a passionate imperialist.[98] He noted in his autobiography that while in South Africa at the time of the Boer War, he acquired a political faith in imperialism. He "was more than a convert, [he] was a fanatic."[99] The work involved administering the notorious concentration camps (which he claimed to have turned into "health resorts") where thousands of Boers and Black Africans died.[100] He also distributed land to potential settlers. Buchan hoped to be made governor general of the Union of South Africa but had to accept the appointment in Canada instead.[101]

As governor general, he made a few speeches to Ukrainian and other European groups of non-British heritage, urging them to retain their cultures.[102] He also encouraged more young Canadians to join the Colonial Service, "for that service is as much the right of Canada as it is of Britain."[103]

John Buchan, writer, governor general, and white supremacist, in his governor general's uniform. He described a Canadian Indigenous group as "tenuous growths, fungi which had no hold on the soil." | *Yousuf Karsh, Library and Archives Canada, 1987-054*

Some of his literature reflects his racist and white supremacist views.[104] *Prester John*, a novel about the defeat of a fanatical Black preacher who leads a rebellion, is racist to the core. It concludes with a speech from the hero passionately expounding on "the white man's duty": "the difference between the white and the black, the gift of responsibility, the power of being in a little way a king." He proclaims, "So long as we know this and practise it, we will rule not only in Africa alone but wherever there are dark men who live only for the day and their own bellies."[105]

In 1937, as governor general, Buchan toured northern Canada. The tour inspired *Sick Heart River*, a classic text on the sacrifice inherent in the civilizing mission, published posthumously in 1941.[106] Somewhat improbably, a British barrister gives up his life to save an Indian band. The book describes the band's dysfunction, the pride of two Métis brothers in their Scottish but not their Indigenous heritage, and how the hero took charge.[107] Buchan writes of the British protagonist, "From the beginning he dominated them, and the domination became in the end, on their part, almost worship."[108]

John Buchan wearing
an Indigenous
headdress, 1937. |
*Yousuf Karsh, Library
and Archives Canada,
R613-591, e010751819*

In one passage in the book, Buchan takes the racial hierarchy to an absurd level as the hero sits brooding in the flicker of the firelight:

> He saw the Indians as tenuous growths, fungi which had no hold on the soil. They existed on sufferance; the North had only to tighten its grip and they would disappear. Lew and Johnny [the Métis brothers], too. They were not mushrooms, for they had roots and they had the power to yield under strain and spring back again, but were they any better than grassy filaments which swayed in the wind, but might any day be pinched out of existence ... And Galliard [a French Canadian]? He had deeper roots, but they were not healthy enough to permit transplanting ... Compared to his companions Leithen suddenly saw himself founded solidly like an oak.[109]

In summary, according to Buchan, the English visitor was rooted in the Canadian soil like an oak, the French Canadian had deep roots but could not be transplanted, the Métis brothers also had roots but might be displaced, and the Indigenous people were like "fungi which had no hold on the soil."

Despotism for the Dependent Empire

Hugh Clifford, a colonial administrator closely connected to Malaya, vividly described the ideal for colonial rule over dependent peoples in a chapter of his book *Studies in Brown Humanity*. The chapter is titled "At the Heels of the White Man":

> We find vile misrule and a government which is so incompetent and impotent that it is incapable of even oppressing its subjects completely, or upon any organised system, and we replace it by a high-class, triple-action, automatic revenue-producing administration that equally presses upon all alike. We give the poor and hitherto undefended, rights of the very existence of which they had never formerly dreamed ... We educate, we vaccinate; we physic, we punish the Wicked, and we reward the Good. We administer the native till we make him almost giddy.[110]

In practice, British rule rarely attained this ideal of replacing inefficient, oppressive government with efficient administration "[pressing] upon all alike" and conferring new rights. Clifford himself recognized this reality and blamed it on the fact that subordinates of other races had to be used to carry out the administration.

Britain (including within that term the dominions) preached the doctrines of the rule of law, liberalism, and democracy and claimed their benefits but ruled Indigenous peoples despotically. There were some signs early in the nineteenth century that British liberalism might extend to India, but that was not to be.[111] By the 1830s, the forces of reaction had prevailed. James Mill, the author of the leading history of India, was quoted in Parliament in 1833 by Thomas Macaulay, politician and historian, as saying that it was "utterly out of the question" for Indians to have representative government.[112] Such government was standard for settler colonies from their establishment (although the franchise was limited). How could that double standard be justified?

Obviously influenced by his background as a senior East India Company official, Mill's son, John Stuart Mill, provided the explanation.[113] In "Representative Government," written in 1861, he included a chapter on the government of dependencies, observing that there were colonies that had not reached the stage where they were fit for representative government. In those cases,

Canada and Colonialism

government by the dominant country was "as legitimate as any other if it is the one which in the existing state of civilisation of the subject people most facilitates their transition to a higher state of improvement."[114] A "vigorous despotism" may be the best mode of government. The greatest hope of a dependent people for advancement may depend on having "a good despot." However, this goal was not achieved through government by the British people or their ministers: "such a thing as government of one people by another does not and cannot exist." Government by ministers would be about the worst form of government. Instead, government should be delegated to autonomous bodies of experts, like the officials at his former employer, the East India Company, who had lost power following the Indian Rebellion of 1857.[115]

J.S. Mill set out his famous defence of individualism and liberal values in "On Liberty," published in 1859. He advanced the principle that "the only purpose for which power can be rightfully exercised over any member of a civilised community, against his will, is to prevent harm to others. Over himself, over his own body and mind, the individual is sovereign." However, these were empty words for the great majority of those living in the British Empire because Mill, and most Britons, excluded them from the civilized world. He continued:

> It is perhaps, hardly necessary to say that this doctrine is meant to apply only to human beings in the maturity of their faculties ... we may leave out of consideration those backward states of society in which the race itself may be considered as in its nonage ... Despotism is a legitimate mode of government in dealing with barbarians, provided the end be their improvement, and the means justified by actually effecting that end.[116]

So far as the Indigenous peoples of the Dependent Empire and the settler colonies were concerned, Mill's "On Liberty" was a manifesto for despotism, not liberty.

Just as Mill was required to exempt the Dependent Empire from his defence of liberal values, so was Albert Dicey, a leading constitutional lawyer, credited with the "rule of law" doctrine.[117] One writer summarized, "In Dicey's account, the rule of law was a distinguishing feature of English civilisational superiority, one that justified and underpinned the exercise of British imperial rule. And yet Dicey was forced to acknowledge that the exigencies of imperial governance required arbitrariness and formal inequality at odds with the rule of law and the liberal Empire it was supposed to uphold."[118] In the words of a recent book on the nineteenth-century British Empire, "Liberalism was appropriate for Britons at home and overseas but only to a certain extent for colonized subjects of colour. Imperial subjects needed certain cultural and educational correctives before liberal governance could ever work its progressive magic among them."[119]

In sharp contrast to the situation in the settler colonies, including Canada, with their representative and later responsible forms of government, the Dependent Empire was ruled despotically. There were a baffling number of variations in the form of government. Most were "Crown colonies," in which the governor had final and effectively absolute power subject only to the politicians in London.[120] He embodied the executive power of the colony and was the commander-in-chief of its armed forces. He usually had an executive council that could advise him, and a legislative council to pass legislation on specific topics. The governor nominated some members, some were government officials, and some were elected either directly by a narrow electorate or indirectly by business or other groups. In 1938, a senior Colonial Office official, Sir Charles Jeffries, described the forms of government based on the regulations for the colonial services. He noted that a fundamental characteristic of the colonial system was that the governor was "the single and supreme authority responsible to and representative of His Majesty."[121] (In fact, the personal powers of a governor exceeded those of the monarch within Britain and the dominions.) Another senior colonial official described the powers of the governor as "direct personal rule. All power and responsibility are centred in him."[122] To symbolize his authority, he was entitled to wear a unique ceremonial costume including a distinctive helmet with white swan's feathers.

Colonial rulers defended their despotism and the exclusion of Indigenous people from government. Alfred Lyall, lieutenant governor of the North-Western Provinces in India in the 1880s, thought that the immense majority of Indians preferred a "simple despotism" like his.[123] Viceroy George Curzon, an especially imperious imperialist, did not purport to speak for Indian people. Instead, he justified their lack of power by their "inferiority." He said in 1901 that the real strength of his position lay in "the extraordinary inferiority in character, honesty and capacity of the [Indians]. It is often said why not make some prominent native a member of the Executive Council? The answer is that in the whole continent there is not an Indian fit for the post."[124] The population was then over 240 million! Justifying the autocratic system, the prominent imperial historian Reginald Coupland said it was "essential that the Governor's will should in the last resort prevail in everything" so he could ensure that the will of the UK Parliament ("a democratic authority") would prevail.[125] Of course, this convoluted argument of using democracy in the UK to justify despotism overseas ignores the lack of colonial representation in that Parliament.

Canada and Colonialism

Sometimes there were a few representatives of the local people on the executive and legislative council, but they were outnumbered by officials who did as the governor instructed and by unofficial members representing the British community. John Darwin, a historian of empires, explains, "The convenience of the Crown colony method was that it could be tailored to a very diverse set of possessions by adjusting the choice and number of unofficial members and by widening or narrowing the scope of legislative council business. A moderately skilful governor could head off discontent or find a new ally by using his power of appointment."[126] Furthermore, the governor or the imperial government could overrule any legislation that the legislative council might pass. Writing of British rule in Africa, George Padmore, a fierce West Indian critic of imperialism, said in 1936 that it was "as 'totalitarian' as any fascist state, with the Governor as absolute dictator."[127] For example, in Kenya, Indigenous people had no representative on the legislative council except a missionary appointed by the governor.[128]

One consequence of the immense power of the governor was that he could pursue a completely different policy from his predecessor, leading, according to one author, to chronic instability in many parts of the Empire.[129] Some governors lacked relevant experience, since they were former politicians, although others had extensive experience.[130] The centre of colonial social life, governors lived lives of luxury in their residences, surrounded by servants and with little direct contact with ordinary people.[131]

This despotic system resulted in draconian legislation intended to ensure the survival of imperial rule by limiting opposition. For example, in India, the *Bengal State Prisoner's Regulation* of 1818 authorized detention without trial of anyone for various purposes, including "the security of the British dominions ... from internal commotion."[132] In 1870, Justice Norman of the High Court of Calcutta rejected a legal challenge to its validity. He held that the danger to the security of the British dominions was permanent and so justified the permanent suspension of the right to personal liberty.[133] This regulation remained in effect for over a century and was supplemented by other provisions permitting such detention.

The *Indian Penal Code,* enacted in 1860, had numerous provisions dealing with offences pertaining to challenges to British rule.[134] One writer has counted forty-nine provisions for crimes concerning dissent against the state.[135] Another states that the code's priority "was the smooth and safe functioning of the imperial regime not the punishment of crimes against individuals."[136] Section 124A dealing with sedition was added in 1870.[137] It became an offence to bring, or attempt to bring, into hatred or contempt, or to excite or attempt to excite, dissatisfaction against the government established in British India. The punishment was transportation for life (forced relocation to a foreign country) or imprisonment for up to three years plus a fine. In a prosecution against the prominent Indian scholar and nationalist Bal Gangadhar Tilak in 1897, the judge said the English law on sedition did not apply. He explained to the jury that, in India, "the offence consists in exciting or attempting to excite in others certain bad feelings towards the Government." In his view, those "bad feelings" could be equated to disloyalty.[138] Twenty-five years later, the provision was used against another prominent Indian leader, Mahatma Gandhi. He pleaded guilty and said the imperial system was "an effective system of terrorism and an organised display of force on the one hand, and the deprivation of all powers of retaliation or self-defence on the other." Gandhi described Section 124A as "perhaps the prince among the political sections of the Indian Penal Code designed to suppress the liberty of the citizen." Some of India's most loved patriots had been convicted under it and he was privileged to join them.[139] The *Vernacular Press Act* was passed in 1878 to regulate the press and so limit opposition to the government. The government used its control of the army, police, and prisons to enforce this despotic rule. Even criticism of the government's ineffective response to famine in 1896 resulted in arrests and imprisonment.[140] Similar repressive legislation was passed in other dependent colonies, showing how hollow was the claim that the rule of law prevailed in the Empire.[141]

Colonial judges did not enjoy the formal recognition of independence that existed in the UK, Canada, and the other settler colonies, which is usually considered a crucial part of the rule of law. According to a detailed study, the principle of judicial independence "continued to be a contested matter until dusk settled on colonial rule" in the non-white Empire.[142] However, as a practical matter, this uncertainty was of limited significance as judges were part of the colonial establishment. In India, officers of the East India Company and its successor, the Indian Civil Service, performed judicial functions as magistrates and senior judges despite, in most cases, their lack of legal training.[143] Throughout the rest of the Empire, the powers of district officers also included acting as magistrates. These powers even extended to trials of suspects they had arrested themselves. In any event, the law gave such sweeping powers to the governor and other officials that judges and magistrates had little ability to limit or reverse their decisions, even if they were minded to do so. A court in India was required to accept an order of the Governor General in Council as "full justification [for any] act, except so far as the order extends to any European British subject."[144] Also, courts could not make rulings in claims that were considered to be based on political relations with foreign states, such as treaties or annexations. Therefore, when the Punjab was annexed and the ruler deposed, the court refused to consider a claim for property and a pension.[145]

◄◄ • ► ►

To return to the scene that opened this chapter from the 1911 coronation of George V as King and Emperor of India, the Canadian North-West Mounted Police and Indian troops may have jointly honoured their common monarch in London, but they did so under very different circumstances. The Canadians would return to a self-governing and virtually independent country. The Indians would return to a colony ruled despotically by men sent out from the imperial capital, including some from Canada and other settler colonies.

The Rulers and Their Rule

In *Bush and Boma*, J.C. Cairns describes his experiences during the 1950s in Tanganyika (now Tanzania) as a district officer and member of the Colonial Service.[1] He writes of working in the district office or *Boma*, far from other districts, which are accessible only by dirt roads and the occasional steamer; of the local people who rely on him and address him as *Bwana* or boss or master; and of the heat that causes everything to fade, including the Union Jack that hangs limply in the centre of the courtyard. He also writes of his home in Canada, how he will miss Africa and Africans when he returns, and how some Canadians are very ignorant of Africa. An engaging, well-written book, it forms part of an enormous literature of such memoirs from colonial officials who served around the Dependent Empire, and a broader literature on colonial administration.[2] How were such men (and they were virtually all men) chosen? What training did they receive? What were their lives like?

The Colonial Services

Even before self-government, administration in the settler colonies did not involve any large number of colonial officers sent out from London. Apart from the most senior officers, locally qualified staff were used. In most dependent colonies, by contrast, the senior officials were mainly expatriates, although they relied upon more junior clerical and other local staff. In India, the legal system employed tens of thousands of local judges, assistant magistrates, record-keepers, and police officers, but their powers were limited compared with

European (i.e., white) officials, including, in the case of judges, their jurisdiction over trials of Europeans.[3] In the words of one historian, "Indians could be judges but not lawmakers, and they always earned less than Europeans."[4]

The administrators were almost exclusively male. Writing in 1938, one senior official noted that there were some administrative positions that a woman could fill with success, and some areas, such as medicine, education, and nursing, in which women were superior. However, the Colonial Service, taken as a whole, was not one in which a woman could be expected to perform the ordinary duties effectually, or be available for free interchange with other officers.[5] Given this limited role for women in colonial administration, it is a bit surprising that for over thirty years the leading authority on such administration was Margery Perham. She was a fellow of Nuffield College, Oxford, and taught many training courses to administrators.[6] She was a conventional imperialist in most of her views, with a somewhat gruff manner. But she stressed that the ultimate purpose of British rule in Africa was to enable Africans to achieve self-government. According to a recent biography, "it is this moral insistence, communicated over her long career to governors, Colonial Service officers, soldiers, settlers, students, Africans, missionaries, and the British public that comes through in a defining way as comprising the essence of her life and legacy."[7]

So far as Indigenous peoples were concerned, the men recruited in London and sent out to the colonies *were* the government. The real burden of administration fell on the man in the field, usually known as the district officer. In the words of William Macmillan, a professor of colonial studies, "The lowest rank in the administrative hierarchy is that on which the efficiency of the whole most of all depends."[8] We shall see in Chapter 6 that a similar situation prevailed in Canada. An enormous amount of power was delegated to "the man on the spot," around whom a great deal of romantic mythology arose. However, it should be noted that the men in the colonies ultimately reported to officials in their head office in London. This was the India Office for India, the Colonial Office for most of the other dependencies, and the Foreign Office for a few others.[9] It was not a very tidy arrangement. The main concern of the head offices was the selection of governors, drafting their instructions, and attempting to deal with infringements.[10]

Each colonial head office had a minister responsible to Parliament, but, in practice, much power rested with the senior bureaucrats. James Stephen was the permanent under-secretary of state for the Colonial Office from 1836 to 1847, having joined the office in 1813 as legal counsel. He was the most important civil servant in that office at a time of fundamental change in colonial policies.[11] A critic, Charles Buller, mercilessly satirized him in a book published in 1840 that advocated the system of responsible government. According to Buller, Stephen controlled the office through a mastery of colonial affairs that his superiors lacked: "No pile of despatches with their multifarious enclosures, no red-taped heap of Colonial grievances or squabbles can scare his practised eye. He handles with unfaltering hand the papers at which his superiors quail."[12] Buller called Stephen "Mr. Mothercountry" because it was Stephen, not the Crown, Parliament, the public, the Colonial Secretary, or the parliamentary under-secretary, who truly represented Mother England and ruled the colonists before self-government.

Some senior colonial officials "were a true elite of scholar-official mandarins."[13] Stephen left the Colonial Office to become a professor of history at Cambridge, and his successor, Herman Merivale, was a professor at Oxford. Another official was Arthur Berriedale Keith, who excelled in the civil service examinations, obtained doctorates in law and Sanskrit, and, after leaving the Colonial Office, went on to become a professor of both law and Sanskrit at Edinburgh University. Keith was a leading authority on the constitutional law of the Empire, particularly that relating to Canada and the other dominions.[14] His work was relied upon by Prime Minister Mackenzie King during King's dispute with the governor general of Canada in 1926 over the latter's refusal to dissolve Parliament and call an election.[15]

Colonial administration was often initially part of the military administration, as in Canada until the 1830s, when it became a separate civil administration. It may also have been a part of the commercial operations of large trading firms, such as the East India Company, the Hudson's Bay Company, and the British South Africa Company. During the second half of the eighteenth century, the role of East India Company officials became less that of merchants and soldiers and more that of administrators who collected taxes and maintained law and order. The Company recognized the need for professional administrators and established systems to select and train them. It set up a college at Haileybury that became a model for the future education of colonial administrators in Asia when the Indian Civil Service took over administration from the Company in 1858.[16] Competitive examinations were introduced in 1855 to replace a system of patronage where jobs had been given out by those in power. Training included courses on Indian history, law, and languages at university. There was also a test of riding skills and a medical examination. Oscar D. Skelton, who went on to become a senior Canadian civil servant greatly influencing the country's relationship with the UK, passed the academic and riding tests but failed the medical. It was said that this failure to join the elite ranks

Canada and Colonialism

of the Indian Civil Service soured him toward the Empire.[17] Members of the Indian Civil Service formed an intellectual elite – the so-called heaven-born.[18]

In contrast, the rest of the Dependent Empire was managed by administrators who glorified the cult of the amateur. This lack of professionalism continued until reforms were carried out, especially in the 1940s, relating to the administration of colonies under the Colonial Office. Likewise, undiluted patronage prevailed until the 1930s, when formal interviews were instituted, although the correct connections remained important.[19] In her magisterial survey of the British Empire, Jan Morris described the administration of the non-Asian colonies, known generally as the Colonial Service:

> Jobs in Africa and the lesser tropical colonies went by a kind of patronage. The private interview was the chosen method ... There was no training programme – men were expected to learn their trade on the spot: many subtleties of native life and custom escaped this slapdash novitiate, and British colonial officers were frequently ignorant about complexities like customary law and land tenure. As a whole, the Crown Colonies were ruled by willing all-rounders of very varied quality ... They were recruited more for character than brainpower: it was said that a candidate with a first-class degree would actually be regarded as suspect.[20]

There are many accounts, true and fictitious, of the lives of colonial field officers, especially from Africa.[21] What emerges most clearly is the extent of the power wielded over the Indigenous peoples, underpinned by paternalism and an associated belief in the inferiority of those peoples. The senior administrator, Lord Lugard, alludes to this belief in his account of the qualities that must be shown:

> The white man's prestige must stand high when a few score are responsible for the control and guidance of millions ... There is no room for "mean whites" in tropical Africa. Nor is there room for those who, however high their motives, are content to place themselves on the same level as the uncivilised races. They lower the prestige by which alone the white races can hope to govern and to guide.[22]

In his view, the necessary qualities could be found in the "class that has made and maintained the British Empire ... English gentlemen" produced by a "public" school (which, of course, is the perverse use of English to describe private education in the UK) and probably a university education.[23] About 80 percent of colonial administrators came from "public" schools.[24]

The generic district officer has been described as "usually a practitioner of the public-school code and cultural ethos, even though not always from a public school ... A distinct [upper] middle-class club."[25] The successful applicants were overwhelmingly the sons of professionals such as doctors, lawyers, and parsons. A 1948 appointments handbook referred to the merits of applicants from "stock that has proved its worth, generation to generation."[26] British Conservative politician and historian Kwasi Kwarteng (best known for his recent short and economically disastrous reign as Chancellor of the Exchequer) explains that the empire "openly repudiated ideas of human equality and put power and responsibility into the hands of a chosen elite, drawn from a tiny proportion of the population in Britain."[27] Their privileged education likely had a significant impact on how they carried out their duties. One writer comments, "More and more, scholars are realizing that [public schools] are at the heart of any discussion of how the Empire worked."[28] Such schools saw it as their role to prepare their students for service in the Empire. This preparation included inculcating the required superior attitude for rule over "the subject races." Nazi educators were so impressed that they modelled their own elite schools, the Napolas, in part on the British public schools and arranged exchange visits with them.[29] A German handbook prepared (likely by the Gestapo) for the invasion of the UK described the schools as "calculated to rear men of inflexible will and ruthless energy who regard intellectual problems as a waste of time but know human nature and how to dominate other men in the most unscrupulous fashion."[30] Public schools were also imported into Canada and other colonies.

The schools moulded "an authoritarian personality, accustomed to giving orders and having them obeyed."[31] They constituted "the first steps set on the steady and inevitable progress towards the positions of command over the majority."[32] Students naturally regarded themselves as superior to all those of lesser social status. This class prejudice and feelings of racial superiority made it difficult for them to consider Indigenous peoples as anything but inferiors. Anthony Kirk-Greene, a former colonial administrator who became an Oxford academic generally favourable toward the Empire, said innate class consciousness rather than blatant racial rejection could explain the hostility toward educated Africans. They were regarded as educated above their social status.[33] Racial and class bias also explained the negative assessments of applicants to the Colonial Service who did not fit the model. Notes in their files included the following: "Baboo – worse than usual," "Eurasian – discouraged," "fearfully vulgar," "not quite a gentleman."[34] Personal appearance was also carefully scrutinized.

Recruiters made comments such as "a weak and selfish mouth" and "a flabby lip."[35] Successful candidates had to have a firm handshake.[36]

The Colonial Service was almost exclusively British (including all those of British descent) down to the 1940s. A few Africans were appointed to senior positions before 1900. A policy was then adopted to reduce their numbers.[37] In the 1920s, Gordon Guggisberg, a Canadian-born governor, proposed a twenty-year plan for localization in the Gold Coast (Ghana). It was not implemented.[38] In contrast, Indians were appointed to the Indian Civil Service as early as 1867. The new charter for the East India Company in 1833 expressly stated that race and religion would not disable anyone from being employed by the Company. But in practice the policy was to exclude Indians from senior positions. Exams were only held in London. Apart from the cost, this limitation violated a restriction forbidding some orthodox Hindus from travelling over water. Low age limits to take the exams also made it difficult for Indians to acquire sufficient proficiency in English and English academic subjects. By the end of the 1880s, there were still only a handful of Indians in a service of 900 ruling over 250 million Indians and, by 1915, still only 63 Indians had ever been appointed. Exams were held in India from 1922, and efforts were made to increase the percentage of Indian officers. As a result, they comprised a quarter of members in 1932, but in 1939, they still accounted for less than half of the 1,300 members.[39] Their low numbers were a major grievance of the self-government movement.

One man, Major Sir Ralph Dolignon Furse, controlled the hiring and training of Colonial Service members from 1919 to 1948. After an education at Eton and Oxford and service in the Guards, he joined the Colonial Office and became responsible for recruitment. An insufferable snob, he fought ceaselessly, strenuously, and successfully against competitive examinations and meritocracy.[40] He insisted instead on patronage, references, and interviews, so favouring those with the right connections. The overriding stated criterion for recruitment and promotion was "character and personality." This vague term could be used to weed out those perceived as racially and socially inferior and any candidate who might be overly critical of the status quo. It was a trump card that could always be used to ensure that "the right sort" received the job. Intelligence was not a necessary requirement and was sometimes seen as a liability. The right connections could help those who were "remarkably stupid."[41]

Furse was instrumental in making it easier for Dominion applicants to join the Colonial Service. As a result of his efforts, including a visit to Canada in 1922, the Dominion Selection Scheme was put into effect.[42] The scheme arose as the result of a visit in 1920 to London of W.L. Grant, the principal of Upper Canada College. The college, a private elitist school, was a centre of imperialist culture. One of Grant's predecessors was George Parkin, who was probably the leading imperialist campaigner in Canada, and Stephen Leacock taught there. Grant wanted a process that would enable suitable Canadian graduates to apply to the imperial services without having to go to England at their own expense for the interview. As a result, selection committees were established in Canada to conduct the interviews, although the final decision was made in London.

Explaining the scheme, Furse thought it would increase awareness in Canada of the problems and achievements of the administration of Indigenous peoples.[43] Leo Amery, who was then parliamentary under-secretary of state at the Colonial Office, said that he looked forward "to the result of this modest little experiment in taking Canada into partnership in 'the White Man's Burden.'"[44] He also expressed the hope they had "done something which in the long run will help to strengthen Canada's recollection of the fact that she owns an Empire."[45] Lord Devonshire, secretary for the colonies, told the House of Commons in 1923 that he was confident the scheme would be a success in benefitting the colonial services because "there will be a clearer understanding in Canada of the needs, the opportunities, and the resources of the Empire."[46]

It is difficult to know just how successful the Dominion Selection Scheme was. No records appear to have been kept of how many colonial officers born in Canada applied through it and how many applied through the normal course. Indeed, it is difficult to know how many officers were born in Canada, since they shared common status as British subjects with those born in the UK or elsewhere in the Empire. In 1926, Amery, who was now the secretary for the colonies, said there was a "small but steady stream" of Canadian appointments.[47] Many of them appear to have been to technical positions, such as in medicine and engineering, although there were administrative appointments as well.[48] Having in mind the policy of Canada and other dominions to exclude non-white immigrants, Arthur Berriedale Keith, a prominent writer on imperial matters, raised the question, "How far is it proper to appoint to colonial positions men coming from Dominions whose national policy excludes the colonists, though British subjects, from entry or settlement?"[49]

The primary duties of colonial officers were collecting revenue, acting as magistrates, and, as required, working with the police and the army to maintain law and order. At times, riot control was a prominent feature of their lives.[50] Kirk-Greene said that, "chronologically, there was a shift of emphasis, say from tax gathering before 1914 through economic development after 1935 to social development and 'politics' after 1945, but underpinning all colonial administration was the imperative of the [district officer's] responsibility for law and order. Without that, nothing else was possible."[51]

In the first half of the twentieth century, which saw Labour governments in Britain and growing independence movements around the Empire, the role of colonial officers changed, as Kirk-Greene noted, in line with the new policies of promoting economic development and, after the Second World War, preparing Indigenous peoples for self-government within the Empire/Commonwealth.[52] Breaking with the long-standing policy that colonies had to be self-sufficient, the central government in London passed legislation in the 1940s to make funds available to promote economic development.[53] Training courses for colonial administrators and promotion of greater professionalism sought to equip them for the new challenges. One internal memorandum prepared by Furse noted the growing presence of educated people within colonial territories. It warned of the danger posed by "the Uninstructed White."[54] Paternalism was still present, however, even as it was being denied. In the words of Alan Burns, a senior administrator with experience around the Empire and relatively liberal in his views, "The main thing in my opinion is to find out what Colonial peoples want, and if their wants are not too unreasonable to let them have their way ... The time is long past when we can get away with the attitude that 'Daddy knows best'; and we must remember that children are perverse enough to grow up."[55]

As noted, the Indian Civil Service was a professional administration from its early days. In contrast, the Colonial Service lacked professionalism and preferred to stress character, common sense, and a jack-of-all-trades approach. This situation started to change after the First World War and was especially notable after the Second World War, when a "Modern Colonial Service" was created. An essential part of this development was the recruitment of specialists with professional qualifications and experience. In addition to the Colonial Administrative Service, there were no fewer than nineteen professional services, such as agriculture, education, forestry, police, and public works. One district officer who joined the Colonial Service after the Second World War observed: "Gone were the days when the District Officer could properly be termed the maid-of-all-work: treasurer, magistrate, prosecutor and defence counsel, road-builder and tax collector all rolled into one. The post-war District Officer was likely to be the leader of a District Team of professionals."[56]

Related developments to make the Colonial Service more professional were recruiting better-educated officers and providing better training rather than learning on the job and relying on character and common sense. As these steps were taken to bring the Colonial Service in line with the Indian Civil Service, candidates who might have applied for the latter began applying to the Colonial Service as the inevitability of early Indian independence became obvious. In his history of district officers in Africa, Anthony Kirk-Greene summarizes the change in their educational background and expected sympathy for the new goal of preparing for independence: "If 'fire in their bellies' had been a feature, at times almost a qualification of the founding [district officers], from 1930 intellectual competence and personal empathy were prize attributes in the final model of the [district officer] in Africa."[57] Applicants to the Colonial Service were expected to be university graduates, although exceptions were made for ex-servicemen who could show similar intellectual ability.[58] A more competitive selection process replaced the earlier system of patronage.

The changes that took place after the end of the Second World War were reflected in what Kirk-Greene describes as "a sudden and silent revolution."[59] On the night of June 17, 1954, the Colonial Service, which had existed since 1837, was replaced by Her Majesty's Overseas Civil Service. Although the full implications would take some years to work out, especially as different colonies gained independence at different times, the change symbolized the beginning of the end of British colonial administration. Members of the former Colonial Service were encouraged by generous financial arrangements to take employment with the governments of the territories involved. They became more like civil servants in London than archetypal colonial district officers. The British end of administration would become one in which "there would no longer be any regular establishment, only a series of contract or loan appointments."[60] Colonial theory regarding Indigenous peoples had also changed: no longer was the colonial mission expressed as a duty of protection and civilization, as with Merivale in 1839, but rather an exercise in economic development and preparation for independence.[61]

Colonial Administrators

Colonial administrators were reasonably well remunerated and generally enjoyed a standard of living that they could not hope to enjoy in the UK. An Indian Civil Service officer received a pension that was transferred to his widow for her life and then passed to any unmarried children for their lives. In return, the district officers in the field had lonely and sometimes difficult, dangerous lives, although not as dramatic as that led by Sanders of the River, "the righter of wrongs," in the books of Edgar Wallace set in West Africa.[62]

Especially in the early days, life could be short for Europeans in the tropics. One poignant example is provided in the collection of letters published in 1910

Canada and Colonialism

and written by one recently arrived administrator in Nigeria, who died at the age of twenty-five from diphtheria. The introduction, written by the Canadian-born High Commissioner, Sir Percy Girouard, stated, "This young officer's name can be placed upon the roll of men given up by British mothers, wives and loved ones to the service of their country."[63] Illness, physical and mental, was a constant concern in many places. Just as Indigenous peoples had not acquired immunity from European diseases brought by contact, Europeans lacked immunity to those of the Dependent Empire. Medical assistance was difficult to obtain in remote areas. One academic who had an accidental and unauthorized peek into personnel files noted, "Many of these illnesses were psychological in origin, the product, it seems, of isolation, of loneliness and the absence of the comforts of home. A few of these tragedies ended in a return voyage to Liverpool in a strait jacket."[64] Heavy drinking was widespread.[65]

Much of the work was mundane and bureaucratic. A sense of the office environment of these men is conjured up in the over seventy pages of advertisements in the *Colonial Office List* of 1901 for the stationery products of Harrison & Sons of Pall Mall. Included are advertisements for red tape costing two shillings for a dozen pieces of narrow width, goose quill pens, and the patent label dampener.[66]

Colonial administrators, and especially the district officers, were, and still are, often held up as examples of all that was good about the Empire. In some accounts, they achieve almost saintly status. The Spanish-American philosopher George Santayana wrote, "Instinctively the Englishman is no missionary, no conqueror ... Never since the heroic days of Greece has the world had such a sweet, just, boyish master."[67] Edmund Morel, who campaigned so vigorously to end the horrors of rule by King Leopold of the Belgians in the Congo, added his praise. He described the colonial officers in Nigeria as "a handful of quiet men, enthusiastic in their appreciation of the opportunity, strong in their sense of duty, keen in their sense of right, firm in their sense of justice." He was moved to conclude that when one sees such a man "living in a leaky mud hut, holding, by the sway of his personality, the balance even between fiercely antagonistic races ... then one feels that permanent evil cannot ultimately evolve from so much admirable work."[68]

Rudyard Kipling, the leading imperial poet and novelist, claimed that some Indian Civil Service officers literally worked themselves to death: "[They] die, or kill themselves by overwork, or are worried to death or broken in health and hope in order that the land may be protected from death and sickness, famine and war, and may eventually become capable of standing alone." These hardships were endured in a spirit of self-sacrifice: "If an advance be made all credit is given to the native, while the Englishmen stand back and wipe their fore-heads. If a failure occurs the Englishmen step forward and take the blame."[69] According to the colonial administrator Lord Lugard, district officers had "an almost passionate conception of fair play, of protection of the weak, and 'play-ing the game.'"[70] The academic Margery Perham claimed they could be "relied upon to be humane, uncorrupt [and] diligent."[71] Churchill also saw them as "incorruptible [and] ... impartial between races, creeds and classes."[72] His pol-itical opponent Arthur Creech Jones, another former Secretary of State for the colonies, agreed with this sentiment and concluded that "the great dedication of many of the members of the Colonial Service and the devotion and service rendered deserve our mead of recognition."[73]

There were less favourable evaluations of the colonial administrators. Writ-ing recently, the Indian politician Shashi Tharoor provides a blistering criti-cism of British rule and a penetrating analysis of why it was so successful for so long with so few rulers – in 1931, 168,000 Britons (including 60,000 in the army and police, and only 4,000 in civil government) ran a country of 300 mil-lion. He quotes Eric Hobsbawm, a Marxist historian with a grudging respect for the achievements of the Empire: the European empires were "so easily won, so narrowly based, so absurdly easily ruled thanks to the devotion of a few and the passivity of the many."[74]

Rejecting the praise so often bestowed on the Indian Civil Service, Tharoor describes it as "all-pervasive, overpaid, obtusely process-ridden, remarkably in-efficient and largely indifferent to the well-being of the people for whose gov-ernance it had, after all, been created."[75] He explains the success of British rule as due to "an extraordinary combination of racial self-assurance, superior mil-itary technology, the mystique of modernity and the trappings of enlighten-ment progressivism – as well as, it must be said clearly, the cravenness, cupidity, opportunism, and lack of organized resistance on the part of the vanquished – that sustained the Empire, along with the judicious application of brute force when necessary."[76] Tharoor observes how so much power was bestowed on young, inexperienced British colonial officers with little knowledge of the local languages or conditions: "A twenty-four-year-old district officer found himself in charge of 4,000 square miles and a million people."[77]

According to Tharoor, colonial administrators "were ... as a rule, singularly smug and self-satisfied and insufferably patronizing in their attitudes to Indians (when they were not simply contemptuous) ... The British ruled nineteenth-century India with unshakeable self-confidence, buttressed by protocol, alco-hol and a lot of gall."[78] They were "good at manipulating the paperwork created by the new rules but had little interest in the well-being of their subjects nor the capacity to establish their authority other than by reference to their rules. When these were violated, they could only take recourse in the forcible imposition of law and order."[79]

This recent criticism of the limits of the bureaucratic mind echoes some criticism of the time. In the words of Ramsay MacDonald, the Labour politician, colonial administrators were "the finest race in the world for keeping in old ruts, and that in itself is some qualification for the offices they hold. But they are also the least imaginative and sympathetic of men."[80] Professor Harold Laski thought they had a mind that rarely questioned the historical assumptions of the Empire or looked to innovation in fundamentals.[81] Another professor, William Macmillan, wrote that even the junior officers in Africa were members of a tiny ruling caste, living a life apart, seldom answered back to, with little opportunity for free discussion, and overly deferential to their superiors.[82] Leonard Barnes, a critic of the Empire, thought they were men of good intelligence and general ability, but they were not suitably equipped to handle the complex problems of race and culture and administration to which their official lives were devoted.[83] Nationalist leaders were generally highly critical.[84] From his prison cell, Jawaharlal Nehru, the independence leader, referred to the Indian Civil Service as "neither Indian, nor civil, nor a service."[85]

George Orwell summed up his view in *Burmese Days:*

> The poor devils are no worse than anybody else. They lead unenviable lives; it is a poor bargain to spend thirty years, ill-paid, in an alien country, and then come home with a wrecked liver and a pine-apple backside from sitting in cane chairs, to settle down as the bore of some second-rate Club.
>
> On the other hand, the sahiblog [British in the East] are not to be idealized ... The real work of administration is done mainly by native subordinates; and the real backbone of the despotism is not the officials but the Army. Given the Army, the officials and the business men can rub along safely enough even if they are fools. And most of them *are* fools. A dull, decent people, cherishing and fortifying their dullness behind a quarter of a million bayonets.[86]

This was a harsh judgment but perhaps closer to the truth than the more romantic view of Wallace and other authors.

There is evidence that some colonial officials went beyond bureaucratic mediocrity and became tyrants. Some exploited their power to abuse local women.[87] In 1903, an Assistant Native Commissioner in Southern Rhodesia was dismissed for serious misconduct that included threatening a girl's father with arrest if she refused to live with him. The Colonial Office ignored the recommendation of Milner, the High Commissioner, advising that he be let off as lightly as the circumstances allowed.[88] Instead, he was dismissed. The reasoning of the Colonial Office seemed to have as much to do with prohibiting any sexual relationship between colonial officers and Black women as punishing him for his conduct. A senior official of the office minuted, "the simple and cast-iron rule should be that any white men having connection with, or behaving indecently to, any black women will be at once fired out of the service."[89]

As noted, one criticism with significant practical consequences was the lack of understanding of Indigenous peoples by many of their rulers. According to Ramsay MacDonald, "Nine-tenths of them return from their foreign appointments without having understood the mind of the natives they were ruling. One meets them in the Islands of the Seas, pining for home, surrounded by English influences."[90] Writing in 1918, one senior colonial administrator acknowledged the lack of contact the "vast majority" of European officials had with local people. This was unavoidable, as "ordinary social intercourse between natives and Europeans is impossible and indeed inexpedient except in rare cases." The Indigenous people met were generally not typical at all.[91] According to Norman Leys, a medical doctor who was a member of the colonial administration in Kenya in the early decades of the twentieth century and spoke from personal experience, "knowledge of African life and readiness to defend the rights and interests of Africans are not the qualities that mark men for promotion."[92] In a lecture given in 1930, the famous archaeologist and anthropologist Louis Leakey claimed that, putting aside deliberate unfairness, this lack of knowledge meant that "practically every administrative officer I know is continually doing things which are considered by the natives as grossly unjust and unfair, and moreover which usually are in fact unfair and unjust and unwise."[93]

In contrast, colonial officials could socialize with the local European residents. It was often a criticism that they identified with European interests (although many settlers thought officials hostile to them and too sympathetic to the Indigenous people). A Fabian Society publication of 1942 referred to complaints that the Colonial Service had identified itself with the interests and prejudices of Europeans with vested interests in the colonies, and lacked sympathy with the legitimate aspirations of the peoples.[94] Laski thought there was a definite hostility in the Service to the normal British ideas of civil liberties.[95]

Canadian Governors

Imperial administrators were included in the lecture given in 1866 by the biographer Henry Morgan on British Americans who had distinguished themselves in the service of the Empire.[96] He referred to Sir Charles Darling, governor of Victoria in Australia and Sir William Winniett, governor of the Gold Coast. Darling was born in Annapolis Royal, Nova Scotia, in 1809, and, after serving in the British Army, was governor of several colonies in the West Indies, South Africa, Newfoundland, and Victoria. He became involved in controversies in Victoria, including over convict labour and local politics. As a result, he was abruptly removed from office in 1866. In the words of his biographer, "As a vice-regal representative, a constitutional head of state and an officer of the British government Darling had been a failure."[97] Also born in Annapolis Royal, Winniett had a more successful career. He joined the Royal Navy and served in North America and on the coast of West Africa, being appointed governor of the Gold Coast from 1845 to his death in 1850. During this time, he was active in suppressing the slave trade. Another colonial administrator, Sir William Douglas Young, was born in British Columbia in 1859. He had a variety of appointments in the Colonial Service and retired as governor of the Falkland Islands.

Some prominent imperialists were keen to include non-British Europeans, including French Canadians, in the British imperial system. Alfred Milner wrote, "The French Canadian need not cease to be a French Canadian, but he may be a British soldier or administrator all the same and he will have abso-lutely the same scope and opportunities as his competitors of British blood."[98] Understandably, French Canadians were not generally enthusiastic supporters of the British Empire. However, there were exceptions, and a few made careers in other parts of the Empire.[99] Percy Girouard was one of them. He was excep-tional in many ways and lived a fascinating life worthy of a comprehensive biography that has yet to be published, although aspects of his life have been covered in some detail.[100] That life took him from Quebec to England and then to the Sudan, South Africa, Nigeria, and Kenya.

Trained as an engineer at the Royal Military College in Kingston, Ontario, Girouard served in the British Army. He subsequently became a governor in both West and East Africa. He thus gained direct experience of how the British Empire distinguished between dependent colonies considered unsuitable for European settlement and to be exploited for their resources, and those col-onies viewed as "a white man's country" and so intended to become settler colonies. His life also intersected at critical times with prominent imperialists like Kitchener, Churchill, and Milner, as well as Indigenous peoples. Girouard's views concerning race, cultural supremacy, the use of force, and systems of rule were those of a conventional imperialist. But he successfully used uncon-ventional engineering methods to defend and expand the Empire, including in the campaign to reconquer the Sudan and in the Boer War during the 1880s and 1890s. His skills earned him the praise of Winston Churchill in his account of the Sudan campaign.[101] Girouard had built a railway at breakneck speed across the desert – so different from his native Quebec – that enabled General Kitchener's successful re-conquest.

In his youth, he was the image of a dashing Army officer, with a full moustache and habitually using a monocle. He received early recognition, with a knighthood at thirty-three. A contemporary journal described his career as "so brilliant as to be almost without precedent."[102] In his middle years as governor, he stood out for his distinguished and dapper appearance. There is a 1909 photo of him being welcomed at the Nairobi railway station by Lord Delamere, the flamboyant leader of the settler community.[103] Dressed all in white and wearing a pith helmet, Girouard conjures up the splendour of Empire. One contemporary who worked under him in Kenya wrote, "He has brains. But he is vain, absurdly fond of popularity, dearly loves the rich and titled."[104] A man of great energy, intelligence, and self-confidence, he was not intimidated in the least by powerful men.

The reverse side to this boldness was an impatience with control by others, including senior officials at the Colonial Office to whom he reported. He was less than truthful in keeping them advised of his actions, and ultimately paid with the loss of his governorship in Kenya for upsetting and potentially embarrassing the Colonial Secretary. The matter that finally led to his forced resignation was the movement of the Maasai in 1911 from one of their two reserves to the other so that settlers (with whom Girouard strongly identified) could obtain the former, where the land was of better quality. This event, which has received much attention, was crucial for the future development of Kenya and remains a cause of unrest.[105] Pressure and threats were used to induce the Maasai to make the move. However, it was Girouard's misleading statements to the Colonial Office about promises of land made to some settlers that led to the demand for his resignation from the Colonial Secretary. He died in relative obscurity. His life was one of both great success and failure.

Gordon Guggisberg was another Canadian appointed to be a governor in the twentieth century.[106] His career did not have the dramatic rise and fall of Girouard's, although, like Girouard, he died in relative obscurity, alone in an English seaside boarding house. His private life was also unhappy. Like Girouard, he was a military engineer with the British Army, and his biggest successes were due to his engineering abilities. His term as governor of the Gold Coast (now Ghana) from 1919 to 1927 also had a lasting impact on the country he ruled. He, too, ran into some difficulties with Colonial Office officials, but

Percy Girouard, Quebec-born soldier, engineer, and colonial governor, in 1899. He had great success and failure as a governor, resigning in disgrace from his post as governor of Kenya following the forced removal of the Maasai from their lands. | *McCord Stewart Museum, II-129700*

in his case it was due to his relatively progressive ideas. Guggisberg was later appointed governor of British Guiana, but he served only eight months in this role before leaving in an ambulance due to ill health. One writer described his appearance as "every inch the classic colonial governor of common perception, tall, proud and distinguished."[107] He was a stickler for protocol, often appearing in full regalia. Unlike Girouard's, his career as governor can be considered a success, especially for his far-sighted views on education and health care for Africans, and on economic development. Two biographies have been published. Both are complimentary, and one is even titled *Beloved Imperialist*, but, as we shall see, he was not without critics.

Within days of his arrival in Accra, Guggisberg set out his mission in a speech to the legislative assembly: "I am an engineer, sent out here to superintend the construction of a broad Highway of Progress along which the races

Gordon Guggisberg, Ontario-born soldier, engineer, and colonial governor. He was described as a "beloved imperialist," and an Ashanti chief erected his headstone. | Illustrated London News, *January 25, 1930*

of the Gold Coast may advance."[108] He was successful in pursuing that object-ive. Within a month, he presented a ten-year development plan, including a deep-water harbour to export raw commodities. The port at Takoradi opened in 1928, after his term had ended, but it was his achievement. He also oversaw the development of railways and the first major modern hospital in tropical Africa at Korle-Bu, Accra. A statue of Guggisberg was erected outside the hospital on its fiftieth anniversary in 1973 by a post-independence government. Another success was Achimota College, which opened in 1927, combining primary, secondary, and college education. The college flew in the face of the general opposition among imperialists to "over-educating" Africans. It num-bers many prominent African leaders among its students, including Kwame Nkrumah, who led Ghana to independence in 1957. Yet another unusual in-itiative commenced by Guggisberg was the recruitment of more Africans into the civil service. He also made changes to the legislative assembly that in-creased African membership, although the European representatives still out-numbered them.

His progressive views should not be overstated. He firmly believed in the superiority of Europeans and the civilizing mission. He thought that the races of British tropical Africa "are all in varying degree emerging from primitive conditions ... There cannot be a moment's doubt of their incapacity today to stand by themselves." It was a part of Britain's "self-imposed task of tutelage and development" to enable them to do so by creating the required leadership through education and character training.[109] He admitted to running a "grandmotherly administration," explaining that its purpose was to prevent "a child running before it can walk."[110] An advocate of indirect rule, he encouraged conservative, traditional rulers and opposed demands for more democracy from educated nationalist African leaders.

Guggisberg received high praise, including from Ghanaians and other Africans. As noted, a statue was erected in his honour following independence, which may have been an unprecedented honour for an imperial representative. A recent article by Ghanaian scholars praises his governorship as an example to future governments.[111] Nnamdi Azikiwe, the man who helped lead Nigeria to independence, and the country's first president, paid tribute to Guggisberg in his influential book *Renascent Africa*. He wrote, "This administrator, during his regime, attempted in his humble way to solve human problems in the only feasible way – the *human way*," explaining that he did not abuse his powers.[112] The two biographies of Guggisberg are favourable. One describes him as "Africa's most successful colonial governor."[113] The other recognizes his limitations but considers him thirty years ahead of his time in the economic development and reforms he introduced.[114]

Against this praise must be placed several criticisms. One writer accuses him of discrimination against African medical officers.[115] Another of neglecting the northern part of the colony in his economic development.[116] Yet another that, under him, the Gold Coast was more antagonistic to trade unions than the other colonies, noting that he had cautioned the Colonial Office to "do nothing to hasten the growth of unionism."[117] George Padmore, the West Indian critic of imperialism who advised President Nkrumah upon independence, was highly critical of the steps Guggisberg took to undermine African nationalists. Padmore wrote that Guggisberg "served the aims of the imperialists by divorcing the chiefs from the intelligentsia and driving a wedge between the educated urban and illiterate rural communities," arresting the onward march toward self-government.[118] Recently, Guggisberg has been criticized for the lack of recognition for African soldiers who died fighting for the Empire in the First World War, based on his advice that "the average native of the Gold

Coast would not understand or appreciate a headstone."[119] (A somewhat ironic comment since his own headstone was the gift of those people.)

Weighing all these assessments, it seems fair to say that he was a great success as governor, given the times, his faith in imperialism, and his conservative views. He introduced economic, social, and political initiatives that had a lasting impact on the development of Ghana. In particular, he promoted planned economic growth and encouraged higher education for Africans when other imperialists opposed it. But he was still a man of his times.

After his death, an Indigenous leader visited his grave in the municipal cemetery at Bexhill-on-Sea on the south coast of England and was shocked to find that it was unmarked because Guggisberg's family could not afford to erect a gravestone. He arranged for a stone of red granite to be erected with the words, "This memorial was erected by the paramount chiefs and people of the Gold Coast and Ashanti."[120] The grave is now sadly neglected and overgrown.

Methods of Rule

Colonial rule relied on different tools to introduce and enforce that rule. We have seen Orwell's comment that "the real backbone of the despotism is not the officials but the Army." Force or, more often, the threat of force was the ultimate tool. Law, however, was the formal basis of British rule. It was both imported and indigenous, each being transformed to meet the local circumstances. Colonial law consisted of statutes and regulations made in London or locally by the governor and legislature. Some of this legislative activity was impressive, matching the breathtaking developments taking place in physical infrastructure such as railways. The work of Henry Maine, professor and author of the influential book *Ancient Law* (which set out his argument on the progress of the law from status in "primitive" societies to contract in modern societies), was especially noteworthy.[121] As the legal member of the Governor's Executive Council, he supervised over two hundred enactments for British India from 1862 to 1869. One contemporary said they were to have "a permanent influence upon some hundred and fifty millions of men."[122] The law also included cases decided by courts in the colonies and the UK, especially by the Judicial Committee of the Privy Council, which acted as the court of last resort. In practice, day-to-day rule relied on the governor exercising his power as the Crown's representative in the colony.[123] In most territories, there were plural legal systems, as Indigenous peoples continued to be governed in many matters, such as family and inheritance, by Indigenous or religious laws.

Canada and Colonialism

However, those laws were often misunderstood or modified to fit the needs of the colonizers.

The complex and sometimes contradictory role of the law in colonization, including in Canada, has been summarized by anthropologist Sally Engle Merry:

> European law was central to the colonizing process but in a curiously ambiguous way. It served to extract land from precolonial users and to create a wage labor force out of peasant and subsistence producers. Yet, at the same time, it provided a way for these groups to mobilize the ideology of the colonizers to protect lands and to resist some of the more excessive demands of the settlers for land and labor ... It was an unequal contest, however, in which colonial officials and settler populations exerted vastly greater power than colonized groups.[124]

Law was one way of introducing aspects of British society into the colonies. Land law, for example, incorporated centuries of development in Britain. It imported individualistic values of private ownership into traditional societies that valued more the collective well-being of the community and shared access to resources.[125] Criminal law served to directly enforce imperial order. Criminal courts also served "as classrooms where litigants and the public alike were taught ... to distinguish between acceptable and deviant behaviours – as defined by dominant groups – and to accept culturally constructed categories as natural."[126] As with other areas of law, there was a cultural impact on colonial societies that helped to create something of a reflection of British society and, especially in the settler colonies, contributed to the British World.

The basic policies pursued by colonial administrators to rule Indigenous peoples can be divided into three very broad forms: direct rule, indirect rule, and local self-government.[127] In practice, as noted by J.S. Furnivall in 1948, "there is no sharp line between direct and indirect rule, and we find the same power adopting different systems in the same place at different times, and in different places at the same time."[128] For example, there was indirect rule in Malaya but direct rule in the adjacent Straits Settlement. In Furnivall's view, the choice was often governed by convenience rather than by principle.[129]

Direct rule was administration directly by the colonial authorities. Nearly two-thirds of British India was under direct rule, while the balance, made up of over five hundred "native" or princely states, was under indirect rule. Direct rule left little role for the Indigenous peoples to play in their governance. A colonial administrator noted in 1918, "The number of posts which could be filled by educated natives must always remain few and must be posts which do not carry high responsibility ... Under Direct Rule, therefore, the native, even the educated native, can never take any but a small share in the Government."[130]

In practice, direct rule over large areas was often impractical and ineffectual. Professor Macmillan wrote, "It suddenly came to me as a revelation that except as an arbitrary power in the background much so-called 'direct' rule was in effect no rule at all. Having struggled to remote villages by execrable roads ... I realized that visits at intervals of six months or a year by the officers who were piloting me were the only links these villages had with authority of any kind, other, perhaps, than an occasional policeman. The rest of the time they were left entirely to their own devices."[131] As another writer pointed out, "Some areas of formal empire were scarcely ever penetrated during the imperial period. Legislation and administrative orders were frequently entirely ineffectual beyond the immediate ambit of the boma or district office."[132] British rule only became apparent when challenged or the area required special attention.

Indirect rule was rule by the British authorities using Indigenous rulers and bodies for many matters.[133] Robert Clive, a founder of British rule in India, explained, "We may be regarded as the spring which, concealed under the shadow of the Nabob's name, secretly gives motion to this vast machine of government without offering violence to the original constitution."[134] Writing in 1935, imperial historian Reginald Coupland described the situation: "With their 'royal' pomp and panoply, their troops of armed retainers, the prostrate crowd at their palace gates, their trumpets and their drums, [the Indigenous rulers] still had the stage: the Resident is hidden in the wings."[135] The role of the British officer (often called the Resident or Political Officer) was supposed to be that of an unobtrusive adviser.

In India, they were part of the Indian Political Service that represented British rule in the Indian princely states.[136] The Indian Political Service officers were recruited from both the army and the Indian Civil Service. Despite their supposedly limited role, they generally expanded their authority and became more intrusive in the affairs of the princely states.[137] As a result, the Indian rulers often became mere puppets. In his memoirs as a district officer in India in the later decades of the nineteenth century, John Beames explained how Britain solved the "problem" of the theoretical independence of the princely states. First, the government issued rules to be followed by the states without any consultation and then, on the rare occasion they were not followed, sent in some sepoys (Indian soldiers) to enforce them, including jailing the rajah and annexing the state.[138] Niall Ferguson, a historian, notes that the playboy maharaja – wealthy, westernized, and weakened – became a familiar figure throughout India. "In return for running their kingdoms and granting them a generous allowance, the British expected only one thing: supine loyalty."[139]

Malaya and most of the African colonies were also under indirect rule. Some powers would be retained by or delegated to local bodies such as sultans and chiefs, often using tribal courts to administer what were described as traditional laws.[140] Indirect rule is mainly associated with the activities of Lord Lugard in northern Nigeria.[141] As in India, even where indirect rule applied in theory, some colonial administrators could not avoid the temptation to intervene in administration so that the rule became "direct."[142] Indigenous leaders had to ask for advice from the colonial administrators and then act on it in many matters.[143] Traditional leadership and law were sometimes based on what the British authorities wanted them to be or mistakenly thought they were. To some extent, they were part of an invented tradition.[144] For societies that did not have rulers, such as the Igbo of southern Nigeria, or were not organized in "tribes," the British created chiefs and tribes.[145]

The limits of the "rule" exercised by the local authority should be noted. It was not sovereignty, and the British were obviously the paramount rulers.[146] In the words of historian Ashley Jackson, "No indigenous leader, no matter how powerful, would be allowed to treat with a foreign power or to possess military power, and the functions of the central treasury and colony-wide levels of government and administration were exclusively British."[147] Nor would such a leader be permitted to rule over Europeans: "That an Indian should rule Europeans ... is unthinkable," to quote a relatively moderate colonial official in 1913.[148] One senior colonial administrator in Nigeria stressed that local chiefs were "not independent rulers; they are merely the delegates of the Governor, whose representative is the Resident."[149] The British reserved the right to declare overriding martial law or states of emergency to deal with any challenges to their ultimate rule. They also reserved the right to recognize and replace local rulers and modify the local laws by exercising their paramount authority.

Different rationales have been given for the emergence of indirect rule. Tharoor suggests that the British sought to create social hierarchies in the colonies similar to their own class systems: indirect rule devolved power to "an entire hierarchy of greater and lesser imitation 'gentlemen.'"[150] The most elaborate explanation is given by political scientist Karuna Mantena, who argues that it was a reaction to concerns that changes introduced by the British were leading to a dissolution of the existing society which, in turn, was a serious threat to the stability of the imperial order. Therefore, imperial rule became implicated in a political strategy of protecting, preserving, and rehabilitating traditional society. "That empire could be simultaneously cause and cure for the crisis of native society became an alibi for permanent imperial rule ... The structure of imperial domination was masked through its insinuation into native structures of authority."[151] She comments that, "even as it enabled the consolidation of direct imperial rule across Africa and Southeast Asia, in its most laudatory representations indirect rule and its deference to the logic of native traditions would be heralded as a practice of cultural tolerance and cosmopolitan pluralism."[152]

George Woodcock suggested that Indian experience had conditioned African practice for different reasons: "By the late Victorian period British administrators even in India had come to distrust the western-educated [Indians] ... The African administrators sought to avoid the Indian dilemma by their system of indirect rule."[153] Most commentators see the origins of indirect rule in necessity and cost. In Africa, especially, there were insufficient British officers and qualified local people for the British to rule without relying heavily on local leaders. British tropical Africa, with 43 million people, was governed by 1,200 administrators.[154] According to Furnivall, "Indirect rule through a local chieftain is the simplest and cheapest way by which a western power can obtain economic control."[155] In some cases, such rule may have given an air of authority to the imperial government. As one historian explains, "imperial authority was most successfully established whenever it was able to work with the grain of the colonial peoples' own notions of legitimacy."[156]

Much praise has been bestowed on indirect rule and, in the late 1800s and early 1900s, it acquired an almost cult-like following. One senior colonial administrator in East Africa said that, in Tanganyika, "adopting and modernizing the existing indigenous tribal authorities ... off we went with the enthusiasm of religious revivalists ... [Indirect rule] helped to create a cult, and its devotees were in some danger of becoming a sort of orgiastic order of monks – if there can be such a thing."[157] Margery Perham described it as "the most comprehensive, coherent and renowned system of administration in our colonial history."[158] According to another writer, its principal value to the British was that it provided a justification for the British colonial order that was outwardly progressive.[159] Officials in the field were often enthusiastic over indirect rule partly because it made their work easier and meant they could avoid handling routine matters.[160]

On the other hand, there has also been much criticism, sometimes fierce. For example, George Padmore denounced indirect rule as

Tyrannical and non-democratic ... Blacks have absolutely no voice in the affairs of the state. They have one duty, and that is to obey authority ... The chief is *the* law, subject only to one higher authority, the white official stationed in his state as advisor ... No oriental despot ever had greater power than these black tyrants, thanks to the support they receive from the white officials who quietly keep in the background.

... Under the African system, the chiefs had certain definitely prescribed authority, rigidly controlled by the elders and councillors according to Native law and customs.

Indirect rule serves as a convenient smoke-screen behind which [officials] can collect taxes and exploit the Blacks without openly making themselves offensive to the Africans.[161]

In his very detailed survey of the problems of Africa in 1938, the senior colonial administrator Lord Hailey said, "The scheme of indirect rule has not only its unsolved problems, but some noticeable points of weakness," mainly because of the "inefficiency" of traditional African authorities. He called for more study.[162]

Modern critics note that indirect rule was backward-looking, focusing "too much on the experience of the past and too little on the exigencies of the future."[163] It had no relevance to the future independent nation-states and no place for Western-educated Indigenous people.[164] During the struggle for independence, the traditional rulers were often rejected as collaborators by nationalist leaders. At best, they were regarded as belonging to the past, without the knowledge or skills required for nation-building or modern urban conditions. It has been suggested that traditional rulers slowed the process of involving more Indigenous people in administration.[165] One writer concluded that "indirect rule in all its forms ... sought to freeze colonial societies, to slow and control the pace of change. Its long-term positive influence was limited."[166]

Local self-government was considered a step toward ultimate independence within the Empire. It was prominent as part of the reforms made to colonial policy in the final decades of the Empire.[167] Politicians often described these reforms as creating a "partnership" between the colonizers and the colonized. A turning point occurred in February 1947 when the secretary for the colonies issued a dispatch announcing a policy of local government to replace indirect rule. It had to be "local because the system of government must be close to the common people and their problems, efficient ... to raise the standard of living, and democratic because it must not only find a place for the growing class of educated men, but at the same time command the respect and support of the mass of the people."[168] It was essentially based on the British local government system, with elected councils rather than traditional leaders. The following year, this statement appeared in the report on the Colonial Empire:

> The central purpose of British colonial policy is simple. It is to guide the colonial territories to responsible self-government within the Commonwealth in conditions that ensure to the people concerned both a fair standard of living and freedom from oppression from any quarter.[169]

In other words, the Dependent Empire was to receive local government as a step toward a form of the responsible government within the Empire/Commonwealth that Canada had received nearly a century before. Commentators have interpreted this reform as an attempt to bring in local representatives of the "ordinary" people to balance the demands of more radical leaders at the centre. It was a policy of "managed reform," not intended to end British rule but to preserve it.[170]

In addition to formal methods of rule, it is necessary to consider more informal practices such as pomp and ceremony, symbolism, and rituals of different sorts. In *The Spectacle of Empire*, Jan Morris states, "Spectacle was always an instrument of British imperialism." She explains, "It had become a maxim of British imperial method that ostentatious effect was not only necessary to survival, but essential to domination too."[171] The former viceroy of India, Lord Curzon, said it was easy to denounce such displays "as savouring of useless pomp or meretricious splendour. They are not so regarded in the East, where sovereignty is invested with natural reverence, and has always been accustomed on ceremonial occasions to associate itself with public ceremonies and rejoicings."[172] The historian David Cannadine describes the Empire as about "processions and ceremony, plumed hats and ermine robes; about chiefs and emirs, sultans and nawabs, viceroys and proconsuls; about thrones and crowns, dominion and hierarchy, ostentation and ornamentalism."[173] He sees class and status as at the heart of the Empire. Pomp and ceremony were essential to the lifestyle of the colonial viceroy or governor, complete with regal government houses, swarms of servants, fleets of limousines, gun salutes, and protocol.[174]

Writer Paul Rich generally shares this view and stresses the role played by "public" school rituals like prize days, which were reflected in elaborate ceremonies such as durbars in India. In his view, "the rich symbolism of schooldays prepared colonial administrators for staging the Imperial drama."[175] As public schools spread throughout the Empire, these symbols, rituals, and performances were also exported. He notes, for example, how St. George's School, founded in 1930 in Vancouver, applied to the College of Heralds for a grant of arms, and comments: "What is ... remarkable is that a school thousands of miles from London would seek a grant from a King of Arms and confirmation by the College of Heralds. This dramatizes the ritualistic concern of the public schools."[176]

Protocol produced the proper pecking order and put people in their place. The Warrant of Authority for British India, issued under the royal signature, listed the positions of colonial officials over several pages, from the top tier of governor general and viceroy at number 1 to lowly officers of the Bengal pilot service at number 63. Local rulers were also listed in order of importance and received an appropriate number of gun salutes, ranging from the Maharaja of Baroda with twenty-one guns to the Sabwa of Yawnghwe at nine guns.[177]

Ritual robbed the colonized of their self-confidence: "The ritualistic paraphernalia of Empire contributed to the insecurity felt by colonial subjects who were always being put off balance by coming to the dinner party in the wrong clothes ... Much of the public schoolboy's success depended on the way his ritualistic behaviour produced this lack of confidence and almost paranoiac self-criticism in the natives."[178] An American author noted with amazement in 1939 that it was maintained "in all seriousness that the evening dress of England, with its starched shirts and collars so pernicious in the tropics, is essential for the maintenance of racial superiority and self-respect."[179]

Some writers refer to the "schlock and awe" campaign exemplified in such displays as the three gigantic durbars held in India to mark imperial occasions. They dazzled with officials and soldiers dressed in elaborate ceremonial costumes and maharajas in colourful regalia.[180] The 1911 *Handbook for Travellers in India, Burma and Ceylon*, the indispensable guide to that country, contained an advertisement headed "To the Durbar by Canadian Pacific," claiming that no more delightful route could be suggested.[181] It showed a highly decorated elephant (including the tusks) with an equally elaborately decorated carriage or howdah. The durbar in question was an extravagant coronation of the new British monarchs in Delhi at a lavish ceremony designed to evoke the Mughal rulers.

Durbars were copied on a lesser scale in Africa. Governor Lugard's visit to Kano in 1913 was welcomed by a procession that included fifteen thousand horsemen, an uncounted number of footmen, eight hundred West African Frontier Force troops, and three hundred mounted infantry with lances.[182] Bad news could also be disguised by a display of splendour. When the British government granted a charter in 1890 to the British South Africa Company, recognizing its "right" to control lands in the future Zimbabwe, a letter from

CPR advertisement promoting the All Red Route from London to India via Canada for the 1911 durbar, a grand display of imperial splendour. | *Reprinted from* A Handbook for Travellers in India, Burma and Ceylon, *8th ed.* *(London: Murray, 1911).*

Queen Victoria with the news was conveyed to King Lobengula "by a military mission consisting of five officers and men from the Royal Horse Guards. They arrived in Bulawayo in a gaudily painted four-wheeled coach adorned with the royal monogram and drawn by eight mules. Dressed in plumed helmets and glistening breastplates, they presented the letter to Lobengula."[183] It was effectively his death sentence.

In Canada, pomp and ceremony were used by governments to further their rule over Indigenous peoples. According to the Manitoba Indian Brotherhood in 1968, this approach was employed during the signing of the prairie treaties: "The Indian was impressed by the pomp and ceremony and the authority of the officials ... the respect and ceremony with which the officials were dealing with the Indians lulled the Indians into a passive mood."[184] Uniforms and medals were distributed to the chiefs. In attendance were North-West Mounted Police officers, who had adopted a uniform of scarlet tunic and blue trousers patterned on the traditional British army uniform, which had acquired symbolic importance among First Nations.[185] Above all of them was the embodiment and ultimate symbol of Empire, both in Canada and throughout the

Canada and Colonialism

NWMP lancer illustrating the spectacle of Empire, 1875. | *Library and Archives Canada, R9266-3771a*

▼ Chief's badge with an enamelled Union Jack at its centre. This badge was given to chiefs and councillors to commemorate the signing of Treaty 9 in 1910. | *Library and Archives Canada, 1986-79-1630*

▲ Red Crow of the Blood Tribe, in treaty uniform, 1895. "Indian Chiefs" received uniforms and medals as part of treaty signing. | *Steele and Company, Glenbow Library and Archives Collection, Libraries and Cultural Resources Digital Collections, University of Calgary, CU191769*

Empire: the monarch. In particular, there was Queen Victoria, the "Great White Mother," who was said by treaty negotiators to take a maternal interest in her Indigenous "children."[186] Royal tours inevitably included meetings with apparently admiring Indigenous groups. The admiration was not always reciprocated. Queen Victoria's great-grandson, the future King Edward VIII, privately described his contempt for the Indigenous peoples he met on his tours. He made racist comments about the Māori and Aboriginal Australians and complained about camping on a Saskatchewan Indian reserve surrounded by "hundreds of the mouldy local tribe."[187]

As with the Roman Empire, there was an element of "bread and circuses" in the British Empire. The governed came to expect their rulers to provide a spectacle or performance. A commonly cited example is given by George Orwell in his essay "Shooting an Elephant." As a police officer in Burma, he felt compelled to shoot an elephant that had killed a man but was now under control. He did so not because it was necessary or he wanted to but because it was expected of him by the villagers. He wrote:

> And it was at this moment, as I stood there with the rifle in my hands, that I first grasped the hollowness, the futility of the white man's dominion in the East. Here was I, the white man with his gun, standing in front of the unarmed native crowd – seemingly the leading actor of the piece, but in reality I was only an absurd puppet pushed to and fro by the will of these yellow faces behind.[188]

The puppet master had become the puppet.

5

Canadian Participation in the Empire

A picture appeared in the *Illustrated London News* in 1870 of emigrants about to depart for Canada. The accompanying text explained that "the Ganges, a fine screw-steamer, of 1899 tons register, W.S. Mason, commander, left the Victoria Docks, on Wednesday week, at eleven o'clock, having on board a large party of emigrants connected with the East-End Emigration Club, a society acting in union with the Committee of the British and Colonial Emigration Fund." It went on to note that, close at hand, was another steamer, the *Tweed*, displaying bunting in gay profusion, also destined to start for Canada the next morning with another large party of emigrants under the auspices of the same societies. There were 757 souls on board the *Ganges*. Charitable organizations had substantially borne the cost of the voyage. Also, the Poplar Board of Guardians, which administered the Poor Law and workhouse in the impoverished district of the East End of London, had made a contribution. The emigrants themselves, being "somewhat superior to the usual class," had contributed £3 per adult.

The artist captured the features of many of the people present. Some are dressed in top hats and appear wealthy. These are probably representatives of the charities, seeing off their charges. The emigrants are dressed in working-class clothing, and many look anxious and sad. What thoughts must have been going through their minds as they contemplated leaving, likely forever, their homes and families for an uncertain future? Most of them have children. Are they thinking of their futures in a new land? Where in the newly confederated colonies of British North America would they settle? What would their lives be

Emigrants leaving the Victoria Docks in London for Canada, 1870. |
Illustrated London News, *May 7, 1870*

like? Would they differ much from that which they had known? In many ways, life would not be different. They were leaving the British Isles but not the British Empire nor the British World. Leaving the British Isles did not make them less British. It would take a couple of generations before their descendants saw themselves primarily as Canadians. It is unlikely the emigrants gave much thought to the Indigenous peoples in their new land.

Migration and Settlement

Migration from Britain to British North America grew dramatically after 1830.[1] It had picked up after 1815, following more than twenty years of war. Over 200,000 people left the British Isles (including Ireland) for British North America between 1815 and 1830. The numbers then took off, although totals

Canada and Colonialism

fluctuated over the following decades. Between 1831 and 1900, the numbers were: 322,485 in the 1830s; 429,044 in the 1840s; 235,285 in the 1850s; 192,250 in the 1860s; 232,213 in the 1870s; 395,160 in the 1880s; 328,411 in the 1890s. From 1901 to 1914, the total was 1,865,807. A total of 4,213,362 immigrated to British North America/Canada during the nineteenth century, or 19 percent of the total emigration from the UK of about 22 million.[2]

The increase in the British population was, at times, explosive. The European population of British North America was only about half a million in 1806 and a million in 1831. Most recent immigrants had come from the United Kingdom. A massive increase in immigration, overwhelmingly from the UK, and the natural increase meant this population grew to almost 4 million by 1871. Just over 60 percent of the new Dominion's residents were of British origin, and 84 percent of immigrants had come from the British Isles.[3] This increased population transformed British North America from scattered settlements in isolated British colonies to a new country – a country that was a leading member of the British World, although still legally a colony. It also reduced the Indigenous population to a minority in their own lands. It has been estimated that by 1821, Indigenous people formed not much more than 10 percent of the population of Upper Canada. By 1867, they were a minority in all of eastern Canada, although still the majority in the West for a few more decades.[4]

Emigration was encouraged by numerous guidebooks published in the nineteenth century. However, large-scale British settlement in what became Canada still had to overcome some negative accounts. William Cobbett, the English reformer, described British North America (with some exceptions) in his *Emigrant's Guide*, published in 1829, as "wretchedly poor: Heaps of rocks covered chiefly with fir trees. These countries are the *offal* of North America; they are the head, the skins, the shanks and hoofs of that part of the world; while the United States are the sir-loins, the well-covered and well-lined ribs and the suet."[5] The many boosters of emigration overcame this type of bad press with their own version of creative writing: "From 1820, prospective immigrants were assured that Upper Canada was 'totally free of ferocious animals.' Its rattlesnakes were few, absent, or lacking in venom; its bears were 'timorous and inoffensive' and fading away like the Indians in any case ... Far from dreading winter, settlers 'hail its near approach with the greatest of pleasure.'"[6]

In the numerous guidebooks aimed at future settlers in British Columbia and Vancouver Island following the discovery of gold in the late 1850s, writers likewise downplayed the threat of violence from Indigenous peoples.[7] Some were breathless in their enthusiasm: "It is a land where a sudden transformation is about to take place! and it is a land whither thousands of the civilized inhabitants of the globe are rushing in hot haste to gather of the new found spoil!"[8] A book published by the Agent-General for BC in 1875 was much more restrained but still encouraging. It gave detailed information on matters like the *Land Act* of 1874, which made "most liberal provision for the acquisition by settlers of land, either as Free Homesteads, or by purchase," and noted that the Indigenous peoples were "quite quiet, over the whole mainland and island; rather saucy on the west coast of Vancouver Island and in Queen Charlotte Island."[9]

Migration was also promoted by land companies and other private organizations. The most successful of the land companies was the Canada Company, incorporated in 1826. It acquired over 2 million acres of land in Upper Canada on which it built roads and schools, distributed publicity material throughout the UK, and transported migrants. During the 1880s, the Canadian Pacific Railway received 25 million acres of land in western Canada. It devised several schemes to attract immigrants, including transport on company ships and trains, and ready-made farms complete with house, barn, shed, fencing, and fifty acres of ploughed and sowed land.[10] British women were even wooed to the prairies by promises of more masculine men. One Scottish journalist enthused, "It is refreshing to eyes accustomed to the tired, anxious faces, and listless or stilted gait of the average Briton, to look on the manly Titans of the west. They are Britons, yes, but Britons of larger body and larger heart than those at home."[11] Charities sponsored the relocation of disadvantaged people, including children. Much migration relied on private networks and assistance to get migrants established in their new homes.

Government promotion of migration from the British Isles varied over the decades depending on the governments in office and the needs of the economy. The British government sometimes undertook sponsorship to alleviate economic and social pressures (especially after the First World War). Sometimes Canadian federal and provincial governments did so to attract settlers and thus aid development. During his election campaign of 1878, John A. Macdonald announced the National Policy, which included increased population growth and immigration, especially to settle western Canada. Government promotion included newspaper advertisements, posters, lectures, and agents posted to English cities. The *Empire Settlement Act* of 1922 was an attempt, largely unsuccessful, to coordinate and encourage migration from the UK to the settler colonies, including Canada. The scheme included assisted passage,

Canada and Colonialism

training, and financial aid. It faced opposition from some Canadians, who saw it as thrusting unemployed migrants upon them, and was abandoned in 1930.[12]

During the time of the Empire, preference was generally given to British immigrants over other European immigrants. The British Isles remained the predominant source of immigrants to Canada until the late 1950s. Sometimes, however, an insufficient supply from the UK led to recruitment from countries outside the Empire, such as hardy eastern Europeans destined for the prairies. Ethnic considerations and the preference for British immigrants were not abandoned until 1967.

Non-Europeans were discouraged or effectively forbidden, as was prospective immigration from China and India. Immigration policy was summarized in 1908 by the poet Robert Stead:

They are coming, coming, coming from the land of Who-Knows-Where,
Black and white and many-tinted, brown and yellow, dark and fair,
... As I roll 'em out Canadians – all but the yellow and brown.[13]

Preventing immigration from India was problematic, as Indians, like Canadians, were British subjects. However, despite this status, the government implemented discriminatory measures against Indian immigrants. These measures were designed by future prime minister Mackenzie King, then a senior civil servant, to ensure that "Canada should remain a white man's country."[14] Section 38 of the *Immigration Act* of 1910 gave powers to the Governor-in-Council (the Canadian cabinet) to refuse entry to "immigrants belonging to any race deemed unsuited to the climate or requirements of Canada."[15] With the knowledge that there were no available direct routes from India to Canada, the government required immigrants to travel continuously to Canada from a port of embarkation in their home country. In 1914, the British Columbia Court of Appeal rejected legal objections brought by some of those on board the *Komagata Maru*. This boat carried prospective immigrants from India and, in a challenge to the Canadian requirement, it had come from Hong Kong and not an Indian port. The passengers unsuccessfully argued that, as British subjects, they had a legal right to land anywhere in the Empire and the refusal of the Canadian authorities to allow them to do so was illegal. Following the legal defeat, the boat was forcibly turned back from Vancouver by HMCS *Rainbow,* the first vessel of the new Canadian navy.[16] Soldiers had paraded on the *Rainbow* and the pier with their rifles in a show of force. In the opinion of one of the judges, the Parliament of Canada was "safe-guarding the people of Canada

Vancouver harbour, with the naval cruiser HMCS *Rainbow* and the *Komagata Maru* in the distance. The Canadian navy and soldiers ensured the forced return of Indian immigrants in 1914. | *Leonard Frank, Vancouver Public Library Archives, 6229*

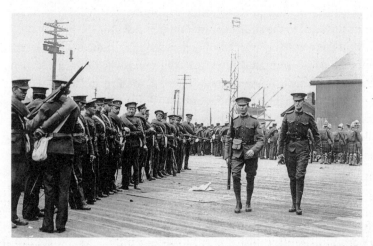

Soldiers on parade at a Vancouver pier as a show of force to ensure the return of Indian immigrants on board the *Komagata Maru* in 1914. | *Canadian Photo Company, Vancouver Public Library Archives 123*

from an influx, which it is no chimera to conjure up, might annihilate the nation."[17] Even progressive writers such as James Woodsworth, a founder of what became the New Democratic Party, thought that such "essentially non-assimilable elements ... should be vigorously excluded."[18]

Canada's discrimination against Indians caused some mild friction with the government of British India. One retired member of the Indian Civil Service asked, "How can we expect that Indians should feel pride in the solidarity of the Empire when their membership does not even privilege them to set foot in many of its lands?"[19] Anger in India over the treatment of the passengers on the *Komagata Maru* added to the growing strength of the movement in India for self-government and, ultimately, independence, discussed in Chapter 7. Kurdit Singh, the organizer of the voyage, protested, "When even the slum dweller of London could freely move to India as well as Canada why should not we? We are insulted, we are dishonoured, we are disgraced in all parts of the wourld [sic] because we have no Government that will feel for indignities inflicted on us."[20] The answer to his question was, of course, the racism that permeated imperialism in Canada as elsewhere. Indians may have been British subjects (i.e., subjects of the British King), but they were not "British" nor considered members of the British World like Canadians of British ancestry.

Settler Colonialism

In his famous and influential denunciation of colonialism, the Martinique political philosopher Frantz Fanon wrote, "In the colonies, the foreigner imposed himself using his cannons and machines. Despite the success of his pacification, in spite of his appropriation, the colonist always remains a foreigner."[21] He was wrong as far as large parts of the British Empire, including Canada, were concerned. Colonialism originally referred to establishing colonies by settlement in foreign lands, such as the American, Canadian, Australian, and New Zealand colonies. The essence of successful colonialism in these places was the very opposite of what Fanon wrote.

Settler colonialism transformed colonists into permanent residents and citizens of the new nation they created in a land they made their own. This transformation was illustrated in an address given in September 1858 by Governor James Douglas to a large congregation of miners at the foot of the Fraser Canyon in British Columbia. He assured them of the protection of British law and then, addressing the British miners, said that he was "commanded to say to all Her Majesty's Native born subjects that this is their country." As the geographer-historian Cole Harris commented:

Considering where he was, and when, this was an extraordinary statement. It was not just that a new colony was being added to the Empire; rather, settlers were welcomed to a colony that was to become "their country" approximately as England or Scotland had been. British Columbia was to be added, in effect, to the geography of a greater Britain, part of a greater Europe, the locus of civilization.[22]

To some extent in Canada, colonialism also transformed Indigenous peoples into outsiders or foreigners in the new societies created in their traditional lands. This process was acknowledged between 1950 and 1966, when the Department of Citizenship and Immigration had responsibility for Indian Affairs and developed programs "to make Canadian citizens of as many as possible of the descendants of the original inhabitants of this country," in the words of Prime Minister Louis St. Laurent.[23]

In contrast to the Dependent Empire (and the unsuccessful settler colonies in southern Africa), in which the colonists were always a minority population (although a dominant one), colonists in the successful settler colonies became the majority, and the Indigenous peoples a minority. Also, most of the colonists in the Dependent Empire were transients (although sometimes staying decades or even generations), intending to take resources from the colonies to benefit British businesses. Colonists in the settler colonies came primarily to settle permanently and to exploit the resources for themselves. Colonists in the Dependent Empire looked to Indigenous peoples for their labour to exploit resources. Colonists in the settler colonies generally saw the Indigenous peoples as obstacles to settlement, to be pushed out of the way to await their fate of either dying out (a widespread view at the time) or assimilating at some unknown future time through measures such as residential schools and the promotion of agriculture. They preferred to hire labourers of British, or at least European, ancestry when available. (This is not to deny the contribution that Indigenous people did make as workers, which has been documented elsewhere).[24] British colonists in the Dependent Empire – traders, plantation owners, and administrators – were ultimately forced to leave (as they were in the unsuccessful settler colonies in Africa). But colonists in the other settler colonies, including Canada, were outstandingly successful and created new societies originally modelled after Britain ("new Britains") that remain today.

Settler colonies were and are the permanent and most successful legacies of the British Empire.[25] The settlers created their new societies at incredible speed, but this was at the cost of existing communities. Australian anthropologist Patrick Wolfe put it this way: "Settler colonialism has both negative and positive dimensions. Negatively it strives for the dissolution of native societies. Positively, it erects a new colonial society on the expropriated land base ... settler colonizers come to stay: invasion is a structure not an event ... Settler colonialism destroys to replace."[26] Settlers had no desire to adopt an Indigenous way of life. Instead, they aimed to reshape the lands to make them familiar, with British plants and animals to the extent possible. But, of course, they had to make some adaptions, however unwillingly, to their changed circumstances.

The British politician William Gladstone explained the objective of colonization in the settler colonies. It was "to reproduce the likeness of England – to reproduce its laws and manners as they are doing in Australia, New Zealand, North America and the Cape, thereby contributing to the general happiness of mankind."[27] John Ruskin, the enormously influential writer and art critic, raised colonization to a fever pitch in his 1870 inaugural lecture at Oxford:

> And this is what [England] must either do, or perish: she must found colonies as fast and as far as she is able, formed of her most energetic and worthiest men; – seizing every piece of fruitful waste ground she can set her foot on, and there teaching these her colonists that their chief virtue is to be fidelity to their country; and that their first aim is to be to advance the power of England by land and sea: and that, though they live on a distant plot of ground, they are no more to consider themselves disfranchised from their native land, than the sailors of her fleets do, because they float on distant waves.[28]

This lecture profoundly influenced that great practical imperialist and multi-millionaire Cecil Rhodes, who kept a copy as one of his most cherished possessions.[29] No doubt a similar patriotism inspired many colonists who set their sights on Canada.

British Identity

Until 1947, there was no separate Canadian citizenship. Canadians were British subjects, like those born in the UK, India, or any other colony (although the concept of Canadian citizenship had been used for the limited purposes of immigration).[30] A separate Canadian identity took time to develop. There was no official Canadian flag until 1965 and no official national anthem until 1980. Posters for the First and Second World Wars showed Canadian soldiers fighting under the Union Jack.[31] Canadians of British ancestry saw themselves as British. R.B. Bennett, future prime minister of Canada, declared to a meeting of the Empire Club in Toronto in 1914, "I hold myself as much a

Britisher this night as though I was born within the sound of the Bow Bells. (Applause.) ... This is the British Empire, and we are Britons whether we were born in the British Isles, or in Canada, or in Australia, or in New Zealand, we are Britishers."[32] The son of John Buchan, governor general of Canada, said that, in 1935, "if you asked anyone in Toronto or Vancouver about his nationality," he was "as likely to say 'British' as 'Canadian.'"[33] The sense of being Canadian was a sub-identity similar to that of being English, Scottish, or Welsh. Being British and Canadian, like being British and Scottish, were dual identities and did not preclude other identities based on a person's region of birth or religion. Different individuals may have identified more with one or other of these multiple identities.

A separate (and ultimately predominant) Canadian identity became more pronounced in the second half of the nineteenth century and continued into the twentieth. In 1905, Richard Jebb, a political scientist, referred to "colonial nationalism" and the "independent national instincts in the four principal self-governing colonies in varying stages of evolution."[34] This rise of colonial national identity "did not contradict or undermine imperial Britishness. One person might have a number of concurrent identities."[35]

Imperialists welcomed colonial nationalism. Prominent imperialist Alfred Milner told a Canadian audience in 1908 that he did not fear the growth of Canadian patriotism, and he thought Canadians should be imperialists for the love of Canada, since they would see that the Empire gave the country more worldwide influence and power.[36] Earl Grey, Canada's governor general, wrote to Prime Minister Wilfrid Laurier the next year saying, "As a rule of course Nationalism is a step towards Imperialism, and it is the recognition of this truth which has made me, a race Imperialist, do everything in my power to promote Canadian Nationalism."[37] As prime minister, R.B. Bennett claimed in 1930 that he would be "a poor Britisher if I were not a Canadian first."[38] This view was repeated by John Buchan as governor general.[39] The campaign of Canadian nationalists was generally not to separate from the Empire but to assert equality and gain a louder voice in it.[40] They were encouraged by imperial representatives, who saw patriotic pride in the British Dominion as a means of promoting a greater responsibility toward the Empire.[41]

However, Canadian Britishness was not Englishness or Scottishness. Canadian historian W.L. Morton was quoted as saying in 1964, "British we were, but English in the sense of southern English we never were ... Our Britishness, then, was not Englishness, but a local brew which we called Canadian."[42] This distinct identity was acknowledged early on. One of the writers often credited with the concept of a British World or Greater Britain was J.R. Seeley, a professor at Cambridge. In his bestselling book *The Expansion of England*, published in 1883, he observed, "People cannot change their abodes ... without changing their ideas and habits and ways of thinking, nay without somewhat modifying in the course of a few generations their physical type. We know already the Canadian and the [Australian] are not quite like the Englishmen."[43] But these differences did not change their Britishness (or Englishness, as he preferred), and, indeed, he thought they should be included in the population of Britain. As Jan Morris points out, in 1897 "there was no exact dividing line between a Canadian Briton and a British Briton."[44] They shared the same citizenship; usually honoured the same ideals, flag, anthem, and monarch; had similar educations; and read similar newspapers. They were also governed by similar political institutions and laws, made in the UK or modelled on them.

Canadians Working and Doing Business in the Empire

In a speech to the Canadian Club in Winnipeg in 1908, Alfred Milner described the freedom to move around the Empire as one of the benefits of being a white imperial subject:

> The man of white race who is born a British subject can find a home in every portion of the world where he can live under his own flag, enjoying the same absolute freedom, and the same protection for person or property as he has always enjoyed, using his own language and possessing from the first moment that he sets foot there the full rights of citizenship.[45]

It was true that Canadians had less incentive than those from the UK to leave their home, given the opportunities in Canada and across the border. Sara Jeannette Duncan, the Canadian author of many novels on British India and Canada, who lived many years in India, noted that "Canada has room at home and a climate fit to live in: Canadians take root beside their tamaracks and their children after them."[46] However, many Canadians did exercise their right of freedom of movement.

In an 1866 lecture on the role of British North Americans in the Empire, Henry Morgan said, "Go where we will throughout the world, we will find a representative of these Provinces holding some important position or performing some useful profession or function."[47] He gives numerous examples. In many cases, the individuals he wrote about brought skills and experience that reflected the Canadian environment and economy. Canadian historian Phillip Buckner points out that there were "Canadian-born scientists, engineers, miners, doctors and mineralogists wherever the British flag (which was also of course the Canadian flag) flew."[48] There were a variety of professions and businesses. Morgan lists colonial administrators, a prominent journalist in India, a member of parliament in Victoria (Australia), the Chief Justice of Gibraltar, medical practitioners, lawyers, a poet, shipbuilders, and surveyors.

This pattern continued for the remainder of the Empire. In some cases, Canadian soldiers went to fight in other colonies and decided to stay in those colonies in new lines of work. For example, former Canadian soldiers helped survey the Gold Coast and Nigeria.[49] Canadians in senior positions included the chief transport officer in Nigeria, the commander of the Gold Coast police, the chief engineer and general manager of the Kenya and Uganda Railways and Harbour, and the head of the Nigerian Health Department.[50] A French Canadian commanded the local defence force for Mauritius.

Many Canadians were attracted to southern and eastern Africa. In 1903, shortly after the Boer War, while in the bush, John Buchan, a future governor general of Canada, was surprised by "three huge Canadians, who came in the darkness and encamped by our fire." He noted that "the Canadians had been all over the world and in every profession, but of all trades they liked the late war best, and made anxious inquiries about Somaliland. They were the true adventurer type, – long, thin, hollow-eyed, tough as whipcord."[51] Others who had fought in the Boer War also stayed on, sometimes as settlers. Over a thousand Canadians joined the South African Constabulary, a paramilitary force like the North-West Mounted Police. They were led by Sam Steele, who had established his reputation with the NWMP in the Yukon. The Constabulary's commander, Robert Baden-Powell, had been impressed by the Canadians who had served with him at the famous Siege of Mafeking and was eager to recruit them. Their experiences in South Africa were mixed, however, and some returned disillusioned and bitter.[52]

Canadian companies were free to establish or expand their operations throughout the Empire, and some took advantage of this opportunity. Canadian businessmen such as Samuel Cunard, Garfield Weston, and Lord Beaverbrook were highly successful, using the UK as the centre of their extensive business empires. Beaverbrook owned the mass-circulation British newspaper *The Daily Express* and boasted that it had never failed to preach the imperial doctrine.[53] He led a "crusade" for preferential tariffs to promote trade within the Empire, which were agreed at the Imperial Economic Conference held in Ottawa in 1932. The Canadian Pacific Steamship Company carried mail to Hong Kong and operated its own steamships, the Empress Line. These vessels and the railway across Canada formed a vital section of the "All-Red Route" connecting the British World.[54] The railway became a major link in international trade and transport. Sun Life Insurance, based in Montreal, opened offices throughout the world.[55] Canadian banks soon dominated the West Indies after opening branches in the 1880s.[56]

Weston and Beaverbrook were also politicians in London, as were several other Canadian Britons. In 1924, there were seventeen elected to the imperial parliament.[57] Andrew Bonar Law, born in New Brunswick, became the UK prime minister that year. However, he served for only a few months due to illness.[58] As Conservative and Unionist leader, he had earlier spoken of his Canadian birth and upbringing as an advantage: "Ladies and gentlemen, as you probably know, most of you, I was born in Canada [Cheers]. I spent the early years of my life there. Among the many disqualifications for the position which I now hold – and no one feels them more strongly than myself – that is not a disqualification [Cheers]. It is an advantage [Cheers]."[59] Bonar Law was a patron of Beaverbrook, who became minister of information during the First World War and held various cabinet positions during the Second World War. Beaverbrook, in turn, was the patron of R.B. Bennett, Canadian prime minister from 1930 to 1935, who moved to England in 1938, became an active member of the House of Lords, and is the only Canadian prime minister buried outside the country.[60]

Serving the Empire did not require Canadians to leave Canada. Settling and developing the country were regarded as imperial achievements. One parliamentarian proudly proclaimed in 1913:

> We have started preparing the soil, preparing the country to be the home of hundreds of millions of British born and men who come to this country and become British subjects, and in making homes for them under the British flag ... we were serving the Empire in building the Canadian Pacific railway, in constructing the canal system of Canada, in making the St. Lawrence the great avenue of trade it is today, in building the Transcontinental railway, in developing the great Northwest, in dividing it into provinces and in giving them educational and other facilities.[61]

The British World

The leading article in a special supplement to *The Times* to celebrate the 1939 visit of King George VI and Queen Elizabeth to Canada commented: "The average Canadian will argue that there is a Canadian State, a Canadian people, and a Canadian nation. In the same breath he will claim that nation as British,

King George VI and Queen Elizabeth meeting in Calgary with Stoney Tribe members during the 1939 Royal Tour. The Stoney had brought a picture of Queen Victoria. This would have demonstrated their historic relationship with the British Crown. | *National Film Board of Canada, Library and Archives Canada, 1971-271 NPC*

nurtured on and maintaining British traditions." In its advertisement in that supplement, the Province of British Columbia claimed to be the "most British of all the Provinces, with seventy per cent of its population British or of British extraction, it presents an atmosphere of Security and Stability which is definitely home-like ... To the prospective Settler, it offers conditions closely comparable to the choicer parts of rural England ... British in all its loyalties, standards and usages."[62] Canada was a British nation and part of the British World that was at the core of the Empire.[63]

For the bulk of its history, and to an extent that is difficult to imagine today, Canada considered itself "British" and a part of the "British World," consisting of the "mother country" in Europe and the other British settler colonies. This sense of belonging to a British World goes back to the early settlers, including the Empire Loyalists, who rejected rebellion in the United States and moved north to settle in Upper Canada. They were supplemented by the strident Britishness of some other migrants, such as those from Ulster who established the Orange Order as a strong voice in Canadian politics. In 1891, John A.

Canada and Colonialism

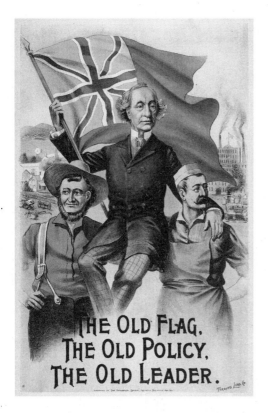

**THE OLD FLAG,
THE OLD POLICY,
THE OLD LEADER.**

1891 campaign poster of John A. Macdonald waving a British flag as a display of imperial loyalty. Macdonald was the architect of Canadian Indian policy. | *Library and Archives Canada, e010934529*

Macdonald fought and won an election using the slogan "The old flag, the old policy, the old leader," and declaring, "A British subject I was born, a British subject I will die!"[64] The campaign poster showed him literally wrapped in the flag.[65]

The language of family was widely used to describe the relationship between the United Kingdom and the settler colonies. In a lecture on "The Imperialist Creed," given in 1897, Alfred Milner said that imperialists wished "the kindred peoples under the British flag to remain one united family for ever."[66] Family relationships were depicted by showing the UK as the mother and the settler colonies as adult daughters. The metaphor was illustrated by Kipling's poem "Our Lady of the Snows," celebrating Canada's quasi-independence: "Daughter am I in my mother's house/But mistress in my own." As the settler colonies became more assertive and demanded a say in imperial as well as internal affairs, the terminology tended to become that of "sister nations." However, there was little doubt that the UK was the most senior sister. The family metaphor was sometimes expressed in different terms, as when an English journalist in 1905 referred to "Jake Canuke" as the grown-up son in the firm of John Bull

THE EMPIRE NEEDS MEN!

AUSTRALIA
CANADA
INDIA
NEW ZEALAND

All answer the call.
Helped by the YOUNG LIONS
The OLD LION defies his Foes.
ENLIST NOW.

A First World War recruitment poster showing Canada as a young lion with the old lion of Britain, 1915. | *Library and Archives Canada, 1983-28-401*

and Sons.[67] Other analogies could also be used: during the First World War, posters showed the UK as a large roaring lion flanked by smaller but equally ferocious cubs identified as Australia, Canada, India and New Zealand, with the caption, "All answer the call. Helped by the young lions/ The old lion defies his Foes."

A combination of factors kept the British World together. Many writers stressed the common racial identity.[68] Milner probably expressed this best in a document (his "Credo") found among his papers and published after his death in *The Times*:

> I am a British (indeed primarily an English) Nationalist. If I am also an Imperialist, it is because the destiny of the English race, owing to its insular position and long supremacy at sea, has been to strike roots in distant parts of the world. My patriotism knows no geographical but only racial limits. I am an

Imperialist and not a Little Englander because I am a British Race Patriot. It seems unnatural to me ... to lose interest in and attachment to my fellow-countrymen because they settle across the sea.

I feel myself a citizen of the Empire. I feel that Canada is my country, Australia my country, New Zealand my country, South Africa my country, just as much as Surrey or Yorkshire.

... The British State must follow the race, must comprehend it, wherever it settles in appreciable numbers as an independent community. If the swarms constantly being thrown off by the parent hive are lost to the State, the State is irreparably weakened. We cannot afford to part with so much of our best blood.[69]

In his lecture on "The Imperialist Creed," Milner declared that the peoples of the settler colonies were "not foreigners to us, or to one another, but fellow-citizens; and as such we want them to remain. One throne, one flag, one citizenship. These are things of inestimable value."[70]

A shared culture was central to the British World. Children in the city of Victoria in Canada and the state of Victoria in Australia grew up gazing at the same wall map showing their Empire with a quarter of the world in red. They read similar books that recited British (mainly English) history and imperial glories, such as *Our Empire Story* by Henrietta Marshall, published in 1908, which remained in print until the 1950s. It reflected the prevailing prejudices. The Métis are described as very ignorant and the "Red Man" as causing "horror and terror."[71] One prominent Canadian historian, Arthur Lower, said of his early youth, "I don't think anybody ever suspected that there was any other kind of history."[72] Another, George M. Wrong, who did much to advance the study of Canadian history, was committed to British imperialism.[73] The emphasis on British history continued until the 1950s and was an essential part of the curricula of early Canadian universities.[74]

Private school education modelled on the "public" school system of the UK spread to Canada and other countries. The schools promoted the imperial spirit. In particular, George Parkin, the headmaster of Upper Canada College for some years, was a leading spokesman for the imperial federation movement. He described himself as "a wandering Evangelist of Empire."[75] One writer says he did more for the British Empire than any other man of his times.[76] The historian Jean Barman has given a detailed account of similar schools in British Columbia and their influence in *Growing Up British in British Columbia*. She estimates that there were fifty such schools in the province and perhaps three thousand similar schools across the Empire, and suggests that they may have been critical to the maintenance of British influence.[77]

Other common imperial institutions included the political and legal systems modelled on the Parliament in Westminster and the senior courts in London. Parliamentarians in Ottawa and members of provincial legislatures followed the procedure of the Mother Parliament. Judges and lawyers modelled the law, their behaviour, and their dress on the English practice.[78] In his preface to *The British Tradition in Canadian Law*, Justice Bora Laskin (later to head the Supreme Court of Canada) wrote, "The British Monarch, the British Cabinet, the British Parliament and such British courts as the House of Lords and the Judicial Committee of the Privy Council ... have played major roles in the establishment of Canadian legal institutions and in the directions taken by Canadian law."[79] Until 1949, when the Supreme Court of Canada assumed this role, the final court of appeal for Canada was the Privy Council. But this did not end the British influence. Even at the ceremony to celebrate the laying of the cornerstone of the new Supreme Court building in 1939, the minister of justice promised that the Canadian judiciary would "remain the protagonists of British ideals, of British traditions and British justice."[80]

Turning to the military, Canadian militiamen were "steeped in the trappings of British military culture." They "dressed in scarlet tunics and British-styled accoutrements, drilling with British weapons and equipment, and were disciplined in accordance with the *Queen's Regulations and Orders for the [British] Army*."[81] Until 1908, an officer from the United Kingdom commanded them. It was widely recognized that Canada's security was dependent on the strength of the Empire. Frank Oliver, a prominent member of Parliament who became the minister in charge of Indian Affairs, made the connection clear in 1902:

> The maintenance of the prestige of Great Britain is just as necessary to the peace and welfare of Canada as it is to the peace and welfare to the county of York in England. So long as Canada is a part of the empire, the safety of Canada depends upon the strength of the empire. Anything that weakens the empire weakens Canada, endangers Canada, and hurts every citizen of Canada.[82]

We will see that many Canadians took part in defending the Empire, both as members of the British Army and as members of Canadian forces.

There were special occasions, usually associated with the monarchy, on which membership in the British World would be celebrated, such as Queen Victoria's Diamond Jubilee of 1897.[83] The Canadian press enthusiastically covered the Jubilee and made much of Prime Minister Laurier's leading role in London and his receipt of a knighthood from the Queen.[84] It was the cause of

popular rejoicing within Canada. Royal births, marriages, deaths, and coronations were also widely covered in Canadian newspapers, as were royal tours.
Throughout the Empire, oaths of allegiance were sworn to the British monarch
(as they still are in Canada).

Empire Day on May 24 (Queen Victoria's birthday) was first celebrated in
Canada, as proudly claimed by Colonel George Denison, a colourful Canadian
supporter of imperial federation and forerunner of the Colonel Blimp cartoon
character. The author of a leading history of cavalries, Denison threatened opponents with the sword and was said to treat politics like a cavalry charge. He
wrote that the idea of Empire Day "has spread throughout the empire, but that
meeting in the National School [in Toronto in 1899] was the beginning of the
movement."[85] The idea of Clementina Fessenden, another ardent imperialist, it
became an annual holiday and helped to unite the Empire.[86] The Ontario minister of education explained its purpose and importance in a pamphlet distributed in 1928: "The purpose of Empire Day is to develop the sense of national
and imperial unity and to enlarge the ideas and ideals of citizenship ... I cannot
see Canadians giving up that primary principle on which their country is built,
that is their determination to remain British. As British, Canada will continue
to live."[87] Today, the annual Commonwealth Day passes without note in Canada, except for the raising of the Union Jack on federal buildings, airports, and
military bases, and press releases from the prime minister and governor general. Few Canadians could say, or care, when it occurs or recognize the Commonwealth flag.[88]

Many less formal connections existed. There were, of course, family connections that found expression in correspondence about matters large and
small.[89] Both powerful and ordinary Canadian families might have branches
in the UK and other colonies. In her history of the family of James Douglas,
British Columbia's first governor, Adele Perry shows that it played out in
Demerara, Barbados, Lower Canada, Oregon, Red River, and British Columbia.[90] Prime Minister Justin Trudeau is a descendant of one of the British
founders of Singapore.[91] The connection with the British Asian Empire was
also illustrated by the remarkable story of Esca Brooke Daykin. He was born in
Sarawak in 1867, the son of a Malay mother and Charles Brooke, one of the
"White Rajahs," who were personal and hereditary rulers of parts of North
Borneo. Initially taken to England, he moved to Ontario, where he became a
floorwalker in a department store in Ottawa. He died a sad man rejected by his
wealthy and powerful family.[92]

Several organizations promoted imperial values, such as the Imperial Order
Daughters of the Empire, the Empire Club of Canada, the Canadian Clubs, the

Girl Guides, and the Boy Scouts. The Imperial Order (now simply the IODE) was founded in 1900 to support Canadian soldiers fighting in the Boer War. Its role has been examined in detail by Katie Pickles, who explains how "the Order constructed a hegemonic Anglo-Canadian identity that was based on mimicking Britain."[93] The Empire Club of Canada was founded in 1903 as a forum for speakers, including Winston Churchill. The Canadian Clubs, founded in Toronto in 1897, also hosted imperialist speakers. In *The Canadian Boy Scout* (1911), Robert Baden-Powell, founder of the scouting movement and prominent imperialist, noted encouragingly that "if the Canadian boys rise to men worth their salt, Canada will have the place of honour in [the] Empire."[94]

Imperial heroes and victories were widely celebrated by the erection of monuments and the naming or renaming of towns, streets, and mountains. This is why we have Kitchener in Ontario and Wolseley in Saskatchewan, and streets named after Boer War generals in Ladysmith on Vancouver Island, itself named after a famous battle fought in that war. Mount Edith Cavell in Jasper National Park is named after a heroic British Red Cross nurse killed by a German firing squad in 1915.[95] Mount Girouard, also in the Rockies, pays tribute to Canadian imperialist Percy Girouard. William Stairs, the Congo mercenary, is commemorated by a street in his birthplace of Halifax, Nova Scotia; a plaque at his old college, the Royal Military College in Kingston; Ontario; and an island at Parry Sound, Ontario.

Books and newspapers were crucial in keeping members of the British World up to date on developments of concern to all, such as imperial campaigns. This task was made easier as communications improved.[96] Also, many networks throughout the Empire connected business, religious, educational, scientific, and professional groups.[97] For example, Tamson Pietsch has studied the networks that existed among academics in the United Kingdom and the settler colonies. She describes how they were made up of connective mechanisms consisting of libraries, scholarships, leave-of-absence programs, appointment practices, and institutional associations. These mechanisms enabled "scholars to sustain connections and build careers that straddled the distances of empire."[98] Imperial exhibitions, such as that at Wembley, London, in 1924, were designed in part to strengthen the bonds between the imperial centre and the colonies, celebrate imperial unity, and promote trade. Canada had a prominent place at the 1924 event.[99] Its exhibits included a life-sized sculpture of the Prince of Wales (with his favourite Canadian horse) made of three thousand pounds of Canadian butter.

The sentiment of belonging to the British World was itself a significant connection. Writing in 1934, Alfred Zimmern, an English academic, said that

BRITISH EMPIRE EXHIBITION. WEMBLEY.
H.R.H. PRINCE OF WALES AND RANCH MODELLED IN BUTTER; (CANADIAN SECTION).

A life-sized sculpture in butter of the Prince of Wales and his favourite Canadian horse exhibited by Canada at the 1924 British Empire Exhibition in London. | *Glenbow Library and Archives Collection, Libraries and Cultural Resources Digital Collections, University of Calgary, CU1233650*

the tie of kinship had been steadily weakening. However, there was still an attachment to England itself as an ancestral home: "The cottages and meadows of the 'old Country,' its lanes and its parks, its downs and its cliffs, were felt to be a kind of patrimony of Greater Britons overseas. So too with the social tradition and inheritance of English life, its old universities and cathedrals, the Monarchy, the House of Commons, and the unwritten constitution."[100] There was also an attachment to the wider Empire. Canadian parliamentarians proudly described distant parts of the Empire as their possessions, referred to a "worldwide empire such as ours," and described themselves as "the proud possessor of an empire."[101] One claimed that "it is just as much ours as it is the empire of the British people living in any part of it."[102] Stephen Leacock declared, "We carry visions of far-away oceans and harbours" and wrote that there was a "humbler imperialism" held by decent people, an inspiration of participating in a "wide Empire, in distant possessions which they never see ... In Canada, for example, we insist on owning part of St. Helena, and refuse to let go our grip on Togoland and Guiana."[103]

Historians have noted that this sense of imperial patrimony contributed to a form of Britannic nationalism shared by those of British ancestry throughout the Empire, including Canada. To them, as observed by John Darwin, "the 'Empire' was not an alien overlord, but a joint enterprise in which they were, or claimed to be, partners."[104] Jan Morris wrote that "British Canadians were proud to share the glory of the British super-nation, but not anxious to share its responsibilities."[105] Taken together, the members of the British World were, in the words of James Belich, "a virtual nation, an ephemeral second United States, Britain plus-Dominions, whose Dominion citizens considered themselves co-owners of London, the Empire, and British-ness in general."[106] So far as non-British peoples were concerned, this Britannic nationalism could lead, in Darwin's words, to "an aggressive sense of cultural superiority as the representatives of a global civilisation then at the height of its prestige."[107]

As with any partnership, the key questions were how equal the partners were and what were their responsibilities. Canada was especially assertive in claiming a larger say in how the Empire was run, although it also sought to avoid incurring any expense or responsibility for defence. Writing in 1891, the Canadian lawyer O.A. Howland declared, "We, the freemen of the Empire, claim all the qualities and incidents of a full equal Imperial citizenship, whether our homes are in Great Britain, in Canada or in Australia."[108] Leacock proclaimed a few years later, "I ... am an Imperialist because I will not be a Colonial."[109] In other words, he was not prepared to be a second-class member of the Empire like the dependent peoples (including Indigenous peoples in Canada).

Sometimes Canadians projected an image of wanting to take over from the United Kingdom as the senior partner. John Fraser, an English journalist, wrote in 1905 that Canadians had "a great respect for the 'old man' but thinks him slow and behind the times. He wants to shake the 'old man' up a bit and show him how to run the Empire properly."[110] It was common to predict that the Empire's centre would move to Canada, which could accommodate a much larger population than the UK. One member of Parliament said he dissented "from the view that Canada's destiny is independence." Instead, he looked forward "to that day when Canada will be the dominating and controlling factor in the affairs of our empire."[111]

Leacock, however, went too far in an article he contributed to an English newspaper in 1907.[112] The article described the relationship between the UK and the dominions as similar to that of an aging farmer, who was too set in his ways to run the farm, and his concerned adult sons. It contained this conclusion: "The old man's got too old and he don't know it, can't kick him off the place; but I reckon that the next time we come together to talk things over the boys have

Canada and Colonialism

got to step right in and manage the whole farm." Not surprisingly, this humour was not appreciated by some imperialists in the UK. Winston Churchill called it "offensive twaddle." The Canadian press was also critical. John Ewart, a lawyer and advocate of dominion equality within the Empire, wrote a detailed and thoughtful response. He said Churchill's criticism was well-deserved and described Leacock as "a perplexed imperialist" for his muddled thinking.[113]

Even English imperialists accepted that at some future time the centre of the Empire might move to a Dominion city such as Vancouver.[114] It was not to be. The end of the British World came with the end of the Empire, discussed in Chapter 7.[115]

Dedication to Empire

Canadian support for the Empire was widespread, and there were few critics. Politicians, influential Canadians, newspapers, and writers expressed their approval with greater or lesser fervour. The general public appear to have regarded the Empire as a fact of life. They were more intent on their own lives and largely indifferent to the politics of the Empire, but their interest was aroused

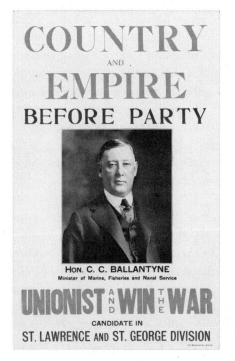

A 1917 election campaign poster urged Canadians to consider "country and Empire before party": vote "Unionist and win the war." | *Library and Archives Canada, 1963-135*

by imperial events such as wars and royal births, marriages, deaths, visits, and coronations.

Prime Minister Macdonald expressed his dedication to the Empire during a debate on the Washington Treaty of 1871, which settled disputes between the UK and the US, including one regarding fishing in Canadian waters. The treaty was negotiated by imperial diplomats, and the prime minister had been an observer. Some Canadians thought it failed to protect their interests. Macdonald responded, "If England does call on us to make a financial sacrifice; does find it for the good of the empire that we, England's first colony, should sacrifice something, I say that we would be unworthy of our proud position if we were not prepared to do so."[116] As already noted, he won an election twenty years later by draping himself in the "old flag." Robert Borden, who also became a Conservative prime minister, declared, "Like Sir John Macdonald, I was born a British subject, I shall remain a British subject, I hope to die a British subject. I trust the day will never come when the British flag will cease to float over this Canada of ours."[117]

Liberal politicians were generally less vocal in their support for the Empire because they were more dependent than the Conservatives on votes in Quebec, where the majority French-speaking population did not share the enthusiasm of English-speaking Canadians for Mother England. Despite their relative silence, they also showed support for the Empire when it was necessary to do so. At the outbreak of the First World War, Wilfrid Laurier, then in opposition, declared to Parliament that Canadians had always known "that when Great Britain is at war, we are at war." He stated that Canada, "a daughter of old England," could only respond "in the classical language of the British answer to the call to duty: 'Ready, ay Ready.'"[118] His successor as Liberal prime minister, William Lyon Mackenzie King, who served over twenty-one years in that position, was likewise generally restrained in his expressions of backing for the Empire but gave vital aid during the Second World War.[119] His diaries show resentment of Churchill's "centralized Imperialism" but continued support for the Empire generally.[120]

Several influential speakers proclaimed the depth of their enthusiasm, such as J.W. Flavelle, a prominent businessman, chair of the Bank of Commerce, chairman of the Munitions Board of Canada during the First World War, and one of the last Canadians to receive a hereditary title. In a speech he gave in 1917 at the University of Toronto, Flavelle described the Empire as "a great civilizing force" providing "power and usefulness and efficiency in unselfish service."[121] Some prominent Canadian imperialists, such as George Parkin and

Stephen Leacock, went on the lecture circuit in the UK and the other dominions, as well as in Canada, to promote imperialism.

Speaking tours of Canada by English politicians such as Joseph Chamberlain,[122] Alfred Milner,[123] and Churchill,[124] as well as by Frederick Young, a pioneer of the imperial federation movement in England, in which they touted imperialism, appear to have received an enthusiastic reception from Canadian business groups.[125] In 1901, after a speech in Winnipeg, Churchill wrote to his mother, "They are furiously British."[126] This may have been due, at least in part, to the confirmations Churchill gave that, as a partner in the Empire, they had an interest in imperial affairs and that "the Empire belongs as much to Canada ... as it does to the Mother Country."[127]

Newspapers often reflected the sense of imperial pride and patrimony. Celebrating the decisive victory of British forces in Egypt in 1882, the *Ottawa Daily Citizen* proudly declared, "Belonging to the Empire [is] our proudest boast. Ours its greatness, ours its wealth, ours its treasure, ours its security, ours its renown."[128] The Boer War likewise brought forth feverish imperial sentiment in many newspapers.[129]

In an article in *Studies in Canadian Literature*, academic Barrie Davies explored the impact of the Empire on Canadian literature between Confederation in 1867 and the 1950s. He concluded that "a significant proportion of Canadian writing propounded or responded to the intoxication, hangover, and withdrawal from the heady Imperial brew."[130] Davies found it difficult to discover a Canadian prominent in politics, enterprise, or letters who was not even more excited about the Empire than his English counterpart, "probably because it seemed the way to prominence and power on the world's stage."

Some of this literature now appears as pure propaganda, such as poems by Wilfred Campbell and Robert Stead. Some of it was well-written fiction, such as the novels of Sara Jeannette Duncan. Some of it consisted of works intended as serious political or economic analysis, such as the books and essays of celebrated writer Stephen Leacock, who wrote more in his capacity as a university professor than as a humorist, although they do not lack humour. Despite their differences, all of these authors shared a belief in the virtues and glory of the Empire. This belief extended even to poet Pauline Johnson (Tekahionwake), although her work contains a degree of ambivalence reflecting her mixed ancestry as the daughter of a Mohawk father and English mother.

The Canadian laureate of Empire was Wilfred Campbell, who, among other works, produced *The Sagas of Vaster Britain*.[131] Included was a poem, "England," in which he claimed for Canadians "a part in the glory and pride and aim/Of the Empire that girdles the world." In "The Lazarus of Empire," he bemoaned the inferior role of "the poor beggar Colonial" feeding on "the crumbs of [Britain's] fame," and urged Canadians to "take up the burden of empire." Another poem pleaded with England "to show the way ... We are not alien ... Pass us not by."[132] Robert Stead's collection *The Empire Builders and Other Poems* included "Manhood's Estate," celebrating the transfer of control over military bases from Mother England to Canada:

> *I pronounce his absolute liberty, I remove my slightest ban,*
> *And I give him the keys of a continent with the bidding, "Be a man!"*
> *... Yet manhood honors his mother's name and loves his mother still.*[133]

Pauline Johnson was dedicated to the Empire. She took pride in being "born in Canada, beneath the British flag." One poem described how, under Queen Victoria's banner of purity and honour, the Empire conferred the "benediction of vast liberties."[134] The Mounties were praised for keeping "the peace of our people and the honour of British law."[135] But Johnson also defended Indigenous rights. She told a London reporter, "The whole continent belongs to us by right of lineage. We welcomed you as friends, we worshipped you, and you drove us into a little corner."[136] The conflict between her views on imperialism and Indigenous rights is expressed in her 1885 poem "A Cry from an Indian Wife":

> *Go; rise and strike, no matter what the cost;*
> *Yet stay. Revolt not at the Union Jack;*
> *... Go forth, and win the glories of the war*
> *... By right, by birth we Indians own these lands.*[137]

Ontario-born Sara Jeannette Duncan has been described as the "Novelist of Empire."[138] She was a committed imperialist and wrote often and favourably on the British Empire and especially British India, where she lived after her marriage.[139] As she explained in a letter in 1903, "Is it any wonder that my sentiments are Imperial, with a husband in India and a family in Canada and everybody else in England!"[140] One biographer, Misao Dean, writes that "she made no bones about her commitment to the future of the Empire and her personal identification with British history and British mission," and her "interest in and support of the Imperial Federation movement is another factor that lends support to the idea that she thought of herself as a particularly Canadian citizen of Empire."[141]

The prominent author and imperialist Sara Jeannette Duncan. She was described as the "novelist of Empire" and wrote *The Imperialist* and many stories about British India. | *Johnston and Hoffman, Library and Archives Canada, C-046447*

Pauline Johnson was a celebrated author of British and Mohawk descent who both celebrated the British Empire and asserted Indigenous land rights. 1895. | *Cochran, Library and Archives Canada, 1952-010 / e010857301*

Editorials on events in South Africa written by Duncan and her husband in their newspaper, *The Indian Daily News,* show support for British imperialism, including the actions of Cecil Rhodes, which are excused with the comment that "Much goes to the making of Empire which should not be too closely scrutinized."[142] Like imperialists generally, she was a racist, and her novels contain many derogatory remarks and stereotypes about Indigenous people in Canada and Indians from the subcontinent. She was also critical of British characters who sympathized with Indian nationalism. Positive comments were reserved for Indians who served the Empire, such as judges. Her best-known novel, *The Imperialist,* was set in small-town Ontario, with a plot that revolves around the unsuccessful election campaign of an outspoken imperialist and explores some of the conflicting emotions evoked by imperial and national issues.[143]

Stephen Leacock's most famous literary work, *Sunshine Sketches of a Little Town,* bears some resemblance to *The Imperialist* as they are both based on elections in small-town Ontario. Both writers were fervent imperialists and, during their day, enjoyed considerable popularity, although Leacock was much more successful. Duncan's writings (leaving aside newspaper articles) were mainly confined to fiction, and unlike Duncan's novels, which explored issues of imperialism, the topic is largely missing in Leacock's works of fiction. Instead, he wrote several books and articles as a serious advocate for imperialism.[144] However, they seem lightweight for his position as a professor of political economy at McGill, earning this wry comment from another professor, Frank Underhill: he "still remains our leading humourist when it comes to writing serious books about Canadian social problems."[145]

In "Greater Canada, an Appeal," published in 1907, when Leacock made the famous statement that he was an imperialist because he would not be a colonial, he explained: "This Colonial status is a worn-out, by-gone thing."[146] Addressing England, he exclaimed, "We will be your colony no longer," and pleaded, "Make us one with you in an Empire, Permanent and Indivisible." He then demanded "the imperialism of any decent citizen that demands for this country its proper place in the councils of the Empire and in the destiny of the world." This was followed by the declaration, "The time has come to be done with this colonial business, done with it once and forever. We cannot in Canada continue as we are. We must become something greater or something infinitely less." Less emotionally, his 1930 book *Economic Prosperity in the British Empire* proposed measures to integrate the economies of the Empire and so promote prosperity.[147] Ten years later, at the outset of the Second World War, Leacock wrote another book, *Our Empire*, to encourage pride in the Empire and support for the war effort.[148]

Canadian critics of Empire were few.[149] The most prominent were Henri Bourassa and the English-born intellectual maverick Goldwin Smith. Bourassa was a French Canadian politician who opposed Canadian participation in the Boer War. In 1903, he founded the Ligue Nationaliste Canadienne (Canadian Nationalist League) to advocate autonomy for Canada, although it would remain within the Empire.[150] He set out his views in a book, *Great Britain and Canada*, which poured scorn on imperialists on both sides of the Atlantic. It denounced British imperialism as "a lust for land-grabbing and military dominion."[151] (Opposition had its lighter side. Bourassa was heckled by someone who reminded him that the sun never set on the glory of the British Empire, to which he shot back, "That only goes to prove that not even God trusts the British in the dark.")[152] A former professor at Oxford and Cornell, Smith was a long-standing and outspoken critic of imperial policy generally and as it applied to Canada. He went so far as to advocate union with the United States.[153] In the twentieth century, Canadian criticism of the Empire remained muted and, as in the UK, appears to have been mainly on the left.[154] Some Canadians might be described as "closet anti-imperialists" who recognized that their views were contrary to majority opinion and so sought greater autonomy for Canada rather than independence outside the Empire. Among them was Oscar D. Skelton, senior civil servant in External Affairs and trusted adviser to Mackenzie King as prime minister.[155]

Probably for most of the time of the Empire, Canadians (like people in the UK) just accepted imperialism as a fact.[156] Their lives were, of course, impacted by being part of the Empire in matters both large and small, from migration to music halls.[157] The majority were likely indifferent or apathetic to imperial politics until stirred into action by the crisis of war or excited by imperial expansion. Duncan's *The Imperialist* shows how the imperial sentiments of the voters of an Ontario town were trumped by more local interests. There were differences among the different Canadian communities. Quebec was generally lukewarm, at best, in its support of the British connection. During the Boer War, for example, many French Canadians opposed participation by Canada in the conflict. That led to competing riots in Montreal by French Canadians opposing the war and English Canadians in favour. Indifference to the Empire increased as non-English communities grew, and some English-speaking Canadians identified more with North America than Britain. In 1938, on the eve of the Second World War, one writer reviewed the different groups, noting that the Canadian views of and attitudes toward Britain and the Empire were mixed and varied. However, he predicted accurately that "the Imperialists, because they are vocal and aggressive, will carry Canada into that crisis with them."[158]

Fighting for the Empire

Canadian support for the Empire went beyond rhetoric. Individual British North Americans/Canadians were involved as members of the British Army in imperial conflicts around the world, including the Battle of Trafalgar in 1805, the Indian Rebellion of 1857, and in Africa at the turn of the century. Canadian contingents also fought in the major imperial conflicts of the Boer War (1899–1902) and the two World Wars. In a lecture delivered in 1866, Henry Morgan commented, "In the British Service there has not been a battle or engagement of any consequence for the last hundred years in which some British American has not taken part."[159] This was to remain the case for the next ninety years, until the Suez Crisis of 1956 saw Canada refusing to join the British invasion of Egypt.

For most of the nineteenth century, the British North American colonies depended on the British Army for defence, assisted by volunteer militiamen.[160] Any British Americans/Canadians who wanted to see full-time active service could join the British Army and serve overseas. Several became officers.[161] The Royal Military College (RMC) was founded in Kingston, Ontario, in 1874 following the withdrawal of British forces from Canada. Some of its graduates went on to serve in the British Army on imperial campaigns. A number were recruited in the 1880s to fill gaps in the officer corps.[162] Thereafter, "Canada continued to serve as a regular and frequent source for the recruitment of soldiers for the Empire throughout the late nineteenth, and early twentieth centuries."[163] A book published in 1891 lists almost two hundred Canadian commissioned officers who served in the British Army or Royal Navy, with brief biographies.[164] It also gives an account of the Leinster Regiment of the British Army, which owed its origins to a regiment raised in Canada for the Indian Rebellion of 1857.

In his lecture, Morgan gave examples of British North Americans who had served or were serving in the British Army or Royal Navy. They had fought in Afghanistan, the East Indies, the West Indies, and other parts of the Empire. He mentions Admiral Westphal, born in Nova Scotia, who served with Nelson at Trafalgar and was wounded at that famous battle. Westphal was placed next to the dying hero and their blood mingled. He went on to see action in the West Indies and other parts of the Empire. Admiral Watts was another admiral born in Nova Scotia. He was part of the British Navy in the West Indies and during the War of 1812 with the United States. A Victoria Cross was awarded to Alexander Dunn of Upper Canada for his bravery during the Charge of the Light Brigade at the Battle of Balaclava in the Crimean War of 1854. A few years later, he raised a regiment to fight in the Indian Mutiny. After being promoted to the rank of colonel, he became the first Canadian to command a regiment of the British Army. He was killed in 1868 in what is now Eritrea.[165]

Major-General John Inglis was another celebrated military hero. He took command of the British garrison at Lucknow, in the state of Awadh (which had been annexed by the East India Company only the year before) during the famous siege by Indian soldiers or sepoys, and became known as the "Hero of Lucknow." This siege was a central event of the rebellion of 1857, which was to end rule by the East India Company.[166] The siege and its relief were to go down as a key event in the history of the Empire. Jan Morris describes how the ruined residency, the home of the imperial representative, became "the great shrine of the [rebellion] and perhaps the supreme temple of British imperialism ... in

Major-General John Inglis, the hero of the Lucknow siege of 1857, with his wife and children. | Illustrated London News, *November 28, 1857*

which a small garrison, with its women and children, had held out in appalling conditions against an overwhelming force of mutinous sepoys." Messages from Inglis, written partially in Greek and smuggled out in quills, described their increasingly desperate situation: "My force is daily diminishing from the enemy's musketry fire and our defences are daily weaker."[167] The story of the siege and the relief of Lucknow was known to every Victorian schoolboy.[168] Tennyson paid tribute in "The Defence of Lucknow":

> *Women and children among us, God help them, our children and wives!*
> *... 'Hold it for fifteen days!' We have held it for eighty-seven!*
> *And ever aloft on the palace roof the old banner of England blew.*[169]

The scene of the great event became a place of pilgrimage and was written up in great detail in *Murray's Handbook*, the guide to British India.[170]

Inglis was born in Halifax, Nova Scotia, in 1814 and fought in the 1837 rebellion in Canada and in the Punjab in 1848. He is commemorated in Halifax with a street that connects with Lucknow Street. After taking command of the garrison in July 1857 upon the death of Sir Henry Lawrence from a shell, Inglis held it for eighty-seven days until the arrival of relief forces. Lawrence had selected him for his abilities over a more senior officer. A Victorian historian of the rebellion described him as in the "prime of his life, an excellent soldier, creative, energetic, and quick-sighted," and praised his "daring obstinacy in resisting, his confident mien and his cool courage."[171] However, Wolseley, who took an active role in the relief, paid him a somewhat backhanded compliment. He wrote that "though by no means an able man in any respect, [Inglis] possessed the pluck and decision to abide by Sir Henry Lawrence's injunction to hold out as long as possible, and never to make any terms with the treacherous enemy around him."[172] Inglis was later promoted to the rank of major-general and received a knighthood. He took command of troops in Corfu but suffered from ill health and died in 1862, aged forty-seven. A plaque in St. Paul's Cathedral, London, shows a portrait of him with an enormous moustache and side whiskers – the very image of a Victorian soldier. His widow kept a diary of the ordeal, published in 1892, that gave a detailed account of their suffering during the siege ("We sat trembling, hardly able to breathe"), the relief ("tremendous cheering was heard"), and the "terrible retribution [that] had fallen on the rebels."[173]

Other British North Americans fought in the rebellion. Two received the Victoria Cross for their actions: William Hall of Nova Scotia (siege of Lucknow, 1857) and surgeon Herbert Reade of Perth, Ontario (siege of Delhi, 1857). Hall, the son of American slaves, was the first Black person to win the medal. He was buried in 1904 in an unmarked grave without military honours and not recognized until 1945.[174]

The Sudan campaign of 1884–85 was an unsuccessful attempt to rescue General Gordon, the personification of the romantic, self-sacrificing, imperial hero. Gordon was under siege in Khartoum, where rebels were attempting to establish an Islamic state.[175] The British forces arrived just three days too late after a long journey down the Nile. The siege took place at the same time as the North-West Resistance in Canada, the second of two Métis-led uprisings against the Canadian government's territorial expansion, and Prime Minister Macdonald compared Louis Riel, who led the resistance, to the Mahdi, who led the Sudan uprising.[176] Gordon, who held very unconventional religious views, seems to have become unhinged as he recorded his deepest and troubled thoughts on telegraph forms that served as his journal.[177] In the margins, he drew satirical cartoons of the politicians who were being driven to distraction by his quest for martyrdom. He disobeyed instructions to evacuate the city to avoid conflict with the Islamic fundamentalists who surrounded it. The tragicomedy of the situation was summarized in an unintentionally humorous poem by William McGonagall, which failed to reach the heights of Tennyson's verse:

　　　　　　　　　　　　　　　　　　　　　Canada and Colonialism

Alas! now o'er the civilised world there hangs a gloom;
For brave General Gordon, that was killed in Khartoum,
He was a Christian hero, and a soldier of the Cross,
And to England his death will be a very great loss.[178]

Several Canadians participated in the Sudan campaign as members of the British Army.[179] Among them was Major-General James Wilson, born in 1852 in Kingston, Ontario, who joined the 1st Brigade, Royal Artillery, in Sudan. His service as a combatant earned him the distinction of being the first officer in Canada's young standing army, the Permanent Force, to see overseas service. Following the Sudan campaign, he returned to Canada to assist in putting down the North-West Resistance.[180]

In addition to individuals who were members of the British Army, Canada's contribution consisted of about four hundred boatmen. A quarter of them were Indigenous men, mainly from Kahnawake.[181] The leader of the British forces, Garnet Wolseley, remembered how well voyageurs had got his troops to Manitoba during the Red River Resistance of 1869–70. He wanted to use their skills again. The boatmen performed very well in navigating boats down the Nile.

Canadian boatmen at breakfast in the Sudan in 1884, in an unsuccessful bid to rescue General Gordon. | Illustrated London News, *November 29, 1884*

However, they added to the sense of farce with their heavy woollen clothing and blue flannel twill shirts despite the heat, and by going AWOL at ports on the trip over. Like the siege and relief of Lucknow, the campaign went down in imperial folklore, especially Gordon's supposedly courageous death on the steps of his building.[182] He received recognition throughout the British World and, despite his failure, joined the pantheon of heroes who inspired imperial patriotism from Canada to New Zealand.

Toward the end of the nineteenth century, the British Army was increasingly involved in "pacifying" Africa. Canadians were very active in these campaigns, as described by Yves Engler in *Canada in Africa*.[183] He lists several Canadians who fought against Indigenous resistance when the British Empire expanded into Africa. Andrew Godefroy, a military historian, has also written on the large number of Canadian soldiers in West African conflicts between 1885 and 1905. As he comments, "Some readers may be surprised to learn that a great number of Canadian soldiers, some of whom would later rise to become generals in Canada's Great War Army [First World War], experienced their first actions and combat in the jungles and swamps of West Africa" on imperial campaigns.[184] They were often graduates of RMC. However, he notes they very likely cared much less whether they were identified as "British" or "Canadian" than the historians who examine them today.[185] He concludes that "Canadians made substantial commitments to imperial defence not just during the flashpoint that was the South African War, but rather constantly during the late 19th and early 20th centuries."[186]

The most prominent of them was Major William Heneker, who fought in no less than a dozen separate campaigns ranging from peacetime military engagements to pivotal battles. He served in South Africa, India, and the North-West Frontier (a province of what is now Pakistan, on the border of Afghanistan) and became a commander on the Western Front during the First World War. After serving as commander-in-chief of Southern Command in India, he retired as a full general.[187] Engler describes how he helped conquer the Benin Empire in what is now southwestern Nigeria, and the destruction and pillage that took place in Benin City and surrounding areas. In 1907, while Heneker was in South Africa, his book *Bush Warfare* was published. It contains the following passage, based on his own experiences:

> The great thing is to impress savages with the fact that they are the weaker, and that it is intended to occupy the country, enforce the will of the white man, and accomplish the object for which the expedition is organized.

Canada and Colonialism

No leniency or half measures are of any use until the savage has felt the power of force. Leniency is treated as a sign of weakness, and half measures as an undecided and wavering policy.[188]

His book became one of the bibles of British forces until the First World War.

The causes of the Boer War or South African War of 1899–1902 were complex and remain controversial. It is often argued that it was fought over the control of the diamonds and gold of southern Africa.[189] The imperialist fervour of the time became jingoistic fever, leading to calls for war in the UK and the British settler colonies, including Canada.[190] The appeal of imperialism was explained by G.E. Foster, a long-time Canadian parliamentarian:

> If there is one thing that thrills in the blood of the Canadian volunteer today it is the subtle symbolism of the flag of the empire. It is not the Maple Leaf, it is not the Australian flag, it is not the flag of the Cape Colony, but it is the flag of that grand old empire which he feels symbolizes the progress of his race as a whole, which symbolizes the permanency and extension of liberty civil and religious.[191]

The Boer War was to mark the high point of popular enthusiasm for the Empire. However, visions of glory vanished when confronted with the reality of determined resistance by the Boers. This resistance resulted in the imperial forces destroying homes and farms to deny supplies to the guerilla fighters. It also led to the degradation and deaths of thousands in concentration camps set up for women and children, captured soldiers, and displaced Africans. Canadian soldiers fought at notable battles, such as the Relief of Mafeking in 1900. Their victory at Paardeberg in 1900 led to Laurier asking the House of Commons, "Is there a man whose bosom did not swell with pride ... that the fact had been revealed to the world that a new power had arisen in the west."[192] The victory was celebrated by an annual day of remembrance until the First World War. Canadian soldiers also took part in the destruction of homes and the running of concentration camps. John Buchan, a future governor general, was involved in administering the camps.

Some of the Canadian soldiers wrote books recounting their experiences.[193] They are full of pride over Canada's involvement and their own participation in the imperial achievements. William Hart-McHarg from British Columbia was representative of Canadians whose support for the Empire ultimately led to the supreme sacrifice. He had qualified and practised as a lawyer. A prize

Canadian soldiers seizing a *kopje* (hill) in a baptism of fire during the Boer War. | *Reprinted from T.G. Marquis,* Canada's Sons on Kopje and Veldt *(Toronto: Canada's Sons, 1900), 165.*

A Canadian nurse, Minnie Affleck, during the Boer War, 1900. | *Library and Archives Canada, C-028733*

shot, he joined the Canadian militia and volunteered to fight in the Boer War. He fought in major battles, including Paardeberg. His book describing his experiences includes this account of his pride at being part of the Grand Army of the British Empire assembled in Pretoria:

> We stood on June 5th as the representatives of the Canadian people in the Grand Army of the British Empire in the surrendered capital of the enemy ... It was one of those unique moments that only come to a man occasionally during a life-time. It will never be forgotten. If anyone asks me what I consider the greatest occasion in my life, I say that it was when I marched past Lord Roberts in Pretoria, June 5th, 1900, with the Royal Canadian Regiment.[194]

Hart-McHarg notes how the Canadian people had cheerfully set about to take up their share of the burden of the Empire.[195] Their support for the Empire was acknowledged as the Canadian troops arrived at the railway station in London. The band of the Scots Guards played "Sons of the Empire" as well as "The Maple Leaf."[196] Hart-McHarg was killed in 1915 at the age of forty-six, at the Second Battle of Ypres, Belgium, a battle in which the Canadian forces earned recognition for their determination and bravery against poison gas and the enemy's greater numbers.[197]

Another veteran of the Boer War commented, "For the first time in Canada's history, she ... had to take her part in a war of the Empire. Gladly did she face her duty, War, War! echoed throughout the Dominion, and in every city, town, hamlet, from Victoria to Charlottetown, young men, the flower of country cried 'We are ready.'"[198] Many of the volunteers had fought in the North-West Resistance or were members of the North-West Mounted Police, such as the renowned Sam Steele.[199] Less celebrated and remembered is Edwin McCormick, Steele's trumpeter and messenger. He enlisted from Toronto at the age of sixteen and later wrote his memoirs recording his experiences. He described one attack as "like the eruption of Mount Vesuvius, as smoke, dirt, rocks and sulphurous gasses shot up from the position."[200] Together with other buglers, he played a vital part in the conflict by giving the calls to action on the battlefield.[201] He also played the "Last Post" as eight Canadian soldiers were laid to rest after the battle of Hart's River. McCormick served two tours of duty but survived into old age.

The Boers may have lost the war, but they won the peace. The real losers were the Africans, who were to suffer under apartheid until the 1990s. Although the British used the Africans for propaganda purposes to arouse opposition to the Boers, who were rightly accused of ill-treating them, the British ultimately abandoned the Africans to the Boers in order to achieve peace. In what has been described as "a momentous commitment," Article 8 of the Treaty of Vereeniging (1902), which ended the war, stated, "The question of granting the Franchise to Natives will not be decided until after the introduction of Self-Government."[202] Of course, the decision made by the Union of South Africa, formed in 1909 and controlled by the Boers, was to deny the franchise. Indeed, the "coloureds" of Cape Province, who had enjoyed the vote, were to lose it.[203] As Milner, who represented the British, had earlier remarked in a private letter, using racially offensive language, "You have only to sacrifice [the Black African] absolutely and the game is easy."[204]

The First World War was to have significant consequences for Canada's ability to have a role in international affairs independent of that of the UK, which had handled such matters for all the Empire.[205] Having said that, it should be noted that there has been a lot of mythology about how the nation was born in the furnace of war and, especially, at the battle of Vimy Ridge.[206] Canada's independence was much less dramatic and heroic than a military victory. We will see in Chapter 7 that it arose out of slow constitutional developments presided over by aging politicians. The First World War was clearly a war between imperial rivals. General Smuts of South Africa (who had moved from Boer commando and key negotiator of the Treaty of Vereeniging to being a member of the Imperial War Cabinet) listed the war aims. He commenced with "Destruction of the German colonial system with a view to the future security of all communications vital to the British Empire."[207]

As the war approached, Canadian prime minister Robert Borden promised London that "the Canadian people will be united ... to ensure the integrity and maintain the honour of the Empire."[208] Wilfrid Laurier, leader of the opposition, told Parliament that "when Great Britain is at war, we are at war."[209] In fact, as with the Boer War, there was a division of views between English and French Canada, and conscription was imposed in the face of strong opposition in Quebec. Support within English Canada was virtually unanimous, as shown by the newspaper coverage.[210] Canada raised an army of over 600,000, and over 300,000 saw action on the Western Front as part of a separate Canadian corps.[211] Recruitment stressed Britishness. In Ontario, a recruiting poster depicted a Canadian officer pointing at the Union Jack and exclaiming: "THIS IS YOUR FLAG – FIGHT FOR IT."[212]

The country suffered considerable casualties, including more than 60,000 dead. It felt it had earned a say in how the war was conducted. This was granted through membership in the Imperial War Cabinet and agreement that the dominions would have an adequate voice in foreign policy.[213] Canada also insisted

First World War recruitment poster for the Ottawa-Carleton Battalion showing the Union Jack flag and the message "This Is Your Flag – Fight for It." | *Library and Archives Canada, 1983-28-895*

on dominion representation at the Versailles peace conference. In a symbolic gesture, it signed separately below Britain, which signed on behalf of the entire Empire. The Canadian representatives got caught up in the general feeling at the conference that territory could be acquired and traded like properties in a game of imperial monopoly. They discussed with the Americans the possibility of exchanging the Alaska panhandle for some of the West Indies. The Canadian prime minister also discussed with the British prime minister the possibility of Canada taking over control of the West Indies.[214] As it turned out, Canada did not add any territory, but Britain, Australia, New Zealand, and South Africa acquired German territory in the Middle East, Africa, and the Pacific.

In contrast, the Second World War can be seen as an anti-imperialist war since it was, in essence, a war to stop Germany, Italy, and Japan from imperial expansion. Nevertheless, it was also, of course, fought to preserve the British

◄ Second World War recruitment poster showing a determined Canadian soldier and the Union Jack flag with the message "Allons-y ... Canadiens!" | *Library and Archives Canada, 1983-30-245*

► Poster promoting Victory Bonds with the Union Jack flag and the message "Come on Canada – Strike a Deadly Blow at Hitler," 1942. | *Library and Archives Canada, 1983-30-763*

Canada and Colonialism

Empire (and other incumbent empires) from that expansion.[215] It succeeded in the short term, but the economic and political cost was too great for the Empire to survive for long. Canada played a critical role in supporting Britain, and Winston Churchill acknowledged this contribution in a speech he made in 1941 to the Senate and House of Commons: "The contribution of Canada to the imperial war effort, in troops, in ships, in aircraft, in food and in finance has been magnificent."[216] It is often said that the United Kingdom stood alone at the outset of the war, but this is not true; it had the support of Canada and other parts of the Empire. As Churchill noted, Canadian participation took many forms, including one billion dollars in financial assistance as well as personnel and material. Canadian enlistment exceeded that of the First World War. This support came at a vital time, and it is unlikely that the allies would have won without it.[217]

▲ Canada provided vital assistance to the UK during the Second World War, although the relationship was not without its strains. This photo shows Winston and Clementine Churchill being greeted by Canadian prime minister Mackenzie King in 1943. | *National Film Board of Canada, Library and Archives Canada, C-007478*

The relationship was not without tension. On occasion, Mackenzie King thought Britain took Canada for granted and did not give adequate recognition.[218] He had some reason for this view, although his own sensitivity to being slighted probably contributed. In a memorandum about keeping the dominions informed on the progress of the war, Churchill said that although there should be "no change in principle, there should be considerable soft-pedalling in practice."[219] There was no Imperial War Cabinet, as there had been during the First World War. In the words of A.P. Thornton, "The Empire was the Empire once more, and to 10, Downing Street returned that imperial control that two generations of Dominion opinion had combined to condemn as sinister."[220] One result of the war was to deepen the Canadian relationship with the United States. Agreements were signed on defence and economic matters. Canada's determination to play a more independent role on international issues and its feelings of nationalism were strengthened. However, the war also reinforced for many the sense of belonging to a family of British nations.[221]

Over a quarter of a million Canadians lived in Britain during the war, experiencing both familiarity and strangeness in what Jonathan Vance describes as "a kind of reverse colonialism."[222] They missed efficient heating systems and were mystified by the class system. They continued to share the same monarch, flag, citizenship, and anthem. But the descendants of those who had boarded the migrant steamer in Victoria Docks bound for Canada a lifetime before were now a different people. Still, one thing remained the same: it is most unlikely that they gave any thought to the Indigenous peoples of the Dominion, who remained largely forgotten. Self-government for Canada included rule over Indigenous peoples, and the next chapter will examine this aspect of Canadian colonialism in some detail.

6

Internal Colonialism in Canada

William Halliday was a stocky man with a reddish pointed beard and blue eyes. A talented photographer, he is best known for his role as an Indian agent who enforced the prohibition in the *Indian Act* of the West Coast feast and gift-giving ceremonies known as the potlatch.[1] Born in Wellington County, Ontario, in 1866, he moved west and became principal of the residential school in Alert Bay, British Columbia. In 1906, he was appointed Indian agent for the Kwawkewlth Agency, responsible for northern Vancouver Island and neighbouring inlets of the mainland, before retiring in 1932. He received a memorandum in 1913 from the Ottawa headquarters of the Department of Indian Affairs, now under the control of newly appointed deputy superintendent Duncan Campbell Scott, encouraging him to enforce the provision in the *Indian Act* outlawing the ceremonies.

Initially enthusiastic, Halliday became frustrated at the resistance from First Nations people and the mild sentences handed down by the courts. He recommended changes in the law, which meant that he could not only charge offenders but convict and sentence them as well in his capacity as a magistrate. Matters came to a head in April 1922 at the trial of fifty-eight First Nations people in Halliday's schoolhouse courtroom, arising from Dan Cranmer's potlatch, one of the largest ever recorded in the area.[2] Twenty-two people served sentences of two months' imprisonment at Oakalla Prison in Vancouver, and many others received suspended sentences. Regalia associated with the potlatch was surrendered or seized and subsequently sent to museums around the world. Halliday felt that he had succeeded in killing the ceremonies, or at least ended their open occurrence.[3] Like other Indian agents and more senior administrators of Indian policy, such as his boss, Scott, he was using his considerable powers over First Nations peoples to fulfil the two objectives of that policy identified by Prime Minister Macdonald in 1887: doing away with the tribal system and promoting assimilation.[4]

Halliday was a faithful servant of the Empire. When a foreign settlement hoisted the red flag of communism, he demanded that it be replaced with the Union Jack and snapped, "Never let me hear of you raising any other flag above that of the Empire."[5] He wrote in 1935 of his experiences, using the classic language of colonial biological racism and class prejudice: "Possibly another reason may be given why the Indians are increasing, and why their physique is improving, but the reason does not reflect creditably on the white people. It is owing to the infusion of white blood that these results are occurring ... It is not the better class of white men who have thus degraded themselves by intermingling with the Indian women."[6]

Indian Agents and Their Work

As with the imperial rule of Indigenous peoples elsewhere in the world, the most crucial person in the administration of Indian policy in Canada was the "man on the spot" – the Indian agent (sometimes known as the Indian superintendent) – who was answerable to more senior officials. As one might expect, those superiors reflected the values and attitudes of the colonial establishment. Before Confederation, many came from Empire Loyalist backgrounds or had served in other branches of the imperial service before they were appointed. For example, James Higginson, superintendent general of Indian Affairs from 1844 to 1846, had served in the Bengal Army and Jamaica, and subsequently in Antigua and Mauritius.[7] As pointed out by one writer, "such men were greatly influenced by intellectual and emotional currents from the country which they regarded with such affection."[8]

Significantly for the history of colonial or "Indian" administration in Canada, the most senior official in the Department of Indian Affairs in the early part of the twentieth century was Duncan Campbell Scott, who retired in 1932 after fifty years. He was widely praised for his administration and mostly left alone to run the department and to enforce, and draft changes to, the *Indian Act*. Scott explained his vision in 1920 to a parliamentary committee considering an amendment to the *Indian Act* that would enable the government to deprive "Indians" of their legal status: "I want to get rid of the Indian problem

Duncan Campbell Scott was a celebrated poet and the senior official in the Department of Indian Affairs. He was a firm believer in the Empire and in the forced assimilation of Indigenous peoples. | *Yousuf Karsh, Library and Archives Canada, PA-165842/ e010752290*

... Our object is to continue until there is not a single Indian in Canada that has not been absorbed into the body politic and there is no Indian question."[9]

A firm believer in the forced assimilation of Indigenous peoples, Scott also believed in the Empire, imperial values, and imperial federalism.[10] Among his heroes was Sir George Grey, who had been prominent as governor in advancing settlement in New Zealand, Australia, and Cape Province, including an invasion of Māori territory and confiscation of their lands. In 1840, Grey wrote his *Report on the Best Means of Promoting the Civilization of the Aboriginal Inhabitants of Australia*. This was a blueprint for their "amalgamation" or assimilation and the destruction of their culture, which he attempted to implement in the colonies he governed. He has also been described as a founder of apartheid in South Africa.[11] Grey was an ardent imperialist. As a member of the New Zealand Parliament, he introduced legislation to promote British annexations in the Pacific.[12] Scott wrote in his newspaper column that he wished Grey could have been governor general of Canada so that "all his activity and experience [could be] working for our interest."[13] That interest was as a great power in the Empire. Scott advised the readers of an American magazine that the "manifest destiny of Canada is to be one of the greatest powers in the Federated Empire of England."[14]

Scott was a noted poet and a member of the group known as the Confederation Poets. Some of his poems reflected his views on Indigenous people. They were written on the theme of the "disappearing Indian," containing references to "a weird and waning race," "tragic savage," and "perished day."[15] In "Half-Breed Girl" and "At Gull Lake," he wrote of the rejection of mixed-race people by both whites and Indigenous people.[16] He was uncomplimentary to Indigenous people generally, describing them as "uncouth," "savage," "wild," "superstitious," and "brutal." As the head of the department, Scott was strict in his supervision of Indian agents and frequently reminded them of their duties, which were frequently unpleasant and harsh on First Nations people, and the possibility of dismissal for non-performance.[17]

The role played by the Indian agent was fundamental to the government's treatment of First Nations peoples.[18] In 1996, the Royal Commission on Aboriginal Peoples observed, "It is clear that their powers and influence were formidable."[19] From the perspective of First Nations peoples, the Indian agent was, in fact, the government's agent – the face of a distant Indian Affairs Department or "Crown." It was the Indian agent who was the point of contact for residents of the reserve.[20] As a study of Indian agents in Ontario commented, "All contact with Indian Affairs was to pass through the agent and he alone would take care of any issue that arose on the reserve ... The effect of this practice was to entrench Indian agents as power brokers between the department and its 'wards.'"[21] They were not simply passive instruments of central power but could play their own considerable part.[22]

The position of the Indian agent, and Indian policy generally, has to be seen in the context of the marginalization of Indigenous peoples in the broader Canadian society. The explosion of settlement across Canada following Confederation overwhelmed them, and they were dispossessed by the resulting demographic changes.[23] First Nations peoples soon became minorities on their traditional lands and were viewed as a disappearing race, an encumbrance and an obstacle to settlement and progress who would soon cease to exist. In the words of the historian James Miller, "So far as nineteenth-century Canadians were concerned, the First Nations throughout southern Canada were now an impediment that had to be cleared away much as the pine forests in the east had to be reduced before production of surplus wheat crops for export was possible."[24] The physical environment of their traditional lands was rapidly changed in the southern parts of the country as land was cleared, resources depleted, and agriculture introduced.

Canada and Colonialism

OUT OF THE WAY!

This 1910 cartoon of a Songhees man sitting in the road with an approaching motorist yelling "Out of the way!" illustrates the prevailing view of Indigenous peoples as obstacles to progress. An agreement was reached the following year to move the original Songhees reserve. | Victoria Daily Times, *May 16, 1910*

WESTWARD AND NORTHWARD, HO!

The greatest wave that ever swept across our great plains.

Settlement swept like a wave across the Canadian West, dispossessing Indigenous peoples from their territories as it went. | Toronto World, *November 14, 1902*

This 1916 poster for the Canadian Patriotic Fund, which shows an Indigenous man declaring "My skin is dark but my heart is white," is emblematic of the widespread racism of the time. | *Library and Archives Canada, 1989-378-1*

First Nations people had little say in the laws that governed their lives. They were denied the vote until the second half of the twentieth century, with a couple of exceptions. The *Indian Act* established a process of enfranchisement for some if they surrendered their Indian status (and received an individual land holding on the reserve) as part of eventual assimilation into the majority society. Also, from 1885 to 1898, some First Nations people in eastern Canada could vote; it was felt by parliamentarians that they were more "civilized" than First Nations people in western Canada as they had been under British influence for longer. Like Indigenous peoples in the Dependent Empire, most were ruled despotically and lacked political power. As one chief from Kahnawake complained, "The basis and scope of our Indian Act is wrong, and injurious to us, because it interferes with our enjoyments of natural and inherent rights. We have no voice whatever in legislation. We are often opposed to it and suffer from its effect."[25] Opposition was not universal. For example, the Grand Council of the Ojibway voted to accept the 1876 *Indian Act* after having made comments on a draft.[26] Usually, as we will see, First Nations opposition was ignored. Non-Indigenous people who sought to help First Nations people were denounced by government spokesmen as "outside agitators who excite the Indians and give them a false conception of their rights."[27]

Most settlers had little to do with their First Nations neighbours and were prejudiced against them (although there were exceptions, like James Teit, a fascinating amateur anthropologist and Aboriginal rights activist).[28] The settler attitude was reflected by Sara Jeannette Duncan in her novel *The Imperialist*, which refers to "drunken Indians vociferous on their way to the lock-up," and contains statements like "You can never trust an Indian."[29] The plot revolves around an election in which the First Nations people vote under the influence of the Indian agent, with the suggestion of corrupt payments.[30] As late as the 1970s, historians largely ignored First Nations peoples in their accounts of the history of Canada except as a problem to be overcome or an insignificant part of the background.[31]

Diamond Jenness, one of Canada's leading anthropologists, wrote in the 1930s of West Coast First Nations peoples: "Socially, they are outcasts, economically they are inefficient and an encumbrance. Their old world has fallen in ruins, and helpless in the face of a catastrophe they cannot understand, they

Colonialism reached all aspects of life, including style of dress, as illustrated by the clothing of this First Nations family on Canada's West Coast. | *Reprinted from William Halliday,* Potlatch and Totem and the Recollections of an Indian Agent *(London: Dent, 1935), page opposite 92.*

vainly seek refuge in its shattered foundations."[32] In this view, First Nations people were to be left in reserves on the margins of the new society, probably to die out or to be assimilated. In any event, to be kept out of the way, under control, and otherwise largely ignored. Their point of contact with the outside world was the Indian agent. It should be noted, however, that, in practice, some First Nations saw little of the Indian agent or the non-Indigenous government generally. The country was big, communications were limited, and there were relatively few agents.

The Indian agent had extensive power over the lives and property of band members, whose independence was correspondingly diminished. The agent's power came formally from the *Indian Act*. "In matters of schooling, management of band monies, reserve lands, wills and estates, local by-laws, community improvements, matters of health and welfare, the Department and especially the Superintendent, were the guiding and controlling powers."[33] An indication

An Indian agent, North-West Mounted Police officers, and Hudson's Bay Company officers meeting at Fort Pitt before the North-West Resistance of 1885. Thomas Quinn, the Indian agent (left), was shot during the Resistance by Wandering Spirit, who was later hanged. Next to him is Inspector Francis Dickens, son of author Charles Dickens, and next to Dickens is James Simpson, son of George Simpson, governor of the Hudson's Bay Company from 1821 to 1860. | *Library and Archives Canada, e007140851-v6*

Canada and Colonialism

of the importance of Indian agents to the scheme of the act is that the 1927 consolidation had about a hundred references to them. Among the most significant powers of the Indian agent was his ability to allocate welfare payments and housing among band members.[34]

Beneath this bureaucratic structure and regulation was the belief that First Nations people were incapable of managing their own affairs. Historian Scott Sheffield reviewed much material produced between 1930 and 1950, especially related to education, to determine the image administrators had developed of the "Indian." He concluded, "What emerges from this wealth of material is an antagonistic and often demeaning image of the wards under their jurisdiction."[35] First Nations people were characterized as lazy, irresponsible, and uncivilized. "Underlying the character traits of the [Indian Affairs Branch's] 'Indian' during the 1930s was a tone, both patronizing and paternalistic, that emphasized not only Native people's subordinate status as wards, but also their perceived cultural and intellectual inferiority."[36] They, therefore, had to be subjected to what was essentially a colonial system of government. Reserves became "a series of internal colonies,"[37] and the department was "cast in a strongly colonial mould."[38] The Indian agent was the Canadian form of the archetypal district officer who ruled Indigenous peoples throughout the British Empire before the Second World War, as discussed in Chapter 4. Indeed, the Canadian version continued until the 1960s, even after the district officer had mainly been replaced by professional administrators preparing colonies for self-government.[39]

One role played by the Indian agent was that of an intermediary between various types of First Nations and non-Indigenous interests. Such interests "revolved mainly around gaining access to Indian land and other natural resources, labour power and souls. These interests were articulated and pursued in a variety of ways and depended on the nature of the communities Superintendents lived and worked in."[40] Rather than letting First Nations people handle such matters themselves, department officials insisted on negotiating contracts for leases, timber, permits, woodcutting contracts, and similar agreements.[41] An example from the Musqueam Band in Vancouver was the role of the Indian agent in negotiating leases and the sale of timber from the reserve. The intermediary role even went so far that local tradesmen would send their bills to the department for payment on behalf of band members from band funds.[42]

Indian agents also had a role in First Nations communities that went beyond their formal powers. In 1979, anthropologist Michael Kew wrote of the Musqueam:

Musqueam people, as did all registered Indians in some degree, came to depend upon the Superintendent for [services under the *Indian Act*] and this dependence extended beyond the sphere of normal business matters and into the inter-personal and even domestic affairs ... The Indian Superintendent was, within the social system of the village, a figure of authority, a step above that of chief and council.[43]

It is little wonder that some Indian agents let this power "go to their heads" or became paternalistic. One of them is quoted as writing that "behind all the seeming indifference of the Indians for the officials of the Department, I am glad to say that in their heart, they know the Department is watching with a fatherly eye to their care and protection."[44]

Indeed, not all First Nations people had a negative view of Indian agents. In his book *Ruffled Feathers*, published soon after the 1969 White Paper on federal Indian policy came out, William Wuttenee of the Red Pheasant First Nation in Saskatchewan, a lawyer and a proponent of integration, said that Canadians should not malign the agents who had performed so well: "In spite of hardships, they stuck to their positions and they helped the Indian in the difficult period of transition from a nomadic culture to a settled life on the land." They acted as buffers between Indigenous people and settlers to ensure fair dealings, and they showed First Nations people the ways of the white man. "To the Indian agent Canada owes much for the progress made, the peaceful settlement of a country, and the ease of cultural transition from the days of buckskin and the feather into the 20th century."[45]

The Royal Commission on Aboriginal Peoples reported in 1996 that some Indian agents were persons of intelligence and integrity who would thwart some department policies, such as the enforcement of the laws banning potlaches and those restricting the use of agricultural machinery. The Commission continued:

By the same token, however, some Indian agents were petty despots who seemed to enjoy wielding enormous power over the remnants of once powerful Aboriginal nations. While much of their apparent disrespect can be attributed to the profound cultural differences between them and the Indian nations they were supervising, it is nonetheless clear that the Indian affairs branch often seemed to attract persons particularly imbued with the zeal associated with the strict morality and social Darwinism exhibited by deputy superintendents general Hayter Reed and Duncan Campbell Scott.[46]

Canada and Colonialism

Historian Jarvis Brownlie called the whole system "a government-sponsored tyranny" and "a primary source of oppression for Aboriginal people."[47] He continued: "Agents had many ways to control band councils if they so wished – by deposing individual members, by delaying relief payments, by refusing loan requests, and so on. The agent's range of powers enabled him to exact petty sorts of revenge on those who crossed him."[48] Another writer observed: "The powers held by an agent made him a formidable opponent: direct and unambiguous opposition by reserve residents could trigger unfavourable forms of retaliation."[49] It made sense to be on good terms with the Indian agent.[50]

Administration of Indian affairs became a goal in itself, and the primary objective of "civilizing Indians" so they could be assimilated was overlooked. There was a failure to develop specific policies, especially after the retirement of Duncan Campbell Scott in 1932. It was left to the schools to do whatever was necessary. In the view of one writer, who considered this issue in some detail, "Ultimately, what becomes clear is that many officials seemed to have abandoned the hope of achieving assimilation in the near future, although they still had to pay lip service to the policy."[51] There was, of course, a fundamental conflict between the interests of Indian agents and other department officials who were preparing "Indians" for assimilation while also preserving their jobs.

Indian agents often lacked the qualifications and experience required to exercise such extensive powers properly. Alan Fry recognized this lack of qualifications in his depressing semi-autobiographical novel about an Indian agent, based on his own background as an agent in British Columbia. The interview process for employment did not require much in the way of experience: "He had expected more penetration into what was after all a fearfully limited experience of the people themselves for someone now offering to make a life's work of solving their problems, but his brief association with a few individuals seemed in some ways to be sufficient."[52] Once employed, "he did worry at times ... about the extent to which he was making decisions in areas where more normally someone with professional qualifications ought to have been in charge." The professional people at the regional office "were few in number and spread thin; for much of the work, they could not be available and it was often a case of make your own decision or do without."[53]

There were few formal qualifications for Indian agents. Those hired were simply expected to be familiar with the office procedures and filing system of the Indian Affairs Branch.[54] There were "no special programs and no employees trained in long-range economic development. In fact, apart from a few engineers and surveyors, the department's staff had little training for their work."[55]

Patronage appears to have been the basis of recruitment up to the Second World War. As a result, some department officials were woefully under-qualified to adequately represent the interests of those for whom they were responsible. One author explained, "While [the Indian agents] were often patronizing, arbitrary, and autocratic, their main failing was that they were ineffectual in protecting Indian interests."[56] They fell far short of the ideal described by professor, and later senior colonial official, Herman Merivale in his 1840 lecture on colonialism. He called for "officers of the higher grade and highest importance" able to take the initiative.[57] Too often, they and their wards were at a severe disadvantage when dealing with better-qualified and experienced businessmen who knew how to look after their interests.

With the extensive powers granted to the Indian agent came a corresponding lack of authority on the part of band councils and a lack of respect for them.[58] Indian agents exercised significant authority over meetings of band councils. They called council meetings, acted as the chair, and expressed their views on matters before the council. Indian agents did not have a vote but could urge headquarters to veto band council decisions of which they disapproved.[59] The Indian agent in the novel written by Fry observes: "Band councils were often a farce. They were frequently elected in indifference, knowing little and caring less what their responsibilities might be. They went through the formalities of their work under [the Indian agent's] persuasion while he carried out all the substance of it."[60] This attitude was criticized by another writer: "He was right about the indifference, but not for the right reasons ... The lack of interest in band councils and their responsibilities was due largely because the substance of leadership had been taken away from them decades before, and had been handed over to Indian agents."[61] To some extent, chiefs and councillors became agents of the Indian agent. Chiefs and councillors signed a declaration under the *Indian Act,* promising to well and truly serve the Queen, obey all her laws and regulations, endeavour to prevent contraventions by any band member, and report any infractions to "the Indian agent over me."[62] This reflected the view of Alexander Morris that the numbered treaties he negotiated made chiefs and councillors "in a sense officers of the Crown" by paying them an annual salary.[63]

The Indians of British Columbia, a report commissioned by the Department of Citizenship and Immigration then responsible for the Indian Affairs Branch and published in 1958, was critical of the policy of direct administration that was "by far the most common in the Province," and of its associated paternalism. The principal authors – H.B. Hawthorn, C.S. Belshaw, and S.M. Jamieson, professors of anthropology and economics at the University of

British Columbia[64] – described the meeting procedures of band councils, not-ing the limited facilities and the fact that meetings were usually convened by the Indian agent and held in his presence. He prepared the agenda and the minutes and did not often approach councils to obtain their views on matters of policy.[65] The report declares:

> We have been astonished to find that ... all business of a financial kind is trans-acted through the superintendent's office, and that officials of the band council seldom come face to face with representatives of the groups with whom they have business. This is one of the most revealing lacks in the administration of Indian Affairs, since it documents with clarity our contention that the focus of administrative action is not the education of the Indian, except in a narrow formal sense, but the manipulation of his property.[66]

Also, "on every major issue, it is the superintendent and his staff who obtain the data, who sign the contracts, who see to it that the band makes no mis-takes."[67] The report made unfavourable comparisons between "Indian" admin-istration in British Columbia and colonial administration elsewhere, including the failure to follow the system of indirect rule described in Chapter 4.

The *Indian Act*

The *Indian Act* was at the heart of the system of internal colonialism adminis-tered by the Department of Indian Affairs through Indian agents. Canada's first prime minister, John A. Macdonald, was crucial to the creation and early ad-ministration of that legislation. He was also personally involved in the non-Indigenous settlement of Canada as a large-scale land developer and speculator.[68] Macdonald is best known as one of the fathers of Confederation and Canada's first prime minister. He also served as minister of Indian Affairs for much of the time he was prime minister, a position he held between 1867 and 1891 except for five years in opposition. This meant he was one of the longest-serving ministers and was involved in Indian Affairs for forty years. He played a pivotal role in developing both pre- and post-Confederation Indian policy, including changes to the *Indian Act,* promotion of residential schools, and banning First Nations ceremonies.[69] In the words of J.R. Miller, a historian of the relationship between Indigenous peoples and the government:

> Macdonald ... had a lengthy and influential role in dealing with First Nations in Canada. He moved adoption of what was probably the most enduring

element of policy a decade before Confederation. And, as prime minister, and as superintendent-general of Indian Affairs after 1867, he was instrumental in determining the shape and scope of Western treaties, reserve policy, economic "development" on reserves, and a swath of government program[s] that targeted First Nations' cultural identity, spiritual practices, and traditional governance. For good or ill, Macdonald was an architect of Canadian Indian policy. The foundation that he and his government laid would last largely unaltered until the middle of the twentieth century.[70]

Pre-Confederation policy was centred on the 1857 *Gradual Civilization Act*. It sought to assimilate First Nations people into non-Indigenous society. This approach continued for over a century despite their opposition. In introducing the legislation, Macdonald argued that it was a vital step in promoting the civilization of First Nations people.

Thirty years later, Macdonald explained the strategy followed by his government: "It is extremely inexpedient to deal with Indian bands ... as being in any way separate nations. They are governed by Canadian statutes ... The great aim of our civilization has been to do away with the tribal system and assimilate the Indian people in all respects with the inhabitants of the Dominion, as speedily as they are fit for the change."[71] Assimilation would not be easy. "Indians are Indians," he told Parliament, "and we must submit to frequent disappointment in the way of civilizing them."[72] "The general rule is that you cannot make the Indian a white man," although he allowed that education could enable some of them to succeed.[73] However he thought this would take generations.[74] "It is only by slow and patient coaxing and firmness at the same time alone that you can manage the Indians."[75] "There is only one way – patience, patience and patience ... In the course of ages – it is a slow process – they will be absorbed in the country."[76] The continuity represented by Macdonald's long involvement in Indian Affairs, his belief in racial and cultural supremacy, his denial of Indigenous sovereignty (First Nations as "separate nations"), his wish "to do away with the tribal system," and his promotion of assimilation were central features of Indian policy during the dispossession and assimilation stages. This policy was expressed primarily in the *Indian Act*, its predecessor legislation, and numerous amending provisions.

Under that legislation, Canadian authorities sought to control virtually all aspects of the lives of First Nations people from the cradle to the grave.[77] In his study of the history of the early legislation, James Milloy summarizes its impact:

Canada and Colonialism

The Canadian federal government ... took extensive control of reserves and tribal nations. Traditional Indian government was dismissed and replaced by Indian-agent-controlled models of white government. The ultimate control of finance and land use passed into federal hands. Governmental powers left with the tribes placed them, in the multi-layered Confederation, well below the position of a respectable municipality.[78]

In the view of Squamish hereditary chief Joe Mathias, an Indigenous leader, and Gary Yabsley, an Aboriginal law specialist, "From an Indian perspective, this legislation represents nothing less than a conspiracy. Examined as a whole, it exhibits a clear pattern founded in a conscious intent to eliminate Indians and 'indianness' from Canadian society."[79]

Among other things, the act provided for the registration of Indians; loss of Indian legal status; membership in bands; the allocation, management, sale, and lease of reserve lands; the management and distribution of band funds; limits on the sale of agricultural products and timber by Indians and the sale of alcohol to them; their education; the distribution of their property on death; the practice of their culture; and election of chiefs and band councils, and the delegation of limited municipal-type powers to them.[80] Through the act, the minister of Indian Affairs obtained extensive powers to make decisions for individuals and bands. The act conferred additional powers on the Governor-in-Council (the Canadian cabinet), including a broad authority to make regulations that superseded the bylaws made by band councils.[81]

The *Indian Act* occupied centre stage in the Canadian colonial legal attack on the First Nations way of life. It paralleled developments in other colonies, although none of them appear to have had such comprehensive legislation, except South Africa. Having noted the widespread conception of Indigenous peoples as wards in a state of tutelage, which prevailed in virtually all European colonies in Africa and Asia, one author wrote that the act "captures in miniature and precise ways the general outline of larger juridical constructs of subordination that, at one time, were applied to the greater portion of human beings throughout the planet." He concluded: "It can truly be said, therefore, that the Indian Act and the Indian Department together generated a culture that was an extreme distillation of Canada's colonial heritage and, at times, a veritable caricature of the most grotesque features of colonialism in action."[82]

Despite the central importance of the *Indian Act,* it should be remembered that numerous other laws supported colonialism and subordinated Indigenous peoples. For example, a stream of legislation in British Columbia had two consistent aims. First, the government took over access to resources that had previously been under the control of First Nations peoples; second, it gave settlers preferential access to these resources. These aims were reflected in fisheries, game, land, and resource laws.[83] First Nations people had no say in this legislation, having been denied the vote.[84] Even in areas without treaties, such as most of British Columbia, they were dispossessed of their lands and effectively restricted to reserves. At the same time, legislation expressly denied them the opportunity to acquire interests in land under the newly introduced legal system.[85] Indigenous laws were rarely recognized, and were certainly ignored in the granting of interests in land and resources to the settlers.[86]

Sometimes control was exercised by Indian agents and the police based on policy without any legal authority. This was the case with the pass system in effect from the 1880s to the 1930s, especially in the prairie provinces. This system required First Nations people who wanted to leave their reserve to obtain a pass signed by the Indian agent, who was sometimes located some distance away and might refuse the request. People without a pass or in violation of its terms could be taken into custody and summarily returned to their reserve.[87]

The *Indian Act* was designed to promote and enforce the government's approach of treating First Nations peoples as wards of the state and making them dependent on it, causing a resulting loss of control over their lives, lands, and resources. Indian policy was also designed to replace their communal values and traditions (Macdonald's "tribal system") with the more individualistic values of the settler society. In 1889, Edgar Dewdney, the superintendent-general of Indian Affairs, who played an important role in the relationship with First Nations peoples and settling the West, commented on "the growth of advanced ideas among the Indians," shown by a willingness to accept individual lots on reserves rather than communal ownership. In his report, Hayter Reed, the Indian commissioner who was instrumental in introducing the pass system and expanding the residential school system, added: "The work of sub-dividing reserves has begun in earnest. The policy of destroying the tribal or communist system is assailed in every possible way and every effort made to implant a system of individual responsibility instead."[88]

Colonial Origins

The origins of the current *Indian Act* go back to the early Victorian era and the start of the expansion leading to the height of the British Empire at the end of the era. This broader colonial context is crucial to understanding the legislation. First Nations activist Harold Cardinal pointed out, "The authors of the

Indian legislation were men who grew up in the imperialist, colonial era of the nineteenth century, and the act faithfully reflects their environment."[89] The early decades of the nineteenth century were the formative years for Canadian Indian policy as they were for much imperial policy. The first *Indian Act* with that name was passed in 1876, but its contents can be traced back to 1839 and the *Crown Lands Protection Act* of Upper Canada (now Ontario).[90] The basic policy behind the legislation of protection, paternalism, and assimilation resulted from commissions of inquiry conducted in the Canadas commencing with the Darling Report in 1828.[91] One historian describes the Bagot Commission Report of 1844, the most significant of about six reports, "as a distant echo of subsequent legislation in later decades."[92]

To protect reserve lands against trespass and damage from the rapidly growing settler population, the *Crown Lands Protection Act* was passed in Upper Canada in 1839. It treated "the lands appropriated for the residence of certain Indian Tribes" as Crown lands.[93] The legislation followed the paternalistic approach advocated by an extensive inquiry carried out by the Parliamentary Select Committee on Aboriginal Tribes in British settlements around the world, discussed in Chapter 2.[94] In practice, the restriction on trespass was difficult to enforce as settlers ignored it, and court decisions limited its scope.[95] Despite its limited practical impact, by treating the Crown as the formal owner of reserve lands with powers to appoint a commissioner to punish trespass by non-Indigenous people, the legislation established an important element of guardianship and government control over reserve lands that remains today.[96] It also took away the control that the First Nations had enjoyed historically over their lands and severely diminished their powers of self-government.

It is noteworthy and ironic that this legislation was passed in the same year as the Durham Report that led to internal self-government for the settlers through a system of responsible government.[97] The report called for "a system of responsible government as would give the people a real control over its own destinies ... The government of the Colony should henceforth be carried on in conformity with the views of the majority in the Assembly."[98] However, this "real control over [their] own destinies" was not to apply to the Indigenous peoples of the colonies.[99]

To implement the recommendations of the Bagot Commission, the government passed further legislation in 1850 to protect Indian reserve lands.[100] It became an offence in Upper Canada to deal directly with First Nations people for their lands. The legislation also expanded the provisions regarding trespass on reserve lands.[101] The lands were made exempt from taxation and seizure for debts.[102] This exemption was intended for the protection of First

Nations people. However, it limited their ability to obtain financing to improve their lands. A significant provision of the legislation for Lower Canada (now Quebec) was the appointment of a commissioner of Indian lands with absolute control over leasing and rentals.[103] This detailed control of the management of reserve lands established another critical element of government control over reserve properties that remains today.[104] A further notable provision was the first statutory definition of "Indian."[105] This provision as amended established the precedent that the government would decide who was legally considered an "Indian" and would do so following the patrilineal tradition of Europe, meaning that status could only be passed on through a father to his children. First Nations women who married non–First Nations men lost their status, as did their children. Both of these features of the Lower Canadian legislation were reflected in the various versions of the *Indian Act* that followed.[106]

However, implementation of the schemes for protection was still limited. In 1856, commissioners noted that few proposals had been tried or investigated and they were, "therefore ... still groping in the dark."[107]

The *Gradual Civilization Act* of 1857 promoted by Macdonald applied to the united Province of Canada (now Ontario and Quebec).[108] Its operating premise was that by eventually removing all legal distinctions between First Nations people and non-Indigenous people through the loss of Indian status (a process known as enfranchisement), and by promoting the acquisition of individual property by First Nations people, it would be possible over time to assimilate them as individuals. Eventually, First Nations communities would cease to exist.[109] From the perspective of eligible First Nations people, they were faced with a choice of giving up their First Nations status and communal rights in order to be free of the legal disabilities attached to such status, including ineligibility to vote. Something of the feelings evoked by the prospect of the loss of status was conveyed in a letter written by Frederick Ogilvie Loft (Onondeyoh), a Mohawk leader. He wrote to the then minister responsible for Indian Affairs, "It is my desire most respectfully to submit to you my most earnest dissent and disapproval of being enfranchised, on principle and ethics of it which involves denationalization. To be branded as an outcast from the bosom of my kin and native heath, would be to inflict a stigma on my conscience that could never be expiated."[110]

Under the 1857 act, to encourage enfranchisement of those who satisfied a demanding test of being literate, free of debt, and of high moral character, the superintendent-general of Indian Affairs could allot to enfranchised First Nations people up to fifty acres of reserve land. First Nations people saw this scheme as part of an attack on communal land rights and vigorously opposed it.[111] One leader described it as an attempt to "break them to pieces."[112] The sections for voluntary enfranchisement remained mostly unchanged in future versions of the *Indian Act*. There were relatively few voluntary enfranchisements, so the provisions were later supplemented by others for compulsory enfranchisement of First Nations people considered to be fit.[113]

Three years later, the *Indian Lands Act* was passed.[114] This act transferred authority for First Nations peoples and their lands from the Colonial Office in London to the colonial legislature. The transfer was not smooth: "The unsteady determination of the Colonial Office, thoroughly matched by the reluctance of colonial politicians to accept responsibility for Canada's Indian population, had caused several delays in the transfer of authority."[115] There was also much wrangling over responsibility for the fiscal deficit of the Indian Department. However protracted, it was still a significant turning point. It marked a departure from a fundamental principle of colonial administration that the imperial government should protect Indigenous peoples from the settler-dominated colonial governments. In place of this principle, the competing demand for colonial control of land prevailed. First Nations opposition to the transfer was ignored.[116] The legislation extended colonial laws on public lands to Indian land, and so confirmed government ownership and control and the non-recognition of property concepts applying under Indigenous law.[117] It also gave government control of the use of funds arising from the surrender of reserve lands.

Under the terms of the Canadian Confederation of 1867, "Indians, and Lands reserved for the Indians" were placed within federal and not provincial jurisdiction.[118] This was the only provision relating to Indigenous peoples. They were not consulted on it or any other aspect of the Canadian constitution passed by the UK Parliament. The new federal government soon introduced the first national legislation to consolidate the civilization and assimilation policy of the previous colonial legislatures. Parliament passed this legislation in 1868: *An Act providing for the organization of the Department of the Secretary of State of Canada and for the management of Indian and Ordnance Lands.*[119] In addition to consolidating much of the previous legislation, this act brought Nova Scotia and New Brunswick into the scheme initially developed for the Upper and Lower Canadas.

The following year saw the passage of the *Gradual Enfranchisement Act 1869*.[120] In it, Parliament acknowledged assimilation as the objective of Indian policy. The act included enfranchisement provisions similar to those in the *Gradual Civilization Act* of 1857.[121] The most significant changes, however, were intended to implement Macdonald's "great aim ... to do away with the

tribal system" by replacing traditional governments. Provisions that were incorporated into later versions of the *Indian Act* conferred on elected councils
limited municipal-style powers over public health; order and decorum at public assemblies; "intemperance and profligacy"; trespass by cattle, roads, bridges,
ditches, and fences; schools and other public buildings; and pounds.[122] The objective of the legislation was summarized by William Spragge, deputy superintendent, as "establishing a responsible for an irresponsible system" and so
paving "the way to the establishment of simple municipal institutions."[123] The
authority given to band councils was limited and that of the federal government was extended. There were no powers of enforcement, and all council
powers were "subject to confirmation by the Governor in Council."[124] Government officials decided to which bands the elected system would apply, and
the consent of band members was not required. First Nations were generally
opposed to the changes, but the government persisted and expanded the system.[125] The governor could also depose chiefs for dishonesty, intemperance, or
immorality.[126] None of these terms were defined, giving officials broad discretion. In 1874, Parliament extended the legislation to Manitoba and British
Columbia upon their inclusion in Confederation.[127]

The *Indian Act* of 1876 and Amendments

The decades between 1870 and 1890 brought significant changes in senior Indian Department personnel, the consolidation of Indian legislation, new legislation, and an expanded role for the department's central office in Ottawa.
These changes resulted in part from the purchase of Rupert's Land and the
North-Western Territory from the Hudson's Bay Company, and the westward
expansion of non-Indigenous settlement. The acquisition of these vast lands,
with their First Nations populations who had previously been largely left alone
by the company, necessitated a more comprehensive legislative and bureaucratic approach to the control and administration of Indian affairs.[128] Once
these changes were implemented, and the prospect of any repetition of the
1885 North-West Resistance receded, the department was largely left to itself
for many decades, with Indian affairs receiving little attention from the politicians or public except when the costs of the department were considered. It
was something of a backwater.[129] The long-serving member of Parliament G.E.
Foster complained in 1909 that "It is only once a year in parliament that we can
devote half an hour to a talk on the Indian question when these estimates are
being considered."[130]

The first act to be called the *Indian Act* was passed in 1876 as a consoli-dation of the existing Indian legislation.[131] With further consolidations in 1880, 1886, 1906, and 1927, and numerous amending statutes (about thirty in total), it was to remain substantially in effect until the revision of 1951. "Civilization" leading to assimilation was the objective. The minister of the Department of the Interior, David Laird, stated in the department's 1876 Annual Report:

> Our Indian legislation generally rests on the principle, that the aborigines are to be kept in a condition of tutelage and treated as wards or children of the State. The soundness of this principle I cannot admit. On the contrary, I am firmly persuaded that the true interests of the aborigines and of the State alike require that every effort should be made to aid the red man in lifting himself out of his condition of tutelage and dependence, and that it is clearly our wis-dom and our duty, through education and every other means, to prepare him for a higher civilization by encouraging him to assume the privileges and re-sponsibilities of full citizenship.[132]

Debate on the draft act was not contentious, and it met widespread approval from the parliamentarians who, of course, did not include any First Nations people. The 1876 act was more detailed and clearer than earlier legislation but did not make any radical changes.[133] "Its general approach and basic philoso-phy ... revealed little change since 1830."[134] Additional steps were taken to en-courage assimilation through enfranchisement.

A new Department of Indian Affairs to replace the Indian Branch of the Department of the Interior was created by the 1880 consolidation.[135] Generally, the consolidated act of 1880 merely restated the provisions of the 1876 act. However, a significant section gave the Governor-in-Council the ability to de-cide how money from the sale of reserve lands or other resources would be spent, denying that power to band governments.[136] Power was also given to replace hereditary chiefs determined under traditional practices with chiefs elected under the act, who were to be the spokesmen for the band.[137]

An amendment in 1884 gave power to the superintendent-general to pro-hibit the sale or gift of ammunition to First Nations people in Manitoba or the North-West Territories.[138] This was a time of growing unrest in the area, which was to lead to the North-West Resistance, and the execution of Louis Riel, the Métis leader, the following year. A further amendment expanded the powers of the minister to lease lands without a surrender from the band.

Poundmaker (front row, right), Mistahimaskwa (Big Bear) (front row, second from left), and Mistahimaskwa's son (front row, left) with Canadian officials and priests at the Regina NWMP barracks following the suppression of the North-West Resistance, 1885. | *O.B. Buell, Library and Archives Canada, C-001872*

The North-West Mounted Police was founded in 1873 to keep order in the new North-West, including preventing any Indigenous resistance. This photo shows NWMP officers and Indigenous scouts, Black Eagle and Elk Facing The Wind, at Fort Macleod, Alberta, 1890. | *Steele and Company, Glenbow Library and Archives Collection, Libraries and Cultural Resources Digital Collections, University of Calgary, CU1138291*

Another amendment attacked First Nations culture in British Columbia, an initial restriction that would later be expanded. It banned the gift-giving ceremonies known as the "Potlatch" and the "Tamanawas" dance, another traditional spiritual ceremony.[139] Explaining the legislation, Macdonald claimed the potlatch was the cause of a great deal of misery and demoralization and involved "all kinds of orgies."[140] It was this legislation that Indian agent William Halliday was to enforce so vigorously. Parliament extended the prohibition a decade later to cover other traditional dances, including the Sun Dance performed by several First Nations in the prairies.[141] In practice, these prohibitions drove the ceremonies underground, and they were revived and openly carried out following the removal of the bans in 1951.[142]

The *Indian Advancement Act* was also passed in 1884. Its full title summarizes its purpose: *An Act for conferring certain privileges on the more advanced Bands of the Indians of Canada, with the view of training them for the exercise of municipal powers.*[143] Like earlier legislation, it was designed to substitute a colonial form of government for Indigenous forms. However, it was only to apply to "advanced" bands in eastern Canada. The Governor-in-Council had the power to move them to a "one-year" elective band council following a municipal government model. Band councils could legislate in additional areas, including public health and taxation of the real property of band members. Continuing the pattern of paternalism, the superintendent-general, acting through Indian agents, was given the ability to direct all aspects of the elections and to call, participate in, and adjourn band council meetings, although he did not have a vote.[144] As a result of resentment against this further interference into their affairs, few bands elected to come under the purview of the act.

In 1885, changes were made to the federal franchise by the *Electoral Franchise Act* to permit First Nations men owning real property with a value of at least $150 to vote in federal elections.[145] The opposition Liberals were against the extension of the franchise, especially to First Nations men in the western bands, some of whom had taken part in the North-West Resistance of that year. They accused Macdonald of currying votes. According to David Mills, their spokesman, the legislation would have given the vote to "men who are massacring women and children in the North-West."[146] As enacted, the act was limited to members of eastern bands.[147] It was repealed in 1898 by a Liberal government.[148] The Conservative opposition leader, Sir Charles Tupper, claimed that Wilfrid Laurier's "first important act [as prime minister] is to take away the franchise from a large body of British subjects in this Dominion who at the present time enjoy it."[149] However, despite the jibe, no subsequent government of either party restored to First Nations people the franchise generally until 1960.[150]

Longer-lasting amendments in 1894 established the legal foundation for the expansion of the notorious residential school system that has had, and continues to have, such detrimental impacts on First Nations communities. The amendments were intended to secure the compulsory attendance of children at school and permitted "the arrest and conveyance to school, and detention there, of truant children," and the punishment of parents and guardians who failed to send their children to school. In addition, the legislation gave the Governor-in-Council the power to make regulations to establish industrial and boarding schools.[151] Such schools had existed since the 1830s and had received government funding.[152] In 1883, Macdonald had explained their purpose in words dripping with the racial supremacy that dominated the thinking of rulers throughout the Empire:

> When the school is on the reserve the child lives with its parents who are savages; he is surrounded by savages, and though he may learn to read and write, his habits, and training and mode of thought are Indian. He is simply a savage who can read and write. It has been strongly pressed on myself, as the head of the Department, that Indian children should be withdrawn as much as possible from the parental influence, and the only way to do that would be to put them in central training industrial schools where they will acquire the habits and modes of thought of white men.[153]

The amendments strengthened government support for the schools, which were predominantly run by churches. The legislation had been promoted by Hayter Reed, now deputy minister of Indian Affairs, who enthusiastically encouraged officials to use their new powers.[154] The intent of these institutions was to assimilate the children, who were forbidden to speak their languages and were separated from their families and cultures.

The growing needs of settler communities for more land and services, and their opposition to having reserves near them, led to further legislation.[155] This legislation was enthusiastically promoted by Frank Oliver, who was both minister of the interior responsible for migration and settlement and the superintendent-general of Indian Affairs from 1905 to 1911. He had long been clear regarding the need for more land to be made available to settlers. "Now is the time," he wrote in one of his newspaper editorials in 1881, "for the government to declare ... whether the country is to be run in the interests of the settlers or the Indians."[156] During his term as the responsible minister, he decisively answered that question, although there really had been no doubt. Changes to the *Indian Act* were made to induce First Nations to surrender reserve lands. An

Canada and Colonialism

Residential school at Alert Bay, British Columbia, proudly displaying the Union Jack, 1929. Such schools did enormous harm to Indigenous people. | *Reprinted from William Halliday, Potlatch and Totem and the Recollections of an Indian Agent (London: Dent, 1935), page opposite 192*

amendment in 1906 permitted the distribution to band members of 50 percent of the proceeds of land sales, instead of the previously specified 10 percent.[157] Other legislation permitted the expropriation of reserve land without any requirement for a surrender by band members, a requirement that has been in place since the Royal Proclamation of 1763. This exception was extended by an amendment in 1911 that authorized any company, municipality, or other authority with statutory expropriation powers to exercise those powers on reserves.[158]

Under another amendment made at the same time, if a judge found that it was "expedient" to do so, he could make an order to relocate a reserve within or adjoining a municipality of at least eight thousand people. Again, no band consent or surrender was required.[159] In introducing the proposed legislation, Oliver explained, "It is not right that the requirements of the expansion of white settlement should be ignored, – that is, that the right of the Indian should be allowed to become a wrong to the white man."[160] Nor would First Nations be permitted to appoint a lawyer to represent them. Oliver thought that allowing First Nations people to have their own lawyers was "a very dangerous proposal." He explained that, "if the sound judgment of the Indians could be depended upon to be exercised in the protection of their own interests, there would be no necessity for the Indian Act or for the supervision that parliament has placed over them."[161] Opposition from Indigenous groups was again rejected.[162] The government's efforts to encourage surrenders was highly successful. By 1913, over a fifth of the land set aside under the treaties for prairie First Nations had been surrendered.[163]

During and after the First World War, the powers of Indian agents to control expressions of culture and manage Indian reserve property continued to grow. It was made an offence in the western provinces and the territories to participate in dances outside of a First Nations person's own reserve or to wear an "aboriginal costume" without the consent of the superintendent-general.[164] An amendment in 1918 further extended the power of the superintendent-general to lease reserve lands without a surrender by the band members if the lease was to enable cultivation or grazing on uncultivated lands.[165] In 1919, the superintendent-general was given the power to issue leases of surface rights in a reserve in connection with the mining of precious metals. Again, there was no requirement to obtain a surrender or band consent. At first, compensation for damage was to be paid, but this requirement was later dropped.[166]

The 1920s saw further restrictions. One amendment in 1920 significantly increased the government's powers over school attendance for First Nations children, including at residential schools.[167] Provisions were passed to enable compulsory enfranchisement. They were opposed by First Nations leaders such as Frederick Loft (Onondeyoh), an army veteran and a founder of the League of Indians of Canada, which was critical of the Department of Indian Affairs.[168] Scott was unsuccessful in his attempt to enfranchise his opponent and remove him as a threat.[169] Another restriction resulted from a committee of the Senate and House of Commons appointed in 1927 to look into land claims in British Columbia.[170] Despite all the evidence to the contrary that was placed before it, the committee found that the province had been acquired by conquest, denied the existence of Aboriginal title, and asserted that First Nations groups had accepted the policy of the government "without demur." The committee claimed that "designing white men" had deceived them "to expect benefits from claims more or less fictitious." It concluded that "the matter should now be regarded as finally closed."[171] Restrictions on receiving payment to pursue land claims were introduced in the same year. They prevented the retention of lawyers, thus avoiding any judicial determination of the validity of such claims.[172] Another consolidation of the *Indian Act* took place in 1927.[173] Just as 1930 can be seen as the height of the territorial extent of the British Empire as discussed in Chapter 2, it can also be seen as the height of restrictions under the *Indian Act*.

An amendment in 1936 gave further powers to the Indian agents to preside at and direct band council meetings. The agent was given a casting vote if there was an equality of votes in council elections.[174] A further amendment authorized the superintendent-general to make additional regulations covering specific topics, including regulations incorporating by reference provincial laws.[175] In *The Historical Development of the Indian Act,* John Leslie and Ron Maguire comment, "Essentially, the Superintendent-General acquired the power to apply existing provincial laws to reserves as he saw fit."[176] This was the beginning of a trend in favour of enlarging the jurisdiction of the provinces over First Nations that continues today.

Few further changes were made to the legislation until after the Second World War. In 1950, amendments to the *Dominion Elections Act* extended the federal vote to First Nations people, but only if they were willing to give up their exemption from the taxation of reserve property, which many First Nations considered a treaty right.[177] The requirement for a waiver was not removed until 1960, when First Nations people became generally entitled to vote in federal elections.[178]

Commenting on the numerous amendments made between 1876 and 1950, Richard Bartlett, a professor of law, writes:

> The astonishing feature of the amendments up to 1950 is how little, despite their frequency, they sought to accomplish. They were always preoccupied with details and never contradicted the basic rationale of the Indian Act, which demanded "civilization" and responsibility from the Indian population while denying them control over the forces affecting their lives.[179]

The Revised *Indian Act* of 1951

Following a review by a joint committee of the Senate and House of Commons and some consultations with First Nations, a revised *Indian Act* was eventually passed in 1951.[180] The more draconian provisions, such as banning potlaches and discouraging land claims, were dropped. However, the revised act remained fundamentally the same as the original *Indian Act* of 1876 that, as we have seen, reflected yet earlier legislation. Assimilation and destruction of the tribal system remained the goal, as had been stated by Macdonald in 1887. The number of discretionary powers that the minister could exercise was reduced, but his powers and those of the Governor-in-Council remained formidable.[181] The minister could still impose a system of elected band councils to replace customary systems of government.[182] The powers of band councils remained very limited and unclear compared with those of a municipal council. An important extension of provincial power was included in section 88, which made First Nations people subject to "all [provincial] laws of general application." Among other things, this led to the "Sixties Scoop" in which large numbers of Indigenous children were taken into care just as the residential school era was ending.[183]

Historian John Leslie summarizes the "eerie continuity" of the government's approach to First Nations people from the 1830s to the 1960s – an approach based on their assimilation (recast as "integration") into the mainstream society without special rights (save for limited historical treaty rights):

> Despite attempts at camouflage by non-Native policy-makers, the basic tenets of post-war Indian policy maintained an eerie continuity with the nineteenth century, particularly in terms of philosophy, policy objectives, and administrative practices ... the fundamental objective of post-war Indian policy remained essentially the same as framed by government officials in the 1830s: give Indian people access to education, instil notions of private property, confer political and civil rights and, like recent European immigrants, Indians will become self-supporting citizens.[184]

The 1960s and the White Paper of 1969

In 1966, the federal government commissioned another report under the chairmanship of Professor Harry Hawthorn to review the situation of First Nations in Canada. The report concluded that the system established by the various historical *Indian Acts* was one of "internal colonialism," with the Indian Affairs Branch described as a "quasi-colonial government,"[185] which was involved in a "holding operation"[186] rather than in promoting active self-government. The report commented that, despite a century of band council experience, the limited and supervised nature of the powers available to bands meant that "it remains essentially true that most Indian communities are administered rather than self-governing."[187]

The Hawthorn Report recommended significant changes to Indian policy and, in particular, the recognition of First Nations peoples as "Citizens Plus" with special rights and status in addition to the rights of Canadians.[188] It rejected the policy of assimilation. These recommendations were generally well received by First Nations peoples and by officials in the Department of Indian Affairs and Northern Development.[189] However, the most far-reaching recommendations regarding special rights and ending assimilation policies were dismissed by the government, as shown by the *Statement of the Government of Canada on Indian Policy* ("the White Paper") announced in June 1969.[190]

Canada and Colonialism

The White Paper was issued as part of the Liberal's "Just Society" program.[191] It reasserted the policy of assimilation and rejected any unique legal status for "Indians," which it saw as the cause of their disadvantaged position. The White Paper declared, "The separate status and the policies which have flowed from it have kept the Indian people apart from and behind other Canadians." It claimed they had travelled "the road of different status, a road that has led to a blind alley of deprivation and frustration." It proposed, instead, that they take "a road that would lead gradually away from different status to full social, economic and political participation in Canadian life." This proposal meant Indian status would be terminated to remove "the legislative and constitutional basis of discrimination." The Department of Indian Affairs would also be abolished. Likewise, section 91(24) of the *British North America Act*,[192] which gave the federal government the power to legislate for "Indians, and Lands reserved for the Indians," would be repealed. Resistance by Indigenous peoples caused the government to withdraw the White Paper and brought the displacement and assimilation era to an end. This ushered in the era of reconciliation.

The 1951 *Indian Act* and revisions were consolidated in 1970,[193] and again in 1985.[194] There have been amendments to specific sections but relatively few significant changes. Despite the movement toward reconciliation, this colonial legislation continues in force, like some Victorian spectre rattling its chains on Indian reserves across the country.

◄◄•►►

We considered in Chapter 3 the acquisition of self-government powers within Canada, and this chapter has considered their exercise with regard to First Nations peoples. Chapter 7 will continue the discussion by examining Canada's acquisition of independence and the path to self-government and independence in the dependent colonies and especially India. It will then examine how the Indigenous peoples of Canada have fared to date with regard to self-government and the process of "reconciliation."

Independence, Self-Government, and Reconciliation

In 1927, Lester Pearson was a young professor of history and, like most of his contemporaries, an imperialist.[1] He was later to become a Liberal prime minister of Canada and would receive a Nobel Prize for his work in resolving the 1956 Suez Crisis, caused by the UK invasion of Egypt. Concluding a lecture, he said he looked forward with confidence a hundred years ahead to a course on the successful solution of Britain's imperial problems in the twentieth century.[2] There were a few dissenters, such as the author of a 1905 pamphlet purporting to be a history of the decline and fall of the Empire written by a Japanese historian in 2005.[3] However, most other imperialists also looked forward to a long-term continuation of the Empire. It was not to be.

George Woodcock, the Canadian writer, historian, literary critic, philosopher, and anarchist, appears to be unique in giving Canada central stage as the culprit in his book *Who Killed the British Empire?*[4] He maintains that "it was ... Canada, even more than Ireland, [that] acted as a pioneer in initiating the long chain of modifications in status among the British possessions that led to the final liquidation of the Second Empire."[5] In his view, there was a causal link between independence in Canada and the independence of India in 1947, which was a key step toward the end of the Empire:

> Gandhi's task would have been immeasurably more difficult if the struggle he began in India in 1919 had not followed a century of Canadian work for colonial independence ... Without the example of Canada's struggle and its development of the concept of dominion status, India would not have made that

half-step to freedom she had already achieved in 1935 with provincial self-government, and without that half-step her liberation after the war would have been a longer and perhaps a much more violent process.[6]

Woodcock wrote widely on many topics in over forty books, including several that covered Canada and India, a country he visited often and knew well. He may have been overly dramatic in both the title of his book and his reference to "Canada's struggle." Still, he was correct that India followed the steps taken by Canada toward self-government and independence.[7] However, India's journey was much later, more hard-fought, went further, and ultimately led to a different and more definitive form of independence. Within Canada, the journey toward self-government for Indigenous peoples has trailed far behind that of India and the other former dependent colonies, and there is much distance still to go. As highlighted by the Royal Commission on Aboriginal Peoples, given their minority status and the small size of Indigenous groups, they are not nation-states seeking independence from Canada, unlike India.[8]

Canada's Path to Independence

We saw in Chapter 3 that self-government came easily and early to Canada in the mid-nineteenth century. Despite Woodcock's reference to "Canada's struggle," independence was available for the asking from about that time.

Ambivalent Independence

In strong contrast to the UK's attitude to the Dependent Empire, it did not oppose independence in principle for the settler colonies. From the 1840s, it consistently said their continued presence within the Empire had to be voluntary. The defeat by, and loss of, the American colonies was not forgotten.[9] William Gladstone (when Colonial Secretary) wrote in 1846:

> It is to the free and loyal attachment of the Canadians at large that Her Majesty will ever look for the maintenance of the connection between the Province and this country.
>
> It is not her desire that it should subsist upon a narrower basis than that of cordial good will and reciprocal advantage. The connection of this country with its transmarine possessions cannot be maintained through coercion or through any vexatious thwarting of the social tendencies of the communities by which they are inhabited; nor ought they to be so maintained even if it were possible.[10]

At the same time, the Colonial Secretary instructed the governor of Nova Scotia, "It is neither possible nor desirable to carry on the Government of any of the British provinces in North America in opposition to the opinion of the inhabitants."[11]

In a lecture delivered in 1858, James Stephen, who had been the most senior official in the Colonial Office, acknowledged that the Canadian colonies might insist on being "as independent in form and in name as they are already in truth and reality. And when that demand shall be so made, is there a man among us who would discharge, I do not say a single cannon, but so much as a single lucifer-match, to resist it? May the union be perpetual; but if it shall ever cease to be spontaneous and cordial, it will also cease to be valuable."[12] He had earlier expressed his view that "it remains for Canadians to cut the last cable which anchors them to us. But it is for them, not for us to take that step, and to assume the consequent responsibility."[13] There was a reluctance to do so. The benefits of remaining a settler colony, especially the defence provided by the imperial government at no cost, were too great.

A decade later, a declaration was made at the highest level that expressly recognized Canada's growing independence. Lord Granville, the Colonial Secretary, stated the government's view:

> It has been more and more felt on both sides that Canada is part of the British Empire because she desires to be so, and that under the influence of this conviction the attachment of the Colonies to Great Britain had grown with the growth of their independence. Her Majesty's Government value the existing relations as the symbol and support of that attachment. They value it while it is valued by the Canadians and while it is useful to the Canadians. They have no desire to maintain it for a single year after it has become injurious or distasteful to them.[14]

In private correspondence, he wrote that the best solution to the lingering threat of annexation by the United States "would probably be that in the course of time and in the most friendly spirit the Dominion should find itself strong enough to proclaim her independence."[15] Sir John Young, the governor general, delivered a speech in Quebec in 1869 in which he declared that Canada was "at the present moment ... in reality independent" and England would give effect to the wishes of Canada's statesmen on the proper form of the alliance.[16] A few years later, the Earl of Dufferin, another governor general, referred to Canada's earlier lack of self-confidence and assertion compared with the United States and welcomed the growing feeling of independence, which was not "antagonistic to our interests."[17] Some British politicians went further and actively urged independence in order to cut the costs of defending Canada.[18]

Clearly, any effort made by Canada to obtain greater independence was pushing on an open door. The support for Canadian self-government and, if desired, independence did not mean that there were no attempts by some government departments in the British government to assert their ever-decreasing authority, but when this happened, the Colonial Office stepped in to uphold Canada's point of view.[19] Also, UK politicians had no hesitation in seeking a contribution from Canada for common imperial expenses, especially for naval protection.

Canadian politicians also made statements confirming Canadian independence but in somewhat more ambivalent terms. In 1896, Sir Charles Tupper (soon to be prime minister) told the House of Commons:

> I need not remind you that, so far as government is concerned, Canada is practically independent. I need not remind you that, so far as measures relating to the internal life of Canada are concerned, we have practically the uncontrolled administration of our own affairs ... I need not remind the House that under this improved status, foreign affairs touching Canada are to a large extent placed under our control.[20]

Explaining Canadian support for the Boer War in 1900, Laurier announced to the House:

> What we have done, we have done ... in the plenitude, in the majesty of our colonial legislative independence. I claim for Canada, this, that in the future, Canada shall be at liberty to act, or not to act, to interfere or not to interfere, to do just as she pleases; and that she shall reserve to herself the right to judge whether or not there is cause for her to act ... We are independent, as I said in London, absolutely independent.[21]

Despite the words "absolutely independent," the earlier reference to "our colonial legislative independence" expresses the sense of continuing attachment to the Empire but with the right of Canada to decide independently what to do. It was independence within the Empire. Three years later, Laurier somewhat inconsistently described Canada as "a dependency of the British Crown." He was expressing his disapproval of the Alaska boundary settlement, in which a British judge had found against Canada: "So long as Canada remains a dependency of the British Crown the present powers we have are not sufficient for the maintenance of our rights."[22]

The Conservative prime minister, Robert Borden, was more sympathetic to British wishes for a unified imperial policy. However, he shared the view that the policy could no longer be under the sole control of the UK government, especially given the sacrifices made by Canada and the other dominions in the First World War.[23] He also opposed the threat posed by imperial federation to Canadian autonomy. Laurier's successor as Liberal prime minister, Mackenzie King, was more assertive. He saw Canada as "a nation within the British Empire, not Canada a colony," and the British Empire as a "co-operative commonwealth."[24] When the Canadian Parliament independently declared war in 1939, he wrote, "Canada stands as a nation not only among the nations of the British Commonwealth, but as a nation among the nations of the world – a young nation with a bright light in her eyes and the spirit of idealistic youth."[25]

Support for Canadian independence was not universal. In "Greater Canada, an Appeal," a lecture delivered in 1907, Stephen Leacock rejected it: "Nor is it ever possible or desirable that we in Canada can form an independent country ... Independent we could not survive a decade."[26] He later explained, "The smaller destiny of isolated independence is set aside in favour of participating in the plenitude of power possible in [imperial] union."[27] Borden told Parliament two years later, "I am not one of those who look to see the integrity of the British empire menaced by the future independence of Canada."[28] Giving a speech to the Empire Club of Canada in 1914, R.B. Bennett, then a member of Parliament and later prime minister, was so passionate about the responsibilities of being a trustee for the "subject races" of the Empire and the imperial mission of civilizing them and settling immigrants that he cast aside talk of Canadian independence:

> I hold it true that no British statesman will lift his hand if we say we must become independent. Time after time they have said, If the time has come that you must cut the painter and drift out in the open sea, and take upon yourself the high responsibilities and burdens of independence, we will not say you Nay. But I do not believe that finally Canadians desire that we should become an independent people.
>
> ... [What] a trust is ours, what a trust is ours! What a splendid trust it is, to think that you and I are the trustees for posterity, that you and I will one day be measured by the manner in which we have discharged our obligations to those subject races and the millions of people that one day must fill the great fertile fields of the west [of Canada], the great plains of Australia, that will

Canada and Colonialism

cover the great plains of South Africa and New Zealand. If that thought sinks into our minds, how can you and I think of independence, how can we be concerned about an independent Canada? (Applause).[29]

The benefits and responsibilities of being part of the Empire, the ruling part, clearly outweighed the benefits of independence for him. Independence would mean that Canadians were "afraid to accept the responsibilities of our race and breed; afraid to think we are Britons."

Control over Foreign Affairs and Defence

After internal self-government was conceded in the first part of the nineteenth century, the key to greater Canadian independence was control over foreign affairs and defence.[30] Here, there was more tension as the UK government (and some dominion governments) thought that imperial unity depended on having a common policy and shared resources, such as one navy, for which the dominions should pay their share. Gradually, however, it lost the argument as more and more powers were conceded to, or assumed by, the dominions.[31]

Canada's first prime minister, John A. Macdonald, sat in on the negotiation of the Washington Treaty of 1871. British forces were withdrawn from Canada in that year, except for those at the naval bases at Esquimalt and Halifax that policed the Pacific and the Atlantic.[32] Canadian troops put down the North-West Resistance of 1885 without British assistance. The British Navy transferred the naval bases to Canada in 1906. Officials at the Colonial Office responsible for the relationship with Canada were increasingly available for other work. "While the Colonial Office received information from Canada regularly, little of it required decision or substantive response."[33]

By 1907, no treaties bound Canada unless she had assented to them.[34] One commentator said in that year that "Canada is today mistress of her own destinies and can exercise that greatest right of Independence – the right to do as she pleases."[35] A Department of External Affairs was established in 1909. However, its staff, responsibilities, and ambitions were still modest. Its founder, Sir Joseph Pope, wrote, "Canada by herself is not a nation and I hope I may never live to see her one."[36] Amidst controversy, the Canadian Naval Service was formed in 1910 following Laurier's rejection of British attempts to get financial support for a joint imperial navy. From 1887, a series of colonial (renamed "imperial" in 1907) conferences increasingly recognized dominion power in imperial affairs. The conferences witnessed Laurier's successful opposition to attempts by British politicians at centralized imperialism and an imperial federation. Canada was committed to the First World War by a declaration made on its behalf by the governor general, acting as the representative of the imperial government. However, it participated in the Imperial War Cabinet. Following the end of the war, it signed the Treaty of Versailles and became a member of the League of Nations in its own right (which the Americans thought was intended to increase British votes).

Albert Dicey, a leading constitutional scholar, summarized the slow progress toward independence. He wrote in 1885 that the white colonies were "most nearly independent states," although not sovereign because the UK Parliament was visible in the background with power to legislate for the whole Empire and control foreign affairs.[37] Thirty years later, he said they had "as much of independence as is compatible with each Dominion remaining part of the Empire."[38] Canada and the other white colonies were described as "dominions" following the 1907 imperial conference, where Laurier complained about being lumped together with Trinidad and Barbados as a mere colony. The term "dominion" had been used in the *British North America Act 1867* in reference to the monarch's authority over Canada after UK politicians had rejected the Canadian request for "kingdom" as offensive to the republican US. It signified "more than a colony but less than an independent state. Dominion status was a half-way house between dependent status and sovereign status."[39]

Matters came to a head and were resolved in the 1920s.[40] Canadian prime minister Arthur Meighen successfully opposed the renewal of an alliance between Britain and Japan in 1921, a decision with considerable consequences twenty years later.[41] The following year, his successor, Mackenzie King, refused to assist the British when they faced a perceived threat from Turkey at Chanak. In 1923, Canada signed a treaty with the US on halibut fishing without British involvement. In the words of one writer, King "had swum to national independence holding the tail of a halibut."[42] Also in that year, Canada refused to ratify the Treaty of Lausanne, negotiated by the British with Turkey to resolve the conflict that had arisen between the Ottoman Empire and the British Empire and its allies on the grounds that Canada had not been involved in its negotiation. George Bernard Shaw described the UK perspective in 1928:

> Look at Australia, New Zealand, and Canada. We did not dare coerce them after our failure in North America. We provide a costly fleet gratuitously to protect their shores from invasion. We give them preferences in trade whilst allowing them to set up heavy protective duties against us. We allow them to be represented at international congresses as if they were independent nations.

We even allow them access to the King independently of the London Cabinet. The result is that they hang on to us with tyrannical devotion, waving the Union Jack as enthusiastically as the Americans wave their Stars and Stripes.[43]

He suggested that the UK itself might wish to be independent of the Empire.

The dominions, led by South Africa, the Irish Free State, and Canada, had asserted their independence, and it only remained for the form of imperial relations to be changed to confirm this reality. That was to come with the Balfour Formula agreed upon at the imperial conference in 1926. This followed a number of earlier conferences in which progress was slow and uncertain. As Mackenzie King noted, it was a challenge to find sufficient common ground among "a British community of nations ... scattered over the globe" in the "absence of precedent for the experiment in co-operation which members are working out."[44] The formula confirmed that Great Britain and the dominions were "autonomous Communities within the British Empire, equal in status, in no way subordinate one to another." In 1931, the *Statute of Westminster*, passed by the UK Parliament, put that political reality into legal form.[45] This statute said the UK Parliament could not legislate for dominions without their consent, freed them from any limitation on their legislative powers, confirmed their control over foreign affairs, and changed the definition of "colonies" to exclude the dominions. So far as the country, and its non-Indigenous population, was concerned, "decolonization" was now official. At Canada's request, due to disagreement with the provinces over how changes could be made to the constitution, the *Statute of Westminster* prevented Canada from amending its constitution. This prohibition was repealed in 1982 as part of the so-called patriation of the constitution. Despite this self-imposed limitation and the absence of any declaration of independence, Canada's sovereignty and independence can be regarded as a political fact since 1931, although the legal situation remains not entirely free from doubt.[46]

As expressed by Arthur Lower, one of Canada's leading historians, "There is good ground for holding December 11, 1931 as Canada's Independence Day, for on that day she became a sovereign state."[47] Leading constitutional scholar Frank Scott said the *Statute of Westminster* (a UK statute) ensured "complete national independence."[48] At the same time, any pretence of imperial unity was at an end.[49] In 1943, the UK Home Secretary, Herbert Morrison, described Canada and the other self-governing dominions as "in fact, as well as in form, absolute masters of their own political development ... The freedom and independence are real."[50]

Decolonization in the Dependent Empire

In his famous speech made in November 1942 about "the end of the beginning" of the Second World War, Churchill declared, "We mean to hold our own. I have not become the King's First Minister in order to preside over the liquidation of the British Empire."[51] At the end of the war, it seemed that Britain could regain its Dependent Empire to the extent it had been lost during the preceding years. British authorities returned to Singapore, Hong Kong, and Malaya. There were even plans to expand the Empire by occupying Thailand.[52] At the time, it was often predicted that the Empire would then last for a long time.

Imperial beliefs and opposition to independence for the dependent colonies were not confined to conservative politicians such as Churchill. In 1943, Morrison, Labour Home Secretary in the coalition government, said that in many cases "it would be like giving a child of 10 a latch key, a bank account and a shot-gun."[53] Four years later, Alan Burns, governor of the Gold Coast, confidently told a group of district officers:

> We are there to teach and to help, not to govern by the strong hand ... Our main job is to teach the Africans and other Colonials to take our places in the administration of the Colonies. We must try and teach them to do the work that we are doing ourselves, in order that they may replace us. It will be a long time before they are as efficient as we are.[54]

He assured them: "Believe me, the Colonial Civil Service, with all its imperfections, will be needed for many years to come."[55] Giving the Reid Lecture to Acadia University in 1959, one historian of the Empire denied that the British were "empire-builders gone out of business": "Is the British Empire liquidated? No, indeed!"[56] A.P. Thornton, another historian of the Empire, later referred to the 1950s as "the grand climacteric for the imperial idea," although he was not aware of this when he finished his influential book on the British Empire in 1959.[57]

But the process leading to the end of the Empire had already begun. Above all, the Second World War had left Britain economically exhausted and led to the rise of the United States and the Soviet Union as the new superpowers. Churchill himself contributed to the dissolution by signing the Atlantic Charter with Roosevelt in 1941 on board a US cruiser at Placentia Bay, Newfoundland. Article 3 said Britain and the US respected "the right of all peoples to choose

Canada and Colonialism

the form of government under which they will live." Upon returning to England, Churchill said he did not intend these words to refer to the Empire.[58] Of course, this was not how they were interpreted by colonial peoples. They naturally thought "all" meant "all." In *Long Walk to Freedom*, Nelson Mandela described how the charter inspired the African National Congress.[59]

Other key events leading to the end of the Dependent Empire were the reaction to the Amritsar massacre in 1919, causing loss of support in India; Japan's seizure of Singapore in 1942, showing that the British were not invincible; the independence of India and other Asian colonies between 1947 and 1948; the Colonial Office policy in 1948 saying the central purpose of colonial policy was "responsible self-government"; the Suez Crisis of 1956, when Canada under Foreign Minister Lester Pearson joined the United States in condemning Britain's invasion of Egypt; the "Winds of Change" speech by UK prime minister Macmillan in 1960, acknowledging the strength of independence movements in Africa; the support for such movements by the Soviet Union and other communist states; fears by the United States that British opposition would push African countries even further into the Soviet camp, balanced by hopes that the Empire would defeat communism; Britain's (unsuccessful) application to join the European Communities in 1960, signalling its abandonment of the Commonwealth; independence for African colonies between 1960 and 1964; the announcement by Prime Minister Harold Wilson in 1968 of the end of Britain's commitments "east of Suez"; and the return of Hong Kong to China in 1997.[60] All that is left today are scattered rocks and islands around the globe, including the Falkland Islands, over which Britain went to war with Argentina in 1982.

When independence and decolonization came, it tended to follow a pattern. Referring to the autobiography of Ghanaian leader Kwame Nkrumah, Margery Perham, the academic authority on colonial administration, described it:

> The full complement of almost ritual acts are there: the leader's return from education overseas; the organization of a party; the appeal to the masses; the attempts by government at private parley; the uncompromising demands; the sloughing off of moderates and the formation of a wider, more resolute party; the growing threat of force; the disorderly incidents; the imprisonment of the leader; the Commission of Enquiry. Because the leader was in a British prison, he was given facilities to enable him to stand in a general election. He was, of course, elected, and there followed his immediate release by the governor and his assumption of power.[61]

She might have added haggling over the constitution; negotiations and some-times violent conflict with leaders of other parties or ethnic or religious groups brought together by colonial boundaries; possible power sharing or partition; attempts by Britain to get a more pliable leader chosen (sometimes successful); the lowering of the British flag and raising of its replacement at an independ-ence ceremony; British royalty in attendance; and the ceremonial departure by the British governor in full regalia. It all seemed a very polite affair.[62] But the pomp and ceremony of the Empire could not mask the violence that so often marked its end as it marked its beginning and duration, especially in Palestine, Malaya, Kenya, and Cyprus.[63]

Historians differ over the weight to be attached to the factors leading to the end of the Empire. Ronald Hyam summarized them by a sporting analogy: bowled out (by freedom fighters); run out (by over-reach and economic con-straints); retired hurt (failure of will); and booed off the field (by international criticism, especially from the United States).[64] As noted, the main reasons were probably the costs of the Second World War and the superpower status the war provided to the United States and the Soviet Union. Canadian prime minister Mackenzie King noted in his diary that it was "an appalling day for Britain" when she had to seek help from Canada in the form of "ships, ammunition, aircraft, additional land forces etc."[65]

India's Path to Self-Government and Independence

The ultimate path to self-government and independence for India and the De-pendent Empire differed greatly from that of Canada and the other settler col-onies in substance, if not always in form.[66] This was not the original aim. The Indian National Congress, which was to lead India to independence and inspire nationalist movements throughout the Empire, was established in 1885. It was formed mainly at the initiative of Allan Octavian Hume, a former member of the Indian Civil Service, who admired the Canadian system of responsible govern-ment and saw it as a model for India. Part of the stimulus for its establishment was Indian disappointment over the failure of legislation in 1884 (the Ilbert Bill) to extend the jurisdiction of Indian judges over Europeans. The legislation amended the *Code of Criminal Procedure* to allow senior Indian judges to try "European British subjects." This increase in the powers of Indian judges led to outrage in Britain and among Britons living in India, which has been described as "a white mutiny." The legislation was subsequently amended to give the ac-cused the right to have a majority white jury. The racist reaction to the bill alien-ated many educated Indians and the Congress was formed the following year.[67]

Canada and Colonialism

The early objective of the major Indian political organizations was for India to become a self-governing dominion like Canada.[68] This remained the official aim until 1930. For example, in 1916, the Congress and the Muslim League jointly entered into a pact at Lucknow that declared, "In any Council or other body which may be constituted or convened for the settlement or control of Imperial affairs, India shall be adequately represented in like manner with the Dominions and with equal rights." The first paragraph of the Congress report under Motilal Nehru in 1929 demanded, "India shall have the same constitutional status in the community of nations, known as the British Empire, as the Dominion of Canada." (This belief in dominion status was not unanimous: Jawaharlal Nehru, his son, declared in 1928, "The very idea suffocates and strangles me.")[69] As noted in 1936 by Keith, the leading expert on the imperial constitution, Indian leaders had "infinitely more serious difficulties to face than had the colonial statesmen who evolved the system of self-government which has now culminated in Dominion status."[70] There would be no easy acceptance and encouragement of independence for India and the other dependent colonies; only denial and repression until circumstances left little alternative. Britain lacked any commitment to independence and, in the end, it was a scuttle.[71]

Viceroy Dufferin, who had earlier served as Canada's governor general, summed up the general attitude of the British rulers: "You cannot apply constitutional principles to a conquered country, inasmuch as self-government and submission to a foreign Sovereign are incompatible."[72] The attempt by Congress to follow the Canadian path to self-government was expressly rejected by the Secretary of State for India in 1907, with the comment that it was a tremendous and dangerous fallacy to think that "whatever is good for Canada must be good for India ... You might just as well say that, because a fur coat in Canada at certain times of year is a truly comfortable garment, therefore a fur coat is [equally appropriate] in the Deccan" (southern India).[73] The request for India to be treated "on the same footing as our self-governing colonies like Canada" was likewise rejected by the Secretary of State for India in 1909 as a "fantastic and ludicrous dream."[74] Again, in 1912, the viceroy wrote, "Colonial self-government on the lines of the British Dominions is absolutely out of the question."[75] The rejection of the Canadian model of self-government was echoed by Canadian politicians. R.B. Bennett declared in Parliament, "Britain did not desire India or Egypt: she had them forced upon her. To let go our rule in India would be anarchy."[76] Even when statements about self-government were made at the highest level of the British government, they were sometimes no more than cynical lip service for short-term expediency. One viceroy wrote in his diary in 1943 that the British cabinet "was not honest in its expressed desire to make progress in India."[77] Self-government and independence would indeed be a struggle. However, once achieved, India's independence and that of other dependent colonies would be more definitive than Canada's.

We saw in Chapter 3 that India, like the other dependent colonies, was ruled despotically during the nineteenth century. This continued into the new century. Keir Hardie, a founder of the Labour Party in Britain, wrote in 1909 that the government of India "resembles a huge military despotism tempered somewhat by a civil bureaucracy."[78] In that year, some mild reforms, the "Minto-Morley reforms," were made by the *Indian Councils Act 1909*.[79] The act introduced representative elements into the government, similar to those the settler colonies had enjoyed from their formation. It still fell far short of the self-government the Canadian colonies had enjoyed for over half a century.[80] The ideal of such self-government, which was then the objective of most Indian nationalists, was dismissed by the drafters of the reforms as "a mere dream."[81] The reforms increased Indian participation in the government of India but did not introduce anything approaching self-government. One token Indian person was appointed by the British to the viceroy's executive council and two to the Secretary of State's India Council in London. More Indians were added to the legislative council (a move that was not acceptable to the majority of the council); some of them were indirectly elected and not appointed by the viceroy.

These changes did not change the despotic nature of the rule of the viceroy/governor general. According to Bampfylde Fuller, a retired member of the Indian Civil Service, writing in 1913, "If the Governor-General can command the support of the Secretary of State he is in theory as powerful as an Oriental despot. He has statutory powers of overruling his Executive Council, and also of vetoing any legislation of which he may disagree; he may even legislate on his own sole authority, subject to the limitation that laws so made by him do not continue in force for a longer period than six months."[82] He noted that there were then sixty-eight members of the legislative council, of whom thirty-six were officials, with four non-officials appointed by the governor general, twelve elected by provincial councils, and the other sixteen nominated or elected by business and landowning groups or to represent Muslims.[83]

The 1909 reforms made greater but still modest changes at the provincial level. More Indians were added as members of the legislative councils; some of them were elected. Provincial councils now had a majority of Indian members, who outnumbered the official members appointed by the provincial governors. But the councils had no real powers. In the words of Shashi Tharoor, an

Indian politician and historian, the changes "were at best cosmetic alterations to the established system and marginally affected how these Indian councils were constituted and functioned ... They had the right to raise issues ... but not to make any decision; they could express the voice of the Indian public (or at least its élite, English-educated sections) but had no authority to pass laws or budgets."[84] Power remained with the British at both the central and the provincial levels, and the despotism continued.

India's contribution to Britain during the First World War (actively encouraged by Mahatma Gandhi) and an increase in nationalist unrest in 1917 forced further but still limited concessions.[85] These were announced on August 20, 1917, by Edwin Montagu, the Secretary of State for India. He declared in the House of Commons, "The policy of His Majesty's Government ... is that of the increasing association of Indians in every branch of the administration and the gradual development of self-governing institutions with a view to the progressive realisation of responsible government in India as an integral part of the British Empire."[86] This vague, convoluted, bureaucratic language at least signalled some intent at some future, unspecified time to grant responsible government in India as had been recommended by Lord Durham for the British North American colonies almost eighty years earlier. The key words were probably "gradual development." As later acknowledged by the viceroy, "responsible government" implied some form of dominion status, like that of Canada. However, the announcement was not explicit and the relationship between the two was not clear. Nor was it clear that dominion status would be the same for the two countries.[87] It would take over twenty years of civil unrest for Britain to provide that clarification.

Montagu's announcement was implemented in what are known as the Montagu-Chelmsford reforms, legislated in the *Government of India Act 1919*.[88] The legislation made some changes at the central government level, including an enlarged legislative council, but again the more significant changes took place at the provincial level. The franchise for the legislature was expanded, although it was still restricted and based on owning property. A system of diarchy or dual government was introduced. The legislation transferred some matters, such as agriculture, education, and health, to Indian ministers, who became responsible to the elected provincial legislature. Other issues that mattered more to the British rulers, such as taxation and law and order, were reserved to them. It was, at best, diluted responsible government at the provincial level over some matters but subject to the overriding power of the British authorities. After some initial acceptance, Gandhi and his supporters rejected these reforms.

If the Minto-Morley reforms and the Montagu-Chelmsford reforms were intended as carrots to lessen Indian demands for immediate self-government, other legislation represented the stick. *A Prevention of Seditious Meetings Act* was passed in 1907, enabling restrictions on public meetings to discuss "any subject likely to cause disturbance or public excitement or ... any political subject."[89] The *Press Act* of 1910 sought to further control the press.[90] It required newspapers to provide a security deposit to the government, which could be forfeited if they printed something deemed objectionable because, among other things, it brought the government into hatred or contempt or excited disaffection. The printing press and the publication itself could also be forfeited. The *Defence of India Act 1915* removed the right of appeal for certain political offences and provided for internment of suspects.[91] The *Anarchical and Revolutionary Crimes Act* of 1919 (the Rowlatt Act) also contained several provisions that flew in the face of any pretense of respect for the rule of law or civil liberties.[92] The government could make an order to arrest and confine without trial anyone they thought was, or had been, involved in certain offences against the state. This legislation constituted more of the repression that can be traced back to *Bengal Regulation III* of 1818, discussed in Chapter 3, and that continued into the twentieth century. As mentioned in that chapter, Gandhi pleaded guilty to a charge of sedition under section 124A of the *Indian Penal Code* in 1922. He received a term of imprisonment for six years. This was the same as that received by an earlier Indian leader, Bal Gangadhar Tilak, in 1909 under the same section.[93]

Opposition to such legislation was widespread, and it was a protest against the Rowlatt Act that led to the Amritsar (or Jallianwala Bagh) massacre in 1919. Reginald Dyer, the British officer sent to stop the meeting, ordered his soldiers to fire on a peaceful crowd in a confined space. Hundreds of people were killed and over a thousand injured.[94] In his defence, Dyer said the firing was intended to produce "a moral effect," i.e., terror. This event and the support shown for Dyer by many British officials and the public led to increased Indian support for the growing, largely non-violent campaign of non-cooperation, civil disobedience, and boycotts to gain self-government. The campaign met violent suppression by the authorities, including imprisonment of its leaders, such as Gandhi, and hundreds of thousands of its supporters. The police played a crucial role in this suppression of political opposition. Being part of the colonial administration, they were unaccountable to the people, immune from prosecution, and free to use violence. They also had a substantial paramilitary presence.[95]

The disparity between the status of India (and other non-white colonies) and that of the dominions was made clear during the drafting of the Balfour Formula at the imperial conference of 1926. Here, the status of Canada, the Irish Free State, Newfoundland, Australia, New Zealand, and South Africa as dominions or autonomous nations equal with the United Kingdom within the Empire was recognized.[96] But the report of the conference made it clear that this recognition did not extend to India. There was nothing in the report to suggest that those attending contemplated that dominion status would ever be extended to the non-white peoples of the Empire.[97] In 1929, the viceroy, Lord Irwin, made a vague statement that it was "implicit in the Declaration of 1917 [made by Edwin Montagu] that the natural issue of India's constitutional progress as there contemplated is the attainment of Dominion status."[98] This statement led to a backlash in the UK against the extension of such status to India. Churchill said it was "not only fantastic in itself but criminally mischievous in its effects." Two years later, he added that "except as an ultimate visionary goal, Dominion status like that of Canada or Australia is not going to happen in India in any period which we can even remotely foresee."[99]

In any event, dominion status had ceased to be the objective of the campaign against British rule in India. A turning point occurred in 1928 when one of the movement's prominent leaders, Lajpat Rai, was beaten and died during a protest against the Simon Commission, an all-British body sent to review the changes made in 1919. His death, and the British opposition to dominion status, radicalized the movement. For some members of the Indian National Congress, the leading group opposing British rule, self-government within the Empire on the vague dominion model was no longer sufficient. Among other concerns, there was suspicion that Britain would not extend dominion status to India equal to that of Canada. A meeting in December 1928 was the scene of a head-on clash between those willing to accept dominion status and those who wanted nothing short of complete independence. Gandhi made a proposal that averted a split: if Britain did not concede dominion status within a year, the Congress was to demand complete independence and to fight for it, if necessary, by launching campaigns of civil disobedience.[100] Complete independence then became the ultimate goal, although dominion status could be a short-term stepping stone.[101] The Congress declared in 1930, "India must sever the British connection and attain *Purna Swaraj* or complete independence."[102] Also in 1930, Gandhi led his famous march to the sea to make salt in protest against the British monopoly, which resulted in thousands of arrests.

The response of the British to the Indian independence movement was described by Jawaharlal Nehru, one of its most prominent leaders, in 1936: "If their special position was acknowledged and their superiority not challenged, they were gracious and obliging, provided that this did them no harm. But opposition to them became opposition to the divine order, and as such was a deadly sin which must be suppressed."[103] He was both fascinated and irritated by their attitude: "The calm assurance of always being in the right and of having borne a great burden worthily, faith in their racial destiny and their own brand of imperialism, contempt and anger at the unbelievers and sinners who challenged the foundations of the true faith – there was something of the religious temper about this attitude." British rule was to continue until Indians had shown themselves sufficiently loyal to be considered worthy of the self-government enjoyed by Canadians almost a century earlier: "The more we accepted British ideals and objectives the fitter we were for 'self-government.' Freedom would be ours as soon as we demonstrated and guaranteed that we would use it only in accordance with British wishes."

Nehru described British rule as "based on an extreme form of widespread violence and the only sanction is fear. It suppresses the usual liberties which are supposed to be essential to the growth of a people."[104] In his presidential address to the Indian National Congress in 1936, he said that argument gave way to "the policeman's baton and soldier's bayonet and prison and detention camps."[105] Like others who opposed British rule, he was repeatedly imprisoned, spending nearly ten years in jail.[106] Another contemporary writer, Leonard Barnes, was critical of the laws of sedition, high rates of imprisonment, and the lack of a free press and an independent judiciary throughout the colonies.[107] *India in Bondage*, a book by an American-based missionary that was critical of British rule, was published in New York in 1929 and contained a statement that it had been previously published in India and promptly suppressed.[108] Martial law was proclaimed in some areas.[109]

Another reaction to the growing unrest in India was to work on further reforms and a new constitution. This led to another step toward limited self-government in 1935 through the *Government of India Act*, based on the recommendations of the Simon Commission and discussions held at Round Table Conferences between Indian and British representatives between 1930 and 1932. In a move later used in other colonies, the act sought to focus political activity at the local level in order to fragment and weaken the national independence movement. It again enlarged the franchise and delegated more powers to provincial legislatures controlled by Indians. Provincial ministers now had control over more matters for which they were responsible to the elected legislature rather than the governor. However, the governor retained power to take over in some circumstances. Control over the essential matters of finance, defence, and foreign affairs remained with the central government under the viceroy. No Indian legislature could pass a law that questioned the sovereignty of the British Crown in any part of India, and the power of the UK Parliament to legislate for British India was expressly asserted.[110] The act proposed creation of a Federation of India to include the provinces of British India and the five hundred princely states, but opposition from those states meant those provisions never came into effect. Like the Simon Commission report, it was deafeningly silent on possible dominion status for India, as the government steadfastly refused to include a reference to such status.[111] In the words of Keith, this omission "inevitably caused a painful feeling in India."[112] Despite these steps toward self-government at the provincial level, India still remained far behind Canada on the path to both internal self-government and independence.[113]

The stress created by the Second World War finally propelled India to dominion status and then complete independence. Without consulting with the Indian leaders, Lord Linlithgow, then viceroy of India, committed the country to the war as its military power was considered vital. (Canada and the other dominions made their own declarations of war).[114] To gain support, he made a speech in 1940 stating the government's desire to achieve "full dominion status ... of the Statute of Westminster variety" at an unspecified time once the war was over. Although the timing was vague, for the first time the British authorities had recognized that India would be equal to Canada and the other white dominions so far as dominion status was concerned. Indian leaders countered with demands for a new constitution and immediate independence. A new campaign of civil disobedience and non-cooperation was started, followed by further mass arrests.

In 1942, Stafford Cripps, a member of the British cabinet, went on a mission to India and made an offer of dominion status at the end of the war, which could lead to full independence later.[115] A major issue was the respective powers of the viceroy and of the executive council, echoing the debate over responsible government in Canada a century earlier. Congress wanted immediate implementation of a system in which they would gain control of the government, but the viceroy wanted to retain his control. Cripps tried to bridge the gap, but his cabinet colleagues supported the viceroy. In recommending the Cripps mission to his reluctant colleagues in the coalition War Cabinet, the Labour leader, Clement Attlee, had referred to the precedent from Canada's path to self-government: the visit to Canada a century earlier by Lord Durham. In his words, "Lord Durham saved Canada to the British Empire. We need a man to do in India what Durham did in Canada."[116] This was not to happen. The Cripps proposal was rejected by the Indian leaders, with Gandhi describing it as a postdated cheque on a bank that was obviously failing. Despite the rejection, this was another watershed moment as, once offered, it would be difficult for Britain to withdraw the offer of independence. The immediate impact of the failure was the launch by Congress of the Quit India campaign, which led to considerable unrest and violence and was met with further government suppression. It has been described as "the most serious challenge to British imperial authority since the Indian Mutiny/Rebellion of 1857."[117]

Confirmation of post-war self-government came over the next couple of years. Herbert Morrison, the Home Secretary, said in a speech in January 1943 that "the boundary between Dominions and dependencies is not fixed, and the trend is always towards freedom ... after the War [India] can have full self-government for the taking."[118] A more general statement was later made by the Colonial Secretary: "We are pledged to guide colonial people along the road to self-government within the framework of the British Empire."[119] The King's speech on August 15, 1945, opening the session of Parliament, confirmed self-government: "In accordance with the promises made to my Indian peoples, my Government [the recently elected Labour government] will do their utmost to promote, in conjunction with the leaders of Indian opinion the early realization of full self-government in India. They will also press on with the development of my Colonial Empire and the welfare of its peoples."[120]

Dominion status was granted to British India in 1947 by the *Indian Independence Act* as a brief prelude to full legal independence for India (in 1950) and Pakistan (in 1956) as republics.[121] The use of dominion status as an interim step meant a quicker route to a transfer of power as it appealed to the British, who wanted to keep the newly independent countries within their sphere of influence, preferably as monarchies. It also gave the new dominions time to develop their own republican constitutions while they continued to operate under suitably modified British laws.[122] But dominion status was only very reluctantly accepted by the Indian National Congress leaders.[123] The term was avoided by both sides as much as possible, being described in official minutes as "offending phraseology."[124]

The new act partitioned British India into India and Pakistan. It contained provisions similar to those in the *Statute of Westminster* of 1931 that had applied to Canada and the other settler colonies. The legislatures of the new dominions would have full powers to make laws for themselves, including the repeal or amendment of any existing act of the UK Parliament. Their governors general,

Canada and Colonialism

representing the Crown, would cease to have discretion or independent authority. No future legislation of the UK Parliament would apply to the dominions unless extended by a law of the dominion legislature. The UK government would cease to have any responsibility for the new dominions. The princely or "native" states were effectively abandoned by Britain and the treaties with them dishonoured. Those states would be free to join India or Pakistan or, in theory, remain separate. In any event, the treaties with them would lapse. They were all eventually integrated into the new dominions and the princes pensioned off.[125] Until new constitutions were created for each dominion, they would continue to be governed by the 1935 *Government of India Act* passed by the UK Parliament, suitably modified. The birth of the two new dominions was tragically marred by communal violence on a terrifying scale.

The Indian constitution of 1950 ended this half-way house of dominion status and repealed the 1935 act. It commenced by declaring, "We, the People of India, having solemnly resolved to constitute India into a Sovereign Democratic Republic ... Hereby Adopt, Enact And Give To Ourselves This Constitution." Unlike Canada, the constitution was made in India under the

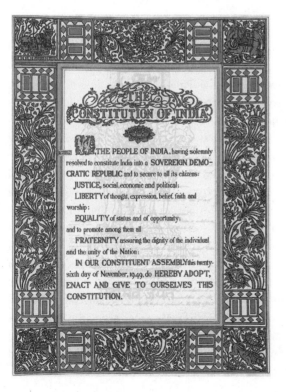

Preamble to the Constitution of India. This made-in-India constitution is beautifully illustrated and kept in a special helium-filled case in the Library of the Parliament. The calligraphy was done by Prem Behari Narain Raizda, and it was illuminated by Nandalal Bose and other artists. | *The Constitution of India, World Digital Library, courtesy of the Library of Congress.*

Indian prime minister Jawaharlal Nehru meeting Canadian prime minister Mackenzie King in Ottawa, 1949. | *Library and Archives Canada, William Lyon Mackenzie King fonds, a122477*

authority of the people of India, with an explicit declaration of sovereignty and an Indian head of state to replace the UK monarch.[126]

Leaders of other independence movements also rejected dominion status except as a stepping stone to complete independence.[127] Kwame Nkrumah was scathing in *Towards Colonial Freedom*, written in 1942. Referring to the argument advanced by Canadian politicians and others, he said some writers spoke of "internal self-government" and gradual evolution to membership in the British Commonwealth. In his view, non-white colonies would never get equal status with Canada and the other dominions. The dominions were "all in league with the financial oligarchy of Great Britain for the exploitation of the colonies." In considering the colonial question, it was necessary to have a clear-cut distinction between the dominions, which were a continuation of the British capitalist system, and those colonies that were exploited by the imperialists: "In the dominions, not only do the capitalists present the colonial extension of the capitalism and imperialism of the mother countries, but their colonial interests, directly or indirectly, coincide." For this reason, he wrote, "the terms 'self-government,' 'dominion status' ... are nothing but blinds and limitations in the way of the struggle of the national liberation movement in the colonies towards self-determination and complete national independence."[128]

Canada and Colonialism

Canada in transition from its British origins: multiracial children in Winnipeg on Dominion Day 1960 (renamed Canada Day in 1982) holding Union Jack flags to celebrate the confederation of British colonies to form Canada on July 1, 1867. | *National Film Board fonds, Library and Archives Canada, e011177410*

Continued Canadian Support for the Empire

The identification of Canada with the British Empire and colonial ideology continued well into the 1960s.[129] Historian Bryan Palmer notes in his account of Canada in the 1960s that as late as the 1950s, "however much the writing was on the crumbling wall of an antiquated, imperialistic understanding of nationhood, the values and attachments of and to this particular identity were still vigorously in evidence throughout Canada ... the older imperialism was often on display."[130]

This display was literally the case when an equestrian statue of Edward VII was removed from India following independence and re-erected by public fundraising in Queen's Park, Toronto.[131] Jośe E. Igartua's study of newspapers, parliamentary speeches, history textbooks, and public opinion polls shows how Canadian identity remained mainly British into the 1950s.[132] The

Citizenship Act of 1946 expressly declared that Canadians remained British subjects and gave preference to all British subjects in matters like elections.[133] Textbooks stressed that Canada's history was part of that of the Empire, and that pupils had responsibilities both to the Dominion and the Empire.[134] An attempt in 1946 to change the name of the annual holiday to celebrate Canadian Confederation from "Dominion Day" to "Canada Day" was unsuccessful in the face of widespread opposition in the press.[135]

In 1956, the *Toronto Daily Star* complained, "Alone among the Commonwealth members we have no flag, no national anthem. We were the last to accept a native son as governor-general, and there are still Canadians who would like to see a Britisher as our chief-of-state. We must be the only country in the world that denied itself the right to amend its own constitution."[136] The Suez Crisis of that year was the opportunity for imperialist jingoism in some Canadian newspapers, which enthusiastically supported Britain's invasion of Egypt.[137] John Diefenbaker's success in the federal election of 1957 "was at least partly due to a desire by many English Canadians to reaffirm the importance of the British connection."[138] Canadian historian Arthur Lower wrote in 1958 that "all little Canadian boys and girls have been subjected from the day on which they start school to an unending steeping in the liquid of imperialism."[139] In 1960, an informal poll at the UK High Commission in Ottawa found that a clear majority of the locally engaged staff (i.e., Canadians) still thought of themselves as British.[140] It was not until 1964 that "the great flag debate of 1964 [over whether the new Canadian flag should include the Union Jack] marked the last hurrah for English-Canadian believers in a British Canada."[141]

Widespread Canadian support for colonialism and antipathy toward anticolonial nationalism in the late 1950s and early 1960s is demonstrated by a study carried out by historian Paula Hastings. She conducted an extensive survey of opinion in the mainstream English-language press and supplemented it with the perspectives of intellectuals, diplomats, and parliamentarians. Her work "suggests that empire apologism, contempt for anti-colonial nationalism, and the misrepresentation of colonial liberation struggles were pervasive."[142] She quotes from articles in the *Vancouver Sun* and the *Edmonton Journal* in 1960 and 1961, which stated that the British Empire had been "the great agency of material civilization" and, on balance, "had been far more a blessing than an evil."[143] Support for the position of Britain, and negative views on anticolonial nationalism, were shared by some officials of Canada's Department of External Affairs.[144] However, Canada's support for the position of the Afro-Asian Commonwealth countries opposing the continued membership of apartheid South Africa in 1961 should be noted.[145]

Several factors ultimately led to Canada's slow withdrawal from the British World after the Second World War: the growing impact of American popular culture and Canada's reliance on US military power and the American economy; fear of Quebec separatism that was fuelled in part by the imperial connection; a greater sense of Canadian identity, accompanied by symbolism such as the Canadian flag and national anthem to replace the British; multiculturalism; and the significant decline in immigration from the United Kingdom compared with that from other parts of the world.[146] In 1965, George Grant published *Lament for a Nation*, in which he wrote of the loss of "the Britishness of Canada."[147] Canada's role as the outpost of Britain in North America was over. However, the Empire continued to cast its shadow over Indigenous peoples in Canada.

Indigenous Peoples and Self-Government

Decolonization in India and other dependent colonies was not without impact in Canada. The Canadian government came under pressure internationally and internally to improve its relationship with Indigenous peoples, who found inspiration in such decolonization for their own struggles.

Canada had been a leader in expelling South Africa from the Commonwealth in 1961 because of its race laws discriminating against Black people. Yet the *Indian Act* had resulted in a Canadian form of apartheid with its race-based, discriminatory laws for "Indians." There was even, as noted in Chapter 6, an early, extralegal pass system controlling the movement of some Indigenous people, which may have influenced South Africa's notorious pass laws. In 1902, a commission from South Africa had visited western Canada to study Canada's system.[148] Claiming that, after South Africa's departure, Canadians had "wallowed in self-congratulation," one journalist said Ottawa's treatment of Indigenous peoples was worthy of "kicking Canada out of the Commonwealth."[149] In the view of the *Globe and Mail*, the "effect of the Indian Act is to produce a real Apartheid."[150] Echoing the reaction to Canadian criticism of Nazi Germany twenty years earlier, the South African government was quick to point to the hypocrisy in Canada's criticism of South Africa's race laws.[151] More generally, sympathy for the position of Indigenous peoples in Canada, and pressure on the federal government to do something, was enhanced by decolonization in the former dependent colonies.[152]

Indigenous peoples in Canada were also becoming more aware of their common bond with Indigenous peoples in other settler societies and in the newly independent former dependent colonies, then known as the "Third

World." George Manuel, a prominent leader from the Shuswap Nation in British Columbia, co-authored *The Fourth World: An Indian Reality*. It set out his views on that relationship and described working with Indigenous peoples in other former colonies. He wrote, "The bond of colonialism we share with the Third World peoples is the shared values that distinguish the Aboriginal world from the nation-states of the Third World."[153] His son, Arthur Manuel, who became a leader himself, wrote that, "while activists of our parents' generation were trying to build unity at home, they were also building new relationships with Indigenous peoples around the world."[154] George Manuel was especially impressed by the progress then being made in Tanzania under Julius Nyerere.[155] In this way, the success of independence movements in the former dependent colonies inspired Indigenous peoples in Canada in their own struggle for greater self-government.

The increased pressure for more self-government powers and greater legal recognition of treaty and Aboriginal rights started as a protest against the 1969 White Paper and the attempt by the federal government to remove the special legal status of "Indian" people, discussed in the previous chapter. This attempt created momentum for Indigenous people to form a more effective movement to seek constitutional protection for Aboriginal rights and title, including an inherent right of self-government. In *The Unjust Society*, a book that received much attention, Harold Cardinal, president of the Indian Association of Alberta, wrote, "The native people of Canada look back on generations of accumulated frustration under conditions that can only be described as colonial, brutal and tyrannical." He described the White Paper as "a thinly disguised programme of extermination through assimilation," and stated that Indian people "will not trust the government with our futures any longer. Now they must listen to and learn from us."[156]

Pierre Trudeau had met his match. Rarely has government policy backfired so badly. The White Paper, which was to end the special legal position of Indigenous peoples, led, instead, to a much larger Indigenous rights movement and to changes that have transformed Canadian laws applying to Indigenous peoples ("Aboriginal law"), and constitutional recognition of Aboriginal and treaty rights. Trudeau had intended to be the undertaker, preparing emaciated Aboriginal and treaty rights for burial; instead, he became the reluctant midwife of a movement that gave these rights new life and a vigour they had never possessed before.

In recent decades, Indigenous peoples have successfully used the court system to gain greater recognition of their treaty and Aboriginal rights and a louder voice in developments affecting their traditional territories. However, they have yet to be successful in gaining constitutional recognition of their right to self-government through the judicial process.

Changes in the constitution, and the failure of attempts at constitutional conferences to define Aboriginal and treaty rights, were critical factors driving the development of Aboriginal rights, including the right to self-government. The Trudeau government became focused on constitutional reform, especially in response to separatist pressure in Quebec resulting from the election of the Parti Quebecois in 1976. Negotiations took place with the provinces over official languages (French and English – not Indigenous), a charter of rights, and an amending formula. According to lawyer Mel Smith, who participated in the constitutional negotiations for British Columbia, "aboriginal rights were not on the agenda."[157]

However, from 1980, a parallel process was conducted simultaneously by a special joint committee of Parliament. Initially, Aboriginal rights were not on the agenda of that committee either. But the New Democratic Party insisted on including a provision recognizing and affirming Aboriginal and treaty rights as a condition of their support for the proposed legislation to amend the constitution. This provision was drafted by lawyers who had been active in representing Indigenous groups and was included in the formal proposal revised in January 1981 by the federal government following lobbying by Indigenous leaders.[158] The proposal also contained an agreement to hold a constitutional conference to identify and define Aboriginal rights. Provincial leaders were opposed to the proposal and launched a court challenge.

On November 5, 1981, the prime minister and nine of the ten provincial premiers reached an agreement on the constitutional amendment (Quebec was the exception). In a glaring error or betrayal, the provision dealing with Aboriginal and treaty rights was not included. This omission led to a vigorous campaign by Indigenous leaders to have the provision reinstated. It also led to a speech criticizing the omission by Thomas Berger, who had been a lawyer for Indigenous peoples and was now a judge of the BC Supreme Court. When the Chief Justice of Canada and the prime minister publicly rebuked him for speaking out, he was forced to resign as a judge and eventually returned to legal practice.[159] The efforts to reinstate the provision were successful, and it was subsequently restored to the draft constitutional amendment with the addition of the word "existing." It now read: "The existing aboriginal and treaty rights of the aboriginal peoples of Canada are hereby recognized and affirmed," which is the wording found in section 35(1) of the *Constitution Act 1982*,

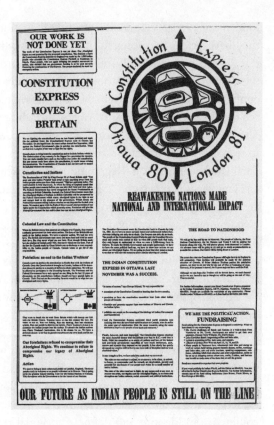

Poster for the Constitution Express, a campaign for greater powers and recognition of rights for Indigenous peoples, from the April 1981 issue of *UBCIC News*. | *Reproduced by permission from the Union of BC Indian Chiefs*

passed by the UK Parliament and proclaimed in force on April 17, 1982.[160] However, the section was so vague and lacking in content that it was often described as "an empty box."

The identification and definition of Aboriginal rights were to be decided at a constitutional conference in 1983. The procedure was set out in section 37 of the *Constitution Act 1982* and became known as the Section 37 process. The first conference resulted in amendments clarifying that "treaty rights" included rights under future as well as existing land claims agreements. Also, this conference determined that there had to be representatives of Indigenous peoples at future conferences before amendments could be made to provisions directly referring to them. It became clear at the meeting that reaching an agreement was going to be very challenging, and three more first ministers' constitutional conferences were scheduled for 1984, 1985, and 1987.[161]

The matter that dominated was whether Indigenous peoples had a right to self-government. This issue then became whether any right to self-government was "inherent," as claimed by Indigenous groups, or delegated by, or "contingent on" (i.e., based on agreement with), the federal and provincial governments. Financing was also a divisive issue. The conferences failed to resolve the identification and definition of Aboriginal rights, including self-government. This failure meant the task would fall to the Supreme Court of Canada by default.[162]

Indigenous anger at the federal and provincial governments' failure to reach an agreement on self-government for Indigenous peoples (a failure they thought was due to a lack of will) was inflamed by the ease with which those governments agreed in 1987 on the Meech Lake Accord. This accord recognized Quebec's status as "a distinct society." To Indigenous people, it appeared their concerns were being treated as secondary to those of Quebec.[163] However, they had the final say on the accord through the lone figure of Elijah Harper, a Cree-Ojibway member of the Manitoba legislature. Prime Minister Brian Mulroney had sought to put pressure on the provincial legislatures to approve the accord by effectively imposing a deadline for approval of June 1990. In his words, he had rolled the dice as the accord required unanimous ratification by the ten provincial legislatures. The prime minister lost the gamble because Harper, holding an eagle feather in his hand, indicated in a soft voice that he would not give the necessary approval for Manitoba MPs to vote on the accord. As a result, the time ran out, the deadline passed, and the accord died.[164] Another prime minister had underestimated the resolve of Indigenous peoples.

In an attempt to appease Indigenous peoples, the next stage in this constitutional saga saw the prime minister, the ten premiers, and national Indigenous leaders meet to agree on a new constitutional package at Charlottetown in August 1992.[165] This detailed accord had provisions recognizing Quebec's distinct status. It also proposed amendments to the constitution that would, among other things, recognize Indigenous governments as one of the three orders of government (in addition to the federal and provincial governments) and recognize an inherent Indigenous right of self-government.

Indigenous peoples had gone from being shut out of the Meech Lake Accord to having their wish list of constitutional amendments included in the Charlottetown Accord five years later. This development almost certainly reflected the federal government's desperation to resolve the Quebec issue. The new accord was defeated in a national referendum held on October 26, 1992, partly as a result of the opposition of the Native Women's Association of Canada, which was concerned about the accord's impact on equality rights.[166] Also adding his voice to the opposition was former prime minister Pierre Trudeau, who denounced the "vague project about a third order of [Indigenous] government."[167]

The Charlottetown Accord was effectively the last attempt at constitutional reform, as fatigue had set in across the country. The Royal Commission on Aboriginal Peoples (RCAP) summarized these years of attempted constitutional reform, stating that "government policies, attempts at legislative reform, and attempts at constitutional reform have failed." However, Indigenous peoples and their rights had emerged from the wings to occupy centre stage of the national drama. In the words of RCAP, they had "forced their way into the debate on the future of our country. It is hard to imagine that Aboriginal proposals for the future of Canada, including constitutional reform, can be ignored when discussions about the basic values of our country resume."[168] But those discussions have yet to resume.

In 1995, the federal government issued a policy statement recognizing the inherent right of self-government as an existing Aboriginal right within section 35.[169] This recognition was based on the view that the Indigenous peoples of Canada have the right to govern themselves when it comes to internal concerns of their communities; matters related to their special relationship to their lands and their resources; and subjects integral to their unique cultures, identities, traditions, languages, and institutions. The policy expressly denied "a right to sovereignty in the international law sense." Although described as "inherent," self-government under the policy is implemented through the negotiation of agreements between Indigenous groups and federal and provincial governments. Further, the negotiations must satisfy some conditions, including the paramountcy of federal and provincial law in some situations.

Following the adoption of the policy, some First Nations have negotiated either modern treaties that give them more government powers or self-government agreements with the federal and provincial governments.[170] Negotiation of these modern treaties commenced in 1975 with the James Bay Agreement following the 1973 decision of the Supreme Court of Canada in the Nisga'a Aboriginal title case, which, although unsuccessful, led to a revival of the treaty process that had been dormant for decades.[171]

RCAP reported in 1996. In its words, "In response to such events as Kanesatake [the Oka crisis over a proposed development], the failure of the Meech Lake and Section 37 processes, the Spicer commission [on Canada's future], and the government of Canada's failure to resolve the growing rift in relations between Aboriginal peoples and the Canadian state, the federal government created this Royal Commission on 26 August 1991."[172] It was charged with finding ways to rebuild the relationship between Indigenous and non-Indigenous people in Canada. The commission had four Indigenous and three

Canada and Colonialism

non-Indigenous members, including a former justice of the Supreme Court of Canada, Bertha Wilson. It took five years and 178 days of hearings to produce its massive final report in five volumes and nearly four thousand pages.[173]

The report is encyclopedic in its coverage and includes detailed reviews of different aspects of the history and contemporary relationship of Indigenous and non-Indigenous people. It is highly critical of the government's policies concerning Indigenous peoples: "The main policy direction, pursued for more than 150 years, first by colonial then by Canadian governments, has been wrong."[174] There are 440 recommendations intended to result in a "renewed relationship between Aboriginal and non-Aboriginal people in Canada."[175]

The commissioners called for a new Royal Proclamation to acknowledge past injustices, recognize the inherent right of self-government, and establish a renewed relationship. To discharge their self-government powers, existing Indigenous groups were to be constituted into about sixty to eighty new nations and provided with adequate resources, including external funding and an enlarged land base. Unfortunately, "almost as soon as the report was released, it was placed on the shelf with all the rest of the reports from Royal Commissions."[176]

Several decisions on Aboriginal law handed down by the Supreme Court of Canada since the 1970s went a long way in clarifying Aboriginal rights to land, hunting and fishing, and treaty rights, as noted below. However, they did little to clarify the existence and nature of any right to self-government. One case decided in 1996, *R v Pamajewon,* gave a restrictive interpretation that required Aboriginal groups to prove the specific matter claimed to be within the right had been a significant part of their distinctive culture before contact with Europeans.[177] This meant that each group had to prove the claimed right was specific and historical rather than part of a generic right to self-government on all matters of contemporary relevance.

In another case the following year, *Delgamuukw v British Columbia,* the Supreme Court avoided the issue.[178] Lower courts had decided that the sovereignty exercised by the Canadian government was constitutionally incompatible with Indigenous self-government.[179] According to this view, all political power in Canada is divided between the federal and provincial legislatures as the result of Confederation in 1867. This division left no space for Indigenous governments except through delegation of powers from one of those two levels of government, such as through the *Indian Act* and other statutes that confer powers on First Nations councils. The law remains uncertain. A 2024 decision of the court again failed to resolve this issue. It involved federal legislation relating to Indigenous children, youth, and families.

In 2018, the federal government issued another policy statement setting out principles to govern its relationship with Indigenous peoples. These principles include acknowledging "that all relations with Indigenous peoples need to be based on the recognition and implementation of their right to self-determination, including the inherent right of self-government."[180] Parliament passed legislation in 2019 that expressly affirmed Indigenous peoples' right to self-determination, including jurisdiction over child and family services.[181] The Attorney General of Quebec challenged the constitutionality of this legislation, claiming there was no inherent right to self-government, and the federal government had no power to legislate for such a right. In 2022, the Quebec Court of Appeal rejected the challenge. It upheld the validity of the legislation with a couple of exceptions.[182] It found that Indigenous peoples did have an inherent right to self-government. However, this right could not be inconsistent with the assertion of sovereignty by the Crown (as in the case of maintaining a military force) or the ability of Canadian governments to infringe any Aboriginal right if justified under the test devised by the Supreme Court of Canada for such infringements. An appeal to the Supreme Court of Canada was heard in December 2022 and a decision given on February 9, 2024.[183] The court upheld the legislation without exception as a valid confirmation by the federal government that Aboriginal rights recognized and affirmed under section 35 included a right of self-government. The legislation promoted reconciliation.[184] It also had significant practical effects.[185] However, the court expressed no view on whether this was a correct interpretation, saying this would be for a future court to decide: "It should be noted that the Attorney General of Canada ... argued that s. 35(1) protects Indigenous peoples' inherent right of self-government 'in relation to child and family services,' ... This Court has not yet addressed the question, and it is unnecessary for it to do so in this case to provide the requested opinion on the constitutionality of the Act."[186] The issue was, therefore, avoided yet again.

Greater international recognition of Indigenous rights, including the right to self-determination, has occurred in recent decades. The United Nations established a Working Group on Indigenous Populations in 1982, which began working on a declaration on the rights of Indigenous peoples in 1985, producing a draft document in 1993. The *United Nations Declaration on the Rights of Indigenous Peoples* (UNDRIP) was adopted by the General Assembly of the United Nations in 2007.[187] Article 3 of the declaration states that "Indigenous peoples have the right to self-determination," and Article 4 affirms the right to autonomy or self-government in matters relating to their internal and local affairs.

Canada voted against the declaration but subsequently dropped its objections and endorsed it three years later in 2010 as an aspirational, non-binding document. In 2021, Parliament passed legislation to affirm the declaration as a source for the interpretation of Canadian law and as a universal international human rights instrument with application in Canadian law.[188] It is important to note that this legislation only applies to matters within the federal jurisdiction. But many issues of great concern to Indigenous groups, such as land and resources, are within the provincial jurisdiction. To date, only British Columbia and Northwest Territories have committed to making UNDRIP apply to their laws and policy. It is unclear what impact the declaration will have on the rights of Indigenous peoples in Canada, and clarification will likely take many years.

Reconciliation in Canada

In recent decades, and especially since the publication of the Truth and Reconciliation Commission ("TRC") report on residential schools in 2015, reconciliation has received much attention in Canada. In general, it refers to non-Indigenous Canadians having a greater awareness of the history and current socio-economic conditions of Indigenous peoples and having a desire to make amends for that history and improve both the conditions of Indigenous peoples and the relationship between Indigenous peoples and non-Indigenous Canadians. Angela Sterritt, an Indigenous journalist, has explained that

> the term has come to describe attempts made by individuals and institutions to raise awareness about colonization and its ongoing effects on Indigenous peoples. Reconciliation also refers to efforts made to address the harms caused by various policies and programs of colonization, such as residential schools. For some, the word represents an opportunity to reflect on the past, to heal and to make right. For others, however, current gestures of reconciliation are merely performative and lack meaningful action to address the harms done by colonization.[189]

Reconciliation activities have extended to changes made by a wide variety of groups and organizations, including greater awareness in schools, universities, governments, and professional bodies of the history and circumstances of Indigenous peoples and the impact of colonialism.[190]

The RCAP report included a chapter on residential schools and recommended a national inquiry into the system. The federal government's response

The raising of the Reconciliation Pole at the University of British Columbia in 2017. The Reconciliation Pole was carved by Haida artist 7idansuu (Jim Hart) and tells the story of residential schools and their impact. | *7idansuu (Edenshaw), James Hart,* Reconciliation Pole: Honouring a Time Before, During and After Canada's Indian Residential Schools, *2015–2017, red and yellow cedar, paint, copper and abalone. Collection of the Morris and Helen Belkin Art Gallery, University of British Columbia, commissioned with support from the Audain Foundation and UBC's Matching Fund for Outdoor Art through Infrastructure Impact Charges, 2017. Photo: UBC Public Affairs/Paul Joseph*

to that report in January 1998 had a Statement of Reconciliation containing an apology and $350 million to facilitate healing. However, the issue of residential schools remained a primary concern to Indigenous people. As a result, hundreds of criminal and civil cases were commenced against the federal government, the individuals who abused the children in those schools, and the institutions that

Canada and Colonialism

operated them. In August 2005, the Assembly of First Nations launched a class-action lawsuit against the federal government on behalf of former students and their families. A financial settlement was announced the following year. It came into effect on September 19, 2007.[191] Other components of the settlement included an apology and an inquiry into residential schools. Prime Minister Stephen Harper gave the apology in Parliament on June 11, 2008.

The inquiry was carried out by the TRC, chaired by Justice Murray Sinclair. The commission spent six years travelling to all parts of Canada and heard from more than 6,500 witnesses. In December 2015, it released its six-volume final report.[192] The commission defined "reconciliation" as "an ongoing process of establishing and maintaining respectful relationships."[193] The report covers many topics related to reconciliation. In addition to residential schools, it discusses Canadian sovereignty, Aboriginal self-determination, Indigenous law, and UNDRIP.

Ninety-four recommendations or "calls to action" in the report were designed to bring about reconciliation. The new federal government of Justin Trudeau (son of Pierre Trudeau) agreed to all of them. They are far-reaching and include recommendations regarding child welfare, education, language and culture, health, and justice; an action plan to implement UNDRIP; a Royal Proclamation and Covenant of Reconciliation; and suggestions for educating lawyers, public servants, and journalists about treaties, Aboriginal rights, and related matters. There are differing views on how many of these calls to action may now be considered complete. A review of the analyses made by the federal government and three independent organizations concluded in 2022 that only between 5 and 13 percent had been completed after seven years, and there was still a very long way to go.[194]

The Supreme Court of Canada has described reconciliation as "the fundamental objective"[195] and "the grand purpose"[196] of modern Aboriginal law. Reconciliation has been defined in different ways by the court. The more common use has been to balance Aboriginal and treaty rights with the interests of non-Indigenous peoples and the sovereignty of the Crown.[197] Since the 1970s, the courts, and especially the Supreme Court of Canada, have played a central role in Indigenous matters and the legal reconciliation process. This has been done mainly through their interpretation and application of section 35 of the *Constitution Act 1982* to recognize and affirm existing Aboriginal and treaty rights.

The most significant changes in the legal position of Indigenous peoples over the last fifty years can be summarized by referring to section 35 and by listing some landmark cases from the court. The *Calder* decision in 1973, on

Aboriginal title,[198] "ushered in the modern era of Aboriginal land law," according to former Chief Justice McLachlin.[199] It was a split decision, and the Nisga'a lost on a technicality. But the decision confirmed the possibility that Aboriginal rights and title still existed in the absence of a clear and plain intention of the government to extinguish them. (Extinguishment is no longer possible after the passage of section 35.) The *Guerin* decision of 1984 dealt with the enforceability of the government's obligations to Indigenous peoples.[200] In that case, the Musqueam successfully obtained a legal remedy for breach of duty by the federal government in managing reserve lands. The court rejected arguments that the band had no legal interest in the land and that the government's obligations to Indigenous peoples were not legally binding. The next year, the court decided *Simon,* which marked the beginning of a line of cases upholding treaty rights in favour of Indigenous groups and construing them liberally.[201]

The Musqueam were also successful in 1990 in *Sparrow* in getting recognition under section 35 of their Aboriginal right to fish.[202] However, the court set out a tough test to satisfy (rights must pre-exist contact with non-Indigenous people and be integral to the group's distinctive culture). It also allowed the government to "infringe" section 35 rights if it could justify the infringement – essentially balancing the section 35 constitutional right against the interests of non-Indigenous Canadians. In 2004, the court gave a detailed account in the *Haida* case of the government's duty to consult Indigenous peoples if it were proposing to make a decision or do something that could adversely affect an asserted Aboriginal or treaty right.[203] This duty was intended as a form of interim relief to protect the asserted right until agreement or litigation resolved the issue. This has become a principal area of Aboriginal law in practice. The *Tsilhqot'in* case of 2014 was the first decision to uphold a finding that Aboriginal title exists.[204] It built on prior rulings to set out what an Indigenous group needs to show to prove title (exclusive occupation at the time of assertion of Crown sovereignty) and what title confers (similar to fee simple but subject to "inherent limits" and only alienable to the Crown).

Colonialism Continues

These legal changes since 1970 have resulted in significant gains for Indigenous peoples. However, they did not change the fundamental colonial relationship between non-Indigenous governments and Indigenous peoples established during the height of the British Empire.[205] The recognition of a fiduciary relationship requires federal and provincial governments to take into consideration that they have legally enforceable obligations to First Nations regarding their exercise of powers. The governments still retain their control but must be more careful in how it is exercised. The courts have interpreted historical treaties in a manner that is more favourable to Indigenous peoples. But those treaties have been upheld as valid surrenders of large areas of land despite some acknowledgment of the concerns relating to their creation. Aboriginal rights (including Aboriginal title) have been recognized and affirmed. But they are difficult to prove. Also, like treaty rights, governments may infringe them if a court decides the infringement can be justified by a test that essentially balances the constitutionally protected rights of Indigenous peoples against the interests of Canadians generally. The Supreme Court of Canada has said that the "settlement of foreign populations," economic development, the building of infrastructure, and the protection of the environment are the types of objective that can justify infringement by governments of Aboriginal title.[206] Critics have argued that this is to justify colonialism.[207] The Supreme Court of Canada has avoided ruling on the issue of what, if any, sovereignty and rights of self-government still exist for Indigenous groups. These legal developments have taken place in the context of a history in which the sovereignty of Indigenous groups has been denied, and they have been largely dispossessed from their traditional lands and limited to reserves.

Some First Nations are subject to modern treaties, self-government agreements, special legislation,[208] or legislation such as the *First Nations Land Management Act*,[209] which limit the government's control and delegate powers to First Nations. However, the majority of First Nations are not parties to such arrangements. They still remain subject to the control of the government set out in the *Indian Act*. As we saw in Chapter 6, that control dates back to legislation passed in 1839, which treated reserve lands as Crown lands; in 1850, giving the commissioner of lands "full power" to manage those lands; and in 1869, replacing traditional government.

The role of the Indian agent was phased out in the 1960s, and changes have been made to the *Indian Act* since the 1970s that moderated some of its provisions. It was amended in 1985 to make changes set out in Bill C-31 that gave bands more control of membership,[210] and in 1988 to clarify and amend the sections dealing with the power of band councils to levy property taxes.[211] The provisions regarding surrenders of reserve lands were amended in 2012 to simplify and clarify the procedure.[212] The minister's power to disallow band council bylaws was repealed in 2014.[213] This was part of legislation with the somewhat misleading name *Indian Act Amendment and Replacement Act*. It did not, in fact, replace the *Indian Act* nor change the fundamental nature of the act as a reflection of Victorian imperial prejudices about the capacity of Indigenous peoples to control their lives and property.

Even those First Nations that have now escaped the worst features of the *Indian Act* through treaties, other agreements, or special legislation do not have control of their traditional territories or recognized sovereignty. Without constitutional protection for self-government, Indigenous people are at the mercy of governments that may repeal or revise any existing recognition and a cloud is cast over the validity of their laws. The shadow of the Empire remains.

Conclusion

Given Canada's involvement in and support for the Empire, some questions arise. What impacts were left by that Empire, and what, if anything, should be done about them? As might be expected, imperialists considered the Empire to be a good thing. Their books are full of statements describing the benefits conferred by it. Lord Lugard, a leading imperial administrator, said it protected the weak from the tyranny of the strong; extended the rule of justice and liberty; protected traders, settlers, and missionaries; checked anarchy and bloodshed; and suppressed slavery and barbarous practices.[1] Another colonial administrator, Alan Burns, added such benefits as treatment of diseases and the provision of education, development funding, railways, and roads.[2] Ralph Furse, who was responsible for the recruitment and training of colonial administrators for many years, included the introduction of cricket.[3] Writing during the Second World War, Stephen Leacock claimed that "our Empire not only contains in its destiny the chief hope for universal peace, but the chief opportunity towards the abiding plenty and prosperity on which alone universal peace can permanently rest."[4]

On the other hand, a couple of leading imperialists were prepared to concede that economic benefits were lacking for the local people. Alfred Milner wrote, "If the question is asked, how much, beyond giving it just laws and honest administration, Great Britain has done for her vast dependent Empire, a true answer cannot be altogether flattering to our national pride."[5] During the Second World War, Margery Perham criticized the lack of attention to economic conditions and referred to the creation of "these tropical East Ends."[6]

She called for a more active role for the state rather than the prevailing laissez-faire policy. A policy of planned economic development was, in fact, later adopted, although too little and too late. As might be expected, leaders of decolonization movements disputed the supposed benefits of the Empire.[7]

Some imperialists were not troubled by imperialism on the grounds that the Indigenous peoples had never enjoyed liberty, and it was better that they be ruled by the British.[8] Historian William Winwood Reade denounced the "sickly school of politicians" who declared imperialism to be a crime, and instead maintained that "the conquest of Asia by European powers is therefore in reality Emancipation."[9] Others defended the Empire on supposedly Darwinian principles of the survival of the fittest, and cared little about benefits for the conquered. Albert Carman, a Canadian journalist and son of the head of the Methodist Church of Canada, was among them. He wrote *The Ethics of Imperialism* in 1905, which has been described as "one of the most hairy-chested presentations of Darwinian imperialism."[10] In that book, Carman explained how the imperialist spirit "teaches the essential inequality of men, the duty of recognising that inequality, the duty of doing unto some others precisely what you hope they will not be able to do unto you, the refusal of equal rights to some people. It sees inferiority of rights in color, race and feebleness – especially in the latter."[11] In his view, humanitarianism was merely "pharisaical chatter."[12] One can detect here an early expression of fascist philosophy.

Modern writers are divided on whether the Empire was a good thing, and the discussion can get quite heated.[13] The conservative historian Niall Ferguson is often attacked as an apologist for the Empire, although he is more balanced than sometimes portrayed. He recognizes that the record was not unblemished and that the Empire did not live up to its ideal of individual liberty. After giving a list of benefits conferred, though, he concludes that the Empire was a good thing: "No organization in history has done more to promote the free movement of goods, capital and labour than the British Empire in the nineteenth and early twentieth centuries. And no organization has done more to impose Western norms of law, order and governance around the world."[14]

In *Inglorious Empire*, Shashi Tharoor disputes Ferguson and rejects the various claims for the benefit of the Empire as far as India is concerned.[15] Tharoor has, in turn, been challenged, especially so far as his arguments based on disrupting economic progress and creating communal division are concerned.[16] Jon Wilson, another writer on British India, says, "The British Empire's greatest legacy was to create some of the most disjointed and chaotically ruled societies in the world."[17]

Canada and Colonialism

Another historian, Piers Brendon, has performed a moral audit of the Empire, setting "its obvious pluses" against "its palpable minuses." Liberalism and the civilizing mission, good administration, and largely peaceful dissolution are set against its coercive and exploitative nature, famines, brutal suppression of resistance, and the slave trade.[18] Brendon concludes that "it seems clear that, even according to its own lights, the British empire was in grave moral deficit," and quotes Edward Gibbon, the great historian of the Roman Empire, who wrote that "The history of empires is that of the miseries of humankind."[19]

As an intellectual exercise, there may be some merit in trying to balance the credits and debits of the Empire. However, it is impossible to assign values to the different components. How do you calculate the cost of destroying the traditional way of life of Indigenous peoples and taking their land? What is the value of lost community and of freedom? How do you value the loss of communal land used for hunting and gathering that cannot be sold under Indigenous laws? What is the benefit of "economic progress" that destroys or distorts a culture, economy, and traditional way of life and leads to extensive adverse socio-economic, health, and economic consequences? How do you value "good administration" that is based on despotism, destroys more democratic traditional governments, and establishes traditions of autocratic government in their place, which still continue?

Further, imperialism is taking control of the lands and lives of peoples of another society based on a belief in racial and/or cultural supremacy, and using force as necessary. Such a predatory, hierarchical world order is systemically immoral. To quote the Nigerian author Chinua Achebe, "It is a gross crime for anyone to impose himself on another, to seize his land and his history, and then to compound this by making out that the victim is some kind of ward or minor requiring protection."[20] Trying to offset this fundamental immorality with benefits conferred on the victims is like trying to excuse slavery because the slave is given shelter and food.

Historian Ronald Hyam argues that the British Empire could not legitimately claim to have been "an ethical empire" since it employed slavery, seized lands, and used shocking brutality, among other things. (However, it did not lack an ethical policy based upon humanitarian principles.)[21] As Ashley Jackson, another historian, says, "Surely it is appropriate to avoid endorsing past actions that we would utterly disapprove of today: we would no longer consider it acceptable to take over someone else's land or kill them – so why endorse what stemmed directly from such actions in the past?"[22] Further, if Russia's imperialist expansion in 2022 into Ukraine was wrong, as confirmed by worldwide condemnation, how is it possible to deny that Britain's imperialist expansion into North America, India, and Africa was also wrong? Some defenders of the British Empire point out that Britain often expanded its empire in areas that had already been colonized, or that some Indigenous or other rulers were more brutal.[23] Such arguments may provide the context of imperialist actions but do not absolve them.

If you accept, as I do, that imperialism is wrong and that Canada bears some responsibility for it, then the question that arises is what, if anything, should now be done as a result?

An important step would be greater public awareness of Canada's history of colonialism – not just as a former colony that received self-government and became independent, but as a colonizer. There should be more education in schools and colleges regarding this history. Official publications should at least record the racist and white supremacist views held by imperialists. Existing statues of John A. Macdonald should be removed or, at the very least, a prominent plaque should be added that explains the harm he did as well as his achievements.[24] No new recognition should be given, as was done as recently as 2012 when a building and parkway in Ottawa were renamed after him.[25] The biographies of governors general on the website of the governor general of Canada should be more balanced and less hagiographic.[26] The role played by Governor Grey in the brutal suppression of Indigenous peoples in Africa should be recorded in place of the bland references that he was administrator for Rhodesia and gained commercial experience as a director of the British South Africa Company. It is unacceptable for the current *Canadian Citizenship Guide* to display John Buchan (Lord Tweedsmuir) as a promoter of multiculturalism without mentioning his racist and white supremacist views and demeaning references to Indigenous peoples in Canada.[27] It is also no longer acceptable for Tweedsmuir Park, a British Columbia provincial park, to be named after him. The National Library webpage on Stephen Leacock should discuss his imperialism.[28] Private bodies, such as the one that presents the annual Stephen Leacock Award, should consider providing information on his imperialist views. This would, at least, raise the question of how "his gentle style of humour" can be reconciled with his brutal expression of racist ideas.[29] Whether street names should continue to be named after imperialists is a matter for local consultation. The benefits of ending the association (which in many cases will have been forgotten) should be weighed against the local disruption.

The question of whether to continue with the British monarch as Canada's head of state should also be thoroughly discussed by Canadians as part of any process of decolonization and democracy generally.[30] The monarchy played a central role in imperial rule. In the words of John Buchan, "The pivot of the Empire is the Crown."[31] An increasing number of Caribbean nations have recently rejected the Crown as part of their own journey to decolonization. To date, there has been no widespread public debate in Canada. The suggestion of change has been dismissed by most Canadian politicians without serious debate as a matter of little importance.[32] One exception is Niki Ashton, an MP who presented the argument in favour of abolition:

> We must recognize the truth when it comes to Canada's ugly history of colonization. That colonization is rooted in the Crown's control, to its benefit. With the *Indian Act,* the reserve system, the residential school system, the pillaging of indigenous resources and the genocide of indigenous peoples, the devastating impacts of colonization are still evident today.
>
> Reconciliation means carrying on a journey of decolonization and this must include ending our ties with the British monarchy. The monarchy is a symbol of colonialism for many indigenous peoples and for many people who have come to Canada from around the world.[33]

Canadians should, at least, have a full and honest discussion of this issue.

There can be no doubt that the impact of colonialism on Indigenous peoples in Canada, as elsewhere in the Empire, was and is profound. In the words of a justice of the Supreme Court of Canada, "The history of Indian peoples in North America has generally been one of dispossession, including dispossession of their pre-European sovereignty, of their traditional land, and of distinctive elements of their culture."[34] The residential schools examined in detail by the Truth and Reconciliation Commission were just a part, although an important part, of that history.[35] Indigenous writers have described these impacts on them and their communities in moving and passionate detail.[36] Jody Wilson-Raybould, who was active in Indigenous politics before becoming Canada's justice minister, has described the effects of colonization on both Indigenous and non-Indigenous people:

> [They] are within each of us, as much as they are in our social realities, culture, laws, politics, and institutions. Patterns of thought and action have been shaped, often in unseen ways, by the experience of colonization. For First Nations people, this is seen in how we have internalized aspects of being an "Indian," often feeling disassociated inside ourselves from our true identities, who we are, and the very places to which we belong.

... For non-Indigenous people, this internal colonization is seen in the ingrained, casual, often unrecognized racism and paternalism that is frequently present in interactions.[37]

She describes it as a shocking thing that in Canada, the central piece of legislation about Indigenous peoples is still the *Indian Act* – "a segregationist, colonial and racist law passed in 1876."[38] She writes that "it is colonial paternalism at its core, resting on the racist belief that Indigenous peoples are uncivilized and cannot govern themselves."[39]

If internal colonialism in Canada was "a bad thing," what can now be done to limit its impacts? First, we must recognize a fundamental difference between external ("Third World") and internal ("Fourth World") colonialism as described by political scientist Alan Cairns:

Although Third and Fourth World peoples were both subject to the hierarchy of imperialism, the latter were never treated as peoples/nations on the road to independence. In Canada, Indian peoples were placed outside the standard working of the majority's constitutional order, and governed in geographically discrete communities by superintendents who were the domestic counterparts of district officers in British colonial sub-Saharan Africa. The system of Indian reserves could be thought of as transitional appendages to the mainstream constitutional order, while the policy of assimilation – for which church-run residential schools were key instruments – eroded cultural diversity. In the context of Canadian domestic imperialism, therefore, the governing logic of the state was that indigenous difference was transitional: to be overcome by state pressure and inducements.[40]

Under this model, "decolonization" would occur when Indigenous peoples had ceased to be different and were assimilated into the majority population of settlers and their descendants. The colonized would gradually disappear. That model was abandoned in the 1970s and is no longer acceptable, raising the question of what "decolonization" now means in the Canadian context.

Decolonization in Canada cannot be the same as the process that took place decades ago for British colonies in Asia and Africa. That process followed the classic definition of "decolonization" from the *Oxford English Dictionary* (OED): "The withdrawal of a colonizing state from its colonies, leaving them independent; the acquisition of political or economic independence by a former colony."[41] Cairns observes that "the Fourth World nationalist project must accommodate itself to an ongoing relationship with the majority population within the same state that was the historic agent of indigenous dispossession."[42] He continues, "In the Third World, the imperial power formally departs; in the Fourth World what was the imperial majority remains behind, perhaps no longer imperial, but still the majority."[43] They have no distant home across the oceans to return to. Most importantly, these settler communities will not be suddenly relegated to minority status, as was the case for minority settler communities in Kenya and Zimbabwe. The previously privileged position of settlers in Africa derived not from their numbers but from their linkage with the imperial presence in the heyday of overseas empire.[44] For Indigenous peoples in Canada, "independence, the logical antithesis to colonialism, is not an available option. This is the crucial tension, or the cruel reality, at the heart of indigenous nationalism in Canada."[45] The Supreme Court of Canada said in a case on Quebec's right to secede from Canada, in passing and without full discussion, that an Aboriginal right of self-determination "cannot in the present circumstances be said to ground a right to unilateral secession."[46]

For the Indigenous peoples of Canada, there will be no lowering of the old flag, speeches and dances at independence celebrations, and the sailing away of the governor general. "Decolonization" for them must mean some application of the secondary meaning given in the OED: "The process of eliminating the effects or influence of colonization or colonialism on the attitudes, assumptions, power structures, institutions, etc., of a formerly colonized people or (later also) a former colonial power or culture; an instance of this." This reality was recognized by George Manuel, a Secwépemc leader, who compared the position of Indigenous peoples in Canada and newly independent countries like Tanzania in his book *The Fourth World: An Indian Reality*, published in 1974. Manuel wrote that the distinction was noted by an African diplomat, who, "pointed out to me that political independence for colonized peoples was only the Third World. 'When native peoples come into their own, on the basis of their own cultures and traditions that will be the Fourth World.'"[47] Manuel interpreted this to mean that instead of Indigenous peoples in Canada creating their own nation-states, Canada "would learn to contain within itself many different cultures and life-ways, some highly tribal and traditional, some highly urban and individual."[48]

What, then, does "decolonization" mean in Canada? How can the harmful effects of colonization be mitigated or reversed? When will Indigenous peoples "come into their own"? It seems to me that only Indigenous peoples are in a position to answer this question, and then only for their own nation.

Some Indigenous leaders have explained what they would regard as "decolonization," and it seems only fitting to give a couple of them the last words. In essence, it comes down to self-determination. George Manuel's son, Arthur Manuel, devotes the final chapter of his book, *The Reconciliation Manifesto*, to what he calls "The Six-Step Program to Decolonization."[49] The critical step is recognition of the right to self-determination, "which is the essential decolonizing remedy to move Indigenous peoples from dependency to freedom."[50] He concludes by saying:

> We will know that Canada is finally decolonized when Indigenous peoples are exercising our inherent political and legal powers in our own territories up to the standard recognized by the United Nations, when your government has instituted sweeping policy reforms based on Indigenous rights standards and when our future generations can live in sustainable ways on an Indigenous designed and driven economy.[51]

Wilson-Raybould also stresses the necessity for self-determination. In her words, "at its core, decolonization in Canada is the right of self-determination."[52] She uses the analogy of a "postcolonial door" to illustrate the continuum of government reform and nation rebuilding. It is represented visually by three doors: "one locked, one partially open, and one fully opened to a new future based on

Copyright Jody Wilson-Raybould, used by permission

The artwork "Building on OUR Success: Navigating Our Way Through The Post-Colonial Door" shows the three doors — one locked, one partially open, and one fully open to a post-colonial future. It originally appeared in *Governance Toolkit: A Guide to Nation Building* and *From Where I Stand,* written by Jody Wilson-Raybould.

self-determination." Opening the door will require the federal and provincial governments, in partnership with Indigenous peoples, to remove legislative and other barriers to Indigenous nation-building in Canada. "Building a shared postcolonial future will depend on [all Canadians] working together while enabling Indigenous Nations to determine their own course."[53]

Acknowledgments

This book was written by me but could not have been published without the much-appreciated contribution of a number of other people. I owe a great and continuing debt to my Indigenous clients, especially the Musqueam of Vancouver. They first opened my eyes to the disastrous impacts of colonialism over forty years ago and deepened my understanding over the many years that I was privileged to serve them. To all of them, I record my thanks, "hay chxw q'a." I also owe a debt to my professional colleagues over those years with whom I had the opportunity to exchange views.

The production of a book is a fascinating process. I have been very fortunate to work more than once with the dedicated staff at UBC Press/Purich Books. On this book, they have included Nadine Pedersen (editor), Katrina Petrik (production editor), and Carmen Tiampo (assistant editor). Lesley Erickson, author and editor, provided invaluable and much needed advice at a critical time on the structuring of the book. The outstanding skills of Audrey McClellan as a copy editor saved me much embarrassment by correcting errors that escaped my repeated reading of the manuscript but which I know would have mysteriously and glaringly appeared immediately after publication to haunt me forever if she had not caught them. I thank Irma Rodriguez for the design and composition of the book; Judith Earnshaw for proofreading, and Judy Dunlop for the difficult task of preparing the index. I am very grateful for the comments received from anonymous reviewers as part of the external assessment process. Their willingness to give their time, knowledge, and expertise without receiving any credit is very commendable and in the best traditions of scholarship.

I owe a debt of gratitude to many other people, in addition to those directly involved in the publication of this book. Librarians at Simon Fraser University, the University of British Columbia, and the Courthouse Library of British Columbia were very helpful and efficient in answering questions and providing materials. Many of the older materials were located in digital format at the Internet Archive, an invaluable collection for researchers. As shown in the credits, illustrations were obtained from sources around the Commonwealth but primarily from Library and Archives Canada. Like any author in history and law, I have relied heavily on previously published works, as listed in the notes. Whether I have agreed with them or not, such works have been instructive and food for thought.

Finally, and as ever, I must record my gratitude to my wife Pui-ah and our sons Christopher and Alistair for all that they have given me.

Notes

Note on Terminology

1 I have attempted to summarize some of the legal issues in Jim Reynolds, *Aboriginal Peoples and the Law: A Critical Introduction* (Vancouver: UBC Press, 2018), 10–14.

Introduction

1 Truth and Reconciliation Commission of Canada (TRC), *The Final Report of the Truth and Reconciliation Commission of Canada,* vol. 1, *Canada's Residential Schools: The History, Part 1, Origins to 1939* (Montreal and Kingston: McGill-Queen's University Press, 2015), 9.
2 *House of Commons Debates,* 28th Parl., 3rd Sess., October 18, 1971, 8545.
3 Eric Hobsbawm, "The Sense of the Past," in *On History* (London: Weidenfeld and Nicolson, 1997), 23.
4 TRC, *Canada's Residential Schools,* 1:11.
5 TRC, *Canada's Residential Schools,* 1:24.
6 Canada, Department of External Affairs, *Statements and Speeches,* no. 60/32, September 26, 1960, quoted in Asa McKercher, *Canada and the World since 1867* (London: Bloomsbury Academic, 2019), 152.
7 Harsha Walia, "Really, Harper: Canada Has No History of Colonialism?," *Vancouver Sun,* September 27, 2009; Christo Aivalis, "Justin Trudeau and Canada's Colonial Baggage: Past and Present," Active History, April 28, 2016, https://activehistory.ca/blog/2016/04/28/justin-trudeau-and-canadas-colonial-baggage-past-and-present.
8 See, generally, Asa McKercher, "The Centre Cannot Hold: Canada, Colonialism and the 'Afro-Asian Bloc' at the United Nations, 1960–62," *Journal of Imperial and Commonwealth History* 42, 2 (2014): 329–49.
9 Stewart Wallace, *The Memoirs of the Rt. Hon. Sir George Foster* (Toronto: Macmillan, 1933), 194.
10 *House of Commons Debates,* 22nd Parl., 5th Sess., vol.1, January 14, 1957, 175.
11 McKercher, "The Centre Cannot Hold," 333, emphasis in original.
12 McKercher, "The Centre Cannot Hold," 341.

13 "King and Country? Three-in-Five Want to Chuck Charles as Canadians Cool towards New Monarch," Angus Reid Institute, April 24, 2023, https://angusreid.org/canada-constitutional -monarchy-king-charles-coronation/; "Royal Pains? Just 37% View King Charles Favourably as Monarch and Monarchy Skids in Favourability since Death of Late Queen," Ipsos, May 4, 2023, https://www.ipsos.com/sites/default/files/ct/news/documents/2023-05/Monarchy %20factum%20-Final.pdf.

14 Alice R. Stewart, "Canadian–West Indian Union, 1884–1885," *Canadian Historical Review* 31, 4 (1950): 369–89; R.W. Winks, *Canadian–West Indian Union: A Forty-Year Minuet*, Commonwealth Papers no. 11 (London: University of London, 1968); Paula Hastings, "Dreams of a Tropical Canada: Race, Nation, and Canadian Aspirations in the Caribbean Basin, 1883–1919" (PhD diss., Duke University, 2010); Paula Hastings, "Rounding Off the Confederation: Geopolitics, Tropicality and Canada's 'Destiny' in the West Indies in the Early Twentieth Century," *Journal of Colonialism and Colonial History* 14 (2013): doi:10. 1353/cch.2013.0022; Paula Hastings, *Dominion over Palm and Pine: A History of Canadian Aspirations in the British Caribbean* (Montreal and Kingston: McGill-Queen's University Press, 2022).

15 Quoted in Hastings, "Dreams of a Tropical Canada," 215.

16 Joseph Pope, *Confidential Memorandum on the Subject of the Annexation of the West India Islands to the Dominion of Canada*, 1917, 4.

17 Hastings, "Dreams of a Tropical Canada," 270. For the opposition from West Indians to the proposed annexation, see Paula Hastings, "Territorial Spoils, Transnational Black Resistance, and Canada's Evolving Autonomy during the First World War," *Histoire sociale/ Social History* 47, 94 (2014): 443–70.

18 Todd Gordon, *Imperialist Canada* (Winnipeg: Arbeiter Ring, 2010); Tyler A. Shipley, *Canada in the World: Settler Capitalism and the Colonial Imagination* (Halifax: Fernwood, 2020).

19 J.H. Hamilton, *The All-Red Route 1893–1953: The Trans-Pacific Mail Service between British Columbia, Australia and New Zealand* (Victoria: Archives of British Columbia, 1956).

20 James (Jan) Morris, *Pax Britannica* (Harmondsworth, UK: Penguin, 1979), 324.

21 For the dispute in the UK, see Sathnam Sanghera, *Empireland: How Imperialism Has Shaped Modern Britain* (New York: Pantheon, 2023); Nigel Biggar, *Colonialism: A Moral Reckoning* (London: William Collins, 2023).

22 See Jim Reynolds, *From Wardship to Rights: The Guerin Case and Aboriginal Law* (Vancouver: UBC Press, 2020).

23 For current definitions, see John Darwin, *After Tamerlane: The Rise and Fall of Global Empires, 1400–2000* (London: Penguin, 2007), 416; Immanuel Ness and Zak Cope, eds., *Palgrave Encyclopedia of Imperialism and Anti-Imperialism*, 2nd ed. (Cham, Switzerland: Palgrave, 2021), vi; Margaret Kohn and Kavita Reddy, "Colonialism," in *The Stanford Encyclopedia of Philosophy* (Spring 2023 edition), ed. Edward N. Zalta and Uri Nodelman, https://plato.stanford.edu/archives/spr2023/entries/colonialism/.

For the original definitions of "to colonise" as "to plant with inhabitants" and of "colony" as "a body of people drawn from the mother-country to inhabit some distant place," see Samuel Johnson, *A Dictionary of the English Language* (London: Printed by W. Strahan for J. & P. Knapton etc., 1755).

Chapter 1: Historical Overview

1 Royal Commission on Aboriginal Peoples, *Report of the Royal Commission on Aboriginal Peoples*, vol. 1, *Looking Forward, Looking Back* (Ottawa: Minister of Supply and Services Canada, 1996), s 3.2 (hereafter RCAP).

2 RCAP, 1:41.

3 RCAP, 1:42. A major exception was the killing of the Beothuks (who became extinct in 1829) by settlers; see Ingeborg Marshall, *A History and Ethnography of the Beothuk* (Montreal and Kingston: McGill-Queen's University Press, 1996), 100–5.

4 RCAP, 1:42.

5 "Wampum was made traditionally of quahog (clam) shells, drilled and threaded into strings or woven into belts ... Wampum strings and belts were used as aids to memory and to validate the authority of persons carrying messages between communities and nations": RCAP, 1:88, note 8.

6 Robert S. Allen, *The British India Department and the Frontier in North America, 1755–1830*, Canadian Historic Sites, Occasional Papers in Archaeology and History 14 (Ottawa: National Historic Parks and Sites Branch, 1975); Robert Allen, *His Majesty's Indian Allies: British Indian Policy in the Defence of Canada, 1774–1815* (Toronto: Dundurn, 1993); Olive Dickason, *Canada's First Nations: A History of Founding Peoples from Earliest Times*, 3rd ed. (Don Mills, ON: Oxford University Press, 2002), chap. 12; P. Whitney Lackenbauer and Craig Leslie Mantle, eds., *Aboriginal Peoples and the Canadian Military: Historical Perspectives* (Kingston, ON: Canadian Defence Academy Press, 2007).

7 See, generally, Terry Fenge and Jim Aldredge, eds., *Keeping Promises: The Royal Proclamation of 1763, Aboriginal Rights and Treaties in Canada* (Montreal and Kingston: McGill-Queen's University Press, 2015).

8 Dickason, *Canada's First Nations*, 160.

9 John F. Leslie, *Commissions of Inquiry into Indian Affairs in the Canadas, 1828–1858* (Ottawa: Indian Affairs and Northern Development Canada, 1985), 1.

10 Leslie, *Commissions of Inquiry*, gives a comprehensive account. See also John Giokas, *The Indian Act: Evolution, Overview and Options for Amendment and Transition* (Ottawa: Royal Commission on Aboriginal Peoples, March 22, 1995), 19; L.F.S. Upton, "The Origins of Canadian Indian Policy," *Journal of Canadian Studies* 8, 4 (1973): 51–61.

11 Flora Shaw, *A Tropical Dependency* (London: Nisbet, 1905), 460–66; Paul E. Lovejoy and Jan S. Hogendorn, *Slow Death for Slavery: The Course of Abolition in Northern Nigeria 1897–1936* (Cambridge: Cambridge University Press, 1993).

12 William Dalrymple, *The Anarchy: The East India Company, Corporate Violence and the Pillage of Empire* (New York: Bloomsbury, 2021); Stephen Bown, *The Company: The Rise and Fall of the Hudson's Bay Empire* (Toronto: Doubleday, 2022). The lands subject to the Hudson's Bay monopoly were roughly doubled in 1821 and extended to the Pacific.

13 The Hudson's Bay Company generally claimed no jurisdiction over Indigenous peoples unless they offended against its traders: Hamar Foster, "Conflict Resolution during the Fur Trade in the Canadian North West 1803–1859," *Advocate* 51 (1993): 871, 874. Of course, its presence had significant impacts on the way of life of Indigenous peoples, including their health: James Daschuk, *Clearing the Plains: Disease, Politics of Starvation, and the Loss of Aboriginal Life* (Regina: University of Regina Press, 2013), 59–77.

14 William Grant, "Canada versus Guadeloupe: An Episode of the Seven Years' War," *American Historical Review* 17, 4 (1912): 735–43.

15 For a detailed discussion of the Darling Report, see E.A. Heaman, "Space, Race, and Violence: The Beginning of 'Civilization' in Canada," in *Violence, Order and Unrest: A History of British North America, 1749–1876*, ed. Elizabeth Mancke, Jerry Bannister, Denis B. McKim, and Scott W. See (Toronto: University of Toronto Press, 2019), 135–58. There were earlier isolated examples of a policy of establishing reserves going back to 1633 at the

mission at Sillery in New France: Reuben Thwaites, ed., *The Jesuit Relations and Allied Documents,* vol. 6 (Cleveland: Borrows Bros., 1898), 145–51.

16 Charles Bagot, Rawson William Rawson, John Davidson, and William Hepburn, *Report on the Affairs of the Indians of Canada, Laid before the Legislative Assembly, 20th March, 1845* (Kingston, ON: Queen's Printer, 1845), Legislative Journal of the Province of Canada 1847, App. T at commencement of Section III, Recommendations.

17 John George Lambton, Earl of Durham, *The Report and Despatches of the Earl of Durham* (London: Ridgways, 1839); F. Bradshaw, *Self-Government in Canada and How It Was Achieved: The Story of Lord Durham's Report* (London: King and Son, 1903).

18 *Gradual Civilization Act,* SPC 1857, c 26.

19 Some writers distinguished India from other non-settler colonies and referred only to the latter as the "Dependent" or "Colonial" Empire: see Reginald Coupland, *The Empire in These Days* (London: Macmillan, 1935), 159.

20 Bampfylde Fuller, *The Empire of India* (London: Pitman, 1913), 195–96.

21 Syed Ahmed Khan Bahadur, *The Causes of the Indian Revolt* (Benares, India: Medical Hall Press, 1873), 11–15.

22 The over five hundred princely states that were ruled indirectly by Britain (see Chapter 4 of this volume) are often excluded from the term "British India."

23 See, generally, Martin Meredith, *The Fate of Africa: A History of the Continent since Independence* (New York: Public Affairs, 2011).

24 Meredith, *The Fate of Africa,* 1.

25 According to one prominent imperial historian, British rule in Africa was typical of such rule in dependent colonies (excluding India) generally. See Coupland, *The Empire in These Days,* 160–61.

26 Harry Johnston, *A History of the Colonization of Africa by Alien Races* (Cambridge: Cambridge University Press, 1899), 278–79.

27 See Winston Churchill, *My African Journey* (Toronto: Briggs, 1909), 45–46.

Chapter 2: The Essentials of the Empire

1 See Stéphanie Ouellet, "1898: The First Christmas Stamp," in *A Chronology of Canadian Postal History,* virtual exhibit on the Canadian Museum of History website, https://www.historymuseum.ca/cmc/exhibitions/cpm/chrono/ch1898ae.html.

2 Lewis Morris, *The Works of Lewis Morris* (London: Kegan Paul, Trench, Trubner, 1890), 476.

3 Stephen Leacock, *Our British Empire: Its Structure, Its History, Its Strength* (London: The Bodley Head, 1940), 26.

4 Lizzie Collingham, *The Hungry Empire: How Britain's Quest for Food Shaped the Modern World* (London: The Bodley Head, 2017), 13.

5 Alfred Zimmern, *The Third British Empire,* 3rd ed. (London: Oxford University Press, 1934).

6 Ashley Jackson, *The British Empire: A Very Short Introduction* (Oxford: Oxford University Press, 2013), 72.

7 C.C. Eldridge, *Victorian Imperialism* (London: Hodder and Stoughton, 1978).

8 Niall Ferguson, *Empire: The Rise and Demise of the British World Order and the Lessons for Global Power* (New York: Basic Books, 2004), 201.

9 Leacock, *Our British Empire,* 215–16.

10 Leacock, *Our British Empire,* 61.

11 George Woodcock, *Who Killed the British Empire? An Inquest* (Toronto: Fitzhenry and Whiteside, 1974), 36.

12 Eric Hobsbawm, *The Age of Empire: 1875–1914* (New York: Vintage, 1989), 74; Jackson, *The British Empire*, 1.

13 Ronald Hyam, *Britain's Declining Empire: The Road to Decolonisation, 1918–1968* (Cambridge: Cambridge University Press, 2006), 3.

14 For the variety of peoples, see Godfrey Langden, *The Native Races of the Empire* (London: Collins, 1924).

15 Zimmern, *Third British Empire*, 18–23.

16 W. David McIntyre, *Colonies into Commonwealth*, rev. ed. (London: Blandford, 1974), 95.

17 James (Jan) Morris, *Pax Britannica* (Harmondsworth, UK: Penguin, 1979), 45.

18 Ferguson, *Empire*, 201.

19 Charles Jeffries, *The Colonial Empire and Its Civil Service* (Cambridge: Cambridge University Press, 1938), xviii.

20 *House of Commons Debates*, 12th Parl., 2nd Sess., February 25, 1913, 3998. For the imperial federation movement, see Duncan Bell, *The Idea of Greater Britain: Empire and the Future of the World Order, 1860–1900* (Princeton, NJ: Princeton University Press, 2007). For the movement in Canada, see Carl Berger, *The Sense of Power: Studies in the Ideas of Canadian Imperialism, 1967–1914* (Toronto: University of Toronto Press, 1970), and for a detailed proposal from the Imperial Federation League in Canada, see Archibald McGoun, *A Federal Parliament of the British People* (Toronto: Blackett Robinson, 1890).

21 Charles Dilke, *Problems of Greater Britain*, 2nd ed. (London: Macmillan, 1890), 1:100.

22 Quoted in Graeme Thompson, "Ontario's Empire: Liberalism and 'Britannic Nationalism' in Laurier's Canada 1887–1919" (PhD diss., University of Oxford, 2016), 246.

23 *House of Commons Debates*, 7th Parl., 2nd Sess., April 7, 1892, 1139.

24 Lord Haldane, "The Work for the Empire of the Judicial Committee of the Privy Council," *Cambridge Law Journal* 1, 2 (1922): 143; Bonnie Ibhawoh, *Imperial Justice: Africans in Empire's Court* (Oxford: Oxford University Press, 2013).

25 *Brown v Les Curé et Marguilliers de l'œuvre de la Fabrique de la Paroisse de Montréal*, [1894] UKPC 70.

26 Royal Commission on Dominion-Provincial Relations, *Report of the Royal Commission on Dominion-Provincial Relations*, book 1, *Canada: 1867–1939* (Ottawa: King's Printer, 1940), 247–52.

27 See Reginald Coupland, *The Empire in These Days* (London: Macmillan, 1935), 178–80. For his role as a promoter of the Empire, see Caroline Elkins, *Legacy of Violence: A History of the British Empire* (New York: Knopf, 2022), 309–11, 357–58.

28 Quoted in D.J. Hall, "Clifford Sifton and Canadian Indian Administration 1896–1905," in *As Long as the Sun Shines and Water Flows: A Reader in Canadian Native Studies*, ed. Ian A.L. Getty and Antoine S. Lussier (Vancouver: UBC Press, 1983), 137.

29 See Ramsay MacDonald, *Labour and the Empire* (London: George Allen, 1907), 52–54.

30 See, generally, Atul Kohli, *Imperialism and the Developing World* (New York: Oxford University Press, 2020).

31 Kwame Nkrumah, *Towards Colonial Freedom* (London: Heinemann, 1962), xv. First published in 1942.

32 George Orwell, *Burmese Days* (New York: Harcourt, 1974), 40. First published in 1934.

33 George Orwell, *The Road to Wigan Pier* (Harmondsworth, UK: Penguin, 1962), 139–40. First published in 1937.

34 Frederick Lugard, *The Dual Mandate in British Tropical Africa* (Edinburgh: Blackwood, 1922), 92, see also 617–18.

35 Margery Perham, *The Colonial Reckoning* (London: Collins, 1961), 102.

36 Coupland, *The Empire in These Days*, 165.

37 Ronald Hyam, *Britain's Imperial Century, 1815–1914: A Study of Empire and Expansion* (New York: Harper, 1976), 105–7.

38 Bernard Shaw, *Fabianism and the Empire* (London: Grant Richards, 1900), 44.

39 Harry Johnstone, *The Backward Peoples and Our Relations with Them* (London: H. Milford/ Oxford University Press, 1920), 59.

40 Sydney Olivier, *The League of Nations and Primitive Peoples* (London: Oxford University Press, 1918), 6.

41 The sense of entitlement can be traced back to at least 1516 and Thomas More's *Utopia*: Jim Reynolds, *Aboriginal Peoples and the Law: A Critical Introduction* (Vancouver: UBC Press, 2018), 8–9.

42 *House of Commons Debates*, 5th Parl., 4th Sess., April 28, 1886, 809–10.

43 Stephen Leacock, *Elements of Political Science* (Boston: Houghton Mifflin, 1913), 261.

44 Shashi Tharoor, *Inglorious Empire: What the British Did to India* (London: Penguin, 2017), 63. For racism and the Empire, see Sathnam Sanghera, *Empireland: How Imperialism Has Shaped Modern Britain* (New York: Pantheon, 2023), chap. 9.

45 Translated into English: Arthur de Gobineau, *The Moral and Intellectual Diversity of Races*, translated by H. Hotz (Philadelphia: Lippincott, 1856).

46 *House of Commons Debates*, 5th Parl., 3rd Sess., May 4, 1885, col. 1589 (John A. Macdonald); For Buchan's views, see especially, John Buchan, *The African Colony: Studies in the Reconstruction* (Edinburgh: Blackwood, 1903).

47 Edward B. Tylor, *Primitive Culture: Researches into the Development of Mythology, Philosophy, Religion, Art and Custom*, vol. 1 (London: John Murray, 1871), 28–29; see also Lewis H. Morgan, *Ancient Society or Researches in the Lines of Human Progress from Savagery through Barbarism to Civilization* (Chicago: Kerr, 1877). For a detailed discussion, see J.W. Burrows, *Evolution and Society: A Study in Victorian Social Theory* (Cambridge: Cambridge University Press, 1966).

48 C.L. Temple, *Native Races and Their Rulers* (Cape Town: Argus, 1918), 31.

49 Johnstone, *The Backward Peoples*, 7–9, 37.

50 Eric Hobsbawm, *The Age of Capital* (London: Abacus, 1977), 313.

51 Reproduced in A. Berriedale Keith, ed., *Speeches and Documents on Indian Policy 1750–1921* (Oxford: Milford/Oxford University Press, 1922), 1:382.

52 Heather Conn, "The Origins of Stanley Park," in *The Greater Vancouver Book: An Urban Encyclopedia*, ed. Chuck Davis (Surrey, BC: Linkman Press, 1997), 52.

53 Quoted in Lugard, *Dual Mandate*, 85.

54 Richard Toye, *Churchill's Empire: The World That Made Him and the World He Made* (New York: St Martin's Griffin, 2010), xii. See also Lawrence James, *Churchill and Empire: Portrait of an Imperialist* (London: Weidenfeld and Nicolson, 2013), 183, 327.

55 Toye, *Churchill's Empire*, xiv, 119.

56 Palestine Royal Commission, Minutes of Evidence Heard at Secret Sessions, Foreign Office file FO 492/19 (1937), National Archives of the United Kingdom, 507.

57 Julia Maitland, *Letters from Madras: During the Years 1836–1839* (London: Murray, 1846), 20.

58 Toye, *Churchill's Empire*, 28–29.

59 W. Winwood Reade, *Savage Africa* (New York: Harper, 1864), 452.

60 Garnet Wolseley, *The Story of a Soldier's Life* (Westminster: Archibald Constable, 1903), 2:288.

61 Quoted in Shula Marks, "War and Union, 1899–1910," in *The Cambridge History of South Africa*, vol. 2, *1885–1994*, ed. Robert Ross, Anne Kelk Mager, and Bill Nasson (Cambridge: Cambridge University Press, 2011), 175.

62 Alan Field, *Verb. Sap.: On Going to West Africa, Northern Nigeria, Southern and to the Coasts* (London: Bale, 1905), 76.

63 Quoted in McIntyre, *Colonies into Commonwealth*, 115.

64 Lugard, *Dual Mandate*, 69.

65 Phillip Buckner, "Presidential Address: Whatever Happened to the British Empire?," *Journal of the Canadian Historical Association* 4, 1 (1993): 27–28.

66 Quoted in John Sutton Lutz, *Makúk: A New History of Aboriginal-White Relations* (Vancouver: UBC Press, 2008), 34. His reign as the "Little Emperor" of the Canadian northwest marked a change in attitudes toward Indigenous peoples by the company: Stephen Bown, *The Company: The Rise and Fall of the Hudson's Bay Empire* (Toronto: Doubleday, 2020), chap. 13.

67 Quoted in Lutz, *Makúk*, 163.

68 Glen Williams, *Blood Must Tell: Debating Race and Identity in the Canadian House of Commons, 1880–1925* (Ottawa: Willow BX Press, 2014).

69 *House of Commons Debates*, 5th Parl., 3rd Sess., May 4, 1885, col. 1589; see also 4th Parl., 4th Sess., May 12, 1882, 1477; 5th Parl., 1st Sess., April 30, 1883, 905.

70 Richard Bartlett, "Citizens Minus: Indians and the Right to Vote," *Saskatchewan Law Review* 44 (1979): 168–75; Anthony J. Hall, *The American Empire and the Fourth World: The Bowl with One Spoon*, vol. 1 (Montreal and Kingston: McGill-Queen's University Press, 2003), 475–80.

71 Williams, *Blood Must Tell*, chap. 5.

72 W.L. Mackenzie King, *Immigration to Canada from the Orient and Immigration from India in Particular*, Sessional Paper No. 36a (Ottawa: King's Printer, 1908). See Kirt Niergarth, "'This Continent Must Belong to the White Races': William Lyon Mackenzie King, Canadian Diplomacy and Immigration Law, 1908," *International History Review* 32 (2010): 599.

73 James Woodsworth, *Strangers within Our Gates or Coming Canadians* (Toronto: Missionary Society of the Methodist Church of Canada, 1909), 191. While in Parliament, Woodsworth did protest against the "racial prejudice and ... racial bigotry" shown in several anti-Asian speeches: *House of Commons Debates*, 14th Parl., 1st Sess., May 8, 1922, 1571.

74 S.B. Steele, *Forty Years in Canada* (London: Herbert Jenkins, 1915), 386.

75 Leacock, *Our British Empire*, 82, 243, 217, 52.

76 Alan Bowker, *The Social Criticism of Stephen Leacock* (Toronto: University of Toronto Press, 1973), xxi.

77 Celia Haig-Brown and David A. Nock, *With Good Intentions: Euro-Canadian and Aboriginal Relations in Colonial Canada* (Vancouver: UBC Press, 2006), 8–21.

78 Scott Sheffield, *The Red Man's on the Warpath: The Image of the "Indian" and the Second World War* (Vancouver: UBC Press, 2004).

79 Quoted in Asa McKercher, *Canada and the World since 1867* (London: Bloomsbury Academic, 2019), 134.

80 George Grant, *Ocean to Ocean* (London: Sampson Low, 1873), 33.

81 *House of Commons Debates*, 4th Parl., 2nd Sess., vol. 2, May 5, 1880, 1991.

82 Wolseley, *Story of a Soldier's Life*, 2:191.

83 John McMullen, *The History of Canada from First Discovery to the Present Time* (Brockville, ON: McMullen, 1855), xiv.

84 John Darwin, *Britain and Decolonisation: The Retreat from Empire in the Post-War World* (London: Macmillan, 1988), 10.

85 George Trevelyan, *The Competition Wallah* (London: Macmillan, 1895), 261.

86 Trevelyan, *The Competition Wallah*, 350.

87 Arthur Berriedale Keith, *Imperial Unity and the Dominions* (London: Oxford University Press, 1916), 190.

88 Stephen Leacock, "An Apology for the British Empire," in *Last Leaves* (New York: Dodd, Mead, 1945), 58.

89 Jonathan Moore, "The Transformation of the British Imperial Administration 1919–1939" (PhD diss., University of Tulane, 2016), 163. See also Anthony Kirk-Greene, "Colonial Administration and Race Relations: Some Research Reflections and Directions," *Ethnic and Racial Studies* 9, 3 (1986): 275–87; Anthony Kirk-Greene, "Not Quite a Gentleman: The Desk Diaries of the Assistant Private Secretary (Appointments) to the Secretary of State for the Colonies, 1899–1915," *English Historical Review* 117, 472 (2002): 622–33.

90 Hyam, *Britain's Declining Empire*, 38–40.

91 Orwell, *Burmese Days*, 30.

92 Tharoor, *Inglorious Empire*, 213.

93 Williams, *Blood Must Tell*, 29.

94 David Gilmour, *The Ruling Caste: Imperial Lives in the Victorian Raj* (London: Murray, 2005), 253.

95 W.F.B. Laurie, "Macaulay's Great Minute on Education," in *Sketches of Some Distinguished Anglo-Indians* (London: Allen, 1888), 174, 183. For a recent biography of Macaulay (and his father), see Catherine Hall, *Macaulay and Son: Architects of Imperial Britain* (New Haven, CT: Yale University Press, 2012).

96 *House of Commons Debates*, 12th Parl., 7th Sess., May 25, 1917, 1764–65.

97 Hobsbawm, *The Age of Empire*, 32.

98 Jeffrey Auerbach, "Empire under Glass: The British Empire and the Crystal Palace, 1851–1911," in *Exhibiting the Empire*, ed. John McAleer and John Mackenzie (Manchester: Manchester University Press, 2015), 111–41.

99 Klaus Knorr, *British Colonial Theories 1570–1850* (Toronto: University of Toronto Press, 1944), 383–88; Alan Lester and Fae Dussart, *Colonization and the Origins of Humanitarian Governance: Protecting Aborigines across the Nineteenth-Century British Empire* (Cambridge: Cambridge University Press, 2014), 77–104.

100 Adam Hochschild, *Bury the Chains: Prophets and Rebels in the Fight to Free an Empire's Slaves* (Boston: Houghton Mifflin, 2006).

101 *House of Commons Debates* (UK), 3rd series, vol. 19, July 24, 1833, col. 1218.

102 Charles Buxton, ed., *Memoirs of Sir Thomas Fowell Buxton* (London: John Murray, 1849), 301–2.

103 William Howitt, *Colonization and Christianity: A Popular History of the Treatment of the Natives by the Europeans in All Their Colonies* (London: Longman, 1838), 506.

104 George Mellor, *British Imperial Trusteeship 1783–1850* (London: Faber, 1951), 249; Ronald Hyam, *Understanding the British Empire* (Cambridge: Cambridge University Press, 2010), 28; Paul Knapland, *Sir James Stephen and the British Colonial System, 1813–1847* (Madison: University of Wisconsin Press, 1953); Herman Merivale, *Lectures on Colonization and Colonies* (London: Longman, Brown, 1842); David McNab, "Herman Merivale and the Native Question, 1837–1861," *Albion* 9, 4 (1977): 359–84.

105 Aborigines Select Committee, *Report of the Parliamentary Select Committee on Aboriginal Tribes* (London: William Bell, 1837). See Zoë Laidlaw, "Aunt Anna's Report: The Buxton Women and the Aborigines Select Committee, 1835–37," *Journal of Imperial and Commonwealth History* 32, 2 (2004): 1–28.

106 Aborigines Select Committee, *Report*, 105.

107 Aborigines Select Committee, *Report*, 3.

108 Aborigines Select Committee, *Report*, 5. For the killing of the Beothuks (who became extinct in 1829) by settlers, see Ingeborg Marshall, *A History and Ethnography of the Beothuk* (Montreal and Kingston: McGill-Queen's University Press, 1996), 100–5.

109 Aborigines Select Committee, *Report*, 4.

110 Hyam, *Understanding the British Empire*, 28.

111 Perham, *The Colonial Reckoning*, 107.

112 Eric Williams, *Capitalism and Slavery* (Chapel Hill: University of North Caroline Press, 1944), 178.

113 See, generally, on the trust concept, Kenneth Robinson, *The Dilemmas of Trusteeship: Aspects of British Colonial Policy between the Wars* (London: Oxford University Press, 1965); Ronald Hyam, "Bureaucracy and 'Trusteeship' in the Colonial Empire," in *The Oxford History of the British Empire*, vol. 4, *The Twentieth Century*, ed. Judith M. Brown and Wm. Roger Louis (Oxford: Oxford University Press, 1999), 255–79; Jim Reynolds, *From Wardship to Rights: The Guerin Case and Aboriginal Law* (Vancouver: UBC Press, 2020), 87–93.

114 *House of Commons Debates* (UK), 5th series, vol. 150, February 14, 1922, col. 964.

115 *House of Commons Debates* (UK), 5th series, vol. 515, May 4, 1953, col. 58.

116 James C. Hales, "The Reform and Extension of the Mandate System," *Transactions of the Grotius Society* 26 (1940): 155.

117 Kenton Storey, *Settler Anxiety at the Outposts of Empire: Colonial Relations, Humanitarian Discourses and the Imperial Press* (Vancouver: UBC Press, 2016), 8.

118 Nnamdi Azikiwe, *Renascent Africa* (London: Cass, 1968). 55. First published in 1937.

119 Jawaharlal Nehru, letter dated January 17, 1936, in *A Bunch of Old Letters* (Bombay: Asia Publishing House, 1958), 142.

120 Nkrumah, *Towards Colonial Freedom*, xvi.

121 Will Durant, *The Case for India* (New York: Simon and Schuster, 1930), 13.

122 Orwell, *Burmese Days*, 39.

123 J.S. Furnivall, *Colonial Policy and Practice: A Comparative Study of Burma and Netherlands India* (Cambridge: Cambridge University Press, 1948), 290.

124 Trevelyan, *The Competition Wallah*, 353.

125 Quoted in Tharoor, *Inglorious Empire*, 174.

126 *House of Commons Debates* (UK), vol. 19, July 10, 1833, col. 536.

127 Herman Merivale, *Lectures on Colonization and Colonies* (London: Longman, Brown, 1842), 2:155.

128 Quoted in Ferguson, *Empire*, 140.

129 Joseph Chamberlain, "The True Conception of Empire," in *Foreign and Colonial Speeches* (London: Routledge, 1897), 244.

130 Quoted in Toye, *Churchill's Empire*, 5.

131 Winston Churchill, *India: Speeches and an Introduction* (London: Thornton Butterworth, 1931), 63, 93.

132 Berger, *The Sense of Power*, 217–32.

133 Rev. James George, *The Mission of Great Britain to the World* (Toronto: Dudley and Burns, 1867), 19.

134 George Parkin, *The Reorganization of the British Empire* (n.p., 1899), 10. Reprint of an article published in *The Century,* November 1888.

135 *House of Commons Debates,* 12th Parl., 2nd Sess., December 17, 1912, 1304 (H.B. Ames).

136 Yves Engler, *Canada in Africa: 300 Years of Aid and Exploitation* (Winnipeg: Fernwood, 2015), chap. 3.

137 Gilbert Sproat, *Scenes and Studies of Savage Life* (London: Smith, Elder, 1868), 290.

138 Quoted in Robert E. Cail, *Land, Man, and the Law: The Disposal of Crown Lands in British Columbia, 1871–1913* (Vancouver: UBC Press, 1974), 183.

139 House of Commons, Sessional Papers, 3rd Parl., 3rd Sess., 1876, vol. 7, paper 9, xii–xiii.

140 Quoted in Cole Harris, *Making Native Space* (Vancouver: UBC Press, 2002), 108.

141 William Kirby, *Canadian Idylls,* 2nd ed. (Welland, ON: self-published, 1894), 66.

142 Quoted in Olive Dickason, *Canada's First Nations: A History of Founding Peoples from Earliest Times,* 3rd ed. (Don Mills, ON: Oxford University Press, 2002), 381.

143 *House of Commons Debates,* 13th Parl., 4th Sess., May 5, 1920, 2055.

144 MacDonald, *Labour and the Empire,* 52.

145 Harold J. Laski, "The Colonial Civil Service," *Political Quarterly* 9, 4 (1938): 541.

146 Quoted in Jackson, *The British Empire,* 127.

147 Lorraine Hansberry, *Les Blancs* (New York: Vintage, 1994), 113.

148 Hyam, *Britain's Imperial Century,* 288.

149 Hyam, *Britain's Imperial Century,* 288.

150 Truth and Reconciliation Commission of Canada (TRC), *The Final Report of the Truth and Reconciliation Commission of Canada,* vol. 1, *Canada's Residential Schools: The History, Part 1, Origins to 1939* (Montreal and Kingston: McGill-Queen's University Press, 2015), 294.

151 Sarah Carter, *Lost Harvests: Prairie Indian Reserve Farmers and Government Policy,* 2nd ed. (Montreal and Kingston: McGill-Queen's University Press, 2019), ix.

152 Bill Waiser and Jennie Hansen, *Cheated: The Laurier Liberals and the Theft of First Natons Reserve Land* (Toronto: ECW, 2023).

153 William Blackstone, *Commentaries,* vol. 1, *Introduction* (Oxford: Clarendon, 1765), section 4, 104. For a detailed discussion, see Kenneth Roberts-Wray, *Commonwealth and Colonial Law* (London: Stevens, 1966), 98–116.

154 Ferguson, *Empire,* 45.

155 For more detailed studies, see James Belich, *Replenishing the Earth: The Settler Revolution and the Rise of the Angloworld* (Oxford: Oxford University Press, 2009); John Darwin, *Unfinished Empire: The Global Expansion of Britain* (London: Penguin, 2013), chap. 4; Marjory Harper and Stephen Constantine, *Migration and Empire* (Oxford: Oxford University Press, 2010).

156 Jackson, *The British Empire,* 41.

157 Tharoor, *Inglorious Empire,* 162–65.

158 Hyam, *Britain's Declining Empire,* 8.

159 James Daschuk, *Clearing the Plains: Disease, Politics of Starvation, and the Loss of Aboriginal Life* (Regina: University of Regina Press, 2013), 47–48, 64.

160 Belich, *Replenishing the Earth,* 178.

161 Knorr, *British Colonial Theories,* 270.

162 Editorial, *Times* (London), February 4, 1862. The editorial was in response to a letter from Goldwin Smith, then a professor at Oxford, arguing for "colonial emancipation." Smith later moved to Canada and continued to oppose colonial policy; see Chapter 5 of this volume.

163 Lorenzo Veracini, *The World Turned Inside Out: Settler Colonialism as a Political Idea* (London: Verso, 2021), 80.

164 Belich, *Replenishing the Earth,* 180.

165 John Mackenzie, *Austral Africa: Losing It or Ruling It* (London: Sampson, Low, 1887), 1:80.

166 A.B. Thruston, *African Incidents: Personal Experiences in Egypt and Unyoro* (London: Murray, 1900), 171.

167 Hamar Foster, "British Columbia: Legal Institutions in the Far West, from Contact to 1871," *Manitoba Law Journal* 23 (1995): 319.

168 Margery Perham, *Lugard: The Years of Adventure 1858–1898* (London: Collins, 1956); *Lugard: The Years of Authority 1898–1945* (London: Collins, 1960).

169 Margery Perham, ed., *The Diaries of Lord Lugard,* vol. 2, *East Africa, December 1890 to December 1891* (Evanston, IL: North West University Press, 1959), 40–46.

170 Frederick Lugard, *The Rise of Our East African Empire* (Edinburgh: Blackwood, 1893), 2:41, 579–80.

171 Lugard, *Dual Mandate,* 15.

172 Temple, *Native Races,* 140.

173 John Mugambwa, "Treaties or Scraps of Paper? A Second Look at the Legal Characteristic of the Nineteenth Century British/African Colonial Agreements," *Comparative and International Law Journal of Southern Africa* 20, 1 (1987): 79–93.

174 See, for example, *Nabob of the Carnatic v East India Company,* 1792 English Reports 1368, and the Maasai court decision reported in Appendix 3 of G.R. Sandford, *An Administrative and Political History of the Masai Reserve* (London: Waterlow, 1918).

175 *R v Syliboy,* [1929] 1 DLR 307 (Co. Ct.), 313.

176 Laura Ishiguro, "Northwestern North America (Canadian West) to 1900," in *The Routledge Handbook of the History of Settler Colonialism,* ed. Edward Cavanagh and Lorenzo Veracini (New York: Routledge, 2017), 125–38.

177 Jean Friesen, "Morris, Alexander," in *Dictionary of Canadian Biography,* vol. 11 (Toronto/ Quebec City: University of Toronto/Université Laval, 1982), http://www.biographi.ca/ en/bio/morris_alexander_11E.html; for sympathetic accounts, see Robert J. Talbot, *Negotiating the Numbered Treaties: An Intellectual and Political Biography of Alexander Morris* (Saskatoon: Purich, 2009) and Michael Asch, *On Being Here to Stay: Treaties and Aboriginal Rights in Canada* (Toronto: University of Toronto Press, 2014).

178 Alexander Morris, *Canada and Her Resources: An Essay* (Montreal: Dawson, 1855), 97.

179 Alexander Morris, *Nova Britannia, or Our New Canadian Dominion Foreshadowed* (Toronto: Hunter Rose, 1884), 5.

180 Morris, *Nova Britannia,* 55–56.

181 Alexander Morris, *The Treaties of Canada with the Indians* (Toronto: Bedford, Clarke, 1880), 292.

182 Richard T. Price, ed., *The Spirit of the Alberta Indian Treaties,* 3rd ed. (Edmonton: University of Alberta Press, 1999). For a discussion of some of the legal issues and further references, see Reynolds, *Aboriginal Peoples and the Law,* 130–39.

183 Sheldon Krasowski, *No Surrender: The Land Remains Indigenous* (Regina: University of Regina Press, 2019), 160.

184 Philip Goldring, *Whisky, Horses and Death: The Cypress Hills Massacre and Its Sequel,* Canadian Historic Sites, Occasional Papers in Archaeology and History 21 (Ottawa: National Historic Parks and Sites Branch, 1979).

185 Daschuk, *Clearing the Plains,* 79–126.

186 *House of Commons Debates,* 5th Parl., 4th Sess., April 15, 1886, 729 (D.M. Cameron).

187 Harold Cardinal, *The Unjust Society* (Edmonton: Hurtig, 1969), 42.

188 Peter A. Cumming and Neil H. Mickenberg, eds., *Native Rights in Canada* (Toronto: Indian-Eskimo Association of Canada, 1972), 125.

189 Quoted in Cardinal, *The Unjust Society,* 36.

190 John L. Tobias, "Canada's Subjugation of the Plains Cree, 1879–1885," *Canadian Historical Review* 64, 4 (1983): 519–48; Jean Friesen, "Magnificent Gifts: The Treaties of Canada with the Indians of the Northwest, 1869–1876," in Price, *The Spirit of the Alberta Indian Treaties.*

191 R. St. J. Macdonald (Chairman), *Native Rights in Canada* (Toronto: Indian-Eskimo Association of Canada, 1970), 110.

192 Morris, *The Treaties of Canada with the Indians,* 34–35.

193 Rudy Wiebe, "Mistahimaskwa (Big Bear, Gros Ours)," in *Dictionary of Canadian Biography,* vol. 11 (Toronto/Quebec City: University of Toronto/Université Laval, 1998), http://www.biographi.ca/en/bio/mistahimaskwa_11E.html; Rudy Wiebe, *Big Bear* (Toronto: Penguin, 2008). The prosecution was unable to show any active participation in the fighting or plundering by Big Bear and, in fact, conceded he had objected; however, the judge said that, unless he had feared his life would be in danger were he to leave, it sufficed that he had remained at the rebel camp. The defence counsel said the conviction made him feel that it was almost "a hopeless task to attempt to obtain from a jury in Regina a fair consideration of the case of an Indian"; Sessional Papers, 5th Parl., 4th Sess., 1886, vol. 13, 52A, 52, 231.

For an account of Big Bear's imprisonment, see Edward James McCoy, "A Lesson They Would Not Soon Forget: The Convicted Native Participants of the 1885 North-West Rebellion" (MA thesis, University of Calgary, 2002). For an account of the North-West Resistance and the trial and imprisonment of Big Bear by a Hudson's Bay Company employee who testified on his behalf, see William Cameron, *The War Trail of Big Bear* (Boston: Small Maynard, 1927).

194 John Darwin, *The Empire Project: The Rise and Fall of the British World System, 1830–1970* (Cambridge: Cambridge University Press, 2009), 268.

195 For accounts of unrest and opposition from Indigenous groups and settlers, see John Newsinger, *The Blood Never Dried: A People's History of the British Empire* (London: Bookmarks, 2006); Richard Gott, *Britain's Empire: Resistance, Repression and Revolt* (London: Verso, 2011); Antoinette Burton, *The Trouble with Empire: Challenges to Modern British Imperialism* (New York: Oxford University Press, 2015).

196 Arthur Keppel-Jones, *The White Conquest of Zimbabwe* (Montreal and Kingston: McGill-Queen's University Press, 1983), 55–102.

197 Ernest Jones, preface to his poem "The New World," 1857, later renamed "The Revolt of Hindostan" (Calcutta: Eastern Trading, 1957). See, generally, on the violent nature of colonialism, Frantz Fanon, *The Wretched of the Earth* (New York: Grove, 1963).

198 Elkins, *Legacy of Violence,* 9.

199 Elkins, *Legacy of Violence,* 13.

200 Elkins, *Legacy of Violence,* 15.

201 Erik Linstrum, *Age of Emergency: Living with Violence at the End of the British Empire* (Oxford: Oxford University Press, 2023), 10–11.

202 Elizabeth Kolsky, *Colonial Justice in British India: White Violence and the Rule of Law* (Cambridge: Cambridge University Press, 2010), 231, 232.

203 Morris, *Pax Britannica,* 236.

204 Wolseley, *Story of a Soldier's Life,* 1:256.

205 Chamberlain, "The True Conception of Empire," 244–45.

206 Quoted in D.A. Low, *Lion Rampant: Essays in the Study of British Imperialism* (London: Cass, 1973), 22.

207 C.E. Callwell, *Small Wars: Their Principles and Practice*, 3rd ed. (London: HMSO, 1906), 41.

208 Callwell, *Small Wars*, 72.

209 Callwell, *Small Wars*, 148.

210 Erik Linstrum, *Ruling Minds: Psychology in the British Empire* (Cambridge, MA: Harvard University Press, 2016), 174–88.

211 Hyam, *Britain's Imperial Century*, 162.

212 Charles Gwynn, *Imperial Policing* (London: Macmillan, 1934).

213 Berger, *The Sense of Power*, 233–58.

214 John Reid, "Empire, Settler Colonialism and the Role of Violence in Indigenous Dispossession in British North America 1749–1830," in *Violence, Order and Unrest: A History of British North America, 1749–1876*, ed. Elizabeth Mancke, Jerry Bannister, Denis B. McKim, and Scott W. See (Toronto: University of Toronto Press, 2019), 117–34.

215 Chris Arnett, *The Terror of the Coast: Land Alienation and Colonial War on Vancouver Island and the Gulf Islands 1849–1863* (Burnaby, BC: Talon, 1999). For an account of such conflicts from the settler's viewpoint, see B.A. McKelvie, *Tales of Conflict* (Vancouver: Daily Province, 1949).

216 *House of Commons Debates*, 5th Parl., 3rd Sess., June 10, 1885, 2422.

217 Steele, *Forty Years in Canada*, 265.

218 Jean Teillet, *The North-West Is Our Mother: The Story of Louis Riel's People, the Métis Nation* (Toronto: Harper Collins, 2019). The transcripts of the trial proceedings can be found in Sessional Papers, 5th Parl., 4th Sess., 1886, vol. 13, no. 52.

219 Bob Beal and Rod Macleod, "North-West Resistance," in *The Canadian Encyclopedia*, last modified July 8, 2021, https://www.thecanadianencyclopedia.ca/en/article/north-west-rebellion.

220 McCoy, "A Lesson They Would Not Soon Forget," 2.

221 Quoted in J.R. Miller, "Macdonald as Minister of Indian Affairs: The Shaping of Canadian Indian Policy," in *Macdonald at 200*, ed. Patrice Dutil and Roger Hall (Toronto: Dundurn, 2014), 332.

222 *House of Commons Debates*, 5th Parl., 3rd Sess., March 26, 1885, 745.

223 Hilaire Belloc, *The Modern Traveller* (London: Edward Arnold, 1898).

224 Stephen Leacock, "The Union of South Africa," *American Political Science Review* 4, 4 (1910): 503.

225 Quoted in Berger, *The Sense of Power*, 249.

226 Joseph Maloney, *With Captain Stairs to Katanga* (London: Sampson, Low, 1893); Janina Konczacki, *Victorian Explorer: The African Diaries of Captain William G. Stairs, 1887–1892* (Halifax: Nimbus, 1994); Roy MacLaren, *African Exploits: The Diaries of William Stairs, 1887–1892* (Montreal and Kingston: McGill-Queen's University Press, 1998); Ian McKay and Jamie Swift, *Warrior Nation: Rebranding Canada in an Age of Anxiety* (Toronto: Between the Lines, 2012), chap. 2.

227 Maloney, *With Captain Stairs to Katanga*, 2.

228 MacLaren, *African Exploits*, 100.

229 MacLaren, *African Exploits*, 114.

230 Shaw, *Fabianism and the Empire*, 31.

231 Quoted in Hyam, "Bureaucracy and 'Trusteeship,'" 271.

232 George Padmore, *How Britain Rules Africa* (London: Wishart, 1936; New York: Negro Universities Press, 1969), 4, 124–30 (citations refer to the 1969 edition). See, generally, on the connection between fascism and colonialism made by Padmore and other anticolonial campaigners in London, Priyamvada Gopal, *Insurgent Empire: Anticolonial Resistance and British Dissent* (London: Verso, 2019), especially chaps. 8–9.

233 Bertrand Russell, *Freedom and Organization, 1814–1914* (London: Allen and Unwin, 1934), 415–16.

234 John Strachey, *The Menace of Fascism* (London: Gollancz, 1933), 80.

235 Quoted in Gopal, *Insurgent Empire*, 372.

236 Jawaharlal Nehru, *The Discovery of India* (Calcutta: Signet, 1946), 386.

237 Norman Baynes, *The Speeches of Adolf Hitler* (London: Oxford University Press, 1942), 2:1623. See also Adolf Hitler, *Mein Kampf* (London: Hurst and Blackett, 1939), 131. Hitler repeatedly offered to protect the British Empire if he was allowed to form his own empire in Europe: William Shirer, *The Rise and Fall of the Third Reich* (New York: Simon and Schuster, 1960), 548–49, 572–75, 746.

238 For a discussion of Nazi Germany and imperialism, see Dirk Moses, *The Problems of Genocide: Permanent Security and the Language of Transgression* (Cambridge: Cambridge University Press, 2021), chap. 7.

239 Richard Overy, *Blood and Ruins: The Last Imperial War, 1931–1945* (New York: Viking, 2022), 205.

240 William Joyce, *Twilight over England* (Berlin: Internationaler Verlag, 1940), 114.

241 "Hitler Sees 'Atrocities' among Canadian Indians," *Globe and Mail,* November 21, 1938.

242 The absence of any clear definition or philosophy of "fascism" also makes analysis difficult: Eric Hobsbawm, *Age of Extremes: The Short Twentieth Century, 1914–1991* (London: Abacus, 1995), 116–18; George Orwell, "What Is Fascism?," in *The Collected Essays, Journalism and Letters of George Orwell,* ed. Sonia Orwell and Ian Angus (New York: Harcourt Brace, 1968), 111–16.

243 Hannah Arendt, *The Origins of Totalitarianism* (New York: Harcourt Brace, 1966), 221; see Karuna Mantena, "Genealogies of Catastrophe: Arendt on the Logic and Legacy of Colonialism," in *Politics in Dark Times: Encounters with Hannah Arendt,* ed. Seyla Benhabib (Cambridge: Cambridge University Press, 2010), 83–112.

244 See Heinrich Krieger, "Principles of the Indian Law and the Act of June 18, 1934," *George Washington Law Review* 3, 3 (1935): 304 (Krieger was a Nazi lawyer); James Whitman, *Hitler's American Model: The United States and the Making of Nazi Race Law* (Princeton: Princeton University Press, 2017), 114–16.

245 Edward Shanks, *Rudyard Kipling: A Study in Literature and Political Ideas* (London: Macmillan, 1940), 97, 263. See George Orwell, "Introduction," in *The Works of Rudyard Kipling* (Ware, UK: Wordsworth, 1972), xvii–xix.

246 Hobsbawm, *Age of Extremes,* 123. See, generally, Paul Nicholls, "John Buchan and the Dictators," *Quadrant,* November 1, 2011, 48.

Chapter 3: Self-Rule and Despotism

1 This is a reference to "The Ballad of East and West"; see Rudyard Kipling, *Ballads and Barrack-Room Ballads* (London: Macmillan, 1897), 3: "Oh, East is East, and West is West, and never the twain shall meet."

2 Alfred Milner, *Questions of the Hour* (London: Hodder and Stoughton, 1923), 146–47, 153.

3 Leonard Barnes, "Skeleton of the Empire," *Fact,* June 1937, 13–14.

4 George Curzon, *The Place of India in the Empire* (London: John Murray, 1909), 9.

5 *House of Commons Debates,* 12th Parl., 3rd Sess., March 2, 1914, 1252 (J.H. Burnham).

6 *House of Commons Debates,* 12th Parl., 3rd Sess., May 30, 1914, 4533 (W.F. Cockshutt).

7 Quoted in Charles Lucas, ed., *The Empire at War,* vol. 1 (Oxford: Oxford University Press, 1921), 57.

8 *House of Commons Debates,* 7th Parl., 3rd Sess., February 23, 1893, 1173 (G.H.R. Cockburn).

9 Ramsay MacDonald, *The Awakening of India* (London: Hodder and Stoughton, 1910), 145–46.

10 Shashi Tharoor, *Inglorious Empire: What the British Did to India* (London: Penguin, 2017), 21; see also John Darwin, *The Empire Project: The Rise and Fall of the British World System, 1830–1970* (Cambridge: Cambridge University Press, 2009), 145.

11 J.R. Seeley, *The Expansion of England* (London: Macmillan, 1883), 11.

12 Joseph Chamberlain, "The True Conception of Empire," in *Foreign and Colonial Speeches* (London: Routledge, 1897), 244.

13 Goldwin Smith, *Canada and the Canadian Question* (London: Macmillan, 1891).

14 Richard Jebb, *Studies in Colonial Nationalism* (London: Edward Arnold, 1905), 276–77.

15 Sara Jeannette Duncan, *Set in Authority* (New York: Doubleday Page, 1906), 14.

16 J.A. Hobson, *Imperialism: A Study* (London: George Allen and Unwin, 1902), 6–7, 36, 125, 274.

17 Jebb, *Studies in Colonial Nationalism,* 277.

18 Stephen Leacock, *Our British Empire: Its Structure, Its History, Its Strength* (London: The Bodley Head, 1940), 84.

19 John Stuart Mill, "Representative Government" [first published in 1861], in *Utilitarianism, Liberty and Representative Government* (London: Allen and Unwin, 1968), 378. See, generally, Duncan Bell, "John Stuart Mill on Colonies," *Political Theory* 38, 1 (2010): 34–64.

20 Stanley R. Stembridge, "Disraeli and the Millstones," *Journal of British Studies* 5, 1 (1965): 122–39.

21 T.E. Kebbel, ed., *Selected Speeches of the Earl of Beaconsfield* (London: Longman, Green, 1882), 2:530.

22 John Darwin, *Unfinished Empire: The Global Expansion of Britain* (London: Penguin, 2013), 201–2.

23 Leacock, *Our British Empire,* 55.

24 Richard Toye, *Churchill's Empire: The World That Made Him and the World He Made* (New York: St Martin's Griffin, 2010), 103.

25 For accounts, see Phillip Buckner, *The Transition to Responsible Government: British Policies in British North America, 1815–1850* (Westport, CT: Greenwood, 1985); Peter Burroughs, *The Canadian Crisis and British Colonial Policy, 1828–1841* (London: Edward Arnold, 1972); Alan Lester, Kate Boehme, and Peter Mitchell, *Ruling the World: Freedom, Civilisation and Liberalism in the Nineteenth-Century British Empire* (Cambridge: Cambridge University Press, 2020), 84–94; George Woodcock, *Who Killed the British Empire? An Inquest* (Toronto: Fitzhenry and Whiteside, 1974), 161–91.

26 Leacock, *Our British Empire,* 46. For an account of the rebellions, see Andrew McIntosh, "Rebellions of 1837–38," in *The Canadian Encyclopedia,* last modified October 4, 2019, https://www.thecanadianencyclopedia.ca/en/article/rebellions-of-1837.

27 Quoted in Lester, Boehme, and Mitchell, *Ruling the World,* 89.

28 John George Lambton, Earl of Durham, *The Report and Dispatches of the Earl of Durham* (London: Ridgways, 1839). For an explanation and defence of the recommendations for

responsible government, see Charles Buller, *Responsible Government for the Colonies* (London: Ridgway, 1840), originally published anonymously. Buller was Durham's chief secretary.

29 G.M. Craig, "Introduction to the 1963 Edition," in *Lord Durham's Report, New Edition* (Montreal and Kingston: McGill-Queen's University Press, 2007), viii.

30 Alfred Zimmern, *The Third British Empire*, 3rd ed. (London: Oxford University Press, 1934), 26.

31 Peter Burroughs, "Imperial Institutions and the Government of Empire," in *The Oxford History of the British Empire*, vol. 3, *The Nineteenth Century*, ed. Andrew Porter (Oxford: Oxford University Press, 1999), 187.

32 Niall Ferguson, *Empire: The Rise and Demise of the British World Order and the Lessons for Global Power* (New York: Basic Books, 2004), 91.

33 W. David McIntyre, *Colonies into Commonwealth*, rev. ed. (London: Blandford, 1974), 46.

34 Piers Brendon, *The Decline and Fall of the British Empire, 1781–1997* (New York: Alfred Knopf, 2008), 84.

35 Ronald Hyam, *Britain's Imperial Century, 1815–1914: A Study of Empire and Expansion* (New York: Harper, 1976), 183.

36 Durham, *Report*, 191, 205, 210.

37 Joseph Howe, *Letters to Lord John Russell* (Halifax, 1839), 4.

38 W.N. Sage, "From Colony to Province: The Introduction of Responsible Government in British Columbia," *British Columbia Historical Quarterly* 3 (1939): 1.

39 James Hillier, "Status without Stature: Newfoundland, 1869–1949," in *Canada and the British Empire*, ed. Phillip Buckner (Oxford: Oxford University Press: 2010), 136–37.

40 Ged Martin, *The Durham Report and British Policy: A Critical Essay* (London: Cambridge University Press, 1972), 99; see also Denis Judd, *Empire: The British Imperial Experience, from 1765 to the Present* (New York: Basic Books, 1996), 52.

41 Durham, *Report*, 207.

42 Ann Curthoys, "The Dog That Didn't Bark: The Durham Report, Indigenous Dispossession, and Self-Government for Britain's Settler Colonies," in *Within and Without the Nation: Canadian History as Transnational History*, ed. Karen Dubinsky, Adele Perry, and Henry Yu (Toronto: University of Toronto Press, 2015), 25–48.

43 Durham, *Report*, 8.

44 Aborigines Select Committee, *Report of the Parliamentary Select Committee on Aboriginal Tribes* (London: William Ball, 1837), 117.

45 Herman Merivale, *Lectures on Colonization and Colonies* (London: Longman, Brown, 1842), 2:158.

46 Herman Merivale, *Lectures on Colonization and Colonies*, new ed. (London: Longman, 1861), 495.

47 *House of Lords Debates*, vol. 151, July 26, 1858, col. 2102.

48 Lester, Boehme, and Mitchell, *Ruling the World*, 186.

49 Mill, "Representative Government," 386.

50 Mill, "Representative Government," 387.

51 McIntyre, *Colonies into Commonwealth*, 84.

52 David T. McNab, "Herman Merivale and Colonial Office Indian Policy in the Mid-Nineteenth Century," *Canadian Journal of Native Studies* 1, 2 (1981): 286.

53 Quoted in J.R. Miller, "Macdonald as Minister of Indian Affairs: The Shaping of Canadian Indian Policy," in *Macdonald at 200*, ed. Patrice Dutil and Roger Hall (Toronto: Dundurn, 2014), 318–19.

54 Patrick Wolfe, "Settler Colonialism and the Elimination of the Native," *Journal of Genocide Research* 8, 4 (2006): 388.

55 Durham, *Report,* 207.

56 Fred H. Hitchins, *The Colonial Land and Emigration Commission* (Philadelphia: University of Pennsylvania Press, 1931); "The Colonial Land and Emigration Commissioners," State Records Authority of New South Wales, https://researchdata.edu.au/colonial-land -emigration-commissioners/166070.

57 Hitchins, *Colonial Land and Emigration Commission,* 49–51.

58 Parliamentary Papers (UK), 1854, vol. 15, no. 47, 355.

59 The Hudson's Bay Company surrendered its land rights to the British Crown, which then transferred them to Canada. The Company's two-hundred-year claim to most of Canada came to an end: *Rupert's Land Act,* 1868, 31 & 32 Vict., c 105 (UK); Stephen Bown, *The Company: The Rise and Fall of the Hudson's Bay Empire* (Toronto: Doubleday, 2020), chap. 17.

60 Daniel Heidt, ed., *Reconsidering Confederation: Canada's Founding Debate, 1864–1999* (Calgary: University of Calgary Press, 2018).

61 Ben Gilding, "The Silent Framers of the British North American Union: The Colonial Office and Canadian Confederation, 1851–67," *Canadian Historical Review* 99 (2018): 349–93. See also Ged Martin, *Britain and the Origins of Canadian Confederation, 1837–67* (London: Macmillan, 1995).

62 Stephen Leacock, "Britain and Canada," in *Last Leaves* (New York: Dodd, Mead, 1945), 69.

63 Lester, Boehme, and Mitchell, *Ruling the World,* 297.

64 *House of Lords Debates,* 3rd Sess., vol. 185, February 19, 1867, 576. The legislation was *British North America Act 1867,* 30 & 31 Vict., c 3.

65 Donald Creighton, *Dominion of the North: A History of Canada* (Boston: Houghton Mifflin, 1944), 312–13.

66 Paula Hastings, *Dominion over Palm and Pine: A History of Canadian Aspirations in the British Caribbean* (Montreal and Kingston: McGill-Queen's University Press, 2022), 7–8.

67 Jerry Banister, "Liberty, Loyalty and Sentiment in Canada's Founding Debates, 1864–1873," in *Violence, Order and Unrest: A History of British North America, 1749–1876,* ed. Elizabeth Mancke, Jerry Bannister, Denis B. McKim, and Scott W. See (Toronto: University of Toronto Press, 2019), 78–92.

68 *Parliamentary Debates on the Subject of the Confederation of the British North American Provinces,* 3rd Session, 8th Prov. Parl. of Canada (Quebec: Hunter Rose, 1865), 43–45.

69 *Parliamentary Debates on the Subject of the Confederation,* 115.

70 Quoted in Janet Ajzenstat, Paul Romney, Ian Gentles, and William D. Gairdner, eds., *Canada's Founding Debates* (Toronto: University of Toronto Press, 1999), 170.

71 Marian Fowler, *Redney: A Life of Sara Jeannette Duncan* (Toronto: Anansi, 1983), 29.

72 Attempts at federation were also made with little success during the 1950s and 1960s in Malaya, South Arabia, Central Africa, East Africa, and the West Indies.

73 Gilbert Sproat, *Canada and the Empire: A Speech* (London: n.p., 1873). For a discussion of Sproat, see Sarah Pike, "Gilbert Malcolm Sproat, British Columbia Indian Reserve Commissioner (1876–1880) and the 'Humanitarian Civilizing' of Indigenous Peoples" (LLM thesis, University of British Columbia, 2018).

74 Joseph Chamberlain, "The Mild Sovereignty of the Queen," in *Foreign and Colonial Speeches* (London: Routledge, 1897), 13.

75 *The Colonial Laws Validity Act 1865,* 28 & 29 Vict., c 63.

76 Arthur Berriedale Keith, *The Constitution, Administration and Laws of the Empire* (London: Collins, 1922), 24; see also K.C. Wheare, *Statute of Westminster and Dominion Status* (London: Oxford University Press, 1938).

77 *Report of the Conference on the Operation of Dominion Legislation and Merchant Shipping Legislation, 1929* (Cmnd. 3479), 9–10, https://nla.gov.au/nla.obj-2722622595/view?partId =nla.obj-2724915757#page/n0/mode/1up.

78 Goldwin Smith, *Canada and the Canadian Question* (London: Macmillan, 1891), 243.

79 Keith, *Constitution, Administration and Laws*, 24.

80 A.P. Thornton, *The Imperial Idea and Its Enemies: A Study in British Power*, 2nd ed. (Basingstoke, UK: Macmillan, 1985), 201.

81 Eirik Brazier, "Guardians of Empire? British Imperial Officers in Canada, 1874–1914," in *Fighting with the Empire: Canada, Britain, and Global Conflict, 1867–1947*, ed. Steve Marti and William Pratt (Vancouver: UBC Press, 2019), 69–85.

82 See Chapter 5 of this volume.

83 Garnet Wolseley, *The Story of a Soldier's Life* (Westminster: Archibald Constable, 1903), 2: chaps. 34–39.

84 Wolseley, *Story of a Soldier's Life*, 2:116.

85 Garnet Wolseley, *The Soldier's Pocket Book for Field Service*, 5th ed. (London: Macmillan, 1886).

86 Wolseley, *Soldier's Pocket Book*, 5.

87 Wolseley, *Story of a Soldier's Life*, 2:222.

88 Eugene Forsey, *The Royal Power of Dissolution of Parliament in the Commonwealth* (Toronto: Oxford University Press, 1943), 131–250.

89 Vincent Massey, the first Canadian-born governor general, was an anglophile, aristocrat, and ardent royalist: Claude Bissell, *The Imperial Canadian* (Toronto: University of Toronto Press, 1986). It may be noted that in 1887, Evelyn Baring, a prominent imperialist, said he regarded a proposal to make an Egyptian prime minister of Egypt "little less absurd than the nomination of some savage Red Indian chief to be Governor-General of Canada"; quoted in The Marquess of Zetland, *Lord Cromer* (London: Hodder and Stoughton, 1932), 164–65.

90 For a detailed review, see Anthony Kirk-Greene, "The Governors-General of Canada, 1867–1952: A Collective Profile," *Journal of Canadian Studies* 12 (1977): 35. See also Barbara Messamore, "The Governors General of Canada 1888–1911: British Imperialists and Canadian 'Nationalists'" (MA thesis, Simon Fraser University, 1991); Barbara Messamore, *Canada's Governors General, 1847–1878: Biography and Constitutional Evolution* (Toronto: University of Toronto Press, 2006).

91 Roy MacLaren, *Canadians on the Nile, 1882–1898* (Vancouver: UBC Press, 1978), 15.

92 David Gilmour, *The British in India* (London: Penguin, 2019), 32. See also Anthony Kirk-Greene, *Britain's Imperial Administrators, 1858–1966* (London: Palgrave Macmillan, 2000), 208.

93 "Earl Grey," Governor General of Canada, https://www.gg.ca/en/governor-general/former -governors-general/earl-grey.

94 Carman Miller, "Grey, Albert Henry George, 4th Earl Grey," in *Dictionary of Canadian Biography*, vol. 14 (Toronto/Quebec City: University of Toronto/Université Laval, 1998), http://www.biographi.ca/en/bio/grey_albert_henry_george_14E.html.

95 Quoted in Martin Meredith, *Diamonds, Gold, and War* (New York: Public Affairs, 2007), 357.

96 Quoted in Piers Brendon, *The Decline and Fall of the British Empire, 1781–1997* (New York: Alfred Knopf, 2008), 576.

97 William Galbraith, *John Buchan: Model Governor-General* (Toronto: Dundurn, 2013); Peter Henshaw, "John Buchan and the British Imperial Origins of Canadian Multiculturalism," in *Canadas of the Mind: The Making and Unmaking of Canadian Nationalisms in the Twentieth Century,* ed. Norman Hillmer and Adam Chapnick (Montreal and Kingston: McGill-Queen's University Press, 2007), 191–213; Daniel Gorman, *Imperial Citizenship: Empire and the Question of Belonging* (Manchester: Manchester University Press, 2006), chap. 3.

98 See, in particular, John Buchan, *A Lodge in the Wilderness* (London: Nelson, 1922), first published in 1906; John Buchan, *Prester John* (New York: Doran, 1910). For discussion, see Guy Vanderhaeghe, "John Buchan: Conservatism, Imperialism and Social Reconstruction" (MA thesis, University of Saskatchewan, 1975); Bill Schwarz, *The White Man's World* (Oxford: Oxford University Press, 2011), 252.

99 John Buchan, *Memory Hold-the-Door* (London: Hodder and Stoughton, 1940), 125.

100 Buchan, *Memory,* 108.

101 Kirk-Greene, "The Governors-General of Canada," 39.

102 Henshaw, "John Buchan," 191–94.

103 John Buchan, *Canadian Occasions* (Toronto: Musson, 1941), 76.

104 An early book in which John Buchan set out his ideas on imperialism and racial supremacy, and his opposition to the franchise for Black people and to mixed-race marriages and mixed-race people ("Nature to the end of time has a care of races but not of hybrids," 30), was *The African Colony: Studies in the Reconstruction* (Edinburgh: Blackwood, 1903).

105 Buchan, *Prester John,* 264. Similar views are found in *A Lodge in the Wilderness,* 179–88.

106 John Buchan, *Sick Heart River* (London: Stodder and Houghton, 1941).

107 Buchan, *Sick Heart River,* 247, 249, 304.

108 Buchan, *Sick Heart River,* 305.

109 Buchan, *Sick Heart River,* 266–67.

110 Hugh Clifford, *Studies in Brown Humanity, Being Scrawls and Smudges in Sepia, White and Yellow* (London: Grant Richards, 1898), 124.

111 Jon Wilson, *India Conquered: Britain's Raj and the Chaos of Empire* (London: Simon and Schuster, 2016), 196–206.

112 *House of Commons Debates* (UK), vol. 19, July 10, 1833, col. 513.

113 Eileen P. Sullivan, "Liberalism and Imperialism: J.S. Mill's Defense of the British Empire," *Journal of the History of Ideas* 44 (1983): 599–617; Caroline Elkins, *Legacy of Violence: A History of the British Empire* (New York: Knopf, 2022), 50–51, 59–65.

114 Mill, "Representative Government," 382.

115 See Abram L. Harris, "John Stuart Mill: Servant of the East India Company," *Canadian Journal of Economics and Political Science* 30, 2 (1964): 185–202.

116 John Stuart Mill, "On Liberty" [first published in 1859], in *Utilitarianism,* 73.

117 For an insightful study of the "colonial mutation" in India of the rule of law doctrine, see Nasser Hussain, *The Jurisprudence of Emergency: Colonialism and the Rule of Law* (Ann Arbor: University of Michigan Press, 2019).

118 Dylan Lino, "The Rule of Law and the Rule of Empire: A.V. Dicey in Imperial Context," *Modern Law Review* 81 (2018): 763–64. For another example of the conflict between liberalism and imperialism, see the discussion of James Fitzjames Stephen in Lester, Boehme, and Mitchell, *Ruling the World,* 275–82. See also Keally McBride, *Mr. Mothercountry: The*

Man Who Made the Rule of Law (Oxford: Oxford University Press, 2016) for the role of James Stephen and his son James Fitzjames Stephen. For a detailed discussion of the rule of law and colonialism based on the brutal suppression of the Jamaican (Morant Bay) Rebellion of 1865, see Rande Kostal, *A Jurisprudence of Power: Victorian Empire and the Rule of Law* (Oxford: Oxford University Press, 2005).

119 Lester, Boehme, and Mitchell, *Ruling the World,* 336–37.

120 For an account of executive power in the dependent colonies, see Kenneth Wray-Roberts, *Commonwealth and Colonial Law* (London: Stevens, 1966), 237–40.

121 Charles Jeffries, *The Colonial Empire and Its Civil Service* (Cambridge: Cambridge University Press, 1938), xxiii.

122 Anton Bertram, *The Colonial Service* (Cambridge: Cambridge University Press, 1930), 18.

123 David Gilmour, *The Ruling Caste: Imperial Lives in the Victorian Raj* (London: Murray, 2005), 239.

124 Quoted in Denis Judd, *The Victorian Empire: A Pictorial History, 1837–1901* (London: Weidenfeld and Nicolson, 1970), 177.

125 Reginald Coupland, *The Empire in These Days* (London: Macmillan, 1935), 162.

126 Darwin, *Unfinished Empire,* 215.

127 George Padmore, *How Britain Rules Africa* (London: Wishart, 1936; New York: Negro Universities Press, 1969), 313. Citations refer to the 1969 edition.

128 Padmore, *How Britain Rules Africa,* 124.

129 Kwasi Kwarteng, *Ghosts of Empire: Britain's Legacies in the Modern World* (London: Bloomsbury, 2011), 3.

130 See, for example, the biography of Alan Burns by Bruce Gilley, *The Last Imperialist: Sir Alan Burns' Epic Defense of the British Empire* (Washington: Regnery Gateway, 2021).

131 Kirk-Greene, *Britain's Imperial Administrators,* 218–22, 230.

132 Bengal Regulation III of 1818 (East India Company).

133 *In the Matter of Ameer Khan* (1870), 6 Bengal Law Reports 392 (High Court of Calcutta).

134 Act No. XLV of 1860 (Legislative Council, British India); W. Morgan and A.G. MacPherson, *The Indian Penal Code (Act XLV of 1860) with Notes* (Calcutta and London: Hay, 1863).

135 Tharoor, *Inglorious Empire,* 94, 84–85.

136 Wilson, *India Conquered,* 301.

137 Act No. XXVII of 1870 (Legislative Council, British India).

138 *Queen-Empress v Bal Gangadhar Tilak,* (1897) 27 Indian Law Reports 112, 134–35 (High Court of Bombay), Justice Strachey.

139 Mulik Raj Anand, ed., *The Historic Trial of Mahatma Gandhi* (New Delhi: National Council of Educational Research and Development, 1987), 46.

140 Wilson, *India Conquered,* 344.

141 Bonny Ibhawoh, "Stronger Than the Maxim Gun: Law, Human Rights and British Colonial Hegemony in Nigeria," *Africa: Journal of the International Affairs Institute* 72, 1 (2002): 55–83.

142 John McLaren, *Dewigged, Bothered and Bewildered: British Colonial Judges on Trial, 1800–1900* (Toronto: University of Toronto Press, 2011), 303. See Kenneth Roberts-Wray, *Commonwealth and Colonial Law* (London: Stevens, 1966) for a discussion of the legal issues.

143 Gilmour, *The Ruling Caste,* 123–34.

144 *Amending Act 1781,* 21 Geo. III, c 70; *Government of India Act 1915,* s 111.

145 *Salaman v Secretary of State,* [1906] 1 KB 613 (Court of Appeal).

Chapter 4: The Rulers and Their Rule

1 J.C. Cairns, *Bush and Boma* (London: Murray, 1959).

2 A general account of Britain's imperial administration is provided in Anthony Kirk-Greene, *Britain's Imperial Administrators, 1858–1966* (London: Palgrave Macmillan, 2000). For a collection of papers from former colonial administrators and academics, see John Smith, ed., *Administering Empire: The British Colonial Service in Retrospect* (London: London University Press, 1999). For comparative accounts, see J.S. Furnivall, *Colonial Policy and Practice: A Comparative Study of Burma and Netherlands India* (Cambridge: Cambridge University Press, 1948); A. Lawrence Lowell, *Colonial Civil Service: The Selection and Training of Colonial Officials in England, Holland and France* (New York: Macmillan, 1900). For bibliographies of materials on the Colonial Service, see Anthony Kirk-Greene, *On Crown Service: A History of HM Colonial and Overseas Civil Services, 1837–1997* (London: Tauris, 1999), 125; Terry Barringer, "'Administering Empire' Annotated Bibliographic Check List," 2nd ed., 2020, https://sas-space.sas.ac.uk/9314/.

3 Jon Wilson, *India Conquered: Britain's Raj and the Chaos of Empire* (London: Simon and Schuster, 2016), 306–17; David Gilmour, *The Ruling Caste: Imperial Lives in the Victorian Raj* (London: Murray, 2005), 48–50.

4 Wilson, *India Conquered*, 310. For the tragic career of one exceptional Indian judge who fell from high office, see Alan M. Guenther, "Syed Mahmood and the Transformation of Muslim Law in British India" (PhD diss, McGill University, 2004).

5 Charles Jeffries, *The Colonial Empire and Its Civil Service* (Cambridge: Cambridge University Press, 1938), 236.

6 For a biography, see C. Brad Faught, *Into Africa: The Imperial Life of Margery Perham* (London: Bloomsbury, 2012).

7 Faught, *Into Africa*, 160.

8 W.M. Macmillan, *Africa Emergent* (Harmondsworth, UK: Pelican, 1949), 193.

9 See, generally, Alan Lester, Kate Boehme, and Peter Mitchell, *Ruling the World: Freedom, Civilization and Liberalism in the Nineteenth Century British Empire* (Cambridge: Cambridge University Press, 2020).

10 John Darwin, *Unfinished Empire: The Global Expansion of Britain* (London: Penguin, 2013), 194.

11 See Paul Knaplund, *James Stephen and the British Colonial System, 1813–1847* (Madison: University of Wisconsin Press, 1953); Keally McBride, *Mr. Mothercountry: The Man Who Made the Rule of Law* (Oxford: Oxford University Press, 2016).

12 Charles Buller, *Responsible Government for the Colonies* (London: Ridgway, 1840), 78–79.

13 Ronald Hyam, "Bureaucracy and 'Trusteeship' in the Colonial Empire," in *The Oxford History of the British Empire*, vol. 4, *The Twentieth Century*, ed. Judith M. Brown and Wm. Roger Louis (Oxford: Oxford University Press, 1999), 259.

14 Ridgway F. Shinn, *Arthur Berriedale Keith, 1879–1944: The Chief Ornament of Scottish Learning* (Aberdeen: Aberdeen University Press, 1990). See, for example, A.B. Keith, *Responsible Government in the Dominions* (London: Stevens, 1909).

15 Shinn, *Arthur Berriedale Keith*, 214–15.

16 Philip Mason, *The Men Who Ruled India* (London: Jonathan Cape, 1985), and Gilmour, *The Ruling Caste*, provide detailed accounts. For Haileybury, see H. Morse Stephens, "An Account of the East India College at Haileybury (1806–1857)," in Lowell, *Colonial Civil Service*.

17 Norman Hillmer, *O.D. Skelton: A Portrait of Canadian Ambition* (Toronto: University of Toronto Press, 2015), 14–16.

18 For first-hand accounts of the Indian Civil Service, see Evan Maconochie, *Life in the Indian Civil Service* (London: Chapman and Hall, 1926); Edward Blunt, *The I.C.S.: The Indian Civil Service* (London: Faber, 1937). For the situation in the decades leading up to the independence of India, see Charles Allen, *Plain Tales from the Raj: Images of British India in the 20th Century* (London: Futura, 1976), especially 42.

19 Kirk-Greene, *Britain's Imperial Administrators*, 129.

20 James (Jan) Morris, *Pax Britannica: The Climax of an Empire* (Harmondsworth, UK: Penguin, 1979), 186–87. Strictly, colonial services, plural, as each colony had its own administration until they were unified starting in 1930: Jeffries, *The Colonial Empire*.

21 For the district officer in Africa, see Anthony Kirk-Greene, *Symbol of Authority: The British District Officer in Africa* (London: Tauris, 2006); Christopher Prior, *Exporting Empire: Africa, Colonial Officials and the Construction of the Imperial State, c. 1900–39* (Manchester: Manchester University Press, 2015).

22 Frederick Lugard, *The Dual Mandate in British Tropical Africa* (Edinburgh: William Blackwood, 1922), 59.

23 Lugard, *Dual Mandate*, 132.

24 Kirk-Greene, *Britain's Imperial Administrators*, 16.

25 Ronald Hyam, *Britain's Declining Empire: The Road to Decolonisation, 1918–1968* (Cambridge: Cambridge University Press, 2006), 10–11.

26 Quoted in Kirk-Greene, *On Crown Service*, 194.

27 Kwasi Kwarteng, *Ghosts of Empire: Britain's Legacies in the Modern World* (London: Bloomsbury, 2011), 2.

28 P.J. Rich, *Elixir of Empire: The English Public Schools, Ritualism, Freemasonry and Imperialism* (London: Regency, 1989), 13. See also Kwarteng, *Ghosts of Empire*, 4–6.

29 Helen Roche, *The Third Reich's Elite Schools: A History of the Napolas* (Oxford: Oxford University Press, 2021).

30 Peter Fleming, *Invasion 1940: An Account of German Preparations and the British Counter-Measures* (London: Rupert Hart-Davis, 1957), 192.

31 John W. Cell, "Colonial Rule," in Brown and Louis, *Oxford History of the British Empire*, 4:233–34.

32 A.P. Thornton, *The Imperial Idea and Its Enemies* (London: Macmillan, 1959), 90.

33 Anthony Kirk-Greene, "Colonial Administration and Race Relations: Some Research Reflections and Directions," *Ethnic and Racial Studies* 9, 3 (1986): 275–87. See also Anthony Kirk-Greene, "The Thin White Line: The Size of the British Colonial Service in Africa," *African Affairs* 79 (1980): 25.

34 Anthony Kirk-Greene, "Not Quite a Gentleman: The Desk Diaries of the Assistant Private Secretary (Appointments) to the Secretary of State for the Colonies, 1899–1915," *English Historical Review* 117, 472 (2002): 622–33.

35 Kirk-Greene, *Britain's Imperial Administrators*, 140.

36 Hyam, *Britain's Declining Empire*, 11.

37 Ronald Hyam, *Britain's Imperial Century, 1815–1914: A Study of Empire and Expansion* (New York: Harper, 1976), 288.

38 Kirk-Greene, *Britain's Imperial Administrators*, 18, 242–53.

39 Kirk-Greene, *Britain's Imperial Administrators*, 88, 242–53.

40 See, generally, his memoirs: Ralph Furse, *Acupuarias: Recollections of a Recruiting Officer* (London: Oxford University Press, 1962).

41 Jonathan Moore, "The Transformation of the British Imperial Administration 1919–1939" (PhD diss., Tulane University, 2016), 147.

42 Ralph Furse, "Note on Liaison with Universities in the Self-Governing Dominions 1929," in *The Government and Administration of Africa, 1880-1939*, vol. 1, *Recruitment and Training*, ed. Casper Andersen and Andrew Cohen (Abingdon, UK: Routledge, 2016), 113; Anthony Kirk-Greene, "Taking Canada into Partnership in 'The White Man's Burden': The British Colonial Service and the Dominion Selection Scheme of 1923," *Canadian Journal of African Studies* 15, 1 (1981): 33–54; Furse, *Aucuparius*, 73–76, 102–4; Moore, *The Transformation of the British Imperial Administration*, 160–62.

43 Kirk-Greene, "Taking Canada into Partnership," 38.

44 Kirk-Greene, "Taking Canada into Partnership," 39.

45 Kirk-Greene, "Taking Canada into Partnership," 42.

46 *House of Lords Debates*, vol. 54, July 12, 1923, 1017–19.

47 Kirk-Greene, "Taking Canada into Partnership," 44.

48 For the memoirs of one Canadian administrator, see Cairns, *Bush and Boma*.

49 Arthur Berriedale Keith, *The Dominions as Sovereign States: Their Constitutions and Governments* (London: Macmillan, 1938), 723.

50 Kirk-Greene, *Britain's Imperial Administrators*, 111, 146, 280.

51 Anthony Kirk-Greene, "Public Administration and the Colonial Administrator," *Public Administration and Development* 19, 5 (1999): 509.

52 For detailed accounts, see Furnivall, *Colonial Policy and Practice*, 484–512. See also Margery Perham, *The Colonial Reckoning* (London: Collins, 1962), 120–29.

53 Charles Jeffries, *The Colonial Office* (London: Allen and Unwin, 1956), 38–46, 150–59.

54 Sir R. Furse, memorandum, February 27, 1943, partially reproduced in *British Documents on the End of Empire*, series A, vol. 1, ed. S.R. Ashton and S.E. Stockwell (London: HMSO, 1996), 27–39; Kirk-Greene, *On Crown Service*, 43.

55 Alan Burns, *Colonial Civil Servant* (London: Allen and Unwin, 1949), 321; see also Furnivall, *Colonial Policy and Practice*, 428. For a biography of Burns, see Bruce Gilley, *The Last Imperialist: Sir Alan Burns' Epic Defense of the British Empire* (Washington: Regnery Gateway, 2021).

56 Charles Allen, *Tales from the Dark Continent: Images of British Colonial Africa in the Twentieth Century* (London: Futura, 1980), xvii.

57 Kirk-Greene, *Symbol of Authority*, 12; Chris Jeppesen, "'Sanders of the River, Still the Best Job for a British Boy': Recruitment to the Colonial Administrative Service at the End of Empire," *The Historical Journal* 59 (2016): 469.

58 Kirk-Greene, *Symbol of Authority*, 36–41.

59 Kirk-Greene, *On Crown Service*, 62.

60 Kirk-Greene, *On Crown Service*, 75.

61 Furnivall, *Colonial Policy and Practice*, 312–18, 484–512. See also Hyam, "Bureaucracy and 'Trusteeship.'"

62 The 1935 movie *Sanders of the River* was subsequently denounced by its star, Paul Robeson, as imperialist propaganda: Martin Bauml Duberman, *Paul Robeson: A Biography* (New York: Ballantine, 1989), 178–81. It was based on the short stories written by Edgar Wallace. Some of William Somerset Maugham's short stories included district officers and commissioners in Malaya: W. Somerset Maugham, *Collected Short Stories*, vol. 4 (London: Pan, 1976), especially "The Back of Beyond" and "The Outstation." The novelist Joyce Cary was a former district officer, and he included district officers as characters in some of his novels, such as *Mister Johnson*, first published in 1939. See, generally, Anthony Kirk-Greene, "The Colonial Service in the Novel," in Smith, *Administering Empire*, 19–48.

63 Martin Kisch, *Letters and Sketches from Northern Nigeria* (London: Chatto and Windus, 1910), ix.
64 Richard Rathbone, "The Colonial Service and the Transfer of Power in Ghana," in Smith, *Administering Empire*, 150.
65 Prior, *Exporting Empire*, 83.
66 *Colonial Office List 1901* (London: Harrison, 1901).
67 George Santayana, *Soliloquies in England* (London: Constable, 1922), 32.
68 E.D. Morel, *Nigeria: Its Peoples and Its Problems*, 2nd ed. (London: Smith, Elder, 1912), 6–7.
69 Rudyard Kipling, "On the City Wall," in *Black and White* (Allahabad: Wheeler, 1890), 73.
70 Lugard, *Dual Mandate*, 132.
71 Perham, *Colonial Reckoning*, 125.
72 Winston Churchill, *India: Speeches and an Introduction* (London: Thornton Butterworth, 1931), 74.
73 A. Creech Jones, "The Colonial Service," in *The Civil Service in Britain and France*, ed. William Robson (Westport, CT: Greenwood, 1956), 89.
74 Eric Hobsbawm, *The Age of Empire: 1875–1914* (New York: Vintage, 1989), 82.
75 Shashi Tharoor, *Inglorious Empire: What the British Did to India* (London: Penguin, 2017), 54.
76 Tharoor, *Inglorious Empire*, 52.
77 Tharoor, *Inglorious Empire*, 55–56.
78 Tharoor, *Inglorious Empire*, 51.
79 Tharoor, *Inglorious Empire*, 55.
80 Ramsay MacDonald, *Labour and the Empire* (London: George Allen, 1907), 26.
81 Harold J. Laski, "The Colonial Civil Service," *Political Quarterly* 9, 4 (1938): 546.
82 Macmillan, *Africa Emergent*, 196.
83 Leonard Barnes, *Empire or Democracy?* (London: Gollanz, 1939), 95.
84 Kirk-Greene, *Britain's Imperial Administrators*, 285–86.
85 Jawaharlal Nehru, *Glimpses of World History*, 4th ed. (London: Lindsay Drummond, 1949), 94.
86 George Orwell, *Burmese Days* (New York: Harcourt, 1974), 68. First published in 1934.
87 Denis Judd, *Empire: The British Imperial Experience from 1765 to the Present* (New York: Basic Books, 1996), 179.
88 Ronald Hyam, *Empire and Sexuality* (Manchester: Manchester University Press, 1991), 171–73.
89 Quoted in Hyam, *Empire and Sexuality*, 173.
90 MacDonald, *Labour and the Empire*, 27.
91 C.L. Temple, *Native Races and Their Rulers* (Cape Town: Argus, 1918), 188–89.
92 Norman Leys, *Kenya*, 3rd ed. (London: Hogarth Press, 1926), 155; Barnes, *Empire or Democracy*, 95.
93 L.S. Leakey, "Colonial Administration in East Africa from the Native Point of View," in *The Government and Administration of Africa, 1880–1939*, 1:302.
94 Fabian Colonial Bureau, *Downing Street and the Colonies* (London: George Allen, 1942), 17.
95 Laski, "Colonial Civil Service," 546–47.
96 Henry Morgan, *The Place British Americans Have Won in History* (Ottawa: Hunter, Rose, 1866), 18.
97 F.K. Crowley, "Darling, Sir Charles Henry," in *Australian Dictionary of Biography*, vol. 4 (Melbourne: Melbourne University Press, 1972).
98 Alfred Milner, *The Nation and the Empire* (London: Constable, 1913), xxxviii.

99 Donal Lowry, "The Crown, Empire Loyalism and the Assimilation of Non-British White Subjects in the British World: An Argument against 'Ethnic Determinism,'" *Journal of Imperial and Commonwealth History* 31 (2003): 102–10; Serge Courville, "Part of the British Empire Too: French Canada and Colonization Propaganda," in *Canada and the British World: Culture, Migration and Identity,* ed. Phillip Buckner and R. Douglas Francis (Vancouver: UBC Press, 2006), 129–41; Colin Coates, "French Canadians' Ambivalence to the British Empire," in *Canada and the British Empire,* ed. Phillip Buckner (Oxford: Oxford University Press: 2010), 181–99.

100 Anthony Kirk-Greene, "Canada in Africa: Sir Percy Girouard, Neglected Colonial Governor," *African Affairs* 83, 331 (1984): 207–39; Robert M. Maxon, "Judgement on a Colonial Governor: Sir Percy Girouard in Kenya," *Transafrican Journal of History* 18 (1989): 90–100; Robert Maxon, *Struggle for Kenya: The Loss and Reassertion of Imperial Initiatives, 1912–1923* (Cranbury, NJ: Associated University Presses, 1993), 36–42; Michael Smith, "Sir Percy Girouard: French Canadian Proconsul in Africa, 1906–1912" (MA thesis, McGill University, 1989); John M. Mwaruvie, "Kenya's 'Forgotten' Engineer and Colonial Proconsul: Sir Percy Girouard and Departmental Railway Construction in Africa, 1896–1912," *Canadian Journal of History* 41, 1 (2006): 1–22; Lotte Hughes, *Moving the Maasai: A Colonial Misadventure* (Basingstoke, UK: Palgrave, 2006); Abdullahi Sara, *Kenya at a Crossroads: Administration and Economy under Sir Percy Girouard, 1909–1912* (Lanham, MD: Lexington, 2015).

101 Winston Churchill, *The River War* (London: Longman Green, 1899), 1:287–88.

102 Editorial, *The King and His Army* 16 (1903): 30.

103 Reproduced in M.P.K. Sorrenson, *Origins of European Settlement in Kenya* (Nairobi: Oxford University Press, 1968).

104 Norman Leys, quoted in Hughes, *Moving the Maasai,* 79.

105 G.R. Sandford, *An Administrative and Political History of the Masai Reserve* (London: Waterlow, 1918), chap. 3, app. 1–3; Leys, *Kenya,* chap. 4; Woolf, *Empire and Commerce in Africa,* 339–43; W. McGregor Ross, *Kenya from Within: A Short Political History* (London: Allen and Unwin, 1927), chap. 8; George Bennett, *Kenya: A Political History – The Colonial Period* (London: Oxford University Press, 1963), chap. 4; Sorrenson, *Origins of European Settlement in Kenya,* chap. 7; Smith, *Sir Percy Girouard,* chap. 6; Hughes, *Moving the Maasai*; Sara, *Kenya at a Crossroads,* chap. 8.

106 R.E. Wraith, *Guggisberg* (London: Oxford University Press, 1967); H.B. Goodall, *Beloved Imperialist: Sir Gordon Guggisberg, Governor of the Gold Coast* (Durham: Penland, 1998).

107 Anthony Kirk-Greene, foreword to Goodall, *Beloved Imperialist,* xvii.

108 Goodall, *Beloved Imperialist,* 88.

109 Gordon Guggisberg, *The Keystone* (London: Waterlow, 1924), 13–14.

110 Wraith, *Guggisberg,* 216.

111 Kwame Osei Kwarteng and Edmund Selorm Sosu, "Economic, Social and Political Developments in Ghana: A Relook at the Guggisburg Era in the Gold Coast (1919–1927)," *Historical Research Letter* 41 (2017): 8–17.

112 Nnamdi Azikiwe, *Renascent Africa* (London: Cass, 1937), 76.

113 Goodall, *Beloved Imperialist,* xi.

114 Wraith, *Guggisberg,* 9, 242.

115 Thomas Gale, "Sir Gordon Guggisberg and His African Critics," *Transactions of the Historical Society of Ghana* 14 (1993): 271–75.

116 N.J.K. Brukum, "Sir Gordon Guggisberg and Socio-Economic Development of Northern Ghana, 1919–1927," *Transactions of the Historical Society of Ghana* 9 (2005): 1–15.

117 Komla Tsey, *From Head-Loading to the Iron Horse: Railway Building in Colonial Ghana* (Bamenda, Cameroon: Langaa, 2013), 116.

118 George Padmore, *The Gold Coast Revolution* (London: Dennis Dobson, 1953), 90–91; see also 39–41.

119 Commonwealth War Graves Commission, *Report of the Special Committee to Review Historical Inequalities* (Maidenhead, UK: Commonwealth War Graves Commission, 2021), 39.

120 Wraith, *Guggisberg*, 334–36.

121 Henry Maine, *Ancient Law: Its Connection with the Early History of Society, and Its Relation to Modern Ideas* (London: Murray, 1861).

122 W.W. Hunter, *Seven Years of Indian Legislation* (London: Trubner, 1870), 5. For a digest of legislation relating to the government of India, see Courtenay Ilbert, *The Government of India* (London: Clarendon, 1898).

123 For accounts of colonial law, see Charles Clark, *A Summary of Colonial Law* (London: Sweet, 1834); A. Berriedale Keith, *The Constitution, Administration and Laws of the Empire* (London: Collins, 1922); Kenneth Roberts-Wray, *Commonwealth and Colonial Law* (London: Stevens, 1966); Ian Hendry and Susan Dickson, *British Overseas Territories Law*, 2nd ed. (Oxford: Hart, 2018). For a collection of essays on aspects of the legal histories of the Empire, see S. Dorsett and J. Mclaren, eds., *Legal Histories of the British Empire* (London: Routledge, 2014).

124 Sally Engle Merry, "Law and Colonialism," *Law and Society Review* 25, 4 (1991): 891. See also Tina Loo, "Don Cranmer's Potlatch: Law as Coercion, Symbol, and Rhetoric in British Columbia, 1884-1951," *Canadian Historical Review* 73 (1992): 125–65; John Comaroff, "Colonialism, Culture and the Law: A Foreword," *Law and Society Inquiry* 26 (2001): 305.

125 Cole Harris, "How Did Colonialism Dispossess? Comments from an Edge of Empire," *Annals of the Association of the American Geographers* 94, 1 (2004): 176.

126 Lesley Erickson, *Westward Bound: Sex, Violence, the Law, and the Making of a Settler Society* (Vancouver: UBC Press, 2011), 41.

127 For discussion of ruling methods used in the British Empire, see Darwin, *Unfinished Empire*, 189–222; Cell, "Colonial Rule"; Casper Andersen and Andrew Cohen, eds., *The Government and Administration of Africa*, vol. 2, *Governance and Law* (Abingdon, UK: Routledge, 2016).

128 Furnivall, *Colonial Policy and Practice*, 276–77.

129 Furnivall, *Colonial Policy and Practice*, 428.

130 Temple, *Native Races*, 58.

131 Macmillan, *Africa Emergent*, 213–14.

132 John M. MacKenzie, "General Editor's Introduction," in Prior, *Exporting Empire*, xvi.

133 For accounts of the complex relationship between the British and Indigenous rulers, see Ronald Robinson, "Non-European Foundations of European Imperialism," in *Studies in the Theory of Imperialism*, ed. R. Owen and R. Sutcliff (London: Longman, 1972), 128–52; D.A. Low, *Lion Rampant: Essays in the Study of British Imperialism* (London: Routledge, 1973).

134 Quoted in Tharoor, *Inglorious Empire*, 43.

135 Reginald Coupland, *The Empire in These Days* (London: Macmillan, 1935), 206.

136 Wilson, *India Conquered*, 232–33; Gilmour, *The Ruling Caste*, 176–77.

137 Michael H. Fisher, *Indirect Rule in India: Residents and the Residency System* (Delhi: Oxford University Press, 1991).

138 John Beames, *Memoirs of a Bengal Civilian* (London: Eland, 1984), 260–61. First published in 1896.

139 Niall Ferguson, *Empire: The Rise and Demise of the British World Order and the Lessons for Global Power* (New York: Basic Books, 2004), 174.

140 A form of indirect rule was briefly government policy in Australia's Northern Territory: Ben Silverstein, *Governing Natives: Indirect Rule and Settler Colonialism in Australia's North* (Manchester: Manchester University Press, 2019).

141 For a detailed discussion with copies of relevant documents, see Anthony Kirk-Greene, *Native Administration in Nigeria* (London: Oxford University Press, 1965). See also Lugard, *Dual Mandate*, 193–229, and Temple, *Native Races*.

142 Frank Swettenham, *British Malaya* (London: John Lane, 1906), 221; N.J. Ryan, *The Making of Modern Malaya* (Kuala Lumpur: Oxford University Press, 1963), 130; Philip Loh Fook Seng, *The Malay States 1877–1895: Political Change and Social Policy* (Singapore: Oxford University Press, 1969).

143 Swettenham, *British Malaya*, 176–77.

144 Martin Chanock, *Law, Custom and Social Order: The Colonial Experience in Malawi and Zambia* (Cambridge: Cambridge University Press, 1985), 145; Terence Ranger, "The Invention of Tradition in Colonial Africa," in *The Invention of Tradition*, ed. Eric Hobsbawm and Terence Ranger (Cambridge: Cambridge University Press, 1983), 211, 247–51; Terence Ranger, "The Invention of Tradition Revisited: The Case of Colonial Africa" in *Legitimacy and the State in Twentieth-Century Africa*, ed. Terence Ranger and Olufemi Vaughan (London: Palgrave, 1993), 5–50.

145 Lugard, *Dual Mandate*, 217.

146 For an account of the legal relationship with the princely states in India, see William Lee-Warner, *The Protected Princes of India* (London: Macmillan, 1894).

147 Ashley Jackson, *The British Empire: A Very Short Introduction* (Oxford: Oxford University Press, 2013), 20.

148 H. Fielding-Hall, *Passing of the Empire* (London: Hurst and Blackett, 1908), 197.

149 Donald Cameron, quoted in Kirk-Greene, *Native Administration in Nigeria*, 26.

150 Tharoor, *Inglorious Empire*, 42.

151 Karuna Mantena, *Alibis of Empire: Henry Maine and the Ends of Liberal Imperialism* (Princeton, NJ: Princeton University Press, 2010), 177.

152 Mantena, *Alibis of Empire*, 178.

153 George Woodcock, *Who Killed the British Empire? An Inquest* (Toronto: Fitzhenry and Whiteside, 1974), 82.

154 Martin Meredith, *The Fate of Africa: A History of the Continent since Independence* (New York: Public Affairs, 2011), 5

155 Furnivall, *Colonial Policy and Practice*, 277.

156 Low, *Lion Rampant*, 20.

157 Philip Mitchell, *African Afterthoughts* (London: Hutchinson, 1954), 127.

158 Margery Perham, *Lugard: The Years of Authority, 1898–1945* (London: Collins, 1960), 138.

159 Cell, "Colonial Rule," 242.

160 Prior, *Exporting Empire*, 147.

161 George Padmore, *How Britain Rules Africa* (London: Wishart, 1936; New York: Negro Universities Press, 1969), 317–18, 323. Citations refer to the 1969 edition.

162 Lord Hailey, *An African Survey: A Study of Problems Arising in Africa South of the Sahara* (London: Oxford University Press, 1938), 537–38.

163 Hyam, *Britain's Declining Empire*, 15.

164 Cell, "Colonial Rule," 242.

165 Kirk-Greene, *Britain's Imperial Administrators*, 242.

166 Cell, "Colonial Rule," 251.

167 Mason, *The Men Who Ruled India*, 271–335.

168 Kirk-Greene, *On Crown Service*, 219–20.

169 Secretary of State for the Colonies, *The Colonial Empire (1947–1948)*, Cmd. 7433 (London: HMSO, 1948), para. 3.

170 Martin Lynn, "Nigerian Complications: The Colonial Office, The Colonial Service and the 1953 Crisis in Nigeria," in Smith, *Administering Empire*, 181.

171 Jan Morris, *The Spectacle of Empire: Style, Effect and the Pax Britannica* (New York: Doubleday, 1982), 11.

172 George Curzon, *The Place of India in the Empire* (London: George Murray, 1909), 16.

173 David Cannadine, *Ornamentalism: How the British Saw Their Empire* (London: Allen Lane, 2001), 126.

174 Kirk-Greene, *Britain's Imperial Administrators*, 222–24.

175 Rich, *Elixir of Empire*, 13.

176 Rich, *Elixir of Empire*, 64.

177 *Thacker's Indian Directory 1934* (Calcutta: Thacker, 1934), 55.

178 Rich, *Elixir of Empire*, 102.

179 A. Grenfell Price, *White Settlers in the Tropics* (New York: American Geographical Society, 1939), 223.

180 Tharoor, *Inglorious Empire*, 46–50.

181 *Handbook for Travellers in India, Burma and Ceylon*, 8th ed. (London: Murray, 1911), "Advertiser," 8.

182 Prior, *Exporting Empire*, 104.

183 Martin Meredith, *Diamonds, Gold and War* (New York: Public Affairs, 2007), 231.

184 Quoted in Harold Cardinal, *The Unjust Society: The Tragedy of Canada's Indians* (Edmonton: Hurtig, 1969), 36.

185 Edward Butts, "North-West Mounted Police," in *The Canadian Encyclopedia*, last modified January 4, 2023, www.the canadianencyclopedia./ca/en/article/north-west-mounted -police.

186 Sarah Carter and Maria Nugent, eds., *Mistress of Everything: Queen Victoria in Indigenous Worlds* (Manchester: Manchester University Press, 2016).

187 Rupert Godfrey, ed., *Letters from a Prince* (London: Little Brown, 1998), 205, 289, 348.

188 George Orwell, "Shooting an Elephant" [first published in 1936], in *Collected Essays* (London: Secker and Warburg, 1961), 9.

Chapter 5: Canadian Participation in the Empire

1 Migration to Canada is covered in Marjory Harper and Stephen Constantine, *Migration and Empire* (Oxford: Oxford University Press, 2010), chap. 2; in Elizabeth Jane Errington, "British Migration and British America, 1783–1867," in *Canada and the British Empire*, ed. Phillip Buckner (Oxford: Oxford University Press: 2010), 140–59; and in Marjory Harper, "Rhetoric and Reality: British Migration to Canada 1867–1967," in Buckner, *Canada and the British Empire*, 160–80. For a history of Canadian immigration policy, see Valerie Knowles, *Strangers at Our Gates: Canadian Immigration and Immigration Policy, 1540–1990*, 4th ed. (Toronto: Dundurn, 2016).

2 John Darwin, *Unfinished Empire: The Global Expansion of Britain* (London: Penguin, 2013), 95.

3 Harper and Constantine, *Migration and Empire*, 11–12.

4 Olive Dickason, *Canada's First Nations: A History of Founding Peoples from Earliest Times*, 3rd ed. (Don Mills, ON: Oxford University Press, 2002), 200, 238.

5 William Cobbett, *The Emigrant's Guide in Ten Letters* (London: self-published, 1829), 41. For a more positive guide, see A.C. Buchan, *Emigration Practically Considered with Detailed Direction to Emigrants Proceeding to North America, Particularly to the Canadas* (London: Colburn, 1828).

6 James Belich, *Replenishing the Earth* (Oxford: Oxford University Press, 2009), 282.

7 Kenton Storey, *Settler Anxiety at the Outposts of Empire: Colonial Relations, Humanitarian Discourses, and the Imperial Press* (Vancouver: UBC Press, 2016), 210–17.

8 W. Parker Snow, *British Columbia: Emigration and Our Colonies* (London: Piper, Stephenson and Spencer, 1858), 1.

9 Gilbert Sproat, *British Columbia: Information for Emigrants* (London: Agent-General for British Columbia, 1875), 7.

10 Lorenzo Veracini, *The World Turned Inside Out: Settler Colonialism as a Political Idea* (London: Verso, 2021), 224.

11 Quoted in Lesley Erickson, *Westward Bound: Sex, Violence, the Law, and the Making of a Settler Society* (Vancouver: UBC Press, 2011), 21.

12 Stephen Leacock, *Our British Empire: Its Structure, Its History, Its Strength* (London: The Bodley Head, 1940), 240–41; Kent Fedorowich, "Restocking the British World: Empire Migration and Anglo-Canadian Relations, 1919–30," *Britain and the World* 9 (2016): 236.

13 Robert Stead, "The Mixer," in *The Empire Builders and Other Poems* (Toronto: William Briggs, 1908), 16.

14 W.L. Mackenzie King, *Immigration to Canada from the Orient and Immigration from India in Particular*, Sessional Paper No. 36a (Ottawa: King's Printer, 1908). See Kirt Niergarth, "'This Continent Must Belong to the White Races': William Lyon Mackenzie King, Canadian Diplomacy and Immigration Law, 1908," *International History Review* 32 (2010): 599.

15 *Immigration Act*, SC 1910 c 27.

16 Gurdit Singh, *Voyage of the Komagatamaru or India's Slavery Abroad* (Calcutta: Gurdit Singh, 1928); Hugh Johnston, *The Voyage of the Komagata Maru: The Sikh Challenge to Canada's Colour Bar* (Vancouver: UBC Press, 2014); Renisa Mawani, *Across Oceans of Law: The Komagata Maru and Jurisdiction in the Time of Empire* (Durham, NC: Duke University Press, 2018); Rita Kaur Dhamoon, Davina Bhandar, Renisa Mawani, and Satwinder Kaur Bains, *Unmooring the Komagata Maru: Charting Colonial Trajectories* (Vancouver: UBC Press, 2019).

17 *In Re The Immigration Act and Munshi Singh* (1914) 6 WWR 1347 (BCCA) per McPhillips JA, 1380.

18 James Woodsworth, *Strangers within Our Gates or Coming Canadians* (Toronto: Missionary Society of the Methodist Church of Canada, 1909), 278.

19 Bampfylde Fuller, *The Empire of India* (London: Pitman, 1913), 384. See, however, the defence of immigration restrictions by a former viceroy of India: George Curzon, *The Place of India in the Empire* (London: John Murray, 1909), 44–45.

20 Singh, *Voyage of the Komagatamaru*, 103.

21 Frantz Fanon, *The Wretched of the Earth* (New York: Grove, 2004), 5. First published in 1961.

22 Cole Harris, *The Resettlement of British Columbia* (Vancouver, UBC Press, 1997), 267–68; reproduced in Cole Harris, *A Bounded Land: Reflections on Settler Colonialism in Canada* (Vancouver: UBC Press, 2020), 222–23.

23 Quoted in Heidi Bohaker and Franca Iacovetta, "Making Aboriginal People 'Immigrants Too': A Comparison of Citizenship Programs for Newcomers and Indigenous Peoples in Postwar Canada, 1940s–1960s," *Canadian Historical Review* 90 (2009): 428.

24 See, for example, Rolf Knight, *Indians at Work: An Informal History of Native Indian Labour in British Columbia, 1858–1930* (Vancouver: New Star, 1978); John Sutton Lutz, *Makúk: A New History of Aboriginal-White Relations* (Vancouver: UBC Press, 2008).

25 Belich, *Replenishing the Earth,* 23. See, generally, Lorenzo Veracini, *Settler Colonialism: A Theoretical Overview* (Basingstoke, UK: Palgrave Macmillan, 2010).

26 Patrick Wolfe, "Settler Colonialism and the Elimination of the Native," *Journal of Genocide Research* 8 (2006): 388.

27 Quoted in Jeremy Mouat, "Situating Vancouver Island in the British World 1846–49," *BC Studies* 145 (2005): 25.

28 John Ruskin, "Lectures on Art," in *The Works of John Ruskin,* ed. E.T. Cook and Alexander Wedderburn (London: George Allen, 1905), 20:42.

29 Richard Symonds, "Oxford and the Empire," in *The History of the University of Oxford,* vol. 7, *Nineteenth-Century Oxford, Part 2,* ed. M.G. Brock and M.C. Curthoys (Oxford: Oxford University Press, 2000), 691.

30 *Immigration Act 1910,* SC 1910 c 27, s 2(f).

31 Mikhail Bjorge, "Anti-fascist Strikes and the Patriotic Shield?," in *Fighting with the Empire: Canada, Britain, and Global Conflict, 1867–1947,* ed. Steve Marti and William Pratt (Vancouver: UBC Press, 2019), 144–45.

32 Empire Club of Canada, *Addresses Delivered to the Members during the Sessions of 1912–13 and 1913–14* (Toronto: Warwick and Rutter, 1915), part 2, 201.

33 Alastair Buchan, "A Memoir," in *Britain and Canada: Survey of a Changing Relationship,* ed. Peter Lyon (London: Cass, 1976), 32.

34 Richard Jebb, *Studies in Colonial Nationalism* (London: Edward Arnold, 1905), 272–73. For a description of Canadian identity in 1907, see André Siegfried, *The Race Question in Canada* (London: Everleigh Nash, 1907), 115–21.

35 Carl Bridge and Kent Fedorowich, "Mapping the British World," in *The British World: Diaspora, Culture and Identity,* ed. Carl Bridge and Kent Fedorowich (London: Cass, 2003), 5.

36 Viscount Milner, *Imperial Unity: Speeches Delivered in Canada in the Autumn of 1908* (London: Hodder and Stoughton, 1909), 7.

37 Quoted in Barbara Messamore, "The Governors General of Canada 1888–1911: British Imperialists and Canadian 'Nationalists'" (MA thesis, Simon Fraser University, 1991), 119.

38 *House of Commons Debates,* 16th Parl., 4th Sess., vol. 2, May 6, 1930, 1826.

39 John Buchan, *Canadian Occasions* (Toronto: Musson, 1941), 80–81.

40 John Darwin, *The Empire Project: The Rise and Fall of the British World System, 1830–1970* (Cambridge: Cambridge University Press, 2009), 147.

41 Messamore, "The Governors General of Canada," 119.

42 Phillip Buckner, "The Long Goodbye," in *Rediscovering the British World,* ed. Phillip Buckner and R. Douglas Francis (Calgary: University of Calgary Press, 2005), 191.

43 J.R. Seeley, *The Expansion of England* (London: Macmillan, 1883), 13.

44 James (Jan) Morris, *Pax Britannica: The Climax of an Empire* (Harmondsworth, UK: Penguin, 1979), 391.

45 Milner, *Imperial Unity*, 18.

46 Quoted in Marian Fowler, *Redney: A Life of Sara Jeannette Duncan* (Toronto: Anansi, 1983), 226.

47 Henry Morgan, *The Place British Americans Have Won in History* (Ottawa: Hunter, Rose, 1866), 10.

48 Phillip Buckner, "Was There a 'British' Empire? The *Oxford History of the British Empire* from a Canadian Perspective," *Acadiensis* 32 (2002): 125.

49 Yves Engler, *Canada in Africa: 300 Years of Aid and Exploitation* (Winnipeg: Fernwood, 2015), chap. 2.

50 Engler, *Canada in Africa*, chap. 2.

51 John Buchan, *The African Colony: Studies in the Reconstruction* (Edinburgh: Blackwood, 1903), 166–67.

52 Carman Miller, *Painting the Map Red: Canada and the South African War, 1899–1902* (Montreal and Kingston: McGill-Queen's University Press, 1993), 368–90; R.M. Macleod, *Sam Steele: A Biography* (Edmonton: University of Alberta Press, 2018), 232–55.

53 Caroline Elkins, *Legacy of Violence: A History of the British Empire* (New York: Knopf, 2022), 262. For a biography of Beaverbrook, see Anne Chisholm and Michael Davie, *Beaverbrook: A Life* (London: Hutchinson, 1992).

54 J.H. Hamilton, *The All-Red Route 1893–1953: The Trans-Pacific Mail Service between British Columbia, Australia and New Zealand* (Victoria: Archives of British Columbia, 1956).

55 Asa McKercher, *Canada and the World since 1867* (London: Bloomsbury Academic, 2019), chap. 3.

56 Walter Stewart, *Towers of Gold, Feet of Clay: The Canadian Banks* (Toronto: Collins, 1982), 187–88; Peter Hudson, "Imperial Designs: The Royal Bank of Canada in the Caribbean," *Race and Class* 52 (2010): 33–48.

57 Jonathan Vance, *Maple Leaf Empire: Canada, Britain and Two World Wars* (Don Mills, ON: Oxford University Press, 2012), 132.

58 R.J.Q. Adams, *Bonar Law* (London: Thistle, 2013).

59 Quoted in Stuart Ward, *Untied Kingdom: A Global History of the End of Britain* (Cambridge: Cambridge University Press, 2023), 59.

60 P.B. Waite, *In Search of R.B. Bennett* (Montreal and Kingston: McGill-Queen's University Press, 2012).

61 *House of Commons Debates*, 12th Parl., 2nd Sess., February 6, 1913, 2809–10 (D.D. McKenzie).

62 *Times* (London), May 15, 1939, v, xxx.

63 Darwin, *Unfinished Empire*, 90.

64 W. David McIntyre, *Colonies into Commonwealth*, rev. ed. (London: Blandford, 1974), 79.

65 It should be noted that the flag shown was the Red Ensign, which was flown by British ships and some colonies, with the Union Jack prominent in the upper corner.

66 Lord Milner, *The Nation and the Empire – Being a Collection of Speeches and Addresses* (London: Constable, 1913), 152.

67 John Foster Fraser, *Canada as It Is* (London: Cassell, 1905), 52.

68 See Bill Schwarz, *The White Man's World* (Oxford: Oxford University Press, 2011); John Mitcham, *Race and Imperial Defence in the British World, 1870–1914* (Cambridge: Cambridge University Press, 2016).

69 *Times* (London), July 27, 1925.

70 Milner, *The Nation and the Empire*, 141.

71 Henrietta Marshall, *Our Empire Story* (London: Jack, 1908), 115, 118.

72 Quoted in Paul Phillips, *Britain's Past in Canada: The Teaching and Writing of British History* (Vancouver: UBC Press, 1989), 4.

73 Carl Berger, *The Writing of Canadian History – Aspects of English-Canadian Historical Writing: 1900–1970* (Toronto: Oxford University Press, 1976), 11.

74 Phillips, *Britain's Past in Canada*, 14, 17.

75 Quoted in Carl Berger, *The Sense of Power: Studies in the Ideas of Canadian Imperialism 1867–1914* (Toronto: University of Toronto Press, 1970), 36. See, generally, Terry Cook, "Parkin, Sir George Robert," in *Dictionary of Canadian Biography*, vol. 15 (Toronto/Quebec City: University of Toronto/Université Laval, 2005), http://www.biographi.ca/en/bio/parkin_george_robert_15E.html; Berger, *The Sense of Power*, 33–41; John Willison, *Sir George Parkin: A Biography* (London: Macmillan, 1929).

76 Richard Howard, *Upper Canada College: Colborne's Legacy* (Toronto: Macmillan, 1979), 385.

77 Jean Barman, *Growing Up British in British Columbia: Boys in Private School* (Vancouver: UBC Press, 1984), 173.

78 Bora Laskin, *The British Tradition in Canadian Law* (London: Stevens, 1969); Philip Girard, "British Justice, English Law, and Canadian Legal Culture," in Buckner, *Canada and the British Empire*, 259–77.

79 Laskin, *The British Tradition in Canadian Law*, xiii.

80 Quoted in Girard, "British Justice," 272.

81 Erik Brazier, "British Imperial Officers in Canada, 1874–1914," in *Fighting with the Empire: Canada, Britain, and Global Conflict, 1867–1947*, ed. Steve Marti and William Pratt (Vancouver: UBC Press, 2019), 69.

82 *House of Commons Debates*, 9th Parl., 2nd Sess., April 22, 1902, 3356.

83 For a collection of essays on celebrations in Canada, including Victoria Day, Empire Day, and Dominion Day, see Matthew Hayden and Raymond Blake, *Celebrating Canada: Holidays, National Days, and the Crafting of Identities* (Toronto: University of Toronto Press, 2016).

84 Kit Coleman, *To London for the Jubilee* (London: Morang, 1897).

85 George Denison, *The Struggle for Imperial Unity: Recollections and Experiences* (London: Macmillan, 1909), 256–57.

86 Molly Pulver Ungar, "Trenholme, Clementina," in *Dictionary of Canadian Biography*, vol. 14 (Toronto/Quebec City: University of Toronto Press/Université Laval, 1998), http://www.biographi.ca/en/bio/trenholme_clementina_14E.html. For the celebration of Empire Day in the UK, see Sathnam Sanghera, *Empireland: How Imperialism Has Shaped Modern Britain* (New York: Pantheon, 2023), chap. 1.

87 Quoted in Vance, *Maple Leaf Empire*, 142.

88 For the Commonwealth flag, see "Foreign Flags in Canada," Canadian Heritage, last modified June 20, 2023, https://www.canada.ca/en/canadian-heritage/services/flag-canada-etiquette/foreign-flags.html.

89 Laura Ishiguro, *Nothing to Write Home About: British Family Correspondence and the Settler Colonial Everyday in British Columbia* (Vancouver: UBC Press, 2019).

90 Adele Perry, *Colonial Relation: The Douglas-Connolly Family and the Nineteenth-Century Imperial World* (Cambridge: Cambridge University Press, 2015).

91 Nadia Wright, *William Farquhar and Singapore* (Penang: Entrepot, 2017), 222.

92 Cassandra Pybus, *The White Rajahs of Sarawak: Dynastic Intrigue and the Forgotten Canadian Heir* (Vancouver: Douglas and McIntyre, 1996).

93 Katie Pickles, *Female Imperialism and National Identity: Imperial Order Daughters of the Empire* (Manchester: University of Manchester Press, 2002), 168–69.

94   Robert Baden-Powell, *The Canadian Boy Scout* (Toronto: Morang, 1911), 279. For the Boy Scouts and similar organizations, see Mitcham, *Race and Imperial Defence,* chap. 6. For the response to Baden-Powell's promotion, see Patricia Dirks, "Canada's Boys – An Imperial or National Asset? Response to Baden-Powell's Boy Scout Movement in Pre-War Canada," in *Canada and the British World: Culture, Migration and Identity,* ed. Phillip Buckner and R. Douglas Francis (Vancouver: UBC Press, 2006), 111–28. For Girl Guides, see Kristine Alexander, "Canadian Girls, Imperial Girls, Global Girls: Race, Nation and Transnationalism in the Interwar Girl Guides," in *Within and Without the Nation: Canadian History as a Transnational History,* ed. Karen Dubinsky, Adele Perry, and Henry Yu (Toronto: University of Toronto Press, 2015), 276–92; Kristine Alexander, *Guiding Modern Girls: Girlhood, Empire, and Internationalism in the 1920s and 1930s* (Vancouver: UBC Press, 2018).

95   Katie Pickles, "Claiming Cavell: Britishness and Memorialization," in Buckner and Francis, *Canada and the British World,* 157–73.

96   Simon Potter, "Communications and Integration: The British and Dominion Press and the British World," in Bridge and Fedorowich, *The British World,* 190–206. For a study of the newspapers of Vancouver Island and New Zealand in the 1850s and 1860s, see Kenton Storey, *Settler Anxiety at the Outposts of Empire: Colonial Relations, Humanitarian Discourses, and the Imperial Press* (Vancouver: UBC Press, 2016).

97   Bridge and Fedorowich, "Mapping the British World," 6.

98   Tamson Pietsch, *Empire of Scholars: Universities, Networks and the British Academic World 1850–1939* (Manchester: Manchester University Press, 2013), 199.

99   For the 1924 exhibition, see Anne Clendinning, "Exhibiting a Nation: Canada at the British Empire Exhibition, 1924–1925," *Histoire sociale/Social History* 39, 77 (2006): 79–107.

100 Alfred Zimmern, *The Third British Empire,* 3rd ed. (London: Oxford University Press, 1934), 98.

101 *House of Commons Debates,* 8th Parl., 5th Sess., February 13, 1900, 377 (J. Charlton); *House of Commons Debates,* 11th Parl., 1st Sess., March 29, 1909, 3518 (R.L. Borden); *House of Commons Debates,* 11th Parl., 2nd Sess., February 17, 1910, 3810 (H.H. McLean).

102 Alex McNeil in a speech to the Imperial Federation League, quoted in Berger, *A Sense of Power,* 107–8.

103 Leacock, *Our British Empire,* 77–78.

104 Darwin, *The Empire Project,* 11.

105 Morris, *Pax Britannica,* 397.

106 Belich, *Replenishing the Earth,* 209.

107 John Darwin, "A Third British Empire? The Dominion Idea in Imperial Politics," in *The Oxford History of the British Empire,* vol. 4, *The Twentieth Century,* ed. Judith M. Brown and Wm. Roger Louis (Oxford: Oxford University Press, 1999), 72.

108 O.A. Howland, *The New Empire: Reflections upon Its Origin and Constitution and Its Relations to the Great Republic* (Toronto: Hart, 1891), 361.

109 Stephen Leacock, *Greater Canada: An Appeal* (Montreal: Montreal News Company, 1907), 2.

110 Fraser, *Canada as It Is,* 52.

111 *House of Commons Debates,* 11th Parl., 2nd Sess., February 23, 1910, 4106–7 (J.W. Edwards).

112 Alan Bowker, *The Social Criticism of Stephen Leacock* (Toronto: University of Toronto Press, 1973), xiv.

113 John Ewart, "Perplexed Imperialist," *Queen's Quarterly* (1907): 90. For a detailed account of his views, see John Ewart, *The Kingdom of Canada* (Toronto: Morang, 1908). See, generally, Roy St. George Stubbs, "John S. Ewart: A Great Canadian," *Manitoba Law Journal* 1 (1962): 3.

114 Joseph Chamberlain, "The True Conception of Empire," in *Foreign and Colonial Speeches* (London: Routledge, 1897), 248; J. Lee Thompson, *A Wider Patriotism: Alfred Milner and the British Empire* (London: Routledge, 2008), 125; see also *Speeches of the Right Hon. Earl Grey, GCMG, in September and October, 1911, and January, 1912* (Ottawa: The Canadian Club, 1912), 34; Richard Jebb, *Studies in Colonial Nationalism* (London: Edward Arnold, 1905), 275; Belich, *Replenishing the Earth*, 467; Paula Hastings, "Dreams of a Tropical Canada: Race, Nation, and Canadian Aspirations in the Caribbean Basin, 1883–1919" (PhD diss., Duke University, 2010), 159.

115 For a detailed account of the diminishment of the ideas of a British World and Britishness, see Ward, *Untied Kingdom*.

116 Quoted in George Parkin, *Sir John A. Macdonald* (Toronto: Morang, 1910), 171–90.

117 *House of Commons Debates*, 11th Parl., 1st Sess., March 29, 1909, 3518.

118 *House of Commons Debates*, 12th Parl., 4th Sess., vol. 118, August 19, 1914, 9–10, reproduced in Arthur Berriedale Keith, ed., *Speeches and Documentation, British Colonial Policy, 1763–1917*, vol. 2 (London: Oxford University Press, 1918), 358, 363.

119 Darwin, *The Empire Project*, 395–97. For Laurier's difficult task of reconciling French Canadian support with the imperialist views of English Canadians, see Graeme Thompson, "Ontario's Empire: Liberalism and 'Britannic' Nationalism in Laurier's Canada, 1887–1919" (DPhil diss., University of Oxford, 2016).

120 *The Diaries of William Lyon Mackenzie King*, July 26, 1945, https://www.bac-lac.gc.ca/eng/discover/politics-government/prime-ministers/william-lyon-mackenzie-king/Pages/search.aspx/. See, generally, Roy MacLaren, *Mackenzie King in the Age of the Dictators: Canada's Imperial and Foreign Policies* (Montreal and Kingston: McGill-Queen's University Press, 2019).

121 J.W. Flavelle, *Canada and Its Relations to the British Empire* (London: Macmillan, 1917), 3.

122 Chamberlain, *Foreign and Colonial Speeches*.

123 Milner, *Imperial Unity*; Thompson, *A Wider Patriotism*, chap. 9.

124 David Dilks, *The Great Dominion: Winston Churchill in Canada, 1900–1954* (Toronto: Thomas Allen, 2005).

125 Frederick Young, *A Pioneer of Imperial Federalism in Canada* (London: George Allen, 1902).

126 Dilks, *The Great Dominion*, 27.

127 Dilks, *The Great Dominion*, 83.

128 Quoted in Engler, *Canada in Africa*, chap. 2, note 15.

129 Robert Page, *Imperialism and Canada, 1895–1903* (Toronto: Holt Rhinehart, 1972), 25–41.

130 Barrie Davies, "We Hold a Vaster Empire Than Has Been: Canadian Literature and the Canadian Empire," *Studies in Canadian Literature* 14 (1989): 18. For Canadian poems published at the height of the Empire, see E.A. Helps, ed., *Songs and Ballads of Greater Britain* (London: Dent, 1913), 3–167.

131 Wilfred Campbell, *Sagas of Vaster Britain* (London: Hodder and Stoughton, 1914).

132 Wilfred Campbell, *The Collected Poems of Wilfred Campbell* (New York: Fleming, Revell, 1905), 297, 303, 305.

133 Robert Stead, *The Empire Builders* (Toronto: Briggs, 1908), 14.

134 Pauline Johnson, "For Queen and Country" and "Canadian Born," in *Pauline Johnson (Tekahionwake): Collected Poems and Selected Prose*, ed. Carole Gerson and Veronica Strong-Boag (Toronto: University of Toronto Press, 2005), 124, 75–76.

135 Pauline Johnson, "Riders of the Plains," in *Canadian Born* (Toronto: George Morang, 1903), 27.

136 Quoted in Veronica Strong-Boag, *Paddling Her Own Canoe: The Times and Texts of E. Pauline Johnson (Tekahionwake)* (Toronto: University of Toronto Press, 2000), 190.

137 Pauline Johnson, "A Cry from an Indian Wife," in *Flint and Feather* (Toronto: Musson, 1912), 17.

138 Thomas E. Tausky, *Sara Jeannette Duncan: Novelist of Empire* (Port Credit: Meany, 1980).

139 Karyn Huenemann, "The Complexities of Sara Jeannette Duncan's Imperialist Attitudes," *Graduate Work in Canadian Studies in Europe, Canadian Cahiers* 7 (2009): 108.

140 Quoted in Fowler, *Redney*, 265.

141 Misao Dean, *A Different Point of View: Sara Jeannette Duncan* (Montreal and Kingston: McGill-Queen's University Press, 1991), 4, 12.

142 Dean, *A Different Point of View*, 140.

143 Sara Jeannette Duncan, *The Imperialist* (New York: Appleton, 1904); a recent version with notes has been published: Sara Jeannette Duncan, *The Imperialist*, ed. Misao Dean (Peterborough, ON: Broadview, 2005).

144 For commentary on Leacock's political views, including imperialism, see Ewart, "A Perplexed Imperialist"; Carl Berger, "The Other Mr. Leacock," *Canadian Literature* 55 (1973): 23–55; Bowker, *The Social Criticism of Stephen Leacock*; David Staines, ed., *Stephen Leacock: A Reappraisal* (Ottawa: University of Ottawa Press, 1986); Gerald Lynch, *Stephen Leacock: Humour and Humanity* (Montreal and Kingston: McGill-Queen's University Press, 1988).

145 Quoted in Margaret MacMillan, *Stephen Leacock* (Toronto: Penguin, 2009), 138.

146 Leacock, *Greater Canada*, 2.

147 Stephen Leacock, *Economic Prosperity in the British Empire* (Toronto: Macmillan, 1930).

148 Leacock, *Our British Empire*, 5.

149 For discussion of critics in the UK, see Bernard Porter, *Critics of Empire: British Radical Attitudes to Colonialism in Africa 1895–1914* (London: Macmillan, 1968).

150 Joseph Levitt, *Henri Bourassa on Imperialism and Bi-culturalism* (Toronto: Copp Clark, 1970).

151 Henri Bourassa, *Great Britain and Canada: Topics of the Day* (Montreal: Beauchemin, 1902), 4.

152 Robert Page, *The Boer War and Canadian Imperialism*, Historical Booklet No. 44 (Ottawa: Canadian Historical Association, 1997), 17.

153 Goldwin Smith, *Canada and the Canadian Question* (London: Macmillan, 1891), 267–80. See also the collection of his letters to the *Daily News* in 1862–63 in Goldwin Smith, *The Empire: A Series of Letters* (Oxford: Henry and Parker, 1863).

154 James Naylor, "Pacifism or Anti-Imperialism? The CCF Response to the Outbreak of World War II," *Journal of the Canadian Historical Association* 8 (1997): 213–37. For opposition in the UK, see Stephen Howe, *Anticolonialism in British Politics: The Left and the End of Empire* (Oxford: Oxford University Press, 1993); Priyamvada Gopal, *Insurgent Anticolonial Resistance and British Dissent* (London: Verso, 2019).

155 Norman Hillmer, *O.D. Skelton: A Portrait of Canadian Ambition* (Toronto: University of Toronto Press, 2015), 7–13.

156 It has been suggested that there is "an argument for saying that the *most* imperialist people, in most senses of the word, were many of those who actually went to the colonies": Bernard Porter, *The Absent-Minded Imperialists: Empire, Society and Culture in Britain* (Oxford: Oxford University Press, 2006), 309.

157 On the impacts of the Empire on the public in the UK, see John Mackenzie, *Propaganda and the Empire: The Manipulation of British Public Opinion 1810–1960* (Manchester: Manchester University Press, 1984); Andrew Thompson, *The Empire Strikes Back: The Impact of Imperialism on Britain from the Mid-Nineteenth Century* (London: Routledge, 2005).

158 Norman MacKenzie, "A Canadian Looks at the Empire," *Political Quarterly* 9 (1938): 553.

159 Morgan, *The Place British Americans Have Won in History,* 15.

160 C.P. Stacey, *Canada and the British Army: A Study in the Practice of Responsible Government,* rev. ed. (Toronto: University of Toronto Press, 1963).

161 Morgan, *The Place British Americans Have Won in History,* 13.

162 Andrew Godefroy, "Canadian Soldiers in the West African Conflict, 1885–1905," *Canadian Military History* 17 (2008): 25.

163 Andrew Godefroy, "For Queen, King and Empire: Canadians Recruited into the British Army, 1858–1944," *Journal of the Society for Army Historical Research* 87 (2009): 135.

164 Hampden Burnham, *Canadians in the Imperial Naval and Military Service Abroad* (Toronto: Williamson, 1891).

165 "Orders and Decorations: Canadian Victoria Cross Recipients," s.v., "Dunn, Alexander Roberts," Veterans Affairs Canada, https://www.veterans.gc.ca/eng/remembrance/medals -decorations/canadian-victoria-cross-recipients.

166 For a detailed description, see Saul David, *The Indian Mutiny 1857* (London: Penguin, 2003). See also James (Jan) Morris, *Heaven's Command: An Imperial Progress* (Harmondsworth, UK: Penguin, 1979), 218–48. For its impact, see Eric Hobsbawm, *The Age of Capital* (London: Abacus, 1977), 151–52.

167 John Clarke Marshman, *Memoirs of Major-General Sir Henry Havelock* (London: Longman, 1861), 392.

168 Morris, *Pax Britannica,* 136, 415.

169 Alfred Tennyson, "The Defence of Lucknow," in *Ballads and Other Poems* (Boston: Osgood, 1880).

170 *Murray's Handbook for Travellers in India, Burma and Ceylon,* 8th ed. (London: Murray, 1911), 292–98.

171 G.B. Malleson, *History of the Indian Mutiny 1857–1858* (London: Allen, 1878), 1:414, 481.

172 Garnet Wolseley, *The Story of a Soldier's Life* (Westminster: Archibald Constable, 1903), 1:291.

173 Julia Inglis, *The Siege of Lucknow* (London: Osgood, 1892), 60, 158, 199. For the scale of this retribution, often directed indiscriminately, see George Trevelyan, *The Competition Wallah* (London: Macmillan, 1895), 251–52.

174 "Orders and Decorations: Canadian Victoria Cross Recipients," Veterans Affairs Canada, https://www.veterans.gc.ca/eng/remembrance/medals-decorations/canadian-victoria -cross-recipients.

175 Michael Asher, *Khartoum: The Ultimate Imperial Adventure* (London: Penguin, 2006).

176 *House of Commons Debates,* 5th Parl., 3rd Sess., March 26, 1885, 745.

177 Lytton Strachey, *Eminent Victorians* (New York: Garden City, 1918), 243; *General Gordon's Last Journal* (London: Kegan Paul, 1885).

178 William McGonagall, "General Gordon, The Hero of Khartoum," in *Still More Poetic Gems* (London: Duckworth, 1980).

179 Roy MacLaren, *Canadians on the Nile 1882–1898* (Vancouver: UBC Press, 1978), 16–18.

180 "MGen JF Wilson (1852–1911)," Royal Canadian Artillery Museum, https://en.rcamuseum.com/mgen-jf-wilson-1852-1911/.

181 Louis Jackson, *Our Caughnawagas in Egypt* (Montreal: Drysdale, 1885); James Deer, *The Canadian Voyageurs in Egypt* (Montreal: Lavell, 1885); C.P. Stacey, *Records of the Nile Voyageurs 1884–1885* (Toronto: Champlain Society, 1959); MacLaren, *Canadians on the Nile*; Anthony P. Michel, "To Represent the Country in Egypt: Aboriginality, Britishness, Anglophone Canadian Identities, and the Nile Voyageur Contingent, 1884–1985," *Histoire sociale/Social History* 39, 77 (2006): 45–77; Carl Benn, *Mohawks on the Nile: Natives among the Canadian Voyageurs in Egypt, 1884–1885* (Toronto: Dundurn, 2009); Peter Pigott, *Canada in Sudan: War without Borders* (Toronto: Dundurn, 2009); Anthony Michel, "The Nile Voyageurs: Recognition of Canada's Role in the Empire, 1884–1885" (PhD diss., Carleton University, 2012).

182 Douglas Johnson, "The Death of Gordon: A Victorian Myth," *Journal of Imperial and Commonwealth History* 10 (1982): 285–310.

183 Engler, *Canada in Africa*, chap. 2.

184 Andrew Godefroy, ed., *Bush Warfare* (Ottawa: Department of National Defence, 2009), xxiii.

185 Godefroy, "Canadian Soldiers," 33.

186 Godefroy, "Canadian Soldiers," 34.

187 Godefroy, "Canadian Soldiers," 31–32.

188 Quoted in Godefroy, *Bush Warfare*, 104.

189 Martin Meredith, *Diamonds, Gold, and War* (New York: Public Affairs, 2007), part 9.

190 For Canada's involvement, see Miller, *Painting the Map Red*; Page, *The Boer War*.

191 *House of Commons Debates*, 8th Parl., 5th Sess., February 6, 1900, 111 (G.E. Foster).

192 *House of Commons Debates*, 8th Parl., 5th Sess., March 13, 1900, 1848.

193 William Hart-McHarg, *From Quebec to Pretoria* (Toronto: Briggs, 1902); T.G. Marquis, *Canada's Sons on Kopje and Veldt* (Toronto: Canada's Sons, 1900); W. Sanford Evans, *The Canadian Contingent and Canadian Imperialism: A Story and a Study* (Toronto: Publisher's Syndicate, 1901). See also E.B. Biggar, *The Boer War: Its Causes and Its Interest to Canadians* (Toronto: Biggar Samuel, 1899).

194 Hart-McHarg, *From Quebec to Pretoria*, 223.

195 Hart-McHarg, *From Quebec to Pretoria*, 117, 48.

196 Hart-McHarg, *From Quebec to Pretoria*, 253.

197 "Lieutenant Colonel William Frederick Richard Hart McHarg," Canadian Virtual War Memorial, Veterans Affairs Canada, https://www.veterans.gc.ca/eng/remembrance/memorials/canadian-virtual-war-memorial/detail/485397.

198 Marquis, *Canada's Sons*, 28.

199 S.B. Steele, *Forty Years in Canada* (London: Herbert Jenkins, 1915), chaps. 18–19.

200 Quoted in Miller, *Painting the Map Red*, 326.

201 "All about Boer War Bugles – Bugles 1," Canadian Anglo-Boer War Museum, https://www.goldiproductions.com/angloboerwarmuseum/Boer93n1_bugles1_intro.html.

202 Leonard Thompson, *A History of South Africa* (New Haven, CT: Yale University Press, 2001), 144.

203 For the consequences on the African population, written by one of the founders of the African National Congress, see Sol Plaatje, *Native Life in South Africa* (London: King, 1916).

204 Quoted in Meredith, *Diamonds, Gold, and War,* 466.
205 For a summary of the literature on Canada and the First World War, see Tim Cook, "Battles of the Imagined Past: Canada's Great War and Memory," *Canadian Historical Review* 95, 3 (2014): 417–26.
206 Ian McKay and Jamie Swift, *The Vimy Trap: Or, How We Learned to Stop Worrying and Love the Great War* (Toronto: Between the Lines, 2016); see also Tim Cook, *Vimy: The Battle and the Legend* (Toronto: Allen Lane, 2017).
207 David Lloyd George, *War Memoirs* (London: Ivor Nicholson and Watson, 1934), 3:1531.
208 Quoted in Ged Martin, "Canada from 1815," in *The Oxford History of the British Empire,* vol. 3, *The Nineteenth Century,* ed. Andrew Porter (Oxford: Oxford University Press, 1999), 544.
209 *House of Commons Debates,* 12th Parl., 4th Sess., August 19, 1914, 9, reproduced in Arthur Berriedale Keith, ed., *British Colonial Policy 1763–1917* (London: Oxford University Press, 1918), 2:358, 363.
210 Mitcham, *Race and Imperial Defence,* 220–21.
211 Mitcham, *Race and Imperial Defence,* 217.
212 Mitcham, *Race and Imperial Defence,* 223, 225.
213 Philip Wigley, *Canada and the Transition to Commonwealth: British-Canadian Relations, 1917–1926* (Cambridge: Cambridge University Press, 1977), 67–95.
214 Margaret MacMillan, *Peacemakers: Six Months That Changed the World* (London: Murray, 2001), 55; Wigley, *Canada and the Transition to Commonwealth,* 44–50.
215 See, generally, Richard Overy, *Blood and Ruins: The Last Imperial War, 1939–1945* (New York: Viking, 2022).
216 *House of Commons Debates,* 19th Parl., 2nd Sess., vol. 228, December 30, 1941, 4479, reproduced in Dilks, *The Great Dominion,* 198.
217 See Mitcham, *Race and Imperial Defence,* 273–74, for a summary of the Empire's contribution to the Allied victory.
218 Richard Toye, *Churchill's Empire: The World That Made Him and the World He Made* (New York: St Martin's Griffin, 2010), 242–43.
219 Reproduced in W.S. Churchill, *The Second World War,* vol. 2, *Their Finest Hour* (London: Cassells, 1949), 631.
220 A.P. Thornton, *The Imperial Idea and Its Enemies: A Study in British Power,* 2nd ed. (Basingstoke, UK: Macmillan, 1985), 317.
221 Buckner and Francis, *Canada and the British World,* 2.
222 Vance, *Maple Leaf Empire,* 4.

Chapter 6: Internal Colonialism in Canada

1 William Halliday, *Potlatch and Totem and the Recollections of an Indian Agent* (London: Dent, 1935); Douglas Cole and Ira Chaikin, *An Iron Hand upon the People: The Law against the Potlatch on the Northwest Coast* (Vancouver: Douglas and McIntyre, 1990), 90–126; John L. Steckley, *Indian Agents: Rulers of the Reserves* (New York: Peter Lang, 2016), 115–44.
2 Tina Loo, "Don Cranmer's Potlatch: Law as Coercion, Symbol, and Rhetoric in British Columbia, 1884–1951," *Canadian Historical Review* 73 (1992): 125–65.
3 Halliday, *Potlatch and Totem,* 194.
4 House of Commons, memorandum from J.A. Macdonald, January 3, 1887, Sessional Papers, 6th Parl., 1st Sess., vol. 16, 20b-37, https://parl.canadiana.ca/view/oocihm.9_08052_20_16.
5 Halliday, *Potlatch and Totem,* ix.

6 Halliday, *Potlatch and Totem,* 226–27.

7 Douglas Leighton, "Higginson, Sir James Macaulay," in *Dictionary of Canadian Biography,* vol. 11 (Toronto/Quebec City: University of Toronto/Université Laval, 1982), http://www. biographi.ca/en/bio/higginson_james_macaulay_11E.html.

8 James Leighton, "The Development of Federal Indian Policy in Canada, 1840–1890" (PhD diss., University of Western Ontario, 1975), 229.

9 Quoted in John Leslie and Ron Maguire, eds., *The Historical Development of the Indian Act,* 2nd ed. (Ottawa: Indian and Northern Affairs, 1978), 114.

10 See, generally, E. Brian Titley, *A Narrow Vision: Duncan Campbell Scott and the Administration of Indian Affairs in Canada* (Vancouver: UBC Press, 1986).

11 Alan Lester, Kate Boehme, and Peter Mitchell, *Ruling the World: Freedom, Civilization and Liberalism in the Nineteenth-Century British Empire* (Cambridge: Cambridge University Press, 2020), 197–99, 204.

12 Keith Sinclair, "Grey, George" in *Dictionary of New Zealand Biography,* first published in 1990, *Te Ara – the Encyclopedia of New Zealand,* https://teara.govt.nz/en/biographies/1g21/ grey-george; Alan Lester and Fae Dussart, *Colonization and the Origins of Humanitarian Governance: Protecting Aborigines across the Nineteenth-Century British Empire* (Cambridge: Cambridge University Press, 2014), 226–69; Alan Lester, "Settler Colonialism, George Grey and the Politics of Ethnography," *Environmental and Planning D: Society and Space* 34, 3 (2016): 492–507.

13 Barrie Davies, ed., *At the Mermaid Inn: Wilfred Campbell, Archibald Lampman, Duncan Campbell Scott in the Globe, 1892–93* (Toronto: University of Toronto Press, 1979), 145–46.

14 Titley, *A Narrow Vision,* 25.

15 Duncan Campbell Scott, "The Onondaga Madonna" and "Wat'kwenies," in *Labor and the Angel* (Boston: Copeland Day, 1898). For Scott as a poet, see John Coldwell Adams, *Confederation Voices: Seven Canadian Poets* (Toronto: Canadian Poetry Press, 2007), chap. 5.

16 Duncan Campbell Scott, "Half-Breed Girl," in *Via Borealis* (Toronto: Tyrrell, 1906); Duncan Campbell Scott, "Gull Lake," in *The Green Cloister* (Toronto: McClelland and Stewart, 1935).

17 Titley, *A Narrow Vision,* 38–39.

18 The term used at the time for Indigenous groups subject to the *Indian Act* was "Indian band"; Inuit and Métis peoples were not subject to the *Indian Act.* Where possible in this chapter, I use "First Nations" to refer to the peoples subject to the act, rather than "Indigenous" peoples, which generally includes Inuit and Métis peoples.

19 Royal Commission on Aboriginal Peoples, *Report of the Royal Commission on Aboriginal Peoples,* vol. 1, *Looking Forward, Looking Back* (Ottawa: Minister of Supply and Services Canada, 1996), 274 (hereafter RCAP).

20 For studies of the role of Indian agents, see Robin Jarvis Brownlie, *A Fatherly Eye: Indian Agents, Government Power, and Aboriginal Resistance in Ontario, 1918–1939* (Oxford: Oxford University Press, 2003); Vic Satzewich and Linda Mahood, "Indian Agents and the Residential School System in Canada, 1946–1970," *Historical Studies in Education* 7 (1995): 45–69; Victor Satzewich, "Indian Agents and the 'Indian Problem' in Canada in 1946: Reconsidering the Theory of Coercive Tutelage," *Canadian Journal of Native Studies* 17 (1997): 227–57; Steckley, *Indian Agents.* For a memoir by an Indian agent, see Halliday, *Potlatch and Totem,* and for a semi-autobiographical novel, see Alan Fry, *How a People Die* (Madeira Park, BC: Harbour Publishing, 1994).

21 Brownlie, *A Fatherly Eye,* ix.

22 Brownlie, *A Fatherly Eye,* 32.

23 John G. Reid, "Empire, Settler Colonialism, and the Role of Violence in Indigenous Dispossession in British North America, 1749–1830," in *Violence, Order and Unrest: A History of British North America, 1749–1876,* ed. Elizabeth Mancke, Jerry Bannister, Denis B. McKim, and Scott W. See (Toronto: University of Toronto Press, 2019), 117–34.

24 James Miller, *Skyscrapers Hide the Heavens*, 4th ed. (Toronto: University of Toronto Press, 2018), 348.

25 Letter to the House of Commons from Mohawk Chief F. McD. Jacobs, quoted in *House of Commons Debates,* 12th Parl., 3rd Sess., April 3, 1914, 2395.

26 Mary-Ellen Kelm and Keith Smith, *Talking Back to the Indian Act: Critical Readings in Settler Colonial Histories* (Toronto: University of Toronto Press, 2018), 26–29, 48–49.

27 *House of Commons Debates,* 16th Parl., 1st Sess., February 15, 1927, 317 (Charles Stewart).

28 Wendy Wickwire, *At the Bridge: James Teit and an Anthropology of Belonging* (Vancouver: UBC Press, 2019).

29 Sara Jeannette Duncan, *The Imperialist* (New York: Appleton, 1904), 5, 428. For the negative portrayal of Indigenous people in Canadian newspapers from 1869, see Mark Anderson and Carmen Robertson, *Seeing Red: A History of Natives in Canadian Newspapers* (Winnipeg: University of Manitoba Press, 2011).

30 See Thomas E. Tausky, *Sara Jeannette Duncan: Novelist of Empire* (Port Credit, ON: Meany, 1980), 153–74, for detailed discussion. In fact, the plot could not have occurred, since the election takes place after the Boer War battle of Paardeberg in 1900, and First Nations people only had the federal franchise between 1885 and 1898, and then only in eastern Canada: see discussion of the *Indian Act* below. Duncan acknowledged her error: Marian Fowler, *Redney: A Life of Sara Jeannette Duncan* (Toronto: Anansi, 1983), 266.

31 James W. Dt.G. Walker, "The Indian in Canadian Historical Writing, 1972–1982," in *As Long as the Sun Shines and Water Flows: A Reader in Canadian Native Studies,* ed. Ian A.L. Getty and Antoine S. Lussier (Vancouver: UBC Press, 1983), 340–57.

32 Diamond Jenness, *The Indians of Canada* (Ottawa: National Museum of Canada, 1935), 350.

33 J.E.M. Kew, "A Synopsis of Musqueam Culture and History" (unpublished manuscript, August 14, 1979), entered at trial of *Guerin v The Queen,* [1982] 2 FC 385, 17.

34 Hugh Shewell, *"Enough to Keep Them Alive": Indian Welfare in Canada, 1873–1965* (Toronto: University of Toronto Press, 2004); Sylvia Olsen, "Making Poverty: A History of On-Reserve Housing Programs, 1930–1996" (PhD diss., University of Victoria, 2016).

35 Scott Sheffield, *The Red Man's on the Warpath: The Image of the "Indian" and the Second World War* (Vancouver: UBC Press, 2004), 20.

36 Sheffield, *The Red Man's on the Warpath,* 23.

37 Kew, "A Synopsis of Musqueam Culture and History," 16.

38 Rolf Knight, *Indians at Work* (Vancouver: New Star Books, 1978), 266.

39 See Chapter 4 of this volume.

40 Satzewich and Mahood, "Indian Agents and the Residential School System," 68.

41 Brownlie, *A Fatherly Eye,* 35.

42 Pleshakov, "'We Do Not Talk about Our History Here': The Department of Indian Affairs, Musqueam-Settler Relations and Memory of a Vancouver Neighbourhood" (MA thesis, University of British Columbia, 2010), 17–27.

43 Kew, "A Synopsis of Musqueam Culture and History," 21–22. For other descriptions of the powers of Indian agents, see Noel Dyck, *What Is the Indian "Problem": Tutelage and Resistance in Canadian Indian Administration* (St. John's: Institute of Social and Economic Research, 1991), 83–84; Fry, *How a People Die,* 79; H.B. Hawthorn, C.S. Belshaw, and S.M.

Jamieson, *The Indians of British Columbia: A Study of Contemporary Adjustment* (Berkeley: University of California Press, 1958), 486; Titley, *A Narrow Vision*, 13–14.

44 John Daly, Indian agent, in 1930, quoted in Brownlie, *A Fatherly Eye*, vi.

45 William Wuttenee, *Ruffled Feathers: Indians in Canadian Society* (Calgary: Bell, 1971), 124.

46 RCAP, 1:274.

47 Brownlie, *A Fatherly Eye*, x, xii.

48 Brownlie, *A Fatherly Eye*, 60; see also Dyck, *What Is the Indian "Problem,"* 88.

49 Dyck, *What Is the Indian "Problem,"* 88.

50 Pleshakov, "'We Do Not Talk about Our History Here,'" 23.

51 Brownlie, *A Fatherly Eye*, 154.

52 Fry, *How a People Die*, 78.

53 Fry, *How a People Die*, 81–82.

54 Brownlie, *A Fatherly Eye*, 33–34.

55 Brownlie, *A Fatherly Eye*, 32.

56 Knight, *Indians at Work*, 266.

57 Herman Merivale, *Lectures on Colonization and Colonies* (London: Longman, Brown, 1842), 2:160.

58 See Brownlie, *A Fatherly Eye*, 56–79. For an account of band councils in British Columbia in 1955, see Hawthorn, Belshaw, and Jamieson, *The Indians of British Columbia*, 445–68. For the powers of band councils under the *Indian Act*, see Wayne Daugherty and Dennis Madill, *Indian Government under Indian Act Legislation, 1868–1951* (Ottawa: Department of Indian and Northern Affairs, 1980).

59 Brownlie, *A Fatherly Eye*, 35.

60 Fry, *How a People Die*, 88–89.

61 Steckley, *Indian Agents*, 149–50.

62 Kelm and Smith, *Talking Back*, 67.

63 Alexander Morris, *The Treaties of Canada with the Indians* (Toronto: Bedford, Clarke, 1880), 286; see also 226, 287.

64 For the background to the report, see Byron King Plant, "A Relationship and Exchange of Experience: H.B. Hawthorn, Indian Affairs and the 1955 BC Indian Research Project," *BC Studies* 163 (2009): 5–28.

65 Hawthorn, Belshaw, and Jamieson, *The Indians of British Columbia*, 455.

66 Hawthorn, Belshaw, and Jamieson, *The Indians of British Columbia*, 458.

67 Hawthorn, Belshaw, and Jamieson, *The Indians of British Columbia*, 460.

68 J.K. Johnson and P.B. Waite, "Macdonald, Sir John Alexander," in *Dictionary of Canadian Biography*, vol. 12 (Toronto/Quebec City: University of Toronto/Université Laval, 1990), http://www.biographi.ca/en/bio/macdonald_john_alexander_12E.html.

69 For Macdonald's influence on Indian policy and legislation, see J.R. Miller, "Macdonald as Minister of Indian Affairs: The Shaping of Canadian Indian Policy," in *Macdonald at 200*, ed. Patrice Dutil and Roger Hall (Toronto: Dundurn, 2014), 312–40, and Donald Smith, "Macdonald's Relationship with Aboriginal Peoples," in the same volume, 58–93.

70 Miller, "Macdonald as Minister of Indian Affairs," 311. The formal association of the government with the residential school program and its opposition to the Red River and North-West Resistances may be added to this list.

71 House of Commons, memorandum from J.A. Macdonald, January 3, 1887, Sessional Papers, 6th Parl., 1st Sess., vol. 16, 20b-37, https://parl.canadiana.ca/view/oocihm.9_08052_20_16.

Macdonald was superintendent-general of Indian Affairs to the governor general. The memorandum related to a claim from the Six Nations, and Macdonald recommended its rejection.

72 *House of Commons Debates,* 5th Parl., 5th Sess., April 27, 1882, 1186.

73 *House of Commons Debates,* 4th Parl., 2nd Sess., May 8, 1880, 1991.

74 *House of Commons Debates,* 5th Parl., 1st Sess., May 9, 1883, 1101; *House of Commons Debates,* 5th Parl., 2nd Sess., April 7, 1884, 1403.

75 *House of Commons Debates,* 5th Parl., 1st Sess., May 9, 1883, 1107.

76 *House of Commons Debates,* 5th Parl., 3rd Sess., June 10, 1885, 2427.

77 See, generally, Richard Bartlett, "The Indian Act of Canada," *Buffalo Law Review* 27 (1978): 581–615; John Giokas, *The Indian Act: Evolution, Overview and Options for Amendment and Transition* (Ottawa: Royal Commission on Aboriginal Peoples, March 22, 1995); Thomas Isaac, *Pre-1868 Legislation Concerning Indians* (Saskatoon: University of Saskatchewan Native Law Centre, 1993); Kelm and Smith, *Talking Back;* Leslie and Maguire, *The Historical Development of the Indian Act;* Leighton, *The Development of Federal Indian Policy in Canada;* John Leslie, "The Indian Act: An Historical Perspective," *Canadian Parliamentary Review* (Summer 2002), 23; John Leslie, "Assimilation, Integration or Termination? The Development of Canadian Indian Policy, 1943–1963" (PhD diss., Carleton University, 1999); John Milloy, *Indian Act Colonialism: A Century of Dishonour, 1869–1969,* research paper for the National Centre for First Nations Governance (May 2008), https://fngovernance.org/wp-content/uploads/2020/09/milloy.pdf; RCAP, *Report of the Royal Commission on Aboriginal Peoples,* 5 vols. (Ottawa: Minister of Supply and Services Canada, 1996), especially vol. 1, chap. 9; John L. Tobias, "Protection, Civilization, Assimilation: An Outline History of Canada's Indian Policy," in Getty and Lussier, *As Long as the Sun Shines and Water Flows,* 39–55; S. Venne, ed., *Indian Acts and Amendments, 1868–1975: An Indexed Collection* (Saskatoon: University of Saskatchewan Native Law Centre, 1981).

78 James S. Milloy, "The Early Indian Acts: Developmental Strategy and Constitutional Change," in Getty and Lussier, *As Long as the Sun Shines,* 57.

79 Joe Mathias and Gary Yabsley, "Conspiracy of Legislation: The Suppression of Indian Rights in Canada," *BC Studies* 89 (1991): 35.

80 See, generally, First Peoples Law, *Annotated Aboriginal Law: The Constitution, Legislation, Treaties and Supreme Court of Canada Case Summaries* (Toronto: Thomson Reuters, 2022).

81 *Indian Act,* RSC 1985, c I-5, ss 73, 81.

82 Anthony Hall, *The American Empire and the Fourth World: The Bowl with One Spoon,* vol. 1 (Montreal and Kingston: McGill-Queen's University Press, 2003), 475, 481.

83 John Sutton Lutz, *Makúk: A New History of Aboriginal-White Relations* (Vancouver: UBC Press, 2008), 237.

84 See, for example, *Qualifications and Registration of Voters Act,* SBC 1872, c 3.

85 *Land Ordinance 1870,* RSBC 1871, c 144, s 3; *Indian Act 1876,* SC 1876, c 18, s 70.

86 Jim Reynolds, *From Wardship to Rights: The* Guerin *Case and Aboriginal Law* (Vancouver: UBC Press, 2020), 63.

87 F. Laurie Barron, "The Indian Pass System in the Canadian West, 1882–1935," *Prairie Forum* 13 (1988): 25.

88 Canada, "Annual Report of Department of Indian Affairs," Sessional Papers, 1890 (no. 12), 6th Parl., 6th Sess., ix, 165. For Edgar Dewdney, see Brian Titley, *The Frontier World of Edgar Dewdney* (Vancouver: UBC Press, 1999), and for Hayter Reed, see Brian Titley,

"Reed, Hayter," in *Dictionary of Canadian Biography*, vol. 16 (Toronto/Quebec City: University of Toronto/Université Laval, 2016), http://www.biographi.ca/en/bio/reed_hayter_16E.html.

89 Harold Cardinal, *The Unjust Society* (Edmonton: Hurtig, 1969), 135.

90 The surrender provisions can be traced back to the Royal Proclamation of 1763.

91 For these inquiries, see John F. Leslie, *Commissions of Inquiry into Indian Affairs in the Canadas, 1828–1858* (Ottawa: Indian Affairs and Northern Development Canada, 1985); G.R. Mellor, *British Imperial Trusteeship, 1783–1850* (London: Faber, 1951), 380–405. Section I of the Bagot Report contains an account of earlier Indian policy: Charles Bagot, Rawson William Rawson, John Davidson, and William Hepburn, *Report on the Affairs of the Indians of Canada, Laid before the Legislative Assembly, 20th March, 1845* (Kingston, ON: Queen's Printer, 1845). For a summary of Indian policy from 1840 to 1867, see Duncan Scott, "Indian Affairs 1840–1867," in *Canada and Its Provinces*, vol. 5, ed. Adam Shortt and Arthur Doughty (Toronto: Glasgow, Brook, 1914), 331–64.

92 Leslie, *Commissions of Inquiry*, 91.

93 *An Act for the Protection of the Lands of the Crown in this Province from Trespass and Injury*, SUC 1839, c 15. Similar legislation was passed in the colonies of Nova Scotia and New Brunswick: *Act to Provide for the Instruction and Permanent Settlement of the Indians 1842* (Nova Scotia) and *Act for the Management and Disposal of the Indian Reserves 1844* (New Brunswick). The Indian legislation of the different British North American colonies was consolidated after Confederation in the *Indian Act*, which followed that of Ontario and Quebec.

94 Aborigines Select Committee, *Report of the Parliamentary Select Committee on Aboriginal Tribes* (London: William Bell, 1837); see Chapter 2 of this volume for a discussion.

95 Sidney Harring, *White Man's Law: Native People in Nineteenth-Century Canadian Jurisprudence* (Toronto: University of Toronto Press, 1998), 68–71; see *Little v Keating* (1842) 6 UCQB (OS) 265.

96 *Indian Act*, RSC 1985, c I-5, s 18.

97 John George Lambton, Earl of Durham, *The Report and Despatches of the Earl of Durham* (London: Ridgways, 1839); F. Bradshaw, *Self-Government in Canada and How It Was Achieved: The Story of Lord Durham's Report* (London: King and Son, 1903).

98 Durham, *Report and Despatches*, 191, 210.

99 Olive Dickason, *Canada's First Nations: A History of Founding Peoples from Earliest Times*, 3rd ed. (Don Mills, ON: Oxford University Press, 2002), 234.

100 *An Act for the better protection of the Lands and Property of the Indians of Lower Canada*, SPC 1850, c 42 (hereafter *Act for the better protection of Lands*); *An Act for the protection of the Indians in Upper Canada from imposition, and the Property occupied or enjoyed by them from trespass and injury*, SPC 1850, c 74 (hereafter *Act for the protection of Indians*).

101 *Act for the protection of Indians*, SPC 1850, c 74, ss 1–2, 10.

102 *Act for the protection of Indians*, SPC 1850, c 74, ss 3–4.

103 *Act for the better protection of Lands*, SPC 1850, c 42, s 3.

104 *Indian Act*, RSC 1985, c I-5, s 53.

105 *An Act for the better protection of the Lands*, SPC 1850, c 42, s 5; *An Act to repeal in part and to amend an Act, intituled, An Act for the better protection of the Lands and property of the Indians in Lower Canada*, SPC 1851, c 59.

106 Giokas, *The Indian Act*, 25.

107 Mellor, *British Imperial Trusteeship*, 409.

108 *Gradual Civilization Act*, SPC 1857, c 26.

109 Giokas, *The Indian Act*, 27.
110 Kelm, *Talking Back*, 124.
111 Miller, *Skyscrapers Hide the Heavens*, 118–20.
112 Milloy, "The Early Indian Acts," 59.
113 *An Act to amend the Indian Act*, SC 1919–20, c 50, s 3. From 1867 to 1920, only 25 families totalling 102 people were enfranchised: Kelm, *Talking Back*, 110.
114 *Indian Lands Act*, SPC 1860, c 151.
115 Leighton, *Development of Federal Indian Policy*, 182.
116 Miller, "Macdonald as Minister of Indian Affairs," 318–19.
117 *Indian Lands Act*, SPC 1860, c 151, s 1–6, 7.
118 *Constitution Act*, 1867 (UK), 30 & 31 Vict, c 3, reprinted in RSC 1985, Appendix II, No 5, s 91(24).
119 *An Act providing for the organization of the Department of the Secretary of State of Canada and for the management of Indian and Ordnance Lands*, SC 1868, c 42.
120 *Gradual Enfranchisement Act*, SC 1869, c 6.
121 *Gradual Enfranchisement Act*, SC 1869, c 6, ss 13–16.
122 *Gradual Enfranchisement Act*, SC 1869, c 6, s 12.
123 Quoted in Daugherty and Madill, *Indian Government under Indian Act Legislation*, Part 1, 1.
124 This overriding control of band council powers by the federal government, through the minister's power to disallow bylaws made by the council, was to remain until 2014. Control still exists over taxation bylaws, which require the minister's consent: *Indian Act*, RSC 1985, c I-5, s 83.
125 William Spragge, deputy superintendent, said in his annual report in 1871 that the legislation had found "little acceptance with the Indian people in general." Quoted in Daugherty and Madill, *Indian Government under Indian Act Legislation*, Part 1, 2.
126 *Gradual Enfranchisement Act*, SC 1869, c 6, s 10.
127 *An Act to amend certain Laws respecting Indians, and to extend certain Laws relating to matters connected with Indians to the Provinces of Manitoba and British Columbia*, SC 1874, c 21, s. 9.
128 Leighton, *Development of Federal Indian Policy*, 506.
129 Leighton, *Development of Federal Indian Policy*, 539.
130 *House of Commons Debates*, 11th Parl., 1st Sess., February 12, 1909, 980.
131 *Indian Act*, SC 1876, c 18; see Dickason, *Canada's First Nations*, 263–65.
132 House of Commons, Sessional Papers, 3rd Parl., 3rd Sess., 1876, vol. 7, Paper 9, xii–xiii.
133 Miller, "Macdonald as Minister of Indian Affairs," 322.
134 Daugherty and Madill, *Indian Government under Indian Act Legislation*, Part 2, 3.
135 *An Act to amend and consolidate the laws respecting Indians*, SC1880, c 28 (hereafter *Indian Act* 1880).
136 *Indian Act* 1880, ss 70, 71.
137 *Indian Act* 1880, s 72.
138 *An Act further to amend "The Indian Act, 1880,"* SC 1884, c 27, s 2 (hereafter *Indian Act* 1884).
139 *Indian Act* 1884, c 27, s 3.
140 *House of Commons Debates*, 5th Parl., 2nd Sess., April 7, 1884, 1399.
141 *An Act to further amend the Indian Act*, SC 1895, c 35, s 6 (hereafter *Indian Act* 1895).
142 Cole and Chaikin, *An Iron Hand upon the People*.
143 *Indian Advancement Act*, SC 1884, c 28.
144 *Indian Advancement Act*, s 9.

145 *Electoral Franchise Act,* SC 1885, c 40; see definition of "person" in s 2 to include "an Indian." For the history of Indigenous people and the franchise in Canada, see John F. Leslie, "Indigenous Suffrage," in *The Canadian Encyclopedia,* last modified March 31, 2016, https://www.thecanadianencyclopedia.ca/en/article/indigenous-suffrage; Elections Canada, *A History of the Vote in Canada,* 3rd ed. (Ottawa: Elections Canada, 2021), 110–12.

146 *House of Commons Debates,* 5th Parl., 3rd Sess., April 30, 1885, 1485 (David Mills, Liberal member and former minister of Indian Affairs).

147 *Electoral Franchise Act,* SC 1885, c 40, s 11.

148 *The Franchise Act,* SC 1898, c 14, s 3. In place of the *Electoral Franchise Act,* the federal franchise was determined by the provincial legislation, which excluded "Indians": *Franchise Act* 1898, s 5.

149 *House of Commons Debates,* 8th Parl., 3rd Sess., April 21, 1898, 3968.

150 *An Act to amend the Canada Elections Act,* SC 1960, c 7, s 1 repealing the restriction found in s 14(e) of the *Canada Elections Act,* RSC 1952, c 23. The franchise was expressly denied to Inuit people in 1934 and restored in 1950: *Dominion Franchise Act,* SC 1934, c 51, s 4(vi); *An Act to amend the Dominion Elections Act, 1938,* SC 1950, c 35, s 1.

151 *An Act to further amend "The Indian Act,"* SC 1894, c 32, s 11.

152 Like the reserve policy, the history of residential schools can be traced back to New France and the 1600s; see Mark Bourrie, "Toxic History," *Globe and Mail,* July 1, 2023.

153 *House of Commons Debates,* 5th Parl., 1st Sess., vol. 2, May 9, 1883, 1107–8.

154 Truth and Reconciliation Commission of Canada (TRC), *The Final Report of the Truth and Reconciliation Commission of Canada,* vol. 1, *Canada's Residential Schools: The History, Part 1, Origins to 1939* (Montreal and Kingston: McGill-Queen's University Press, 2015), 254–56.

155 Bill Waiser and Jennie Hansen, *Cheated: The Laurier Liberals and the Theft of First Nations Reserve Land* (Toronto: ECW, 2023).

156 Quoted in Waiser and Hansen, *Cheated,* 109.

157 *An Act to amend the Indian Act,* SC 1906, c 20, s 1.

158 *An Act to amend the Indian Act,* SC 1911, c 14, s 1.

159 *An Act to amend the Indian Act,* SC 1911, c 14, s 2. Special legislation was also used to relocate reserves: see, for example, *An Act Respecting the Songhees Indian Reserve,* SC 1911, c 24; Kelm and Smith, *Talking Back,* 169–79.

160 *House of Commons Debates,* 14th Parl., 3rd Sess., April 26, 1911, 7826.

161 *House of Commons Debates,* 11th Parl., 3rd Sess., May 4, 1911, 8407.

162 Kelm and Smith, *Talking Back,* 185–88.

163 Peggy Martin-Maguire, *First Nation Land Surrenders on the Prairies, 1896–1911* (Ottawa: Indian Claims Commission, 1998), 27.

164 *An Act to amend the Indian Act,* SC 1914, c 35, s 8.

165 *An Act to amend the Indian Act,* SC 1918, c 26, s 4.

166 *An Act to amend the Indian Act,* SC 1919, c 56, s 1; SC 1938, c 31, s 1.

167 *An Act to amend the Indian Act,* SC 1919–20, c 50, s 1.

168 *An Act to amend the Indian Act,* SC 1919–20, c 50, s 3; Kelm and Smith, *Talking Back,* 109–26.

169 Donald B. Smith, "Loft, Frederick Ogilvie," in *Dictionary of Canadian Biography,* vol. 16 (Toronto/Quebec City: University of Toronto/Université Laval, 2009), http://www.biographi.ca/en/bio/loft_frederick_ogilvie_16E.html.

170 House of Commons, *Special Committees of the Senate and House of Commons to Inquire into the Claims of the Allied Indian Tribes of British Columbia, as Set Forth in Their Petition Submitted to Parliament in June 1926* (Ottawa: King's Printer, 1927) (hereafter *Committee to Inquire into Claims of the Allied Indian Tribes*).

171 *Committee to Inquire into Claims of the Allied Indian Tribes,* ix, xi.

172 *An Act to amend the Indian Act,* SC 1926–27, c 32, s 6.

173 *Indian Act,* RSC 1927, c 98.

174 *An Act to amend the Indian Act,* SC 1936, c 20, s 5.

175 *An Act to amend the Indian Act,* SC 1936, c 20, s 2.

176 Leslie and Maguire, *The Historical Development of the Indian Act,* 126.

177 *Dominion Elections Act,* SC 1938, c 46, as amended by SC 1950, c 35, s 1. The closest that some Indigenous people got to being involved in making the laws that would govern them was to be received as delegations to Parliament: see, for example, *The Diaries of William Lyon Mackenzie King,* May 19, 1948, https://www.bac-lac.gc.ca/eng/discover/politics-government/prime-ministers/william-lyon-mackenzie-king/Pages/search.aspx/.

178 *An Act to amend the Canada Elections Act,* SC 1960, c 7 repealing the restriction found in s 14(e) of the *Canada Elections Act,* RSC 1952, c 23.

179 Bartlett, "The Indian Act of Canada," 585.

180 *Indian Act,* SC 1951, c 49 (hereafter *Indian Act* 1951).

181 Leslie and Maguire, *The Historical Development of the Indian Act,* 150–51.

182 *Indian Act* 1951, s 73.

183 Allyson Stevenson, *Intimate Integration: A History of the Sixties Scoop and the Colonization of Indigenous Kinship* (Toronto: University of Toronto Press, 2021).

184 Leslie, "Assimilation, Integration or Termination," 405.

185 H. Hawthorn, ed., *A Survey of the Contemporary Indians of Canada: Economic, Political, Educational Needs and Policies* (Ottawa: Indian Affairs Branch, 1966), 292, 368.

186 Hawthorn, *Survey of the Contemporary Indians,* 367.

187 Hawthorn, *Survey of the Contemporary Indians,* 270.

188 Hawthorn, *Survey of the Contemporary Indians.*

189 Leslie, "Assimilation, Integration or Termination," 418.

190 *Statement of the Government of Canada on Indian Policy* (Ottawa: Indian Affairs Branch, 1969). See Alan C. Cairns, *Citizens Plus: Aboriginal Peoples and the Canadian State* (Vancouver: UBC Press, 2000), 52.

191 For a comprehensive study of the 1969 White Paper, see Sally M. Weaver, *Making Canadian Indian Policy: The Hidden Agenda 1968–70* (Toronto: University of Toronto Press, 1981).

192 Now known as the *Constitution Act, 1867.*

193 *Indian Act,* RSC 1970, c I-6.

194 *Indian Act,* RSC 1985, c I-5.

Chapter 7: Independence, Self-Government, and Reconciliation

1 For Pearson's imperialism, see John England, *Shadow of Heaven: The Life of Lester Pearson,* vol. 1, *1897–1948* (Toronto: Lester and Orpen Dennys, 1989), 93–94, 135–36. See also Lara Silver, "A Long Goodbye: Pearson and Britain," in *Mike's World: Lester Pearson and Canadian External Affairs,* ed. Galen Perras and Asa McKercher (Vancouver: UBC Press, 2016), 210–25.

2   England, *Shadow of Heaven*, 125. See also Ronald Hyam, *Britain's Declining Empire: The Road to Decolonisation, 1918–1968* (Cambridge: Cambridge University Press, 2006), 1.

3   *The Decline and Fall of the British Empire* (Oxford: Alden, 1905).

4   George Woodcock, *Who Killed the British Empire? An Inquest* (Toronto: Fitzhenry and Whiteside, 1974). For information on this fascinating man, see Douglas Fetherling, *The Gentle Anarchist: A Life of George Woodcock* (London: Douglas and McIntyre, 1998).

5   Woodcock, *Who Killed the British Empire?*, 16.

6   Woodcock, *Who Killed the British Empire?*, 330–31.

7   According to one prominent historian, Canada's pioneering steps constituted "Canada's single but significant contribution to the slow elaboration of human freedom": W.L. Morton, *The Canadian Identity* (Toronto: University of Toronto Press, 1961), 40.

8   See, generally, Royal Commission on Aboriginal Peoples, "A Word from Commissioners," in "Highlights from the Report of the Royal Commission on Aboriginal Peoples: Restructuring the Relationship," 1996, https://www.rcaanc-cirnac.gc.ca/eng/1100100014597/1572547985018#chp4.

9   For a collection of contemporary opinions on, among other things, the entitlement of the Canadian colonies to declare independence, see George Bennett, ed., *The Concept of Empire: Burke to Attlee, 1774–1947* (London: Adam and Black, 1962).

10 Quoted in W. David McIntyre, *Colonies into Commonwealth*, rev. ed. (London: Blandford, 1974), 119–20. For the policy of Gladstone toward Canadian independence while prime minister, see C.C. Eldridge, *Victorian Imperialism* (London: Hodder and Stoughton, 1978), 92–101.

11 Quoted in Woodcock, *Who Killed the British Empire?*, 190.

12 Quoted in Paul Knaplund, *James Stephen and the British Colonial System, 1813–1847* (Madison: University of Wisconsin Press, 1953), 286.

13 Caroline Stephen, *Sir James Stephen: Letters with Biographical Notes* (Eastgate, UK: Bellows, 1906), 144 (letter dated March 20, 1850).

14 Quoted in McIntyre, *Colonies into Commonwealth*, 78.

15 Quoted in E.A. Benians, Sir James Butler, and C.E. Carrington, eds., *The Cambridge History of the British Empire*, vol. 3, *The Empire-Commonwealth* (London: Cambridge University Press, 1959), 22. See also Eldridge, *Victorian Imperialism*, 95–98.

16 "Latest from Quebec, Banquet to the Governor-General," *Globe and Mail*, July 16, 1869.

17 Quoted in David Farr, *The Colonial Office and Canada, 1867–1887* (Toronto: University of Toronto Press, 1955), 294–95.

18 C.P. Stacey, *Canada and the British Army: A Study in the Practice of Responsible Government*, rev. ed. (Toronto: University of Toronto Press, 1963), 141.

19 McIntyre, *Colonies into Commonwealth*, 126. See, generally, Farr, *The Colonial Office and Canada*.

20 *House of Commons Debates*, 7th Parl., 6th Sess., March 3, 1896, 2721–22.

21 *House of Commons Debates*, 8th Parl., 5th Sess., vol. 1, February 5, 1900, 72.

22 *House of Commons Debates*, 9th Parl., 3rd Sess., vol. 6, October 23, 1903, 14817.

23 Speech to Imperial Conference 1917, reproduced in Arthur Berriedale Keith, ed., *Speeches and Documentation, British Colonial Policy, 1763–1917*, vol. 2 (London: Oxford University Press, 1918), 377.

24 *House of Commons Debates*, 14th Parl., 3rd Sess., vol. 3, June 9, 1924, 2936; *The Diaries of William Lyon Mackenzie King*, April 8, 1942, https://www.bac-lac.gc.ca/eng/discover/politics-government/prime-ministers/william-lyon-mackenzie-king/Pages/search.aspx/.

25 *The Diaries of William Lyon Mackenzie King*, September 9, 1939.

26 Stephen Leacock, *Greater Canada: An Appeal* (Montreal: Montreal News Company, 1907), 8.

27 Stephen Leacock, *Elements of Political Science* (Boston: Houghton Mifflin, 1913), 283.

28 *House of Commons Debates,* 11th Parl., 1st Sess., March 29, 1909, 3518.

29 Empire Club of Canada, *Addresses Delivered to the Members during the Sessions of 1912–13 and 1913–14* (Toronto: Warwick and Rutter, 1915), part 2, 200, 204–5.

30 See Norman Hillmer and J.L. Granatstein, *Empire to Umpire: Canada and the World into the 21st Century,* 3rd ed. (Toronto: Nelson, 2008); Asa McKercher, *Canada and the World since 1867* (London: Bloomsbury Academic, 2019).

31 For a detailed discussion of greater autonomy for the settler colonies and relevant documents, see Robert Dawson, *The Development of Dominion Status, 1900–1936* (London: Oxford University Press, 1937); see also Alfred Zimmern, *The Third British Empire,* 3rd ed. (London: Oxford University Press, 1934). For a detailed discussion of the development of the security partnership among Britain and the dominions in the period leading to the First World War, see John Mitcham, *Race and Imperial Defence in the British World, 1870–1914* (Cambridge: Cambridge University Press, 2016), chap. 7.

32 Stacey, *Canada and the British Army,* chap. 9.

33 Ridgway F. Shinn, *Arthur Berriedale Keith, 1879–1944: The Chief Ornament of Scottish Learning* (Aberdeen: Aberdeen University Press, 1990), 65.

34 John Ewart, "Perplexed Imperialist," *Queen's Quarterly* 90 (1907): 93.

35 Ewart, "Perplexed Imperialist," 95.

36 Quoted in Hillmer and Granatstein, *Empire to Umpire,* 50. His successor, Oscar D. Skelton, was much more assertive: Norman Hillmer, *O.D. Skelton: A Portrait of Canadian Ambition* (Toronto: University of Toronto Press, 2015).

37 Albert Dicey, *Lectures Introductory to the Study of the Law of the Constitution* (London: Macmillan, 1885), 109.

38 Albert Dicey, *Introduction to the Study of the Law of the Constitution* (London: Macmillan, 1915), xxxii.

39 W. David McIntyre, "The Strange Death of Dominion Status," *Journal of Imperial and Commonwealth History* 27 (1999): 202.

40 For a comprehensive account, see Philip Wigley, *Canada and the Transition to Commonwealth: British-Canadian Relations, 1917–1926* (Cambridge: Cambridge University Press, 1977).

41 Hyam, *Britain's Declining Empire,* 80.

42 Conrad Black, *Rise to Greatness: The History of Canada from the Vikings to the Present* (Toronto: McClelland and Stewart, 2014), 516.

43 George Bernard Shaw, *The Intelligent Woman's Guide to Socialism, Capitalism, Sovietism and Fascism* (New York: Garden City Publishing, 1928), 159.

44 Quoted in Stuart Ward, *Untied Kingdom: A Global History of the End of Britain* (Cambridge: Cambridge University Press, 2023), 80.

45 22 Geo. V c 4 (UK). For a detailed discussion, see K.C. Wheare, *Statute of Westminster and Dominion Status* (London: Oxford University Press, 1938).

46 *Reference Re Offshore Mineral Rights of British Columbia,* [1967] SCR 792, 816. See, generally, Brian Slattery, "The Independence of Canada," *Supreme Court Law Review* 5 (1983): 369–404; Peter Hogg, *Constitutional Law of Canada,* 5th ed. (Scarborough, ON: Carswell, 2007), s 3.8. The uncertainty over the date of independence is shared by other former dominions. See, for example, W.J. Hudson and M.P. Sharp, *Australian Independence: Colony to Reluctant Kingdom* (Melbourne: Melbourne University Press, 1988); and Deborah Gare,

"Dating Australia's Independence: National Sovereignty and the 1986 Australia Act," *Australian Historical Studies* 29 (1999): 251–66.

47 Arthur Lower, *Colony to Nation*, 4th ed. (Don Mills, ON: Longmans, 1964), 489.

48 F.R. Scott, *Essays on the Constitution: Aspects of Canadian Law and Politics* (Toronto: University of Toronto Press, 1977), 171. The legal situation remained murky in 1931. It took action by South Africa and Ireland to clarify that dominion status included a right of unilateral secession.

49 J.L. Granatstein, *Mackenzie King: His Life and World* (Toronto: McGraw Hill, 1977), 113.

50 "Future of the Colonies," *Times* (London), January 11, 1943.

51 Winston Churchill, "A New Experience: Victory," in *Winston Churchill: His Collected Speeches, 1897–1963*, ed. Robert James (New York: Chelsea House, 1974), 6:6695.

52 Dane Kennedy, *Decolonization: A Very Short Introduction* (Oxford: Oxford University Press, 2016), 35.

53 "Future of the Colonies," *Times* (London), January 11, 1943.

54 Alan Burns, *Colonial Civil Servant* (London: Allen and Unwin, 1949), 323–24.

55 Burns, *Colonial Civil Servant*, 318.

56 C.E. Carrington, *The Liquidation of the British Empire* (Toronto: Clarke, Irwin, 1961), 68, 71.

57 A.P. Thornton, *The Imperial Idea and Its Enemies: A Study in British Power*, 2nd ed. (Basingstoke, UK: Macmillan, 1985), xv.

58 Richard Toye, *Churchill's Empire: The World That Made Him and the World He Made* (New York: St Martin's Griffin, 2010), 213–16.

59 Nelson Mandela, *Long Walk to Freedom* (New York: Little Brown, 1994), 95–96.

60 For studies of the end of the Empire, see John Darwin, *Britain and Decolonisation: The Retreat from Empire in the Post-War World* (London: Macmillan, 1988); Hyam, *Britain's Declining Empire*; Brian Lapping, *End of Empire* (London: Paladin, 1989); Thornton, *The Imperial Idea*; Ward, *Untied Kingdom*; Woodcock, *Who Killed the British Empire?*

61 Margery Perham, *The Colonial Reckoning* (London: Collins, 1961), 60.

62 However, this script was not followed in those colonies where the settlers had sufficient political control to mount an opposition, such as Southern Rhodesia and South Africa, nor in Hong Kong, which was returned to China.

63 Caroline Elkins, *Legacy of Violence: A History of the British Empire* (New York: Knopf, 2022), chaps. 10–13.

64 Hyam, *Britain's Declining Empire*, xiii.

65 *The Diaries of William Lyon Mackenzie King*, May 23, 1940, https://www.bac-lac.gc.ca/eng/discover/politics-government/prime-ministers/william-lyon-mackenzie-king/Pages/search.aspx/.

66 Berriedale Keith, *A Constitutional History of India, 1600–1935* (London: Methuen, 1936). For a recent account, see Walter Reid, *Keeping the Jewel in the Crown* (Edinburgh: Birlinn, 2016). For the relevant documents, see "Historical Constitutions," Constitution of India, https://www.constitutionofindia.net/historical_constitutions. For accounts of the legal steps in the transition from dependence to independence, see Kenneth Roberts-Wray, *Commonwealth and Colonial Law* (London: Stevens, 1966), chap. 6; Ian Hendry and Susan Dickson, *British Overseas Territories Law*, 2nd ed. (Oxford: Hart, 2018), chap. 16.

67 Edwin Hirschmann, *White Mutiny: The Ilbert Bill Crisis in India and the Genesis of the Indian National Congress* (New Dehli: Heritage, 1980); Lawrence James, *The Raj: The Making and Unmaking of British India* (New York: St. Martin's, 1999), 349–52.

68 Edward Moulton, "The Early Congress and the Idea of Representative and Self-Governing Institutions on the Colonial Canadian Model," in *The Congress and Indian Nationalism:*

Historical Perspectives, ed. John Hill (London: Routledge, 1991), 222–53. For a comparison of constitutional developments in Canada and India, see Reginald Coupland, *The Empire in These Days* (London: Macmillan, 1935), chaps. 7–8; D.A. Low, *Lion Rampant: Essays in the Study of British Imperialism* (London: Cass, 1973), chap. 5.

69 Quoted in Sarvepalli Gopal, *Jawaharlal Nehru: A Biography,* vol. 1, *1889–1947* (London: Jonathan Cape, 1975), 111.

70 Keith, *A Constitutional History of India,* viii.

71 Reid, *Keeping the Jewel in the Crown,* chap. 40.

72 Quoted in Moulton, "The Early Congress," 249.

73 Quoted in Moulton, "The Early Congress," 250.

74 Quoted in C.C. Eldridge, *Victorian Imperialism* (London: Hodder and Stoughton, 1978), 228.

75 Quoted in Low, *Lion Rampant,* 153.

76 *House of Commons Debates,* 12th Parl., 2nd Sess., February 25, 1913, 3997.

77 Penderel Moon, ed., *Wavell: The Viceroy's Journal* (London: Oxford University Press, 1973), 23.

78 J. Keir Hardie, *India: Impressions and Suggestions,* 2nd ed. (London: Independent Labour Party, 1909), 71.

79 9 Edw. 7, c 4 (UK).

80 Coupland, *The Empire in These Days,* 122, said the constitutional development of India from 1861 to 1907 "had followed, at a slower pace, the precedent of Canada between 1774 and 1791."

81 Ronald Hyam, *Britain's Imperial Century, 1815–1914: A Study of Empire and Expansion* (New York: Harper, 1976), 240.

82 Bampfylde Fuller, *The Empire of India* (London: Pitman, 1913), 263.

83 Fuller, *The Empire of India,* 263.

84 Shashi Tharoor, *Inglorious Empire: What the British Did to India* (London: Penguin, 2017), 68–69.

85 Bernard Porter, *The Lion's Share: A Short History of British Imperialism, 1850–1970* (London: Longman, 1975), 240–41.

86 *House of Commons Debates* (UK), vol. 97, August 20, 1917, cols. 1695–97; see Richard Danzig, "The Announcement of August 20, 1917," *Journal of Asian Studies* 28 (1968): 19–37.

87 Nicholas Mansergh, *The Commonwealth Experience* (Toronto: University of Toronto Press, 1982), 2:61–70.

88 9 & 10 Geo. 5, c 101 (UK).

89 Act No. IV of 1907 (Governor General in Council, British India).

90 Act No. 1 of 1910 (Governor General in Council, British India).

91 Act No. IV of 1915 (Governor General in Council, British India).

92 Act No XI of 1919 (Indian Legislative Council, British India).

93 Mulik Raj Anand, ed., *The Historic Trial of Mahatma Gandhi* (New Delhi: National Council of Educational Research and Development, 1987), 49.

94 Nigel Collett, *The Butcher of Amritsar: General Reginald Dyer* (London: Bloomsbury, 2005); Kim Wagner, *Amritsar 1919: An Empire of Fear and the Making of a Massacre* (New Haven, CT: Yale University Press, 2019). For a discussion of colonial martial law in the context of the Amritsar massacre, see Nasser Hussain, *The Jurisprudence of Emergency: Colonialism and the Rule of Law* (Ann Arbor: University of Michigan Press, 2019), chap. 4.

95 David Arnold, *Police Power and Colonial Rule: Madras 1859–1947* (Delhi: Oxford University Press, 1986), 230–36. See, generally, David Anderson and David Killingray, *Policing the Empire* (Manchester: Manchester University Press, 1991).

96 See the discussion of the Balfour Formula and the *Statute of Westminster* earlier in this chapter.

97 *Imperial Conference 1926: Summary of Proceedings* (Dublin: Stationery Office, 1926).

98 See R.P. Singh, "The Irwin Declaration of 1929: Its Background and Implications," *Proceedings of the Indian History Congress* 38 (1977): 460.

99 Winston Churchill, *India: Speeches and an Introduction* (London: Thornton Butterworth, 1931), 34, 64.

100 "Motilal Nehru," Past Party Presidents (1985–2010), Indian National Congress, https://www.inc.in/leadership/past-party-presidents/motilal-nehru.

101 Jon Wilson, *India Conquered: Britain's Raj and the Chaos of Empire* (London: Simon and Schuster, 2016), 428–29.

102 "Declaration of Purna Swaraj (Indian National Congress, 1930)," Constitution of India, https://www.constitutionofindia.net/historical-constitution/declaration-of-purna-swaraj -indian-national-congress-1930/.

103 Jawaharlal Nehru, *Autobiography* (London: Lane, 1936), 428.

104 Jawaharlal Nehru, letter dated January 17, 1936, in *A Bunch of Old Letters* (Bombay: Asia Publishing House, 1958), 147.

105 Jawaharlal Nehru, "Presidential Address to the Indian National Congress," *Labour Monthly* 18 (May 1936): 282–305, https://www.marxists.org/history/international/comintern/sections/ britain/periodicals/labour_monthly/1936/05/x01.htm.

106 Tharoor, *Inglorious Empire*, 233.

107 Leonard Barnes, *Empire or Democracy* (London: Gollancz, 1939), 164–69.

108 Jabez T. Sunderland, *India in Bondage: Her Right to Freedom and a Place among the Nations* (New York: Lewis Copeland, 1929), copyright page.

109 Keith, *Constitutional History of India,* 432–34.

110 *Government of India Act,* 1935, 26 Geo. 5, c 2, s 110 (UK).

111 The Simon Report discussed the precedent of federation in Canada but not the growth of self-government and independence: Indian Statutory Commission, *Report of the Indian Statutory Commission,* vol. 2, *Recommendations* (London: HMSO, 1930), 201–2.

112 Keith, *Constitutional History of India,* 316.

113 For a comparison of the 1935 act and progress toward Canadian responsible government, see Coupland, *The Empire in These Days,* chap. 8.

114 Canada's declaration was about a week after the UK's.

115 Trevor Royle, *The Last Days of the Raj* (London: Coronet, 1990), 100–14.

116 Clement Attlee, War Cabinet Paper, February 2, 1942, reproduced in Nicholas Mansergh and E.W.R. Lumby, eds., *Constitutional Relations between Britain and India, 1942–1947,* vol. 1, *The Cripps Mission* (London: HMSO, 1970), 110–12.

117 Kennedy, *Decolonization,* 31.

118 "Future of the Colonies," *Times* (London), January 11, 1943.

119 Quoted in Anthony Kirk-Greene, *Britain's Imperial Administrators, 1858–1966* (London: Palgrave Macmillan, 2000), 316.

120 *House of Lords Debates,* vol. 137, August 14, 1945, cols. 8–12.

121 *Indian Independence Act, 1947,* 10 & 11 Geo. 6 c 30 (UK). Burmese leaders rejected dominion status, and Burma (now Myanmar) left the British Empire on January 4, 1948, as an independent republic under the terms of the *Burma Independence Act 1947,* 11 & 12 Geo. 6 c 33 (UK). Burma had been separated from British India in 1937 under s 46(2) of the *Government of India Act 1935,* 26 Geo. 5 c 2 (UK) and the *Government of Burma Act 1935,* 26 Geo. 5 c 3 (UK).

122 V.P. Menon, *The Transfer of Power* (Bombay: Orient Longman, 1957), 358–70. For the background and the differing objectives of India, Pakistan, and Ceylon in using dominion status, see H. Kumarasingham, "The 'Tropical Dominions': The Appeal of Dominion Status in the Decolonisation of India, Pakistan and Ceylon," *Transactions of the Royal Historical Society* 23 (2013): 223–45.

123 Gopal, *Jawaharlal Nehru*, 356.

124 Ward, *Untied Kingdom*, 107–10.

125 V.P. Menon, *The Story of the Integration of the Indian States* (Bombay: Orient Longman, 1956).

126 A proposal was made in 1950 by constitutional scholar F.R. Scott to pass a Canadian Independence Act with similar provisions: Scott, *Essays on the Constitution*, 250.

127 For a comparison of the process to independence in India and Africa, see Low, *Lion Rampant*, 172–82.

128 Kwame Nkrumah, *Towards Colonial Freedom* (London: Heinemann, 1962), 30–32.

129 For a review of Canadian attitudes to the Empire in 1938, see Norman MacKenzie, "A Canadian Looks at the Empire," *Political Quarterly* 9 (1938): 552–64; and for the relationship in the 1940s and 1950s, see Lord Garner, "Britain and Canada in the 1940s and 1950s," in *Britain and Canada: Survey of a Changing Relationship*, ed. Peter Lyon (London: Cass, 1976), 85–104.

130 Bryan D. Palmer, *Canada's 1960s: The Ironies of Identity in a Rebellious Age* (Toronto: University of Toronto Press, 2009), 19.

131 James (Jan) Morris, *Farewell the Trumpets* (London: Penguin, 1979), 63n.

132 Jośe E. Igartua, *The Other Quiet Revolution: National Identities in English Canada, 1945–71* (Vancouver: UBC Press, 2006).

133 *Citizenship Act*, RSC 1946, c 15. See Igartua, *The Other Quiet Revolution*, 16–29.

134 Igartua, *The Other Quiet Revolution*, 72. See also George Richardson, "Nostalgia and National Identity: The History and Social Studies Curricula of Alberta and Ontario at the End of Empire," in *Canada and the End of Empire*, ed. Phillip Buckner (Vancouver: UBC Press, 2005), 183–94.

135 Igartua, *The Other Quiet Revolution*, 29–33.

136 Igartua, *The Other Quiet Revolution*, 95. The reference to the constitution is to section 7(1) of the *Statute of Westminster 1931*, 22 Geo V, c 4 (UK), which left changes to the Canadian constitution (then the *British North America Act*) to the UK Parliament.

137 Igartua, *The Other Quiet Revolution*, 129.

138 Phillip Buckner and R. Douglas Francis, eds., introduction to *Canada and the British World: Culture, Migration and Identity* (Vancouver: UBC Press, 2006), 3.

139 Quoted in Richardson, "Nostalgia and National Identity," 184.

140 Ward, *Untied Kingdom*, 123.

141 Igartua, *The Other Quiet Revolution*, 173.

142 Paula Hastings, "Distort, Deflect, Deny: Appraising European Colonialism at Empire's End," *Canadian Historical Review* 103 (2022): 203.

143 Hastings, "Distort, Deflect, Deny," 213.

144 Kevin Spooner, "'Awakening Africa': Race and Canadian Views of Decolonizing Africa," in *Dominion of Race: Rethinking Canada's International History*, ed. Laura Madokoro, Francine McKenzie, and David Meren (Vancouver: UBC Press, 2017), 206–27.

145 Dan Gorman, "Race, the Commonwealth and the United Nations: From Imperialism to Internationalism in Canada, 1940–60," in Madokoro, McKenzie, and Meren, *Dominion of Race*, 139–59.

146 See Phillip Buckner, "The Long Goodbye," in *Rediscovering the British World*, ed. Phillip Buckner and R. Douglas Francis (Calgary: University of Calgary Press, 2005), 201–3.

147 George Grant, *Lament for a Nation: The Defeat of Canadian Nationalism* (Toronto: McClelland and Stewart, 1965), 33.

148 F. Laurie Barron, "The Indian Pass System in the Canadian West, 1882–1935," *Prairie Forum* 13 (1988): 26.

149 Kildare Dobbs, "The Case for Kicking Canada out of the Commonwealth," *Maclean's*, May 6, 1961, quoted in McKercher, *Canada and the World since 1867*, 203.

150 "The Lowering of the Color Bar," *Globe and Mail*, January 31, 1962, quoted in McKercher, *Canada and the World since 1867*, 203.

151 "Hitler's Paper Sees 'Atrocities' among Canada's Indians," *Globe and Mail*, November 21, 1938.

152 Sally M. Weaver, *Making Canadian Indian Policy: The Hidden Agenda, 1968–70* (Toronto: University of Toronto Press, 1981), 15.

153 George Manuel and Michael Posluns, *The Fourth World: An Indian Reality* (Don Mills, ON: Collier-Macmillan, 1974), 5.

154 Arthur Manuel and Ronald Derrickson, *Unsettling Canada: A National Wake-Up Call* (Toronto: Between the Lines, 2015), 169.

155 Manuel and Posluns, *The Fourth World*, 244–46.

156 Harold Cardinal, *The Unjust Society* (Edmonton: Hurtig, 1969), 1, 17.

157 Melvin H. Smith, *Our Home or Native Land?* (Victoria: Crown Western, 1995), 143.

158 Ian Waddell, "The Laboured Birth of Section 35," *The Advocate* 66 (2008): 891–95. For an account of the campaign by some Indigenous people from British Columbia to have a say in the constitutional discussions, see Joel Hebert, "'Sacred Trust': Rethinking Late British Decolonization in Indigenous Canada," *Journal of British Studies* 58, 3 (2019): 565–97.

159 Thomas Berger, *One Man's Justice* (Vancouver: Douglas and McIntyre, 2002), 140–64.

160 Enacted as Schedule B to the *Canada Act 1982*, 1982 c 11 (UK).

161 See the National Film Board documentary *Dancing around the Table*, two parts, directed by Maurice Bulbulian (1987), https://www.nfb.ca/film/dancing_around_the_table_1/, https://www.nfb.ca/film/dancing_around_the_table_part_two/.

162 In 1983, a special parliamentary committee recommended (in what became known as the Penner Report) greater autonomy for First Nations, but the recommendation was not implemented; Special Committee on Indian Self-Government, *Indian Self-Government in Canada* (Ottawa: Supply and Services Canada, 1983).

163 James Miller, *Skyscrapers Hide the Heavens: A History of Indian-White Relations in Canada* (Toronto: University of Toronto Press, 1991), 292.

164 The newly elected government of Newfoundland, which had revoked the previous government's approval of the accord, refused to allow the deadline for approval to be extended.

165 For a discussion of the Charlottetown Accord, see Kent McNeil, *Emerging Justice?* (Saskatoon: Native Law Centre, 2001), 161–83.

166 Joel Bakan, *Just Words: Constitutional Rights and Social Wrongs* (Toronto: University of Toronto Press, 1997), 117–33; *Native Women's Assoc. v Canada*, (1992) 57 FTR 115, aff'd (1992) 145 NR 253 (FCA).

167 Pierre Trudeau, *A Mess That Deserves a Big No* (Toronto: Robert Davies, 1992), 72.

168 Royal Commission on Aboriginal Peoples, *Report of the Royal Commission on Aboriginal Peoples*, vol. 1, *Looking Forward, Looking Back* (Ottawa: Minister of Supply and Services Canada, 1996), 200 (hereafter RCAP).

169 Indian and Northern Affairs Canada, *The Government of Canada's Approach to the Implementation of the Inherent Right and the Negotiation of Aboriginal Self-Government* (Ottawa: Indian and Northern Affairs Canada, 1995). The policy was referenced in some subsequent statutes, e.g., *Family Homes on Reserves and Matrimonial Interests or Rights Act*, SC 2013, c 20, preamble.

170 See, for example, the *Yukon First Nations Self-Government Act,* SC 1994, c 35.

171 *Calder v British Columbia*, [1973] SCR 313.

172 RCAP, 1:199.

173 For a detailed and critical review, see Alan Cairns, *Citizens Plus: Aboriginal Peoples and the Canadian State* (Vancouver: UBC Press, 2000), chap. 4.

174 Royal Commission on Aboriginal Peoples, "Highlights from the Report of the Royal Commission on Aboriginal Peoples: A Word from Commissioners," 1996, https://www.rcaanc -cirnac.gc.ca/eng/1100100014597/1572547985018#chp2.

175 RCAP, vol. 5, *Renewal: A Twenty-Year Commitment,* appendix A.

176 Thomas King, *The Inconvenient Indian: A Curious Account of Native People in North America* (Toronto: Anchor, 2012), 171.

177 *R v Pamajewon*, [1996] 2 SCR 821.

178 *Delgamuukw v British Columbia*, [1997] 3 SCR 1010.

179 *Delgamuukw v British Columbia* (1991), 79 DLR (4th) 185 (BCSC), (1993), 104 DLR (4th) 470.

180 Department of Justice, *Principles Respecting the Government of Canada's Relationship with Indigenous Peoples* (Ottawa: Department of Justice, 2018), 5.

181 *An Act respecting First Nations, Inuit and Métis children, youth and families*, SC 2019, c 24.

182 *Reference to the Court of Appeal of Quebec in relation to the Act respecting First Nations, Inuit and Métis children, youth and families*, 2022 QCCA 185.

183 *Reference re An Act respecting First Nations, Inuit and Metis children, youth and families,* 2024 SCC 5.

184 *Reference re An Act respecting First Nations, Inuit and Metis children, youth and families,* 2024 SCC 5, para 92.

185 *Reference re An Act respecting First Nations, Inuit and Metis children, youth and families,* 2024 SCC 5, para 79.

186 *Reference re An Act respecting First Nations, Inuit and Metis children, youth and families,* 2024 SCC 5, para 112.

187 UN General Assembly, *United Nations Declaration on the Rights of Indigenous Peoples*, resolution adopted by the General Assembly, September 13, 2007, https://www.un.org/ development/desa/indigenouspeoples/wp-content/uploads/sites/19/2018/11/UNDRIP_ E_web.pdf.

188 *Act respecting the United Nations Declaration on the Rights of Indigenous Peoples*, SC 2021, c 14, preamble, s 4.

189 Angela Sterritt, "Reconciliation in Canada," in *The Canadian Encyclopedia,* last modified January 23, 2023, https://www.thecanadianencyclopedia.ca/en/article/reconciliation-in -canada.

190 For one approach to reconciliation by an Indigenous leader, see Jody Wilson-Raybould, *True Reconciliation: How to Be a Force for Change* (Toronto: McClelland and Stewart, 2022).

191 For a summary, see *Canada v Fontaine*, 2017 SCC 47, paras. 5–11.

192 Truth and Reconciliation Commission of Canada (TRC), *The Final Report of the Truth and Reconciliation Commission of Canada,* 6 vols. (Montreal and Kingston: McGill-Queen's University Press, 2015).

193 TRC, *Honouring the Truth, Reconciling for the Future: Summary of the Final Report of the Truth and Reconciliation Commission of Canada,* 2015, 16, https://ehprnh2mwo3.exactdn.com/wp-content/uploads/2021/01/Executive_Summary_English_Web.pdf.

194 "How Many of the TRC Calls to Action Are Complete? Don't Ask the Federal Government," Indigenous Watchdog, https://www.indigenouswatchdog.org/2022/04/26/how-many-of-the-trc-calls-to-action-are-complete-dont-ask-the-federal-government/. See also Eva Jewell and Ian Mosby, eds., *Calls to Action Accountability: A 2023 Status Update on Reconciliation* (Toronto: Yellowhead Institute, 2023).

195 *Mikisew Cree First Nation v Canada,* 2005 SCC 69, para 1.

196 *Beckman v Little Salmon First Nation,* 2010 SCC 53, para 10.

197 See Jim Reynolds, *Aboriginal Peoples and the Law: A Critical Introduction* (Vancouver: UBC Press, 2018), 20–22.

198 *Calder v British Columbia,* [1973] SCR 313; see Hamar Foster, Heather Raven, and Jeremy Webber, *Let Right Be Done: Aboriginal Title, the Calder Case, and the Future of Indigenous Rights* (Vancouver: UBC Press, 2007).

199 *Tshilhqot'in v Canada,* 2014 SCC 44, para 10.

200 *Guerin v The Queen,* [1984] 2 SCR 335; see Jim Reynolds, *From Wardship to Rights: The* Guerin *Case and Aboriginal Law* (Vancouver: UBC Press, 2020).

201 *Simon v The Queen,* [1985] 2 SCR 387.

202 *R v Sparrow,* [1990] 1 SCR 1075.

203 *Haida Nation v British Columbia,* 2004 SCC 73.

204 *Tshilhqot'in v Canada,* 2014 SCC 44. This affirmed and restated the earlier *Delgamuukw* decision, [1997] 3 SCR 1010.

205 For a detailed discussion, see Reynolds, *Aboriginal Peoples and the Law.*

206 *Delgamuukw v British Columbia,* [1997] 3 SCR 1010, para 165.

207 Reynolds, *Aboriginal Peoples and the Law,* 110.

208 *The First Nations Commercial and Industrial Development Act,* SC 2005, c 53, passed in 2005, is legislation that may affect the government's control over reserve property for those few First Nations to which it applies.

209 *The First Nations Land Management Act,* SC 1999, c 24, passed in 1999, directly affected reserve property for those First Nations to which it applies.

210 *An Act to amend the Indian Act,* SC 1985, c 27.

211 *An Act to amend the Indian Act (designated lands),* SC 1988, c 23.

212 *Jobs and Growth Act,* SC 2012, c 31, s 208.

213 *Indian Act Amendment and Replacement Act,* SC 2014 c 38, s 7; *Twinn v McKnight,* (1987) 37 DLR (4th) 270.

Conclusion

1 Frederick Lugard, *The Dual Mandate in British Tropical Africa* (Edinburgh: William Blackwood, 1922), 613.

2 Alan Burns, *In Defence of Colonies* (London: Allen and Unwin, 1957), 62–71.

3 Ralph Furse, *Aucuparius: Recollections of a Recruiting Officer* (London: Oxford University Press, 1962), 309. For another defence from a colonial administrator, see Philip Mitchell, *African Afterthoughts* (London: Hutchinson, 1954), 276.

4 Stephen Leacock, *Our British Empire: Its Structure, Its History, Its Strength* (London: The Bodley Head, 1940), 218.

5 Alfred Milner, *Questions of the Hour* (London: Hodder and Stoughton, 1923), 147.

6 Margery Perham, "The Colonial Empire," *Times* (London), March 14, 1942.

7 Nnamdi Azikiwe, *Renascent Africa* (London: Cass, 1937); M.K. Gandhi, *Hind Swaraj or Indian Home Rule* (Madras: Natesan, 1921); Jomo Kenyatta, *Facing Mount Kenya* (London: Secker and Warburg, 1938); Jawaharlal Nehru, *The Discovery of India* (Calcutta: Signet, 1946); Kwame Nkrumah, *Towards Colonial Freedom* (London: Heinemann, 1962).

8 *House of Commons Debates* (UK), 5th series, vol. 17, June 13, 1910, cols. 1141–43 (Arthur Balfour).

9 William Winwood Reade, *Martyrdom of Man* (London: Trubner, 1872), 504–5.

10 Carl Berger, *The Sense of Power: Studies in the Ideas of Canadian Imperialism* (Toronto: University of Toronto Press, 1970), 246.

11 Albert Carman, *The Ethics of Imperialism* (Boston: Turner, 1905), 10.

12 Carman, *The Ethics of Imperialism*, 114.

13 For a recent and comprehensive account of the debate that reflects its unfortunately confrontational tone, see Nigel Biggar, *Colonialism: A Moral Reckoning* (London: William Collins, 2023). Biggar is a priest and former professor of theology and a supporter of the Empire.

14 Niall Ferguson, *Empire: The Rise and Demise of the British World Order and the Lessons for Global Power* (New York: Basic Books, 2004), xxi. For other recent defences of colonialism, see Bruce Gilley, "The Case for Colonialism," *Academic Quarterly* 31 (2018): 167, which was withdrawn from *The Third World Quarterly* amidst controversy (see https://www.tandfonline.com/doi/abs/10.1080/01436597.2017.1369037); the Ethics and Empire Project of the McDonald Centre for Theology, Ethics and Public Life, a research institute at the University of Oxford, https://www.mcdonaldcentre.org.uk/ethics-and-empire; and Jeremy Black, *Imperial Legacies: The British Empire around the World* (New York: Encounter, 2019).

15 Shashi Tharoor, *Inglorious Empire: What the British Did to India* (London: Penguin, 2017).

16 Tirthankar Roy, "Inglorious Empire: What the British Did to India," *Cambridge Review of International Affairs* 31 (2018): 134; Charles Allen, "Who Owns India's History? A Critique of Shashi Tharoor's *Inglorious Empire*," *Asian Affairs* 49 (2018): 355.

17 Jon Wilson, *India Conquered: Britain's Raj and the Chaos of Empire* (London: Simon and Schuster, 2016), 481.

18 Piers Brendon, "A Moral Audit of the British Empire," *History Today* 57 (2017): 44. For an examination of the colonial balance sheet in the political, social, and economic fields from an African perspective, see A. Adu Boahen, *African Perspectives on Colonialism* (Baltimore: Johns Hopkins University Press, 1987).

19 Edward Gibbon, *An Essay on the Study of Literature* (London: Becket and De Hondt, 1764), 1.

20 Chinua Achebe, *The Education of a British-Protected Person* (New York: Anchor, 2010), 7.

21 Ronald Hyam, *Understanding the British Empire* (Cambridge: Cambridge University Press, 2010), 31.

22 Ashley Jackson, *The British Empire: A Very Short Introduction* (Oxford: Oxford University Press, 2013), 121.

23 See, for example, Black, *Imperial Legacies*.

24 For the preliminary report on the restoration of the Macdonald statue in Montreal, see "Démarche d'évaluation du monument à Sir John Alexander Macdonald," Ville de Montréal,

October 26, 2022, https://ville.montreal.qc.ca/pls/portal/docs/page/commissions_perm_v2_fr/media/documents/avispr%c9liminaire_macdonald_20221118.pdf.

25 Trevor Pritchard, "Here's What's Named after Sir John A. Macdonald in Ottawa," *CBC News*, June 3, 2021, https://www.cbc.ca/news/canada/ottawa/map-john-a-macdonald-names-ottawa-1.6050525.

26 "Former Governors General," Governor General of Canada, https://www.gg.ca/en/governor-general/former-governors-general. See Chapter 3 of this volume.

27 Immigration, Refugees and Citizenship Canada, *Discover Canada: The Rights and Responsibilities of Citizenship*. Study Guide (2021), 11, https://www.canada.ca/en/immigration-refugees-citizenship/corporate/publications-manuals/discover-canada/download.html. And see Chapter 3 of this volume.

28 "Stephen Leacock: Humorist and Educator," National Library of Canada, February 1, 2001, https://epe.lac-bac.gc.ca/100/200/301/nlc-bnc/stephen_leacock-ef/2001/index-e.html.

29 "History," The Leacock Medal for Humour, https://www.leacock.ca/history.php#leacock.

30 For a study of the relationship of the monarchy to the end of the Empire, see Philip Murphy, *Monarchy and the End of Empire: The House of Windsor, the British Government and the Postwar Commonwealth* (Oxford: Oxford University Press, 2013). For the monarchy in Canada, see D. Michael Jackson, *The Crown and Canadian Federalism* (Toronto: Dundurn, 2013).

31 John Buchan, "The Law and the Constitution," in *The Empire and the Century*, ed. C.S. Goldman (London: John Murray, 1905), 37.

32 "Prime Minister Justin Trudeau Says Monarchy Offers Canada 'Steadiness,'" *BBC News*, September 19, 2022, https://www.bbc.com/news/world-us-canada-62957626; *House of Commons Debates*, 44th Parl., 1st Sess., vol. 151, October 25–26, 2022, 8812–43, 8859–76, 8908–9. In December 2022, the National Assembly of Quebec removed the requirement for members to swear an oath of allegiance to the monarch: *Statutes of Quebec* 2022, c 30.

33 *House of Commons Debates*, 44th Parl., 1st Sess., vol. 151, October 25, 2022, 8825. It should be noted that some First Nations people are reluctant to diminish the relationship their nations traditionally had with the British monarch; see, for example, Doug Cuthand, "First Nations Will Never Back Abandoning the Queen, Monarchy," *Saskatoon Star Phoenix*, June 3, 2022, https://thestarphoenix.com/opinion/columnists/cuthand-first-nations-will-never-back-abandoning-the-queen-monarchy.

34 Justice Ian Binnie in *McDonald Lumber Ltd v God's Lake First Nation*, 2006 SCC 58, para 106.

35 Truth and Reconciliation Commission of Canada (TRC), *The Final Report of the Truth and Reconciliation Commission of Canada*, 6 vols. (Montreal and Kingston: McGill-Queen's University Press, 2015).

36 See, for example, Harold Cardinal, *The Unjust Society* (Edmonton: Hurtig, 1969); George Manuel and Michael Posluns, *The Fourth World: An Indian Reality* (Don Mills, ON: Collier-Macmillan, 1974); Bev Sellars, *Price Paid: The Fight for First Nations Survival* (Vancouver: Talonbooks, 2016).

37 Jody Wilson-Raybould, *Indian in the Cabinet: Speaking Truth to Power* (Toronto: Harper-Collins, 2021), 50–51.

38 Wilson-Raybould, *Indian in the Cabinet*, 142.

39 Wilson-Raybould, *Indian in the Cabinet*, 55.

40 Alan Cairns, *First Nations and the Canadian State* (Kingston, ON: Institute of Intergovernmental Relations, Queen's University, 2005), 5.

41 *Oxford English Dictionary,* "decolonization, n.," accessed March 14, 2023, https://www.oed.com/view/Entry/48333.

42 Cairns, *First Nations and the Canadian State,* 8.

43 Cairns, *First Nations and the Canadian State,* 9.

44 Cairns, *First Nations and the Canadian State,* 9.

45 Cairns, *First Nations and the Canadian State,* 10.

46 *Reference re the secession of Quebec* [1998] 2 SCR 217, para 125.

47 Manuel and Posluns, *The Fourth World,* 236.

48 Manuel and Posluns, *The Fourth World,* 5–6.

49 Arthur Manuel and Ronald Derrickson, *The Reconciliation Manifesto: Recovering the Land, Rebuilding the Economy* (Toronto: Lorimer, 2017), 275. For a theoretical discussion by an Indigenous scholar, see Aaron Mills, "Rooted Constitutionalism: Growing Political Community," in *Resurgence and Reconciliation: Indigenous–Settler Relations and Earth Teachings,* ed. Michael Asch, John Borrows, and James Tully (Toronto: University of Toronto Press, 2018), 133–74.

50 Manuel and Derrickson, *The Reconciliation Manifesto,* 276.

51 Manuel and Derrickson, *The Reconciliation Manifesto,* 278.

52 Wilson-Raybould, *Indian in the Cabinet,* 53.

53 Jody Wilson-Raybould, *From Where I Stand: Rebuilding Indigenous Nations for a Stronger Canada* (Vancouver: UBC Press, 2019), 7–8.

Suggestions for Further Reading

The endnotes to each chapter give detailed references. The purpose of this brief selected bibliography is to direct attention to those sources that I think will provide the reader with an especially helpful or well-written introduction to, or overview of, the topics covered.

Chapter 1: Historical Overview

Jackson, Ashley. *The British Empire: A Very Short Introduction.* Oxford: Oxford University Press, 2013.

Chapter 2: The Essentials of the Empire

Darwin, John. *Unfinished Empire: The Global Expansion of Britain.* London: Penguin, 2013.

Leacock, Stephen. *Our British Empire: Its Structure, Its History, Its Strength.* London: The Bodley Head, 1940.

Woodcock, George. *Who Killed the British Empire? An Inquest.* Toronto: Fitzhenry and Whiteside, 1974.

Chapter 3: Self-Rule and Despotism

Durham, Lord. *The Report and Dispatches of the Earl of Durham.* London: Ridgways, 1839.

Mill, John Stuart. "Representative Government" (1861). In *Utilitarianism, Liberty and Representative Government.* London: Allen and Unwin, 1968.

Padmore, George. *How Britain Rules Africa.* London: Wishart, 1936. Reprint, New York: Negro Universities Press, 1969.

Chapter 4: The Rulers and Their Rule

Cell, John W. "Colonial Rule." In *The Twentieth Century,* ed. Judith M. Brown and Wm. Roger Louis. Vol. 4 of *The Oxford History of the British Empire.* Oxford: Oxford University Press, 1999.

Kirk-Greene, Anthony. *Britain's Imperial Administrators, 1858–1966.* London: Palgrave Macmillan, 2000.

Chapter 5: Canadian Participation in the Empire

Belich, James. *Replenishing the Earth.* Oxford: Oxford University Press, 2009.

Berger, Carl. *The Sense of Power: Studies in the Ideas of Canadian Imperialism 1967–1914.* Toronto: University of Toronto Press, 1970.

Buckner, Phillip, ed. *Canada and the British Empire.* Oxford: Oxford University Press, 2010.

Buckner, Phillip, and R. Douglas Francis, eds. *Canada and the British World: Culture, Migration and Identity.* Vancouver: UBC Press, 2006.

Morgan, Henry. *The Place British Americans Have Won in History.* Ottawa: Hunter, Rose, 1866.

Chapter 6: Internal Colonialism in Canada

Brownlie, Robin Jarvis. *A Fatherly Eye: Indian Agents, Government Power, and Aboriginal Resistance in Ontario, 1918–1939.* Oxford: Oxford University Press, 2003.

Dickason, Olive, and David McNab. *Canada's First Nations: A History of Founding Peoples from Earliest Times.* 4th ed. Don Mills, ON: Oxford University Press, 2009.

Miller, James. *Skyscrapers Hide the Heavens: A History of Native-Newcomer Relations in Canada.* 4th ed. Toronto: University of Toronto Press, 2018.

Chapter 7: Independence, Self-Government, and Reconciliation

Cardinal, Harold. *The Unjust Society.* Edmonton: Hurtig, 1969.

McIntyre, W. David. *Colonies into Commonwealth.* Rev. ed. London: Blandford, 1974.

Perham, Margery. *The Colonial Reckoning.* London: Collins, 1961.

Royle, Trevor. *The Last Days of the Raj.* London: Coronet, 1990.

Conclusion

Biggar, Nigel. *Colonialism: A Moral Reckoning.* London: William Collins, 2023.

Cairns, Alan. *First Nations and the Canadian State.* Kingston, ON: Institute of Intergovernmental Relations, Queen's University, 2005.

Manuel, Arthur, and Ronald Derrickson. *The Reconciliation Manifesto: Recovering the Land, Rebuilding the Economy.* Toronto: Lorimer, 2017.

Manuel, George, and Michael Posluns. *The Fourth World: An Indian Reality.* Don Mills, ON: Collier-Macmillan, 1974.

Tharoor, Shashi. *Inglorious Empire: What the British Did to India.* London: Penguin, 2017.

Wilson-Raybould, Jody. *From Where I Stand: Rebuilding Indigenous Nations for a Stronger Canada.* Vancouver: UBC Press, 2019.

Index

103; spectacle of Empire, 116; Sudan campaign (1884–85), 79, 104, 150–52, 151(f); treaties, 49–50; trusteeship, 42; violence and force, 57–58, 80, 81(f). *See also* Dependent Empire; despotism; South Africa

Alberta, 131–32, 132(f), 182(f)

Alert Bay (BC), 185(f)

Amery, Leo, 96

Archibald, Adams George, 56

Arendt, Hannah, 64

Ashton, Niki, 231

assimilation. *See* Indigenous peoples, Canada: assimilation

Attlee, Clement, 207–8

Australia: on the "All-Red Route," 7, 116(f), 130–31; colonial governors, 103, 163; colonial possessions, 6, 27, 157; colonialism's long-term effects, 126–27; dominion status, 19, 205; historical overview, 16, 19; immigration policy, 38; indirect rule, 264n140; racism, 37–38, 118, 163

Azikiwe, Nnamdi, 42, 107

Baden-Powell, Robert, 130, 138

Bagot Commission (1845), 17, 177

Balfour, Arthur, 33

Baring, Evelyn, 255n89

Barman, Jean, 135

Barnes, Leonard, 67, 101, 206

Bartlett, Richard, 187

Beames, John, 110

Beaverbrook, Lord, 130–31

beginning of Empire. *See* Empire

Belgian Congo, 62, 99

Belich, James, 48–49, 140, 297

Belloc, Hilaire, 61

Bennett, R.B., 28, 127–28, 131, 194–95, 201

Beothuk people, 41, 240n3

Berger, Carl, 297

Berger, Thomas, 215

Besant, Annie, 38

Big Bear (Mistahimaskwa), 56–57, 56(f), 182(f), 249n193

Biggar, Nigel, 293n13, 297

Blackstone, William, 47

BNA Act. See Constitution Act, 1867 (Canada, was *British North America Act*)

Boer War (1899–1902): overview, 22, 153–56, 154(f); Canadian ties, 22, 81, 130, 138, 146–47, 152–55, 154(f), 193; concentration camps, 81, 153; imperial loyalty, 26, 143, 153–55, 154(f); justifications for, 61–62; post–Boer War, 155–56; racism, 34

books. *See* publications

Borden, Robert, 6, 142, 156, 194

Bourassa, Henri, 146

Brendon, Piers, 229

British Columbia: British culture, 132, 135; Confederation (1872), 72, 75, 180; demographics, 132; elite private schools, 114–15, 135; *Komagata Maru* incident (1914), 123–25, 124(f); responsible government, 72; settler colonialism, 125–26

—INDIGENOUS PEOPLES: Aboriginal title, 186, 223–24; assimilation, 166–68, 167(f); band councils, 180; civilizing mission, 44; Indian agents' powers, 169–70, 172–73, 183; marginalization, 164, 165(f); migration guidebooks on, 121–22; Musqueam people, 8, 169–70, 224; potlatch ban, 161–62, 183; reconciliation, 221, 222(f); reports (1958, 1966), 172–73, 188; residential schools, 185(f), 222(f); resource exploitation, 176; Songhees people, 165(f); terminology, vii–viii, 10, 276n18; treaties, 50, 52, 176; UNDRIP rights, 221; voting rights, 176

British Empire. *See* Empire

British North America Act (1867). See *Constitution Act, 1867* (Canada, was *British North America Act*)

British Overseas Territories, 25

British South Africa Company, 30, 80, 92, 115–16, 230

Britishness: overview, 8–9, 127–42; ancestral home, 138–39; colonial identity, 127–29, 138–39; elite private schools, 93–96, 114–15, 135; vs Englishness or

Scottishness, 128; family metaphors, 133–34, 134(f), 135; key ideas, 8–9; legal systems, 108–9, 136; mobility of citizens, 129–31; nationalism, 134–35, 138–40; organizations, 137–38; public interest in, 141–42; racial identity, 134–35. *See also* monarchy; spectacle of Empire; symbols of Empire
—CANADA: overview, 8–9, 127–47, 211–13; ancestral home, 138–39; British identity, 127–29, 138–40, 211–13; Canadians in Britain, 160; citizenship, 127–29, 140; elite private schools, 114–15, 135; at end of empire, 211–13, 230; French Canadians, 103; imperial loyalty, 132–33, 133(f), 141(f), 142–44; key ideas, 8–9; legal system, 136; literature, 143–47, 145(f); migration and mobility, 119–25, 129–31; monarchy, 136–37; monuments and names, 138, 230; vs multiculturalism, 4, 211(f); organizations, 132, 137–38; public interest in, 141–42, 147, 211–13; publications, 138, 211–12. *See also* monarchy; spectacle of Empire; symbols of Empire
Brooke, Charles, 137
Brown, George, 76
Brownlie, Robin Jarvis, 171, 297
Buchan, John: overview, 80–84, 82(f), 83(f); in Boer War, 81, 130, 153; on fascism, 64; governor general, 79, 81–84, 82(f), 128, 230; on the monarchy, 231; opposition to "educated natives," 46; racism, 81–84, 82(f), 230, 256n104
Buchan, John, works: *The African Colony,* 256n104; *Prester John,* 82; *Sick Heart River,* 82–84; *The Thirty-Nine Steps,* 80–81
Buckner, Phillip, 33–34, 129–30, 297
Buller, Charles, 92
Burma (now Myanmar), 20, 30, 288n121
Burns, Alan, 97, 198, 227
Buxton, Thomas Fowell, 40–41
Buxton report (1837, Select Committee on Aboriginal Tribes), 26, 41, 73–74, 177
Byng, Lord, 78–79

Cairns, Alan, 232–33, 297
Cairns, J.C., 90, 260n48
Calder v British Columbia (1973), 223–24
Callwell, C.E., 58
Cameron, D.M., 54
Campbell, Wilfred, 143–44
Canada. *See* colonialism; settler colonialism: Canada; *and specific topics*
Canada Company, 122
Canadian Pacific Railway, 7, 49(f), 115, 116(f), 122, 130–31
Cannadine, David, 114
Cardinal, Harold, 55, 176–77, 214, 297
Caribbean, 15, 41–42, 231
Carman, Albert, 228
Carnarvon, Lord, 76
Carter, Sarah, 47
Cary, Joyce, 260n62
Cavell, Edith, 138
Cell, John W., 296
ceremony. *See* spectacle of Empire; symbols of Empire
cession of land. *See* Indigenous peoples, Canada: land; treaties
Chamberlain, Joseph, 43, 58, 68, 77, 143
China and Canada's exclusion laws, 34, 123
Christian duty, 40, 43–45, 59. *See also* civilizing mission
Churchill, Winston: on Canadians in wars, 159–60, 159(f); on civilizing mission, 43; on colonial administrators, 100; on conquest, 57; on end of Empire, 141, 198–99; on India, 43, 205; racism, 32–33; tours of Canada, 143
citizenship, 127–29, 140
civilizing mission: overview, 40–46, 107–8; assimilation, 17, 43–45, 46–47, 171, 173–74, 181; Christian duty, 40, 43–45, 59; cleanliness, 39(f); commissions and reports, 15, 17, 177; dependencies, 42–44; despotism, 84–86; duty to protect, 41–45, 73–74, 98; education, 46–47; family metaphors, 107; humanitarianism, 40–43; of *Indian Act,* 181; as justification for colonial harms, 36, 40, 42–44, 54, 59; mandate system, 42;

Denison, George, 137
Department of Indian Affairs. *See* Indian
  Affairs Branch (Canada)
Dependent Empire: overview, 19, 29–31,
  65–69, 84–89, 227–31; civilizing mission, 42–44; colonial administrators,
  90–99, 198; colonialism's long-term
  effects, 227–31; colonists as minorities,
  126; decolonization, 9, 198–200, 232–
  33; demographics, 27, 66, 67, 112;
  despotism, 20, 29, 66, 84–89; direct and
  indirect rule, 20–21, 27, 109–14; duty
  to protect, 41–43, 73–74, 98; economic
  exploitation, 29–31, 46, 67, 126; government, 27–29, 84–89; key ideas, 8–9;
  J.S. Mill on governing, 84–85; as non-
  white colonies, 29; paternalism, 37–38,
  199; plural legal systems, 108–9, 113; vs
  settler colonies, 19, 29, 65–69, 126–27;
  shift to self-government, 9, 29, 113–14;
  spectacle of Empire, 65, 66(f), 114–16;
  taxation, 67–68; terminology, 66,
  241n19. *See also* Africa; civilizing
  mission; despotism; India
Derrickson, Ronald, 297
despotism: overview, 9, 20, 27, 84–89;
  Canadian Indian agents, 170–71; colonial path to self-government, 29, 113–
  14; in dependencies, 29, 84–89; direct
  rule, 20, 109–10; factors in success, 100–
  2; governors' powers, 86–88, 202; justifications for, 84–88; key ideas, 8–9; key
  questions, 229; lack of Indigenous
  peoples in government, 86–87, 202;
  legal systems, 87–89; methods, 27; military power, 86–88, 101, 108; vs representative government, 84–86
Devonshire, Lord, 96
Dewdney, Edgar, 176
Dicey, Albert, 85, 196
Dickason, Olive, 14, 297
Dickens, Charles and Francis, 168(f)
Diefenbaker, John, 5, 212
Dilke, Charles, 28
direct and indirect rule, 20–21, 27,
  109–14
Disraeli, Benjamin, 69

district officers, 91, 94–95, 97–100,
  260n62
Dominion Day, 211(f). *See also* spectacle
  of Empire: Empire Day
dominions: overview, 19, 65–69, 66(f),
  196; Balfour Formula, 197, 205; colonial administrators, 95–96; colonial
  path to self-government, 29, 113–14,
  200–10; defence and foreign affairs,
  195–97; demographics, 27, 67; vs
  dependencies, 29, 65–69; economic
  exploitation, 29–31, 46, 210; in First
  World War, 156–57, 157(f); historical
  overview, 19; independence (1931), 19,
  22, 197, 207, 208–9, 289n136; India's
  goal of status as, 200–9; lack of British
  force against, 18, 62; non-white exclu-
  sions, 196, 205, 210; self-government
  overview, 9, 69–77; spectacle of Empire,
  65, 66(f); terminology, 19, 66, 196. *See
  also* settler colonialism
Dominion Lands Act (1872, Canada), 52
Douglas, James, 125, 137
Dufferin, Earl of, 80, 192–93, 201
Duncan, Sara Jeannette: overview, 143–
  47, 145(f); imperialist, 68, 144–45; *The
  Imperialist*, 145, 167, 272n43, 277n30;
  in India, 46, 129, 145; racism, 145, 167
Dunn, Alexander, 148
Durham, Lord, 70–72, 71(f), 177, 203,
  207–8, 296
Durham Report (1839), 18, 26, 70–75,
  177, 203, 252n28, 296

East India Company (EIC): as colonial
  administration, 16–17, 88, 92, 95; as
  commercial company, 16–17, 25, 30,
  43, 92; despotism, 84–85, 88; end of
  rule, 148; Indian Rebellion (1857), 32,
  85, 148–50, 149(f). *See also* India
economics: overview, 29–31; colonial
  dependence, 77; colonial development,
  103–8, 129–31; colonialism's long-
  term effects, 227–31; exploitation of
  resources, 29–31, 43, 67; key questions,
  229; military costs, 28, 67, 74; slave
  trade, 15–16, 48, 103; taxation, 67–68.

See also East India Company (EIC);
Hudson's Bay Company
education: British culture, ii(f), 24, 27,
135; civilizing mission, 46–47; of colonial administrators, 91–98; economic
motives, 46; elite schools in UK, 93–96,
114–15, 135; leaders of independence
movements, 46; networks of academics,
138; opposition to "educated natives,"
46, 94, 106–8; racial and cultural
superiority, 94–96, 135, 184
— CANADA: Britishness, ii(f), 24, 135;
colonial history, 4–5, 24, 230; elite
British schools as models, 94, 96, 114–
15, 135; racial and cultural superiority,
35, 135, 169, 184; reconciliation, 221–
23, 222(f), 230; textbooks, 35, 135, 212.
See also Indigenous peoples, Canada:
residential schools
Edward VII, King, 211
Edward VIII, King, 118; as Prince of
Wales, 139(f)
Egypt: Anglo-Egyptian War (1882), 143;
Suez Crisis (1956), 148, 190, 199, 212
EIC. *See* East India Company (EIC)
Electoral Franchise Act (1885, Canada), 183
Elizabeth, Queen (wife of King George VI),
131–32, 132(f)
Elkins, Caroline, 57
emigration. *See* migration
Empire: overview, 8–11, 24–29, 227–31;
chronological divisions, 25–26; colonialism's long-term effects, 126–27, 227–
31; common elements, 28; demographics,
27, 112; diversity in, 26–28; expansion
(1830s–1840s), 9–10, 25–26; family
metaphors, 133–34, 134(f), 135; geographical size, 24, 26–27; humanitarianism, 40–41; immorality of, 229–30;
key ideas, 8–9; lack of vision or control,
26–28; as loose federation, 26–28, 69–
70, 77; non-white, dependent colonies,
29, 68–69; settlement of colonies, 47–
49; terminology, vii–viii, 10, 68
Empire, economics. *See* economics
Empire, end of: overview, 23, 25, 190–97,
227–31; Balfour Formula (1926), 197;

in Canada, 140–41, 190–97, 211–13,
230, 232–35; Canada's influence, 190–
97; colonial administration, 98, 113–14;
colonialism's long-term effects, 227–31;
decolonization, 9, 23, 198–200, 232–
35; defence and foreign affairs, 195–97;
independence, 22–23, 199–200; key
events as markers, 25, 199; turn to
Europe, 7; turn to self-government,
22–23, 113–14, 198–200
Empire, foreign affairs and defence. *See*
defence and foreign affairs; military;
violence and force
Empire, government. *See* government
Empire, historical overview: overview,
11–23; chronological divisions, 25–26;
early stages, 13–15; expansion, 9–10,
25–26; Victoria's reign as height, 25, 26
Empire, laws and legal systems. *See* laws
and legal systems
Empire, representatives. *See* administrators, colonial; governors general; Indian
agents (Canada)
Empire, spectacle and symbols. *See* spectacle of Empire; symbols of Empire
Empire Club, 138
end of Empire. *See* Empire, end of
enfranchisement. *See* Indigenous peoples,
Canada: colonial government
Engler, Yves, 152
Englishness vs Britishness, 128. *See also*
Britishness
ethics. *See* morality and ethics
Ewart, John, 141
exhibitions, 40, 138, 139(f). *See also*
spectacle of Empire

Fanon, Frantz, 125
fascism, 62–64, 228, 251n237, 251n242
federation, imperial, 28, 77
federations, 69–70, 72–73
Ferguson, Niall, 47, 110–11, 228
Fessender, Clementina, 137
Field, Alan, 33
First Nations, terminology, vii–viii,
276n18. *See also* Indigenous peoples,
Canada

historical overview, 16–17, 19–20; Indian Rebellion (1857), 20, 32, 85, 148–50, 149(f), 152, 208; key ideas, 8–9; migration, 48; racism, 20, 33–34, 36–39, 63, 67–68, 84–85; rationale for success, 100–2; spectacle of Empire, 65, 66(f), 110–11, 115, 116(f); treaties, 49–50. *See also* East India Company (EIC)

— COLONIAL GOVERNMENT: overview, 84–91; administrators, 16–17, 20, 90–101; civilizing mission, 42–44, 46; despotism, 9, 20, 84–91, 202–3; direct and indirect rule, 20, 109–14; dominion status as goal, 20, 200–8; education of administrators, 92–96, 100; EIC as administrator, 16–17, 20, 95; government reforms (1909, 1919), 202–3; governors general/viceroys, 20, 79–80, 86, 114–15, 201–2, 207; India Office (UK) as authority, 27, 28, 91–93, 95; Indian administrators, 90–91, 95, 97–101, 109–10; Indian National Congress, 38, 200, 206, 208; Indian Political Service, 110; lack of rights, 74, 87; laws and legal system, 87–89, 101, 108, 200–1, 206; military, 67, 110–11; modernization, 97; political organizations, 200–1; press suppression, 88, 204, 206; taxation, 67–68; trusteeship, 42–44; violence and threat of force, 58, 88, 100–1

— INDEPENDENCE AND SELF-GOVERNMENT: overview, 20, 200–10, 209(f), 232–33; British rejection of dominion status, 201–2, 205–8; Canada as model, 29, 190–91, 200–1, 205–8; decolonization, 9, 232–33; dominion status as goal, 200–8; Gandhi's role, 88, 190, 203–5, 208; government reforms (1909, 1919, 1935), 202–9, 288n121; independence (1950, 1956), 208–10, 209(f); key ideas, 8–9; political opposition to British rule, 38, 200–1, 205–8; racism, 84–85, 206; responsible government, 84–85, 190–91, 200–3, 207–8; Second World War's impacts, 207–8; self-government movement overview, 9, 20, 95, 125, 200–10; Simon

Commission report, 205–7, 288n111; violent suppression, 204–6, 208

Indian, terminology, vii–viii, 276n18

Indian Act (1876, Canada): overview, 166–67, 180–89, 225–26, 232; amendments and consolidations, 180–81, 183, 186–89, 225–26; assimilation, 166, 174–76, 181, 184, 187–89; ban on ceremonies, 161–62, 170, 173, 183, 186, 187; band councils, 180, 186–87, 225, 281n124; civilizing mission, 44, 181; colonialism's long-term effects, 231–32; enforcement, 161–62; enfranchisement, 166, 178–79, 186; historical overview, 18; as internal colonialism, 9, 10, 175, 187–88, 232–33; international criticism of, 213; land surrenders, 45, 184–86, 225; laws as precursors to, 17, 174, 177–80; legal status, 162–63, 166, 175, 178–79, 189; minister's powers, 175; opposition to, 166–67; provisions, 174–76, 225–26; recent changes, 225–26; structural racism, 37–38; terminology, vii–viii, 276n18

Indian Advancement Act (1884, Canada), 183

Indian Affairs Branch (Canada): overview, 180–81; expansion (1870–1890s), 180; as internal colonialism, 9, 10, 175, 187–88, 232–33; lack of attention by Parliament, 180; J.A. Macdonald's role, 173–74; minister's powers, 175; officials, 171–72; opposition to, 186; paternalism, 169–70, 172–73, 188; policy overview, 174; D.C. Scott's role, 161–64, 163(f), 170–71; terminology, vii–viii, 276n18; White Paper (1969), 188–89, 214. See also *Indian Act* (1876, Canada)

Indian agents (Canada): overview, 164–73, 186–87; backgrounds, 161–62, 171–72; band government, 172–73, 175, 183, 186–87, 281n124; despotism, 170–71; elimination of position, 225; enforcement of *Indian Act,* 161–62; as internal colonial officer, 9, 10, 169–73; in literature, 161–62, 167, 276n20; pass system, 176, 213; powers, 161–62, 164, 168–73,

delegations to Parliament, 283*n*177; federal/provincial jurisdiction, 179–81, 187–89, 219, 221; justifications for rights infringement, 225; land laws, 52, 176–79, 223–25; landmark cases, 223–25; precursors to *Indian Act,* 17, 174, 177–80; residential schools, 184, 222–23; traditional laws, 52, 54, 176. See also *Indian Act* (1876, Canada)

— RECONCILIATION AND SELF-GOVERNMENT: overview, 213–26, 231–35; Aboriginal title, 186, 223–24; colonialism's long-term effects, 231–35; constitutional rights, 214–18, 216(f); decolonization, 9, 23, 198–200, 232–35; duty to consult, 224; historical overview, 17; *Indian Act* amendments, 225–26; international recognition, 220–21; justifications for rights infringement, 225; land claims, 216; landmark legal cases, 223–25; modern treaties, 218, 225; RCAP recommendations, 218–19, 221–22; reconciliation, 221–26, 230–35; self-government rights, 216–20, 290*n*162; Supreme Court's role, 217, 219–20, 223–25; treaty and Aboriginal rights, 214–16, 219–20; UNDRIP, 220–21, 223; White Paper (1969) response, 188–89, 214

— RESIDENTIAL SCHOOLS: overview, 3–5, 184, 185(f); civilizing mission, 46–47; *Indian Act* provisions, 184, 186; legal actions, 222–23; precursors to, 184, 282*n*152; reconciliation, 222(f); Sixties Scoop as successor, 188; TRC (Truth and Reconciliation Commission), 3–5, 46, 221, 223, 231

indirect and direct rule, 20–21, 27, 109–14

Inglis, John, 148–50, 149(f)

Inuit, vii–viii, 276*n*18, 282*n*150

IODE (Imperial Order Daughters of the Empire), 137–38

Ireland, 120, 197, 205, 286*n*48

Jackson, Ashley, 48, 111, 229, 296

Jamaica, 15, 76, 162, 256*n*118

Jebb, Richard, 68–69, 128

Jeffries, Charles, 86

Jenness, Diamond, 167–68

Johnson, Pauline (Tekahionwake), 143–44, 145(f)

Johnstone, Harry, 21–22, 30–31, 32

Jones, Arthur Creech, 100

Jones, Ernest, 57

Joyce, William, 64

Judicial Committee of the Privy Council, 28–29, 77, 108, 136

Keith, Arthur Berriedale, 37, 77, 92, 96, 201, 207

Kenya, 22, 46, 63, 87, 102, 104

Kenyatta, Jomo, 46, 63

Kew, Michael, 169–70

King, William Lyon Mackenzie: overview, 159(f), 210(f); Canada's independence, 194, 196–97; dissolution of Parliament crisis (1926), 78–79, 92; on end of Empire, 200; immigration policy, 123; imperial loyalty, 142; racism, 34, 123; Second World War, 142, 159(f), 160

Kipling, Rudyard, 64, 99–100, 133, 251*n*1

Kirby, William, 45

Kirk-Greene, Anthony, 94, 96–98, 258*n*2, 296

Kolsky, Elizabeth, 57–58

Komagata Maru incident (1914), 123–25, 124(f)

Kwarteng, Kwasi, 94

Laird, David, 44, 181

land, Indigenous. *See* Indigenous peoples, Canada: land

Laski, Harold, 45, 101, 102

Laskin, Bora, 136

Laurier, Wilfrid: on Canada's independence, 193–94, 196; on Earl Grey, 80; on First World War, 142, 156; on imperialism, 28, 142, 156; knighthood, 136–37; on settler entitlements, 31

Law, Andrew Bonar, 131

Lawrence, Henry, 149–50

laws and legal systems: overview, 28–29, 108–9; blue water thesis, 220; British paramount authority, 27–28, 111;

violence and force: overview, 9, 57–62; at end of Empire, 57–58, 199–200, 204–6, 208–9; against Indigenous peoples, 57–59, 74; legalized, 57–58; spectacle of Empire, 58–59; threats of, 50, 51(f), 55, 55(f), 58–61, 108; against white settlers, 62. *See also* defence and foreign affairs; military

Wallace, Alfred, 32
Wallace, Edgar, 98, 260*n*62
wars. *See* Boer War (1899–1902); First World War; Second World War
Washington Treaty (1871), 142, 195
Watts, George E., 148
Wembley exhibition (1924), 138, 139(f)
West Indies, 6, 37, 41–42, 131, 157, 254*n*72
Westminster, Statute of (1931, UK), 19, 22, 197, 207, 208–9, 289*n*136
Weston, Garfield, 130–31
Westphal, George, 148
white supremacy. *See* racial and cultural superiority
Williams, Eric, 41–42
Wilmot-Horton, Robert, 48
Wilson, Bertha, 219
Wilson, James, 151

Wilson, Jon, 228
Wilson-Raybould, Jody, 231–32, 234–35, 234(f), 297
Winniett, William, 103
Wolfe, Patrick, 126–27
Wolseley, Garnet, 33, 36, 58, 78, 79(f), 138, 150–51
women: authors, 46, 68, 129, 143–47, 145(f); colonial administrators, 91; nurses, 154(f)
Woodcock, George, 26, 112, 190–91, 296
Woodsworth, James, 34, 125, 244*n*73
world wars. *See* First World War; Second World War
Wrong, George M., 135
Wuttenee, William, 170

Yabsley, Gary, 175
Young, Frederick, 143
Young, John, 192
Young, William Douglas, 103
Yukon Territory, 60(f), 61(f)

Zambia (was Northern Rhodesia), 22
Zimbabwe (was Southern Rhodesia), 57, 80, 81(f), 101–2, 115–16, 230, 233
Zimmern, Alfred, 138–39

Printed and bound in Canada
Set in Calibri and Minion by Artegraphica Design Co. Ltd.
Substantive editor: Lesley Erickson
Copy editor: Audrey McClellan
Proofreader: Judith Earnshaw
Indexer: Judy Dunlop
Cover designer: Lara Minja
Cover image: Lion, Trafalgar Square, London. Shutterstock.com/Kamira